Unruly Order

Unruly Order

Violence, Power, and Cultural Identity in the High Provinces of Southern Peru

EDITED BY

Deborah Poole

Westview Press

BOULDER • SAN FRANCISCO • OXFORD

Published in 1994 in the United States of America by Westview Press, Inc., 5500 Central Avenue, Boulder, Colorado 80301-2877, and in the United Kingdom by Westview Press, 36 Lonsdale Road, Summertown, Oxford OX2 7EW

Library of Congress Cataloging-in-Publication Data
Poole, Deborah.
    Unruly order : violence, power, and cultural identity in the high provinces of southern Peru / Deborah Poole.
        p.   cm.
    Includes bibliographical references.
    ISBN 0-8133-8749-3
    1. Indians of South America—Andes Region—Wars.   2. Indians of South America—Andes Region—Politics and government.   3. Violence—Andes Region—History.   4. Ethnicity—Andes Region.   5. Peasantry—Andes Region.   6. Andes Region—Politics and government.   7. Andes Region—Ethnic relations.   8. Andes Region—Social conditions.
I. Title.
F3429.3.W27P66   1994
980—dc20   94-4299
                                                                                                          CIP

Printed and bound in the United States of America

⊗ The paper used in this publication meets the requirements of the American National Standard for Permanence of Paper for Printed Library Materials Z39.48-1984.

10   9   8   7   6   5   4   3   2   1

Contents

Preface and Acknowledgments

This volume began in 1987 as a joint project with Christiane Paponnet-Cantat. Having both just returned from fieldwork in Chumbivilcas, we found ourselves faced with a common set of problems. How did the events and processes we had observed in "our" communities fit into broader regional and national contexts? Were the conflict, violence, and overt abuses of power we had both witnessed peculiar to Chumbivilcas, or were they a feature of life in other southern Andean villages? How was it that the province's *gamonales*, or landlords, had survived an agrarian reform that had supposedly dismantled their haciendas? Were we to believe the Chumbivilcanos' bawdy tales of rustling, banditry, and *machismo*? How were we to reconcile the cowboys, horses, guns, and ballads of Chumbivilcano culture with the prevailing anthropological understandings of Andean indigenous culture? Why was it that so little had been published on the history and ethnography of Chumbivilcas and the other high provinces of Cusco?

Fueled by our innocence concerning the actual work of editing and by our conviction that Chumbivilcas was, in fact, the world's most fascinating place, we resolved to edit a volume that would bring together work by the handful of anthropologists and historians who had studied in the region. We wrote to them asking if they would contribute to a volume addressing the regional formation, history, and culture of the high provinces of southern Peru. Much to our surprise, each of the authors responded not only with enthusiasm but also with abstracts for chapters that would focus on the same issues of violence and conflict that had initially intrigued us as anthropologists in the field. Their proposals confirmed our impressions that violence does indeed play a central role in shaping the forms of power, the modes of daily interaction, and the idioms of ethnic and gender identity that constitute what we might think of as a regional culture within the high provinces of southern Andean Peru. We decided to shift the focus of the volume to violence and its place in *provincias altas* history.

Since that time the volume has undergone a number of other changes. Our initial plans to include chapters on the pre-Columbian and colonial periods gave way to a shorter chronology that has allowed us to explore more closely the modern roots of violence. Though the colonial heritage has certainly been important in shaping some aspects of Andean ethnicity and culture, the central elements of *provincias altas* culture and the roots of its specific forms of violence and coercive power rest in the agrarian class societies and racial discourses that were born with the liberal state and regional capitalist economy of the Republican period.

In the years between conception and birth of this volume, the place of violence within modern Peruvian society has become increasingly difficult to deny. In the 1980s, the dramatic violence of the armed struggle launched by the Peruvian Communist Party "Shining Path" challenged both the Peruvian state and the democratic opposition. Today the violence of military struggle has waned somewhat only to be replaced by the institutionalized violence of Alberto Fujimori's authoritarian regime. Human rights activists, popular grassroots leaders, elected officials, intellectuals, and journalists continue to be subject to harassment, arbitrary detention, and trial by both anonymous judges and military tribunals. Through such practices and their silencing, violence has become an ever more common feature of Peruvians' daily lives. If we add the more publicized violence of Peru's illegal drug economy and the growing wave of criminal violence that has accompanied the massive unemployment, poverty, and desperation fostered by Fujimori's economic policies, it is easy to see that violence is a topic of more than academic interest for those of us who care about the future of Peru and Latin America.

This volume is a modest attempt to explore the social and cultural dimensions of violence in one region of Peru. Its chapters focus on the historical and cultural dimensions of violence as part of what might be thought of as "traditional" Peruvian Andean society. Although the political and criminal violence of recent years is not our specific concern here, our examinations of the routinized discursive and ideological dimensions of violence illuminate some of the mechanisms by which violence has been allowed to flourish in Peruvian society and, conversely, the channels of popular struggle through which violence can be contested and resisted.

In the course of editing this volume, I have counted on the support and assistance of numerous individuals. Christiane Paponnet-Cantat shared fully in editing earlier versions of the book and graciously offered to turn the project over to me when the difficulties of long-distance collaboration became too great. The volume was born of our friendship. I hope that the final product will live up to our initial dream of unraveling the secrets of our beloved *provincias altas*. Ben Orlove provided unending encouragement and guidance as I wended my way through the agonies of editing and the mysteries of academic publishing. Ben, Christiane, and the other contributors to the volume assisted with their patience and good humor over the long *durée*. Gary Urton, Joanne Rappaport, Marisol de la Cadena, Penny Harvey, and Gerardo Rénique provided friendship, ideas, and commentaries for my own chapters in the book. Dorinda Welle helped with several rounds of initial edits. Kellie Masterson and Laurie Milford of Westview Press provided the editorial support with which I was able, finally, to bring this project to life. Support for graphic materials was provided by the Travel and Research Fund of the Graduate Faculty of the New School for Social Research. Finally, my special thanks to Gerardo Rénique, who suffered through life with a reluctant editor and reminded her why it was all worth doing.

Deborah Poole
New York, New York

Introduction

Anthropological Perspectives on Violence and Culture—A View from the Peruvian High Provinces

Deborah Poole

For much of the twentieth century, violence and cultural order have defined the uneasy horizons of social science inquiry. Building on political philosophies inherited from such diverse thinkers as Hobbes, Descartes, Rousseau, and Machiavelli, social scientists have seen violence as something which exists outside of—and thus threatens—the forms of social order and cultural community whose laws and regularities it is their mission to explore.

With the relatively recent theoretical upheavals wrought by both poststructuralism and the more ambiguously defined arena of postmodernism, many social scientists have begun the task of rethinking this traditional divide between violence and the social order. No longer seen as a merely destructive or "anti-social" force, violence, as a form of power, has come to be viewed as productive of subjectivities, truths, histories, and identities—productive, in short, of the social order itself. Culture has been subjected to similar forms of scrutiny. Divorced from the timeless meanings, symbols, and traditions once considered constitutive of "culture" itself, both culture and cultural identity are now more commonly approached in anthropology and other social sciences as inherently contingent phenomena. With no specific locus other than in the minute practices and utterances of individuals or the referential discourses that both validate and generate dispersed forms of power, culture now seems to be less *productive of* identities than *produced by* a seemingly random, and certainly global, set of forces that escape the analytical capacities of any one observer.

1

This book attempts to bring some of these broader theoretical issues down to earth by examining the relationship between violence, culture, and social order in one small corner of the world: the high provinces of southern Andean Peru. As a collective effort, the studies presented here shed new light on the origins, intransigeance, and meaning of violence in an area of the Third World that has recently been afflicted with a seemingly unstoppable spiral of political and social violence. In a more general sense, however, they also suggest some ways in which our questions about violence and culture in the modern world might best be examined through study of the historically specific forms which violence, power, and cultural community have assumed in particular regions of the world. By looking closely at how violence, power, and cultural community are experienced and understood in the Peruvian highlands, we hope to show that the violent practices and discourses which produce subjectivities, histories, cultures, and truths are both actively contested and historically concrete: Both violent acts and the forms of power and cultural identity they generate are carried out by and benefit specific individuals and groups. As such, they are neither natural nor inevitable attributes of any social order.

Conflict, Culture, and Resistance in Andean and Latin American Studies

In recent years, Latin Americanists have begun to reexamine the relationship between indigenous Latin American modes of cultural community and the violent history of European conquest. Whereas the traditions and cultures of the Americas' indigenous peoples were once considered separate from the national histories and "Western" cultural traditions of those countries in which contemporary Indians lived, by the late 1960s anthropologists and historians interested in Latin America had begun to rethink the relationship of the communities they studied to the larger political and economic arenas in which they had historically existed. No longer were Indian communities to be defined as autonomous cultural and social systems. Rather, by reinserting peasant and indigenous communities into national and international histories, scholars began to rethink concepts of local and ethnic community from the related perspectives of class differentiation and intra-group conflict.[1] Privileged topics of study within this conflict oriented reintegration of anthropology and history in Latin American studies included the problems of class formation and export economies, the role of peasants in Mexico's national revolution and Colombia's partisan wars, the problem of rural banditry, and peasant participation in the transition to capitalism.[2] In the Andes, historians reevaluated the causes and impact of nineteenth and early twentieth century peasant uprisings, the role of peasantries in the War of the Pacific, banditry, the articulation of peasant and capitalist economies, and the emergence of contemporary peasant politics in the 1960s and 1970s.[3]

The new focus on the role of political and social conflict in the emergence of rural capitalist economies and contemporary peasant social formations also gave fresh insights into the nature of colonial revolts in Latin America. In Mexico and Central America, historians turned their attention towards such ethnically defined regional conflicts as the caste and mission wars.[4] In the Andes, anthropologists and historians re-examined the eighteenth century colonial uprisings and the earlier sixteenth century messianic uprising known as the Taqui Onqoy.[5] This literature on Andean colonial rebellions emphasized the ethnic structuring of colonial conflict, the importance of religious cosmology, the ambiguous class and ethnic affiliations of the Indians' *mestizo* and criollo leadership, and the class nature of Indian demands for fiscal and economic reform. Most importantly, however, in the context of contemporary peasant militancy, these studies of colonial conflict laid the foundations for conceptualizing an ongoing tradition or ethos of resistance as the new basis for defining Andean cultural continuity (Flores-Galindo 1987; Larson 1983 & 1988; Stern 1982; Stern (ed.) 1987). This new historiography of resistance rejected the notion of unchanging tradition as the basis for defining an authentic indigenous culture. It suggested instead that the elements of a distinctively "Andean" cultural identity lay in the adaptive resistance of an ethnically defined ✓ subaltern population.

The new focus on resistance has given anthropologists and historians a means to account both for the continually changing, emergent, or creative aspects of cultural traditions and identities, and for the intimate relationship of these identities and traditions to the historical record of violent conflict and domination formerly excluded from anthropological definitions of indigenous Andean culture. On the other hand, however, the historians' emphasis on the ethnic parameters of both the resistant population and the culture of resistance which their practices presumably reflect, has reproduced in disturbing ways an older distinction within Latin American historiography and anthropology between indigenous and non-indigenous (or *mestizo*) spheres of cultural and social interaction. In the case of the Andes, this tendency has been reinforced by the privileged position afforded to colonial historiography in the study of rebellions, revolts and resistance. Because modern forms of resistance are envisioned as the continuation of a colonial past in which both cultural and racial lines were, in many respects, more easily drawn, the forms of cultural and ethnic community projected onto nineteenth and twentieth century Andean societies have assumed a misleading polarity in much of the literature. In the process, the boundaries of class and cultural affiliations have been deceptively conflated: "Peasant" and "Indian" become interchangeable identities used to describe the cultural and class contours of a resistant population.

The theoretical and political implications of postulating enduring forms of cultural community as an ethnically defined tradition of resistance have been highlighted by recent events in the Peruvian Andes. Since May 1980, when the guerrilla organization of the Communist Party of Peru ("Sendero Luminoso" [Shining Path]) declared the initiation of its armed struggle against the Peruvian state, Peru has witnessed a decade of escalating political violence that has claimed over 27,000 lives. While much of this war has been played out on a highland geopolitical stage, the parties to the violence have at best only tenuous connections to the indigenous peasantries whom anthropologists and historians had taken to be the principal actors in Andean rural history and culture. Indeed, as I explain in greater detail in my conclusions to this volume, Andean peasants and their community and political organizations have been the principal victims of both Sendero's war and the counterinsurgency campaigns waged by the Peruvian armed forces.

The Andean peasantry's fate in this new scenario of political violence reveals both the usefulness and limitations of those theories of cultural identity and resistance formulated by historians and anthropologists on the basis of the experiences and political agendas of 1960s and 1970s Peru. The historical perspicacity of these theories is demonstrated by the fact that Andean peasant organizations have been targetted by both Sendero and the armed forces precisely because they *do* constitute the principal institutional loci for the local democratic practices and historically proven forms of resistance through which peasants have been able to organize independently of such outside authoritarian forces as Sendero and the Peruvian military.[6] In this respect, Andean historiography and anthropology have helped to strengthen the political and cultural traditions through which peasants attempt to defend themselves and their communities from the violence of both Sendero and the state (Flores-Galindo 1989; Montoya 1986).

Viewed from another angle, however, Peru's "dirty war" also raises important questions about what has been left unsaid about power, ethnicity, and violence itself in the new historiography and anthropology of resistance. Sendero, for example, has recruited both its leadership and militants from a provincial elite and a generation of rural youth whose identities and aspirations often straddle the idealized cultural and ethnic divide which the literature would have us believe separates indigenous peasants from *mestizo* elites. Similarly, although—as I argue in my conclusions to this volume—the authoritarian philosophy of power underwriting Sendero's political-military strategy originates from a distinctively Western European political and philosophical tradition, the partial (and, at times, complete) success which Sendero has had in speaking to an Andean audience cannot easily be explained by invoking the cultural and epistemological divides supposedly separating European and Andean traditions. Nor can the extreme forms of violence which Sendero uses to enforce its claims to power be dismissed as imported forms of terror. Many of the specific idioms and forms of power upon which party members rely in dealing with the peasantry, for example, pull on a regional tradition of coercive local power known as *gamonalismo* (Degregori 1990b; Manrique 1989b & 1990; Poole & Rénique 1991:176–177). As several of the authors in this volume argue, *gamonalismo* must be understood as a historically specific form of power based on both the use of physical violence and the manipulation of certain codes of racial and aesthetic distinction, gender, and authority. These "codes" are neither ethnically bounded nor class defined, but rather form part of a shared understanding of power and authority that links peasants and *mestizos* in what we might think of as a regional "culture of violence."

One of the goals of this book is to take a closer look at the forms of power, ethnicity, and violence that have shaped social and cultural identity in the Peruvian Andes. The different authors in the book look in particular at two key areas in which the notions of cultural community, resistance, and identity might be rethought. The first is the racial discourse that underlies (and motivates) individuals' understandings of ethnic identity and community. The second is the violent practices through which power is continually reconfirmed or "acted out" in Peruvian Andean society. Because these constant reconfirmations and displays of power through violence form part of every individual's sense of self and society, they must— as these studies suggest—be recognized as part of any definition of an "Andean" cultural formation.

Ethnicity and Race in the Peruvian Andes

Building on the longstanding models of New World ethnic relations outlined above, historians—and, to a somewhat lesser degree, anthropologists—have approached Andean ethnicity as an established and, for the most part, stable set of identities arranged along a continuum from "Indian" to "Spanish." As "ethnic" identities, these identities are assumed to be socially constructed, rather than biologically given, and to be based on a combination of culture in the form of customs and beliefs, and a sense of group origins traced through such factors as nationality, language, and religion. Building on this understanding of ethnicity, historians and anthropologists have tended to see both ethnic and cultural identity in the Andes as an inherently social product of group formation or self-identity. As such, identity formation is seen to occur within the context of local communities, in the case of highland peasants and *mestizo*s, or within the newly emergent communities of migrants and laborers found in Lima and other Andean cities.

In Peru, as in many other Latin American countries, however, one of the most important cultural frameworks shaping both personal identity and public understandings of ethnicity and culture is the decidedly non-local discourse of race. While the biological category of race has been long since overturned by, among other things, the theories of socially constructed identity advocated by ethnicity theory, the concept and reality of race as a social and discursive category continues to mold individuals' perceptions of self, other, and society. Racial terminology permeates nearly every aspect of daily life and social intercourse in Peru (Callirgos 1991), while ideologies of racial inferiority and superiority inform dimensions of social practice ranging from the most mundane negotiations of power in small Andean villages to the brutal counterinsurgency doctrines of the Peruvian armed forces. Indeed, given the acknowledged presence of racial and racist discourses in Peru, what is most striking is the absence of any serious discussion in the Andeanist literature of how race affects Peruvians' understandings of such things as culture, power, ethnicity, and resistance itself.

Race is a necessarily divisive and violent dimension of modern social orders (Omi & Winant 1986). It is this aspect of race which anthropologists have had the most difficulty reconciling with traditional approaches to both society and culture in Andean anthropology. Andean culture has frequently been represented in the anthropological literature as a normative order based on ecological harmony, organic reproduction, and forms of consensual and ritual community inherited from the pre-Columbian or colonial past (e.g., Burga 1988; Isbell 1985; Pease 1981; Sallnow 1987). The corporative or collective homogeneity frequently ascribed to such constructions of culture and culturally determined behavior (including resistance) has the effect of identifying "Andean culture" with certain forms of community organization and linguistic affiliation—and, hence, with a specific ethnic group and social class: the Quechua or Aymara-speaking, community-based Andean peasantry. As a result, Quechua and Aymara speaking peasants and Spanish-speaking *mestizo*s have been assumed to move in separate cultural worlds.

Recent critiques of this essentialist view of culture (e.g., Starn 1991), however, have also ignored the ways in which the racial discourse so predominant in Peruvian society essentializes or naturalizes cultural divides for *both* the outside observers of Andean society *and* the Andean *mestizo* and peasant classes. For anthropology, the problem of naturalized or "essentialized" cultural boundaries must not be restricted to a critique of anthropology as a "misrepresentation" of reality. Rather, as several of the authors in this volume suggest, anthropologists need also to examine the ways in which Andean peoples have themselves come to understand their world through the naturalized categories of race and culture. These popular understandings of racial and cultural difference—for example, the divide between Indian and *mestizo*—relate both to local forms of power (e.g., *gamonalismo*) and to national or regional discourses of racial and cultural difference (e.g., *indigenismo* and the nation). By refocussing our anthropological lens on the relationship between such local idioms of power and the divisive racial ideologies that have distinguished Peruvian constructs of the modern nation it becomes easier to understand the all too visible place of violence in Andean history and culture.

Violence in Modern Andean Social Formations

Once considered anathema to both culture and social order, violence has recently been scrutinized anew by cultural and social theorists. Anthropologists and ethnographers, faced with the escalating political and ethnic violence they encounter in the field (Nordstrom & Martin 1992; Sluka 1990), have begun to rethink the meaning of violence as a social and cultural form. Anthropological approaches to the study of violence have, however, varied widely. For some, violence is of interest primarily as a foundational text or ritualized form of social control in primitive societies (Balandier 1986; Clastres 1977; Lenclud & Jamin (eds.) 1984; Verdier 1980), or as a symbolic system of signification (Riches (ed). 1986). For others, violence is an expression of factionalist political and social ideologies (Greenberg 1989), and, as such, forms part of traditional modes of domination (Gilsenan 1986; Jahangir 1989). Such anthropological approaches to violence attempt, for the most part, to fit the observed or ethnographic fact of violence into established theoretical concepts of cultural and social order. Violence is interpreted as one of the many symbolic systems or "texts" that make up "culture"; or, building on anthropological theories of segmentary societies, it is seen to be a culturally recognized means of resolving divisions within the social order.

The anthropological literature on the violence of what have variously been called primitive, traditional, or non-Western societies contrasts sharply with the contemporary literature on violence in Western European history and society. Drawing on a wide array of disciplinary perspectives, this literature adopts a critical perspective on both violence and power that raises important questions regarding the ways in which we conceive and theorize culture itself. Sociological investigation into the phenomena of state terrorism and genocide have led to a rethinking of the ways in which the cultural and political legitimacy of modern nationalist state formations is grounded in violence and war (Corradi, Fagen & Garretón 1992; Smith 1991; van den Berghe 1990; on nationalism and violence, see Anderson 1983). A growing literature on the discursive formations and disciplinary technologies of state and imperial rule has further expanded the boundaries of violence to encompass the very mechanisms and institutions that produce both culture and political order (e.g., Foucault 1979; Mitchell 1988; Said 1978). Within this literature, studies of racism and racial ideologies in the modern nation state have highlighted the centrality of such divisive, and inherently violent, ideologies to modern political systems of rule and domination (e.g., Fanon 1961; Foucault 1991; Omi & Winant 1986; Said 1985). Yet other theorists have pointed to the discursive and philosophical connections between such forms of violence and the European political philosophies informing social science inquiry (Adorno & Horkheimer 1972; Benjamin 1978; Clastres 1977; Deleuze & Guattari 1983; Foucault 1979; Hoffman 1989). Together these new literatures raise a pressing critique of the Enlightenment view of violence as something that is opposed (or historically prior), and therefore external, to a modern social order based on reason and rational rule. They argue instead for a re-examination of violence as a constitutive—rather than aberrant—feature of Western economic, philosophical, and political formations.

Recent anthropological analyses of political, social and state violence in the non-European world have extended such arguments to analyze the ways in which violence has been inscribed in the historical memory, cultural identities, and political ideologies of third world and colonial populations (Carmack 1988; Coronil & Skurski 1991; Feldman 1991; Lavie 1990; Nordstrom & Martin 1992; Taussig 1987 & 1992). From this literature has come a clearer understanding of the ways in which colonial and postcolonial states have used terror and violence to construct both regimes of overt authoritarian domination and systems of democratic rule. By examining the role of violence in the consolidation and reproduction of ideological and cultural hegemony within the modern state, this new anthropology of violence resonates with the philosophical critique of the Enlightenment understanding of "reason"—as the basis of the modern bureaucratic state and its attendant concept of civil society—as an antidote to the violence of "pre-modern" (or pre-rational) governments and states. The importance of the new anthropology of violence, however, goes beyond its correspondence with this more general postmodern "rage against reason" (Bernstein 1992). Rather than simply condemning "reason" for having falsely denied its ties to violence and domination, the new anthropological literature on violence takes as its *starting point* what Michael Taussig (1992:116) has called "the necessary institutional interpenetration of reason by violence" in the modern state. It thus raises the possibility of going beyond the denunciatory—and largely dead-end—positions of the postmodern critique to carry out an empirical examination of the cultural, ideological and discursive channels through which modern forms of political and state power have in practice fused the (supposedly separate) discourses of reason and fear.

Concretely, anthropology's contribution to this questioning of the narrative of modern reason has been twofold. First, anthropologists have by and large insisted that the cultural or expressive dimensions of violence not be separated from the instrumental domain to which social scientists have hitherto confined their analyses of both state violence and more generalized forms of political and social violence. Second, anthropologists have insisted that, as *cultural forms* wielded by both the state and those who would contest state power, violence, terror, and fear inform even such intimate spheres of cultural understanding as individuals' concepts of self, nation, and power. They thus inform as well the modes of "reason" and "rationality" by which individuals construct narratives of causality, history, and power.

A related set of issues emerges from the new Peruvian literature on contemporary political violence. Faced with the immediacy of escalating political and social violence in the 1980s and 1990s, Peruvian sociologists and anthropologists have begun to explore the social (Degregori 1990b; Portocarrero & Oliart 1989; Portocarrero & Soraya 1991), psychological (Rodríguez R. & Castelnuovo 1985), historical (Manrique 1990), and political (Degregori 1990a; Manrique 1989b) contexts which have allowed for the emergence and reproduction of political violence in their country. Several anthropologists have also attempted to outline an indigenous perspective on violence as a disruption of normative relations based on Andean principles of reciprocity (Ansion 1985). The discrepant, and politically situated, understandings of ethnicity and culture which emerge from this Peruvian literature have generated a broader debate on the nature of modernity in Peru (Urbano ed. 1990). A major issue at stake in this highly politicized debate surrounding modernity is the relation between violence, modernity, and the cultural, ethnic, and racial divisions characterizing Peruvian society. While some analysts perceive both political violence and the deep ethnic divides which supposedly fuel that violence as "colonial" (and hence, premodern) legacies impeding the consolidation of a democratic civil society and national culture (Degregori 1991; Portocarrero 1991), others view them more systemically as artifacts of national and regional economic formations in which power has traditionally been negotiated along racial and class lines (Flores-Galindo 1987; Manrique 1990; Montoya 1992).

While the debates about modernity have been in large part fueled by the spectre of Peru's contemporary political violence, analyses of the uses and meaning of violence are still restricted very much to an instrumental reading of violence as a means to achieve specific political (or military) ends. Little attention has been paid, for example, to the ways in which the terror and fear so successfully wielded by both the Peruvian armed forces and the political military organization of the PCP-Sendero Luminoso dovetail with underlying cultural paradigms of racial terror and the nation. Nor have historians or anthropologists looked closely at the ways in which the counterinsurgency state has instrumentalized existing fears of disorder and chaos as a mechanism of social discipline (Lechner 1991). Given both the pervasiveness and complexity of violence in Peru today, what is called for is a more critical understanding of the cultural and discursive dimensions of contemporary violence, the arbitrariness of power, and the uses of fear as a political mechanism.

The studies presented here are concerned with the violence, conflict, and understandings of power and ethnicity that permeate everyday life in the southern Peruvian Andes. As such, this book is an attempt to address some of the gaps in the literature on contemporary Andean and Latin American social formations. This gap can be defined, on one extreme, by the work of those who tend to see the violence perpetrated by "ethnic" conflict, political factionalism, and racism as a residual hangover from Latin America's colonial or pre-modern heritage of conquest (e.g., Rosenberg 1991), and, on the other, by the new anthropology of violence which has focussed almost exclusively on the role of political violence and state repression in perpetuating distinctively modern regimes of domination and rule by fear. Rather than engage in a direct examination of the violence of either of the principal combatants in Peru's ongoing "dirty war," we have preferred to focus our efforts on what James Scott has called the "quiet prehistory of violent conflict" (Scott 1992:63). Of concern in unveiling this "quiet prehistory" are a number of issues left silenced in much of the Andeanist literature. What are the images and idioms of power and authority expressed in Andean daily life? How do these images relate to the notions of racial and cultural difference that inform both violent conflict and the daily negotiations of self and other that constitute Andean community life? Finally, how can we explain the historical pervasiveness of violence itself as a culturally specific form of both conflict resolution and domination in Andean agrarian communities?

Our work departs, then, from most of the recent anthropological and sociological examinations of Third World violence. While these other works have focused on the role of the state or armed insurgencies in shaping the modalities of terror and fear that characterize modern regimes of power in Latin America and other parts of the Third World, our explorations of violence in the southern Peruvian Andes turn an ethnographic and historical lens on the workings-out of fear, race, domination, and violence in either daily life or in the relatively minor conflicts and incidents that shape individuals' sense of self and history. In emphasizing the place of violence in southern Andean society and culture these studies provide eloquent testimony to the ways in which the violence of both Peruvian racial discourse and the historically specific modes of domination and local rule present in the Andean countryside can and do penetrate rationality, reason, and identity in modern Peruvian society.

Regional Perspectives on Culture and Violence

The chapters collected here assume a regional framework for their analyses of violence and cultural identity. This regional focus allows the authors to rethink the nature of cultural identity as it emerges historically in relation to the complex and shifting alliances of state institutions, social classes, ethnic groups, and elite family networks which historians have identified as the basis of regional social systems.[7] This shared focus on a specific region in space, also allows for reflection upon how the localized forms of political, social, and cultural violence discussed in the different chapters develop in relation to each other and over time.

The specific region on which this volume focusses is the *provincias altas* or "high provinces" of southern Peru (Figure I.1). Popular consensus both among residents and scholars of the southern Peruvian Andes agrees on four characteristics defining the *provincias altas* as an identifiable cultural and historical region: They are considered to be geographically remote, economically backward, politically unruly, and culturally primitive. In accordance with these characteristics, the inhabitants of the region are assigned colorful, folkloric personalities which range from the noble bandit and cowboy-style bohemian, to the bloodthirsty criminal, and outlaw cattle-rustler.

While this popular—and only partially imagined—image of the *provincias altas* is given fairly uniform expression by its detractors and admirers alike, the precise geographic boundaries of the region are less easily drawn. As an economic and geographic region, the *provincias altas* unite the *punas*, or high grasslands, of the Departments of Cusco and Apurímac. This catchment area includes all of the Cusco provinces of Chumbivilcas, Espinar and Canas, as well as the southern or upland portions of the Provinces of Canchis and Paruro. In Apurímac, it includes portions of the provinces of Grau, Cotabambas, and Antabamba.

In his survey of the *provincias altas* in Chapter 1, geographer Daniel Gade discusses the historical and ecological arguments for considering this administrative pastiche as a uniform geographic region. Gade examines how such diverse factors as landforms and hydrography, strategic mineral deposits, idiosyncratic land-use patterns, sixteenth century de-

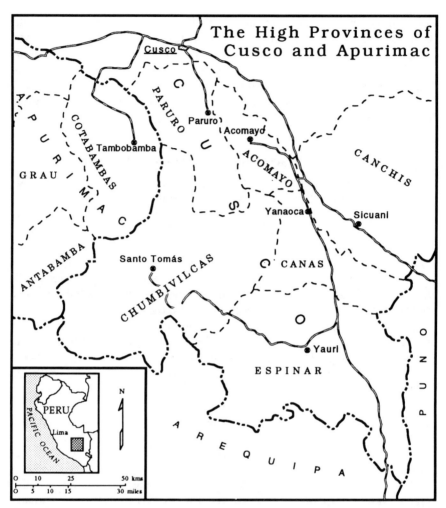

FIGURE I.1   The high provinces of Cusco and Apurímac.

mographic collapse, colonial resettlement policies, and the resulting concentration of economic resources in the higher *puna* areas, have together
shaped the historical conformation of the *provincias altas*. He concludes
that the distinctive feature defining the *provincias altas* is its physical isolation and social character as a "region of refuge." Geographic isolation is
seen to result from a hostile topography in which precipitous canyons,
such as that of the region's major river, the Apurímac, make travel and
communication extremely difficult. Gade is careful to point out, however,
that social isolation in the high provinces has no simple ecological cause
and effect. As he points out, "the human imprint on the land has enhanced

TABLE I.1   Capital, Altitude, and Date of Creation, Southern High Provinces of Cusco and Apurímac

Province	Capital	Districts (no.)	Altitude of capital (meters)	Date of creation
Department of Cusco				
Canchis	Sicuani	8	3,548	1833
Chumbivilcas	Santo Tomás	8	3,661	1821
Espinar	Yauri	7	3,927	1917
Canas	Yanaoca	8	3,923	1833
Paruro	Paruro	9	3,051	1821
Department of Apurímac				
Cotabambas	Tambobamba	5	3,275	1825
Antabamba	Antabamba	7	3,639	1872
Grau	Chuquibambilla	12	3,320	1825

SOURCE: Instituto Nacional de Estadística, *Boletín Estadístico Regional, 1986* (Lima, 1987).

isolation, but it is also explained by isolation. Local and regional patterns of settlement, demography and livelihood may owe much to remoteness, but their particularities may also entrench isolation even further."

The historical period covered in this volume runs from the mid-nineteenth century to the present day. Although, as Gade argues in Chapter 1, events prior to this period certainly helped to define the outlines of present day *provincias altas* society and culture, both the region's marked reputation for violence and its characteristics as a "region of refuge" are products of economic and social transformations that occurred in the mid to late nineteenth century. These transformations included the expansion of the international capitalist wool market, the concomitant rise of a violent form of local political and social power known as *gamonalismo*, and the consolidation of narratives of national and regional identity based on nineteenth century concepts of racial and cultural difference. This volume explores some of the ways in which these social processes have affected the daily lives, cultural identities, and political futures of the inhabitants of Peru's southern *provincias altas*.

Historical Patterns of Ethnicity and Violence in the *Provincias Altas*

At the time of the Spanish conquest, the *provincias altas*, like other areas of the Peruvian highlands, were inhabited by territorial kindreds known as *ayllus*. As the primary social unit of Andean society, the *ayllu* was simultaneously an economic collectivity for landholding and production, an institution for regulating marriages and social reproduction, a religious or rit-

TABLE I.2   Population and Territory, *Provincias Altas*, 1990

Province	Territory (square km.)	Population	Urban (percent)	Rural (percent)	Peasant communities
Department of Cusco					
Canas	2,104	36,721	11	89	60
Canchis	3,999	95,446	48	52	95
Chumbivilcas	5,371	72,823	13	87	64
Espinar	5,311	50,225	22	78	48
Paruro	1,984	34,910	23	77	46
Department of Apurímac					
Cotabambas	2,590	42,791	15	85	28
Antabamba	3,219	14,880	56	44	13
Grau	2,198	27,746	–	–	–
Provincias Altas (Total)	26,776	375,542	32	68	368
PERU	1,285,216	22,332,100	70	30	2,895

SOURCES: Instituto Nacional de Estadística, *Boletín Estadístico Regional, 1980* (Cusco, 1983); Centro de Estudios Bartolome de las Casas (eds.) *Documentos. Rimanakuy Cusco, 1986* (Cusco, 1986); Richard Webb, Graciela Fernandez Baca, *Perú en Números, 1990* (Lima, 1990).

ual entity focussed on a titular sacred mountain and territory, and a hierarchical political unit controlled by hereditary leaders known as *kurakas*. In different historical moments and for different ritual and religious purposes, these *kurakas* and the *ayllus* for whom they served as lords, united into larger social identity groups which the Spaniards referred to as *curacazgos* (from *kuraka*) or *cacicazgos* (from *cacique*, the Nahuatl word for chief). In modernday social science parlance, such early colonial or precolumbian groups are often referred to as "ethnic groups."

Local mythology holds that first the Inca and then the Spanish conquests met with fierce resistance on the part of two of the *provincias altas* more prominent ethnic groups: the K'anas (who were possibly Aymara speakers) and the Chumbivilcas (who spoke their own vernacular).[8] Following Inka conquest of the region, towns such as Colquemarca and Quiñota were built along the frontier between Inka territory and that of the neighboring Chankas. Chumbivilcano speakers from the area surrounding these towns paid tribute to the Inka state by acting as soldiers in the Chanka wars (Acuña 1965(1586)). The K'anas are also credited with a bellicose history of resistance to Spanish domination.

Following the Spanish conquest, Spaniards sought to reorder and control Andean indigenous society through religious conversion, the establishment of nucleated settlements (*reducciones*), labor grants (*encomiendas*), and forced labor corvée (*mita*) to the silver and mercury mines of Potosí and Huancavelica (see Gade Chapter 1). These same colonial institutions through which Spain reorganized Andean social space and economic life were also the sites in which the discourses and practices of ethnic and cultural classification took shape. Spanish civil and ecclesiastic authorities vied with *kurakas* and other representatives of the Andean nobility, for control over labor and resources (Spalding 1984; Stern 1982; for the *provincias altas*, see Poole 1987 & Glave 1987 & 1988). In the *ayllus* themselves, the commoners struggled to retain some autonomy with respect to these competing local powers. These *ayllu* members were classified as "Indians" with the legal status of minors. Their *kurakas*, meanwhile, were assigned a more privileged noble status, albeit one still subsumed to the overarching fiscal and political category of the "Indian Republic." Spaniards or "whites," regardless of their social and class ranking, were placed above the collectivity of "Indians," including nobility.

As Gade describes in Chapter 1 of this volume, Indians resisted the new administrative order and forced labor corvées by fleeing their assigned settlements. In the *provincias altas*, this migration led to the creation of a sizeable population of *forasteros* (foreigners) who could either evade tribute completely or pay smaller head taxes (Wightman 1990). In Chumbivilcas and Canas, Indians returned to their territorially dispersed *ayllu* settlement pattern (Glave 1987 & 1988; Poole 1987). By filing legal claims to their original territories in far off *puna* lands, these Indians succeeded in establishing a *de facto* territorial structure which in many ways ran counter to the Spaniards' ideas of civil order based on centralized communities and nested administrative hierarchies. This territory allowed for the reproduction of prehispanic *ayllu* identities and economic networks specific to the *provincias altas*.

Resistance to Spanish rule also took the form of sporadic violent conflicts between Spaniards and Indians. Litigations over both agricultural and pasture land, disputes over the administration of tribute and *mita* service, and fights over the control of such resources as water, wood, and animals characterized the daily lives of both Spaniard and Indian in the colonial *provincias altas*. Given the distance from colonial administrative and judicial centers, such disputes were often resolved with force and violence. In 1776 in Velille, Chumbivilcas, for example, the Indians rebelled against their corregidor, whom they eventually tried and executed (Poole 1987). Within Indian communities as well, violence in both public and domestic life, though never normatively accepted, came gradually to characterize certain domains of daily life among the colonized population (Stavig 1985).

Occasional uprisings and revolts provided the scenario in which more dramatic forms of violent conflict could unfold. Indians from the *provincias altas* participated actively in the largest and most famous of these revolts. This revolt was led by José Gabriel Condorcanqui or Tupac Amara, a *kuraka* from the high province of Canas and Canchis (then united in the Partido (Province) of Tinta.[9] Tupac Amaru, who claimed Inca noble descent, called for abolition of administrative abuses and for equal economic status for Indian and "caste" merchants such as himself. His call to arms reached Indian populations from all the provinces of southern Peru and Bolivia, each of whom mobilized around issues and grievances specific to their region. These grievances built upon forms of conflict, dispute, and political culture specific to each region and articulated a growing Indian and peasant consensus around the use of violence as a means to effect much needed change.

Analyses of the cultural significance of violence in eighteenth century rebellions, however, have lagged behind the advances made towards understanding the economic and political dimensions of the rebellions. Most such attempts to examine this violence have focussed on the repertoire of symbolic meanings associated with the rituals and Catholic derived sacraments practiced by Indian rebels (Szeminski 1987; Thurner 1991). A less studied aspect of the insurrection, however, involves the equally symbolic theatricality and sacramental brutality of *Spanish* violence (Hinojosa 1989; Walker 1991). It was through such theatrical gestures that the Spaniards retaliated for the role played by the *provincias altas* in the rebellion. Together with Tupac Amaru and his family, two Chumbivilcano generals of Tupac Amaru's army were executed in the plaza of Cusco. Following their public execution and quartering, the Spanish authorities then sent one of Tupac Amaru's legs to Livitaca, Chumbivilcas, as a warning to potential future rebels; to the provinical capital of Santo Tomás they sent an arm from Tupac Amaru's son, Hipólito. With these closing acts of theatricalized brutality the Spaniards sought to inscribe defeat into the historical memory of Peru's southern Andean communities.

Lingering memories of the Tupac Amaru rebellion also cast their shadow over the creole elites in Lima, lending both independence and the ensuing process of nation-building a distinctive character. This character can be summed up in three distinguishing features of Peruvian national identity, each of which bears the mark of the violence that frequently shook Peruvian colonial and early republican society. A first such feature was a continuing elite fear of the Indian masses. Alone of the South American creole elites, Lima's elite resisted independence from Spain in large part out of fear of the Indian and African American soldiers who accompanied the liberating armies. After independence as well, recurrent panics shook Lima as rumours of Indian violence spread, renewing longstanding colonial fears of Indian revenge and slave revolt.

Reinforcing Lima's fear of the Andean highlands and provinces, the early years of republican governance were characterized by the sharply divisive and often violent politics of *caudillo* rule. This second feature of Peruvian national identity pitted regional military leaders, or *caudillos*, against the central government in Lima (Gootenberg 1989). The chaotic political life of early republican Peru set the stage for the third characteristic of Peru's national identity: its centralist narratives of historical progress. In these narratives, the state's "civilizing" force is seen to be continually resisted by a provincial—and particularly Andean—"barbarism" noted for its unruly, violent, and fiercely independent *caudillos* or *gamonales*. The reality of Lima's precarious hold on much of the so-called national territory gave birth to the dominant metaphor of Peruvian cultural and national identity: the cultural and racial divide separating coastal and highland society.

The traditions of violence or combativeness said to characterize the *provincias altas* must be set within this framework of Peruvian national identity and the narratives of progress, civilization, and racial difference that distinguish Peruvian understandings of nation and self. Although violence, rebellion and revolt were features of the colonial era, neither the reality nor image of violence in modern Andean society are organic or necessary outgrowths of an indisputably violent or fractious "colonial heritage." Rather the heritage of conquest and colonialism that has shaped the *provincias altas* is itself a product of the narrative and interpretive strategies which arise from different intellectual, social, and political projects. In the case of the *provincias altas*—and, I would suggest, for that of many other areas in Latin America—these acts of historical interpretation can be explained by examining the ways in which the nineteenth century liberal ideologies of race and the authoritarian discourses associated with such forms of local power as *gamonalismo* have essentialized the cultural and racial characteristics supposedly separating indigenous and *mestizo* populations and cultures.

These acts of interpretation and representation form the topic of the second chapter in the volume. Focussing on a 1931 incident involving the deaths of several policemen and peasants in the community of Molloccahua (Espinar Province, Cusco), anthropologist Benjamin Orlove examines the language and narratives through which *mestizos* have conceptualized the racial and cultural divides separating Indian from *mestizo*, country from town, and civilization from barbarism. The complex layering of historical imagery which surfaces from the *mestizo* accounts of the events in Molloccahua reveals the importance of violence as a narrative and historical trope structuring the ways in which people in Espinar remember and act upon concrete historical events. Occupying a central place in this regional historical imagination is the panoply of ethnic and racial images through which the opposing sides in violent conflicts represent and dehumanize their enemy. Orlove considers how ethnic and social identities are shaped by the narrative mechanisms through which concrete historical acts of violence are essentialized in popular memory. As such, his analysis of the events in Espinar provides important clues for imagining how both racial imagery and the powerful spatial metaphors of city and countryside, civilization and barbarism, have shaped local level perceptions of contemporary political violence.

The narrative strategies and racial imagery explored by Orlove in his analysis of the events at Molloccahua can, in many respects, be said to characterize provincial perceptions of self and other, city and country, *mestizo* and Indian throughout the Peruvian highlands. The question remains, however, as to why the *provincias altas* have retained their particular reputation for violence and how this reputation has both shaped and been shaped by the discourses of national and racial identity uncovered in the accounts from Molloccahua. This question of the specificity of *provincias altas* culture is explored in the following two chapters on the notoriously violent *gamonal* or "*misti*" (*mestizo*) culture of Chumbivilcas and the equally famous indigenous ritual battles practiced throughout the *provincias altas*.

In my own contribution in Chapter 3, I examine the effects of Peru's early period of *caudillo* rule and territorial fragmentation on *provincias altas* society and culture. I argue that the specificity of the *provincias altas* social formation can be traced to the effects of the nineteenth century wool market on the coercive form of personal power which came to be known as *gamonalismo*. Following independence, administrative and economic territory was carved up among those powerful *mestizo* families who controlled access to both Indian labor and state offices on the local and provincial level. The resulting factional and territorial disputes between rival families gave rise to the institutionalization of the armed *pandilla*, or mounted gang. These *pandillas* would later become a distinguishing feature of *gamonal* society in the *provincias altas*. It was through the livestock rustling activities and acts of terror carried out by the *pandillas* that the *gamonales* defined their "mediating" role between Indians and the state. From virtually the beginning of the Peruvian republic, therefore, violence was inscribed at the heart of both local level state political rule and the regimes of domination that would shape perceptions of self and other in *provincias altas* society.

A deciding cultural factor determining both the efficacy and longevity of *gamonal* violence in Chumbivilcas and other parts of the *provincias altas* is the value assigned to certain forms of performative and masculine violence in the region. In discussing the origins of a provincial "folklore of violence" in Chumbivilcas, I argue that the Chumbivilcano *gamonales* retained their hold on political and social power in part through folkloric traditions, songs, legends, and spectacles which celebrate the livestock, horses, arms and masculine bravado constitutive of traditional *gamonal* power. This cultural elaboration of a romanticized or bohemian folkloric ideal based on the same gendered qualities of violence and rebelliousness associated with the *gamonal* created the new idioms of cultural distinction through which *gamonal* culture, and *gamonal* power, would be consolidated.

The reputation for violence attributed to the *provincias altas* as a regional cultural formation, however, is not restricted to the *gamonales* and rustlers of Chumbivilcas. Another, equally important, dimension of the region's popular culture are the ritual battles discussed by Orlove in Chapter 4. Like the *gamonal* violence analyzed in the preceding chapter, ritual battles highlight the performative aspects of violence and the centrality of theatrical traditions to the creation of a regional "culture of violence." The attributes assigned to this "culture of violence," however, vary according to the interpretive scheme used to narrate or represent the events in question. As Orlove argues, the distinct semantic fields surrounding the terms "ritual" and "battle"—one of which connotes notions of order and culture, and the other, violence or disorder—constitute a problem for the anthropologist who seeks to understand the historical origins and meaning of these practices. Their union in the term "ritual battle," however, creates an inherently ambiguous field of meaning which has the positive effect of forcing us to rethink the assumptions and images normally attached to the discrete concepts of symbolic culture (ritual) and instrumental violence (battle). Such a rethinking requires consideration of not only the intellectual and philosophical traditions informing our own notions of culture and violence. It also calls for a parallel re-examination of the social practices, narratives and histories through which Andean peoples have come to their own, often divergent, understandings of these terms. It is only through such an inquiry into the local, historical meanings of ritual battles, Orlove suggests, that we can eventually come to answer the question of why ritual battles exist and why they continue to be practiced in some areas—for example, the *provincias altas*—and not others.

The question of why such practices as *gamonalismo* and ritual battles survive in the *provincias altas* invoke two of the constitutive features of the region's "colonial heritage." The first is the image and reality of the geographical and historical isolation described by Gade in his overview of the region in Chapter 1. The second is the racial or "ethnic" discourses surrounding notions of Indianess and *mestizaje*, self and other, civilization, and barbarism explored in Orlove's and my own chapters on *mestizo* narratives, *gamonal* violence and the ambiguous violence of ritual battles. Peter Gose's ethnographic portrait of Huaquirca (Apurimac) in Chapter 5 provides a more detailed examination of how the racial categories and interpretive politics discussed in previous chapters infiltrate and give shape to daily life in a *provincias altas* community. Gose suggests that "Indian" and *"mestizo"* identities in the Apurimac town of Huaquirca are structured as a semiotics of property enclosure and cultural distinction centered around the European, or Spanish colonial, folk categories of common versus private lands. This incipient recognition of the material basis of class difference, however, dovetails with a cultural discourse centered around attitudes towards labor and reciprocity. Thus, for example, the *mestizos'* insistence on enclosing or fencing their land is interpreted by the peasants of Huaquirca as a refusal to conform to their own "Indian" norms of reciprocal labor obligations, or *ayni*. In this way, Gose suggests, Peru's racial discourse naturalizes local structures of class in terms of a "mythology of conquest" in which class differences are represented as the ethnic or racial categories of "Indian" and "Spanish." It is the intersection between this racialized mythology and language of conquest and the daily reaffirmation of deepseated aesthetic codes of class distinction which explains the *mestizos'* hold on power in Huaquirca. Although the language of cultural superiority or distinction wielded by Huaquirca's *elite* shares much in common with *mestizo* discourse in other parts of Peru, a particular characteristic of this class aesthetic in the *provincias altas* is its melding with local or traditional forms of *gamonal* family power. Here the first factor of spatial remoteness also plays a role for, as Gose argues, the *provincias altas* have functioned as an effective "region of refuge" not so much for a pristine "indigenous" culture, as for a *gamonal* culture which depends for its reproduction on the extra-legal use of violence and the monopoly of local state office.

In the recent agrarian reform of 1970 the conflicting discourses of racial and class difference described in previous chapters, were appropriated and re-worked by the leftist military government of General Juan Velasco Alvarado (1968–1975). Velasco ruled that the term "Indian" was no longer to be used, and that the juridical entitites formed under previous governments as *comunidades indígenas* (indigenous communities) were to be re-named *comunidades campesinas* (peasant communities). Christiane Paponnet-Cantat's analysis of the impact of agrarian reform in the Chumbivilcano district of Capacmarca, discusses the implications of these interventionist state ideologies for ethnic and class relations on the local level. As in other areas of the *provincias altas*, local landowners in Capacmarca employed violence to combat the effects of land reform. Landlords and agents of the state—in this case, rural policemen and teachers with family or personal ties to local *gamonal* families—responded to state intervention by escalating the criminal activities around which local elites had traditionally assured their political and economic dominance in the province. As both Gose and I also conclude from our analyses of *mestizo* culture elsewhere in the *provincias altas*, in such situations where *gamonal* violence comes to form part of a shared cultural discourse of ethnic and class distinction, the *mestizo* elite's monopoly of political and state office is the result, not the cause, of their local power.

José Luis Rénique's analysis of agrarian politics and class conflict in Chapter 7, also argues for the importance of local or "traditional" *gamonal* power as a factor explaining the unfolding of national and regional political initiatives in the Peruvian highlands. Unlike the case described by Paponnet-Cantat for the Cusco *provincias altas*, land reform in the neighboring department of Puno encouraged rural penetration of the state apparatus in the form of cooperatives. Much as occurred in Capacmarca, however, the agrarian reform failed to erradicate old forms of local power. Instead, the hacendados occupied bureaucratic offices in the agrarian reform or retained control over the cooperatives set up by the state. It is this failing, Rénique argues, that explains the state's later inability to respond to peasant initiatives for a restructuring of the cooperatives since the agrarian reform officers, who had ties to local power, blocked any initiative which they saw as empowering the peasantry. Frustration with the state's failure to make promised changes in the cooperatives' administration led some peasants to accept Sendero's violent intervention in the land invasions through which cooperative land was eventually recovered by the communities. The Peruvian state responded to the land invasions with more violence, this time directed towards members of PUM, a legal leftwing party with no connections to Sendero. It was because of their influence in the departmental peasant movement that PUM leaders were accused by both the government and the local hacendados and *gamonales* of "terrorist" activities.

The conflictual dialogue described by Rénique between community based forms of peasant political practice and a regional context of *gamonal* local power, is a scenario which acquires increasing resonance as scholars and politicians attempt to grapple with the complexities of Peruvian social and political violence in the 1990s. During the last few decades, Peru has become increasingly more democratic in terms of the stability of its elected national governments, the role of its expanding electoral opposition and, most importantly, the proliferation of a remarkable network of politically vocal grass-roots and community organizations. Yet at the same time, daily life in Andean Peru has also become more divisive, conflictual, and even habituated to the sight of bloodshed, bombings, and assassinations. The extent to which such violence has undermined Peruvian understandings of political and social process has been underscored by President Alberto Fujimori's ability to use political violence as a pretext for imposing his own highly authoritarian and anti-democratic rule in the aftermath of his April 1992 "self-inflicted *coup d'etat*." As these parallel processes unfold, the challenge for both Peruvians and students of Peru-

vian society and history becomes that of explaining the relation between a
maturing "culture of democracy" embodied in such institutions as national elections, peasant communities, and grass-roots political federations, and an expanding practice of violent coercion with historical ties to
the authoritarian "cultures of violence" characterizing both highland
gamonalismo and coastal *caudillismo*.

The former topic—democratic community—has received a good deal of
attention in an anthropological and sociological literature devoted to describing forms of grass-roots democracy (e.g., Ballon 1986), indigenous
community organization (e.g., Urton 1984; Smith 1989) and Andean ritual
and religion (e.g.,Allen 1989; Isbell 1978; Sallnow 1987). The topic of violence, by comparison, has been treated almost exclusively in the existing
literature on Andean Peru as an episodic or conjunctural exception to the
rule of continuing cultural identities rooted in corporatist ideas of community, ethnicity, and class. The possibilities of understanding the relation between violence and identity have been obfuscated further by the
tendency to see these two domains of Andean experience as separate or
opposed. The first (community consensus) is encoded in the literature
both as ethnically "Indian" and as part of an enduring Andean cultural
subconscious. The second (violence) is understood in exclusively instrumental terms. Little effort has been made to see how these two modes of
political action and discourse—cultural identity and strategic instrumental violence—intersect at the level of both personal experience and national peasant politics.

One goal of the chapters collected here is to bridge this gap between our
appreciation of what anthropologists and historians like to think of as
quintessentially "Andean" concepts of community and popular democracy, and the reality of an increasingly violent social order in which Andean peoples are both actors and victims. Are these historical and ethnographic insights of any value, however, in explaining the specific forms
and rationalities of violence being enacted today by the PCP-Sendero
Luminoso and the Peruvian military and paramilitary forces? In my conclusion to the volume I suggest that, although these military ideologies
answer, in the final analysis, to understandings of power and terror trace-
able to the political philosophies of Enlightenment Europe and the political traditions of the French Revolution, the particular playing out of the
"cycle of violence" they have initiated in Peru can only be understood by
considering the ways in which these military ideologies and Enlightenment derived concepts of power, authority, and historical causality intersect and abut with local ideologies of power and violence in the Andes.
Specifically, through analysis of recent political violence, and particularly
of the political-military organization known as "Sendero Luminoso," I
suggest the need to rework our understanding of historical process in the

Andes in terms of a notion of culture in which both the discursive rules and the repertoire of social actions available to individuals are neither fixed nor ethnically bounded, but rather processually negotiated and inherently ambiguous. The resource being negotiated is power. The discursive rules through which negotiation takes place are derived from multiple traditions of European and Andean political philosophy and practice. Principal among these is the discourse of race and racial difference—itself perhaps the least studied aspect of contemporary Peruvian and Andean societies.

The studies presented in this book represent an initial attempt to rethink the conceptual and theoretical categories we use to discuss culture, identity, and history itself in the Peruvian Andes. Although each chapter focusses on a different aspect of Andean historical and cultural experience, our collective focus on violence and power reflects a growing consensus in Latin American anthropology and history that culture and social order be rethought in terms of the often violent, and always conflictual, systems of domination that have shaped individuals' social identities. It also, however, speaks for the devastating centrality of both political and social violence in modern day Peruvian society. Against the background of Peru's twelve year "dirty war" and the growing authoritarianism of its current government, the highly visible role of both agrarian and political violence in the ordering of Peruvian social and historical experience takes on new resonances. We hope that our cultural and historical analyses of these processes can shed new light on the meanings and forms of violence, racism, and power in the Peruvian Andes today.

Notes

1. The major themes and polemics defining the field of agrarian conflict studies were set by a number of comparative works focussing on both pre- and early modern Europe and the Third World. See, among others, Hobsbawm 1965; Moore 1966; Paige 1976; Scott 1976; Skocpol 1979; Wolf 1969.

2. See for example, on class formation and export economies, Berquist 1986, Roseberry 1983, Smith 1984, and Wolf 1982; on the Mexican revolution and the Colombian Violencia, Knight 1980 and Oquist 1980; on banditry, Slatta 1987; on the transition to capitalism, Deere 1990, Duncan & Rutledge 1978, Mallon 1983, and Stern 1988.

3. On peasant uprisings, see Kapsoli 1977 and Piel 1967; on the War of the Pacific, see Manrique 1981, Bonilla 1988, and Mallon 1983 & 1987; on banditry, see Piel 1982, Poole 1988, Taylor 1986 and Walker 1989; on the articulation of peasant and capitalist economies, see among others Harris 1982, Montoya 1980, and Orlove 1977; on peasant politics, see Albó 1987, Flores-Galindo 1978 & 1987, Handelman 1974, Hobsbawm 1969, Hurtado 1986, and Smith 1989.

4. See, for example, Reed 1964, Hu-DeHart 1981, and Coatsworth 1988.

5. On eighteenth century uprisings, see Campbell 1987, Flores-Galindo (ed.) 1976, Gölte 1980, O'Phelan 1985, Spalding 1984, Stern 1987, and Varese 1968; on sixteenth century messianism, see Stern 1982 and Ossio (ed.) 1973.

6. To date, the most effective form of combatting Sendero in the countryside has been through the patrols, or *rondas*, organized by peasant communities. These *rondas* operate independently and are distinct from the civil patrols (which are sometimes also called *rondas*) organized by the armed forces. See Poole & Rénique 1992:68–70.

7. Anthropologists have tended to frame their study of Andean culture either with focussed community studies or broad comparative analyses which take the Andean highlands of Ecuador, Peru, Bolivia and parts of northern Chile and Argentina as a single culture area. Recent historical and economic work, by comparison, has tended to focus on the regional systems defined by internal markets and political networks; see for example, Larson 1988; Mallon 1983; Manrique 1989a; Montoya 1980; Gonzáles 1982, Sempat 1982, and Slater 1989.

8. As in other areas of the Peruvian Andes, the different "ethnic groups" in the *provincias altas* spoke several distinct vernaculars, including Chumbivilcano, Puquina, Aymara and, in Apurimac, a central Andean dialect of Quechua known as Chinchay Quechua. These languages—whose precise geographic distribution is unkown—mapped onto the overlapping and discontinuous territories of the region's principal ethnic groups. While the local vernaculars were eventually replaced by Quechua under Inka and Spanish rule, the horizontally fragmented nature of this settlement pattern would characterize *provincias altas* society throughout the colonial and early republican periods (Glave 1987; Poole 1987).

9. There is an extensive historiography on Tupac Amaru. For recent evaluations of this literature and the causes of the rebellion, see O'Phelan 1988, Stern 1982, Campbell 1982, and Flores-Galindo (ed.) 1976.

Bibliography

Adorno, Theodor & Max Horkheimer. 1972. *The Dialectic of Enlightenment*. New York: Continuum.

Albó, Javier. 1987. "From MNRistas to Kataristas to Katari." In S. Stern (ed.), *Resistance, Rebellion and Consciousness In the Andean Peasant World, 18th to 20th Centuries*, pp. 379–419. Madison: University of Wisconsin Press.

Allen, Catherine J. 1988. *The Hold Life Has. Coca and Cultural Identity in an Andean Community*. Washington: Smithsonian Institution Press.

Anderson, Benedict. 1983. *Imagined Communities. Reflections on the Origins and Spread of Nationalism*. London & New York: Verso.

Ansion, Juan. 1985. "Violencia y cultura en el Perú." In *Siete Ensayos Sobre la Violencia en el Perú*, pp. 59–78. Lima: Fundación Friedrich Ebert & APEP.

Balandier, Georges. 1986. "An Anthropology of Violence and War," *International Social Science Journal*, 110:499–511.

Ballon, Eduardo (ed.). 1986. *Movimientos sociales y democracia: La Fundación de un nuevo orden*. Lima: CEPES.

— Benjamin, Walter. 1978. "Critique of Violence" (1955). In *Reflections*, pp. 277–300. New York: Schocken Books.

Bernstein, Richard J. 1992. *The New Constellation. The Ethical-Political Horizons of Modernity/Postmodernity.* Cambridge, Mass.: MIT Press.

Berquist, Charles W. 1986. *Coffee and Conflict in Colombia, 1886–1910.* Durham: Duke University Press.

Bonilla, Heraclio. 1978. "The War of the Pacific and the National and Colonial Problem in Peru," *Past and Present*, (November):92–118

Burga, Manuel. 1988. *El Nacimiento de una utopia. Muerte y resurrección de los incas.* Lima: Instituto de Apoyo Agrario.

Burga, Manuel & Alberto Flores-Galindo. 1987. *Apogeo y Crisis de la República Aristocrática.* Lima: Rikchay Peru

Burga, Manuel & Wilson Reategui. 1981. *Lanas y capital mercantíl en el sur. La Casa Ricketts 1895–1935.* Lima: Instituto de Estudios Peruanos.

— Callirgos, Juan Carlos. 1991. "Identidades, estereotipos, tabú: El problema de las razas," *Márgenes*, 8:211–30.

Campbell, Leon. 1987. "Ideology and Factionalism During the Great Rebellion, 1780 to 1782." In S. Stern (ed.) *Resistance, Rebellion and Consciousness In the Andean Peasant World, 18th to 20th Centuries*, pp. 110–42. Madison: University of Wisconsin Press.

Carmack, Robert (ed.). 1988. *Harvest of Violence. The Mayan Indians and the Guatemalan Crisis.* Norman: Oklahoma University Press.

Clastres, Pierre. 1977. *Society Against the State.* New York: Urizen.

Coatsworth, John. 1988. "Patterns of Rural Rebellion in Latin America: Mexico in Comparative Perspective." In F. Katz (ed.), *Riot, Rebellion, and Revolution. Rural Social Conflict in Mexico*, pp. 21–62. Princeton: Princeton University Press.

— Coronil, Fernando & Julie Skurski. 1991. "Dismembering and Remembering the Nation: The Semantics of Political Violence in Venezuela," *Comparative Studies in Society and History*, 33(2):288–337.

Corradi, Juan E., Patricia W. Fagen, & Manuel A. Garretón (eds.) 1992. *Fear At the Edge: State Terror and Resistance in Latin America.* Berkeley: University of California Press.

Deere, Carmen Diana. 1990. *Household and Class Relations. Peasants and Landlords in Northern Peru.* Berkeley: University of California Press.

Degregori, Carlos Iván. 1990a. *Ayacucho 1969–1979: El Surgimiento de Sendero Luminoso.* Lima:Instituto de Estudios Peruanos.

———. 1990b. "Los hijos de la guerra. Jóvenes andinos y criollos frente a la violencia política." In *Tiempos de Ira y Amor*, pp. 185–219. Lima: DESCO.

———. 1991. "El Aprendíz de brujo y el curandero chino." In *Demonios y redentores en el nuevo Perú*, pp. 71–136. Lima: Instituto de Estudios Peruanos.

Deleuze, Gilles & Félix Guattari. 1983. *Anti-Oedipus. Capitalism and Schizophrenia.* Minneapolis: University of Minnesota Press.

Duncan, Kenneth & Ian Rutledge (eds.). 1978. *Land and Labour in Latin America: Essays on the Development of Agrarian Capitalism in the 19th and 20th Centuries.* Cambridge: Cambridge University Press.

Fanon, Frantz. 1961. *Les Damnés de la terre.* Paris: Maspero.

Feldman, Allen. 1991. *Formations of Violence. The Narrative of the Body and Political Terror in Northern Ireland.* Chicago: University of Chicago Press.

Flores-Galindo, Alberto. 1976. *Tupac Amaru II. Sociedad Colonial y Sublevaciones Populares.* Lima: Retablo de Papel Ediciones.

_____. 1978. "Apuntes sobre las ocupaciones de tierras y el sindicalismo agrario, 1945–1964," *Allpanchis*, 11/12:175–85.

_____. 1987. *Buscando un Inca: Identidad y utopía en los Andes.* Lima: Instituto de Apoyo Agrario.

_____. 1989. "Las sociedades andinas: Pasado y futuro." In Confederación Campesina del Perú, *Movilización Campesina: Respuesta Democrática*, pp. 4–9. Lima: Voz Campesina.

Foucault, Michel. 1979. *Discipline and Punish.* New York: Vintage.

_____. 1991. "Faire vivre et laisser mourir: La Naissance du racisme," *Les Temps Modernes*, No.535 (fev. 91):37–61.

Gilsenan, Michael. 1986. "Domination as Social Practice: Patrimonialism in North Lebanon: Arbitrary Power, Desecration, and the Aesthetics of Violence," *Critique of Anthropology*, 6(1):17–37.

Glave, Luis Miguel. 1987. "Comunidades campesinas en el Sur Andino, siglo XVII." In A. Flores-Galindo (ed.), *Comunidades Campesinas: Cambios y permanencias*, pp. 61–94. Lima & Chiclayo: CONCYTEC & Centro Solidaridad.

_____. 1988. "Demografía y conflicto social: Historia de las comunidades campesinas en los Andes del Sur." Lima: Instituto de Estudios Peruanos, Documento de Trabajo No.23.

Gölte, Jurgen. 1980. *Repartos y rebeliones. Tupac Amaru y las contradicciones de la economía colonial.* Lima: Instituto de Estudios Peruanos.

Gonzales de Olarte, Efraín. 1982. *Economías Regionales del Perú.* Lima: Instituto de Estudios Peruanos.

Gootenberg, Paul. 1989. *Between Silver and Guano. Commercial Policy and the State in Postindependence Peru.* Princeton: Princeton University Press.

_____. 1991. "Population and Ethnicity in Early Republican Peru: Some Revisions," *Latin American Research Review*, 26(3):109–157.

Greenberg, James B.. 1989. *Blood Ties. Life and Violence in Rural Mexico.* Tucson: Univ. of Arizona Press.

Handelman, Howard. 1974. *Struggle in the Andes. Peasant Political Mobilization in Peru.* Austin: Univ. of Texas Press.

Harris, Olivia. 1982. "Labour and produce in an ethnic economy, Northern Potosí, Bolivia." In D. Lehmann (ed.), *Ecology and Exchange in the Andes*, pp. 70–96. Cambridge: Cambridge University Press.

Hinojosa, Ivan. 1989. "El Nudo Colonial: La violencia en el movimiento tupamarista," *Pasado y Presente*, 2/3:73–82.

Hobsbawm, Eric J. 1965. *Primitive Rebels: Studies in Archaic Forms of Social Movement in the 19th and 20th Centuries* (1959). New York: Norton.

_____. 1969. "A Case of Neo-Feudalism: La Convención Peru," *Journal of Latin American Studies*, 1(1):31–51.

Hoffman, Piotr. 1989. *Violence in Modern Philosophy.* Chicago: University of Chicago Press.

Hu DeHart, Evelyn. 1981. *Missionaries, Miners and Indians. Spanish Contact with the Yaqui Nation of Northwestern New Spain, 1533–1820*. Tucson: University of Arizona Press.

Hurtado, Javier. 1986. *El Katarismo*. La Paz: Hisbol.

Isbell, Billie-Jean. 1985. *To Defend Ourselves. Ecology and Ritual in an Andean Village*. 2nd edition. Prospect Heights, Ill.: Waveland Press.

Jacobsen, Nils. 1982. Land Tenure and Society in the Peruvian Altiplano: Azángaro. Ph.D. dissertation, University of California, Berkeley.

Jahangir, B.K.. 1989. "Violence and Consent in a Peasant Society." In D. Miller, M. Rowlands, & C. Tilley (eds.), *Domination and Resistance*, pp. 316–324. London: Unwin-Hyman

Kapsoli, Wilfredo. 1977. *Los Movimientos campesinos en el Perú*. Lima: Edit. Delva.

Katz, Friedrich (ed.). 1988. *Riot, Rebellion, and Revolution. Rural Social Conflict in Mexico*. Princeton: Princeton University Press.

Knight, Alan. 1980. "Peasant and Caudillo in Revolutionary Mexico 1910–1917." In D.A. Brading (ed.), *Caudillo and Peasant in the Mexican Revolution*, pp. 17–58. Cambridge University Press.

Larson, Brooke. 1983. "Shifting Views of Colonialism and Resistance," *Radical History Review*, 27:3–20.

———. 1988. *Colonialism and Agrarian Transformation in Bolivia. Cochabamba, 1550–1900*. Princeton: Princeton University Press.

Lavie, Smadar. 1990. *The Poetics of Military Occupation. Mzeina Allegories of Bedouin Identities under Israeli and Egyptian Rule*. Berkeley: University of California Press.

Lechner, Norbert. 1991. "Some People Die of Fear: Fear as a Political Problem." In J.E. Corradi, P.W. Fagen & M.A. Garretón (eds.), *Fear at the Edge. State Terror and Resistance in Latin America*, pp. 26–35. Berkeley: University of California Press.

Lenclud, Gérard & Jean Jamin (eds.). 1984. *Ethnographie de la violence. Etudes Rurales*, No. 95–96.

Mallon, Florencia. 1983. *The Defense of Community in Peru's Central Highlands. Peasant Struggle and Capitalist Transition 1860–1940*. Princeton: Princeton University Press.

———. 1987. "Nationalist and Anti-State Coalitions in the War of the Pacific: Junín and Cajamarca, 1879–1902." In Steve Stern (ed.), *Resistance, Rebellion and Consciousness In the Andean Peasant World, 18th to 20th Centuries*, pp. 232–279. Madison: University of Wisconsin Press.

———. 1992. "Indian Communities, Political Cultures, and the State in Latin America, 1780–1990," *Journal of Latin American Studies*, 24 (Quincentenary supplement):35–53.

Manrique, Nelson. 1981. *Campesinado y Nación: Las guerrillas indígenas en la guerra con Chile*. Lima: C.I.C.-Ital. Peru.

———. 1989a. *Mercado interno y región. La sierra central 1820–1930*. Lima: DESCO.

———. 1989b. "La Década de la violencia," *Márgenes*, 5/6:137–182.

———. 1990. "Violencia e imaginario social en el Perú contemporáneo." In *Tiempos de Ira y Amor*, pp. 49–75. Lima: DESCO.

Mitchell. Timothy. 1988. *Colonizing Egypt*. Cambridge & New York: Cambridge University Press.

Montoya, Rodrigo. 1980. *Capitalismo y no capitalismo en el Perú. Un Estudio histórico de su articulación en un eje regional.* Lima: Mosca Azul.

_____. 1986. "Identidad étnica y luchas agrarias en los Andes Peruanos." In *Identidades andinas y lógicas del campesinado,* pp. 247–78. Lima: Mosca Azul.

_____. 1992. *Al Borde del Naufragio. Democracia, violencia y problema étnico en el Perú.* Lima: Cuadernos de SUR.

Moore, Barrington. 1966. *Social Origins of Dictatorship and Democracy: Lord and Peasant in the Making of the Modern World.* Boston: Beacon.

Nordstrom, Carolyn & JoAnn Martin (eds.). 1992. *The Paths to Domination Terror and Resistance.* Berkeley: University of California Press.

Omi, Michael & Howard Winant. 1986. *Racial Formation in the United States.* New York & London: Routledge & Kegan Paul.

O'Phelan Godoy, Scarlett. 1985. *Rebellions and Revolts in Eighteenth Century Peru and Upper Peru.* Koln: Bohlau Verlag.

Oquist, Paul. 1980. *Violence, Conflict and Politics.* New York:

Orlove, Benjamin S. 1977. *Alpacas, Sheep and Men: The Wool Export Economy and Regional Society in Southern Peru.* New York: Academic Press.

Orlove, Benjamin S. & Glynn Custred (eds.). 1980. *Land and Power in Latin America: Agrarian Economies and Social Processes in the Andes.* New York: Holmes and Meier.

Ossio, Juan (ed.). 1973. *Ideología mesiánica del mundo andino.* Lima: Ignacio Prado Pastor.

Paige, Jeffrey. 1976. *Agrarian Revolution. Social Movements and Export Agriculture in the Underdeveloped World.* New York & London: The Free Press.

Pease, Franklin. 1981. "Continuidad y resistencia de lo andino," *Allpanchis,* 17/18:105–18.

Piel, Jean. 1967. "Un soulevement rural péruvien au xxème siècle: Tocroyoc (1921)," *Revue d'histoire moderne et contemporaine,* XIV(4):375–405.

_____. 1982. *Crise agraire et conscience créole au Pérou.* Paris: Editions du CNRS.

Poole, Deborah. 1987. "Korilazos, abigeos y comunidades campesinas en la Provincia de Chumbivilcas." In A. Flores-Galindo (ed.), *Comunidades campesinas: Cambios y permanencias,* pp. 257–95. Lima & Chiclayo: CONCYTEC and Centro De Estudios Sociales 'Solidaridad.'

_____. 1988. "Landscapes of Power in a Cattle Rustling Culture of Southern Andean Peru," *Dialectical Anthropology,* XII:367–398.

Poole, Deborah & Gerardo Rénique. 1991. "The New Chroniclers of Peru: US Scholars and their 'Shining Path' of Peasant Rebellion," *Bulletin of Latin American Research,* X(2):133–191.

_____. 1992. *Peru: Time of Fear.* London: Latin America Bureau.

Portocarrero M., Gonzálo & Isidro Valentín Soraya I. 1991. *Sacaojos: Crisis Social y Fantasmas Coloniales.* Lima: Tarea

Portocarrero M., Gonzalo & Patricia Oliart. 1989. *El Perú desde la Escuela.* Lima: Instituto de Apoyo Agrario.

Reed, Nelson. 1964. *The Caste War in Yucatán.* Stanford: Stanford University Press.

Riches, David (ed.). 1986. *The Anthropology of Violence.* London: Blackwell.

Rodríguez Rabanal, César & Franca Castelnuovo. 1985. "Sobre la dimensión psicosocial de la violencia en el Perú." In *Siete Ensayos sobre la Violencia en el Perú*, pp. 39–57. Lima: Fundación Friedrich Ebert & APEP.

Roseberry, William. 1983. *Coffee and Capitalism in the Venezuelan Andes*. Austin: University of Texas Press.

Rosenberg, Tina. 1991. *Children of Cain. Violence and the Violent in Latin America*. New York: William Morrow & Co.

Said, Edward W. 1978. *Orientalism*. New York: Pantheon.

_____. 1985. "An Ideology of Difference," *Critical Inquiry*, XII(1):38–58.

Sallnow, Michael. 1987. *Pilgrims of the Andes. Regional Cults in Cusco*. Washington: Smithsonian Institution Press.

Scott, James. 1976. *The Moral Economy of the Peasant: Rebellion and Subsistence in Southeast Asia*. New Haven: Uale University Press.

_____. 1992. "Domination, Acting and Fantasy." In C. Nordstrom & J. Martin (eds.), *The Paths to domination, Resistance and Terror*, pp. 55–84. Berkeley: University of California Press.

Sempat Assadourian, Carlos. 1982. *El sistema de la economía colonial. Mercado interno, regiones y espacio económico*. Lima: Instituto de Estudios Peruanos.

Skocpol, Theda. 1979. *States and Social Revolutions: A Comparative Analysis of France, Russia and China*. New York: Cambridge University Press.

Slater, David. 1989. *Territory and State Power in Latin America: The Peruvian Case*. London: MacMillan.

Slatta, Richard W. 1987. *Bandidos: The Varieties of Latin American Banditry*. New York: Greenwood.

Sluka, Jeffrey A. 1990. "Participant Observation in Violent Social Contexts," *Human Organization*, 49(2):114–126.

Smith, Carol. 1984. "Local History in Global Context: Social and Economic Transitions in Western Guatemala," *Comparative Studies in Society and History*, XXVI(2):193–228.

Smith, Gavin. 1989. *Livelihood and Resistance. Peasants and the Politics of Land in Peru*. Berkeley: University of California Press.

Smith, Philip. 1991. "Codes and conflict: Toward a theory of war as ritual," *Theory and Society*, 20/21(feb.):103–138.

Spalding, Karen. 1984. *Huarochirí. An Andean Society Under Inca and Spanish Rule*. Stanford: Stanford University Press.

Stern, Steve. 1982. *Peru's Indian Peoples and the Challenge of Spanish Conquest. Huamanga to 1640*. Madison: University of Wisconsin Press.

_____. 1987. "The Age of Andean Insurrection, 1742 to 1782: A Reappraisal," In Steve Stern (ed.) *Resistance, Rebellion and Consciousness In the Andean Peasant World, 18th to 20th Centuries*, pp. 34–93. Madison: University of Wisconsin Press.

_____. 1988. "Feudalism, Capitalism and the World-System in the Perspective of Latin America and the Caribbean," *American Historical Review*, 93(4):829–872.

_____. (ed.) 1987. *Resistance, Rebellion and Consciousness In the Andean Peasant World, 18th to 20th Centuries*. Madison: University of Wisconsin Press.

Taussig, Michael. 1987. *Shamanism, Colonialism, and the Wild Man. A Study in Terror and Healing*. Chicago: Univ. of Chicago Press.

———. 1992. *The Nervous System*. New York & London: Routledge.

Taylor, Lewis. 1986. *Bandits and Politics in Peru. Landlord and Peasant Violence in Hualgayoc, 1900–1930*. Cambridge: Centre of Latin American Studies, Cambridge University.

Thurner, Mark. 1991. "Guerra andina y política campesina en el sitio de La Paz, 1781. Aproximaciones etnohistóricas a la práctica insurreccional a través de las fuentes editadas." In H. Urbano (ed.), *Poder y Violencia en Los Andes*, pp. 93–124. Cusco: CERA Bartolomé de Las Casas.

Urbano, Henrique. 1990. *Modernidad en los Andes*. Cusco: CERA Bartolomé de Las Casas.

Urton, Gary. 1984. "Chuta: El espacio de la práctica social en Pacariqtambo, Perú," *Revista Andina*, II(1):7–43.

Valderrama, Ricardo & Carmen G. Escalante. 1981. *El Levantamiento de los Indígenas de Haquira y Quiñota (1922–24)*. Lima: Seminario de Historia Rural Andina, Universidad Nacional Mayor de San Marcos.

Van den Berghe, Pierre (ed.). 1990. *State Violence and Ethnicity*. Niwot, Co.: University Press of Colorado.

Varese, Stefano. 1968. *La Sal de Los Cerros. Notas etnográficas e históricas sobre los Campa de la selva del Perú*. Lima: Universidad Peruana de Ciencias y Tecnología.

Verdier, Raymond (ed.). 1980. *Vengeance et pouvoir dans quelques sociétés extraoccidentales. Vol. I, La Vengeance. Etudes d'ethnologie, d'histoire, et de philosophie*. Paris: Editions Cujas.

Walker, Charles. 1989. "Montoneros, bandoleros, malhechores: Criminalidad y política en las primeras décadas republicanas." *Pasado y Presente*. 2-3:119–137.

———. 1991. "La violencia y el sistema legal: Los indios y el estado en el Cusco después de la rebelión de Tupac Amaru." *In* H. Urbano (ed.) *Poder y Violencia en los Andes*, pp. 125–148. Cusco: CERA Bartolomé de Las Casas.

Wightman, Ann. 1990. *Indigenous Migration and Social Change: The Forasteros of Cusco, 1570–1720*. Durham, NC: Duke University Press.

Wolf, Eric R. 1969. *Peasant Wars of the Twentieth Century*. New York: Harper & Row.

———. 1982. *Europe and the People Without History*. Berkeley: University of California Press.

1

Regional Isolation in the High Provinces of Cusco and Apurímac

Daniel W. Gade

Since 1535, the southern Peruvian sierra has been spatially remote from centers of wealth and power in western South America. Within that highland expanse, certain pockets have experienced intense isolation including the high provinces of Cusco and Apurímac. The geographic sequestration that has gripped this particular zone has gone hand in hand with rank poverty and unrelenting violence. Attacks on people and property in this area have been so common over the years as to form a folk tradition. Yet most incidents of savagery or coercion have never come to the attention of the outside world; journalists have always been few or non-existent and local officials have often been in complicity with one another, if they were not the perpetrators themselves. The relationship of regional isolation to human violence is complex. Describing the physical and human character of the high provinces since the colonial period will help to bring into focus the case studies discussed in subsequent chapters.

Regional Setting

The high provinces, or *provincias altas*, of Cusco and Apurímac form a particularly rugged area that is more isolated than most of the southern sierra. As defined here, the high provinces comprise 18,666 km² to the west of the Vilcanota valley (Fig. 1.1). That valley, a major trough, has long funnelled people, ideas and goods between the regional capital of Cusco and the two other main foci of population in southern Peru: the Lake Titicaca basin with its easy access to Bolivia and, Arequipa, Peru's second largest city, located to the southwest of the high provinces and at a much lower elevation (Flores-Galindo 1977; Glave 1980). Since the Spanish Conquest,

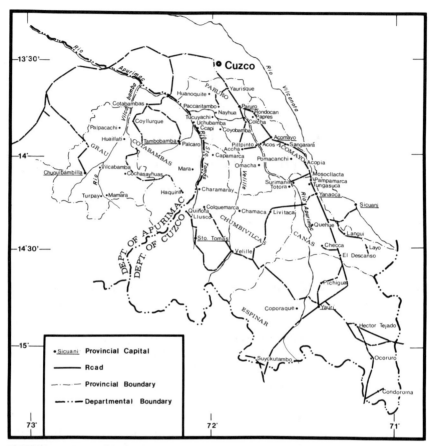

FIGURE 1.1   Zone of the high provinces in the larger context of Southern Peru.

the established lines of communication between those three centers have wedged the *provincias altas* into a marginal position. Five of the provinces—Paruro, Acomayo, Canas, Espinar and Chumbivilcas—are in the Department of Cusco; two other provinces—Cotabambas and Grau—are in the neighboring Department of Apurímac.[1] These units are isolated in varying degrees from the city of Cusco, yet all fall within its orbit of influence (Brisseau 1981). Many old Cusco families once owned haciendas in the high provinces from which they derived their income and some status. Native inhabitants of many estates were regarded as chattel subject to the whim of the *hacendado* (see Gose and Paponnet-Cantat, this volume). Cusco's historic and contemporary role as regional center of education, wholesaling and retailing, departmental capital, and seat of the archdiocese, have given it a very real centrality, even though it is far from being a major source of employment.

The relative strength of the ties connecting urban Cusco to this rural tributary area is a function largely of proximity. Paruro has had the closest relationships with the capital, followed by Acomayo and then Canas. In Espinar and Chumbivilcas, however, it is Arequipa that serves as the primary marketing and wholesaling center. Cotabambas and Grau, although belonging to the Department of Apurímac since 1873, still maintain their primary economic and cultural ties with the city of Cusco, rather than with the smaller and more distant departmental capital of Abancay. Taking the seven provinces as a regional unit, the glue that holds them together as a zone of isolation is their rurality, poverty, difficulty of access, and tradition of violence.

What is he implying?

Land, Resources, and Human Activities

The area west of the Vilcanota valley has three land surface types. First, there are mountain ranges with some snowcapped peaks over 5,000 meters above sea level. Second, between 3,800 and 4,500 meters is a high plateau that can be flat, rolling, or jagged. This vast treeless expanse, or *puna*, is covered with bunch grasses suitable for grazing llamas and alpacas. Lastly are the valleys, some as low as 2,300 meters, etched into the plateau surface by running water. The average altitude of the inhabited areas of the region as a whole varies from 3,341 meters in the Province of Paruro to 4,227 in Espinar.

The deep valleys of the upper Apurímac River and its tributaries form the most notable physiographic feature of the region (Gade and Escobar 1972). A series of canyons impede human movement and in some places exclude it. Principal among these is the gorge carved by the Apurímac River. Unlike the Vilcanota River valley to the east, which has had an important road and railway through its upper portion since earlier in this century, the Apurímac gorge serves almost no function as a transportation funnel along its length (Escobar 1980). The river itself has its source in the Mismi glacier, 5,597 meters above sea level in the Cordillera de Chila in the Department of Arequipa. From there, the incipient torrent abruptly descends to meander across the flat plateau of Espinar. Near Checca (3,600 m) in the Province of Canas, stream incision begins, progressively deepening and widening for about 200 km downstream. In Paruro Province, the main Apurímac valley forms a gaping chasm more than 1,000 meters below the upland surface. The precipitous drop as the river flows north makes it unnavigable to any kind of watercraft and the lack of enough flat land precludes a road or even a pack trail along it. Three major tributaries in the region that feed into the Apurímac have each formed impressive valleys of their own: the 190 km long Velille River; the 150 km long Santo Tomás River; and the 150-km long Vilcabamba River (formerly

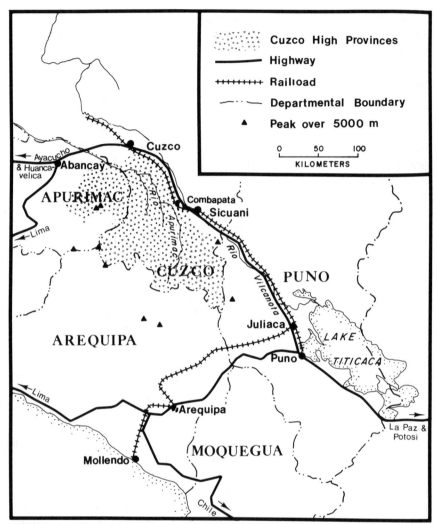

FIGURE 1.2   Basic index map of the high provinces.

known as the Oropesa) (Fig. 1.2). Many other smaller streams flowing into
these three principal tributaries have contributed to a vigorous dissection
of the interfluves in the Provinces of Acomayo, Paruro, Cotabambas, Grau
and part of Chumbivilcas.

The elevation above sea level of a place controls the general temperature level which, in turn, is a major control of its land use. Yauri's (3,915
m) highest average monthly temperature is only 9.3C., whereas in Paruro
(3,084 m) it is 15.7C. (Peru 1986). The orographic effects and latitude posi-

tions explain differences in rainfall receipts. Santo Tomás receives an average of 717 mm a year, whereas Yanaoca gets 919 mm, Acomayo, 889 mm, and Paruro 964 mm. But it is the elevational differences that most account for the effectiveness of that rainfall.

Above 3,800 meters, a short frost-free growing season and frequent hailstorms do not favor an emphasis on agriculture. While hardy Andean cultigens—tetraploid potato (*Solanum tuberosum*), pentaploid potato (*S. curtilobum*) for making dried potatoes or *chuño*, *oca* (*Oxalis tuberosa*), *ullucu* (*Ullucus tuberosus*), *añu* (*Tropaeolum tuberosum*), quinoa (*Chenopodium quinoa*) and *cañihua* (*Chenopodium pallidicaule*)—are grown there, the high rate of crop failure makes dependence on agriculture risky. Abundant wild grasses, on the other hand, provide pasturage for sheep, cattle, llamas and alpacas. Even before the Incas, grazing provided the predominant livelihood above 4,000 meters and today, as well, it is elevation and climate that determine which areas are dedicated to livestock raising. For example, in 1983, Espinar Province, with an average altitude of nearly 3,800 meters above sea level, had 8,900 alpacas, whereas the much lower and warmer Paruro Province had none. Until the nineteenth century, vicuña hunting was a supplementary source of income for *puna* dwellers. The outside demand for wool and meat that began in the late nineteenth century has tended to make the *punas* more commercially oriented than the valleys. Over the past century, individuals have appropriated communal or church-owned lands to form livestock ranches (*haciendas* or, more modestly, *estancias*).

Below 3,600 meters, agriculture is much less vulnerable to the weather extremes and is more productive. Wheat and barley became major crops in the early colonial period, for they grow well without irrigation on slopes which are cultivated periodically and which are given a long fallow. As the favorite food staple of the Spaniards, wheat and wheat flour from Acomayo and Paruro Provinces became an important item of commerce in Cusco and Puno, until displaced by imported Chilean wheat in the nineteenth and early twentieth centuries. Below 3,300 meters, maize has been the major crop wherever irrigation water is available. The elaborate stone terrace systems built for maize cultivation in Cusco's Urubamba valley or Arequipa's Colca valley do not occur in this region. Terraced maize agriculture does occur, however, in Apurímac and parts of Paruro (see Poole 1984 and Gose, this volume). The lack of water for irrigation on many otherwise suitable alluvial fans may explain the rarity of this architectural investment in the region. The Apurímac valley has localized patterns of semi-aridity due to high evapotranspiration.

Below 2,700 meters on the lower slopes and valley bottoms, frost is rare enough to allow such subtropical plants as the orange (*Citrus aurantium*), sweet lemon (*Citrus Limon*), *lucuma* (*Lucuma obovata*), *pakkay* (*Inga* spp.), *cherimoya* (*Annona cherimolia*), sugar cane (*Saccharum officinarum*), and *achira* (*Canna edulis*) to yield under irrigation. These fruits and early maize (*miska sara*) have been prime objects of trade with people at higher elevations. Use of the three broad ecological zones gave rise to an intricate pre-Hispanic pattern of vertical control which has not yet been reconstructed for this region. After the Conquest, that pattern was partially replaced by the interchange of agricultural and other goods at fairs and markets, and through the seasonal movements of llama herders and traders (Custred 1974; Poole 1982; see also Gose, this volume).

Mining

The high provinces have a long history of mineral exploitation. Much of the Spanish interest in this zone was connected to precious metals that, although far overshadowed by the famous silver mines in Potosí (Bolivia), were regionally significant. Most of these mines were later abandoned, but the ruins of mine shafts and water-driven mills to grind the ores are reminders of this former activity. Ironically, the important mines of Cusco's high provinces were in the same administrative districts, or *corregimientos*, from which Indian labor was drawn for the corvée, or *mita*, labor used to work the far off mines of Potosí and Huancavelica (Bakewell 1984; Poole 1987; Wightman 1990).

Colonial Cotabambas (now divided into Cotabambas and Grau Provinces) was well known for its gold and silver production. In the 1690s five mines were in operation, the most important being Cochasayhuas, located at 4,500 meters above sea level. Portuguese miners found large quantities of gold and silver there, the latter extracted from its ore by the amalgam method (Villanueva 1982:50). Operations largely ceased in the eighteenth century, and it was not until 1903 that a company was formed to work it again. Both Espinar (which was part of Canas in the colonial period) and Chumbivilcas also had important colonial mines. Condoroma (at 4,800 m, noted for the endemicity of St. Elmo's fire), Coporaque, Pichigua, and Suyckutambo were silver mining centers. Near the Chumbivilcano town of Colquemarca, placer gold was gotten from the river gravels. Mining generally languished in the eighteenth and nineteenth centuries, often for reasons other than depletion of the ores. Within the past century, many small mines—the bulk of them owned by *hacendados*—have been worked episodically, but quite a few other concessions of known mineral deposits have apparently never been exploited at all.

In the twentieth century, geological prospecting led to the discovery of large deposits of industrial metals. Large copper ore deposits occur in the District of Yauri where the Atalaya, Quechua, Coroccohuayco and Tintaya mines are clustered (Orlove 1985; Peru 1986:93). Tintaya, discovered in 1917 but not worked until 1985, is the largest mine in the Department of Cusco. The Katanga copper mine in the District of Chamaca was expropriated by the government from the Cerro de Pasco Corporation in 1970 and now is worked by a Japanese company. Abundant copper ores have also been discovered in Cotabambas and Grau and iron-bearing deposits have been documented in Chumbivilcas. Given their isolation, these minerals are not likely to be developed any time soon. Throughout the history of this region, mining has been a motive for human exploitation.

Historical Antecedents of Isolation

What correlation is he drawing?

Though violence in the high provinces has a relationship to conditions of remoteness, isolation itself is a slippery concept. Sheer distance is much less a part of the definition than are degrees of accessibility. Taken together they create isolation which has affected regional patterns of settlement, demography, and livelihood. Although the causes of isolation are complex, an historical perspective clarifies some of the patterns and processes that account for it. An undeveloped transport network, depopulation, regional impoverishment, and violence are both outcomes of regional isolation and causes of it.

Rural Settlement Nucleation and Dispersion

The exclusively rural character of the high provinces was part of a colonial design whose legacy has had an isolating effect on the whole region. No provision was made in highland colonial Peru to found cities that might have served as growth poles. The one urban establishment in the southern Peruvian highlands was built by the Spaniards on the Inca foundations at Cusco. The rural settlement of the highlands was thoroughly revamped in 1572 by Viceroy Toledo's edict that "reduced" Indian peasants from their dispersed settlements into newly founded agricultural villages called *reducciones* (Gade 1991; Gade and Escobar 1982). With that massive realignment of where people lived, Toledo sought to facilitate the indoctrination, tax collection, and work assignments of Spain's Indian charges.

In practice, the *reducciones* were divided into kin-oriented *ayllus*—a pre-Hispanic social grouping which allocated labor and governed access to resources. Each *ayllu* had a head man who was responsible for setting up work details. The mosaic of neighborhood *ayllus*, in turn, was organized into one of two moieties, each ruled by a *kuraka* (chief). In a few instances, the moiety split within a *reducción* became formalized as two essentially distinct communities. Accha (Paruro) was divided into the parishes of Accha Hanansaya (Upper Accha) and Accha Hurinsaya (Lower Accha).

Each parish maintained its own church on the main plaza and had separate priests, cemeteries, fiestas, communal pastures, and outlying dependent communities. Likewise in Haquira (Cotabambas), the two moieties, San Pedro and San Martín, each had their own church and priests (Villanueva 1982:36).

*Kuraka*s in turn answered to the *corregidor*, a Spanish official responsible for tribute collection from the Indians in his *corregimiento*. *Corregidores* later forced Indians to buy imported goods in a deeply resented system of
✓ forced consumption known as *reparto*.

It was during Toledo's *reducción* program in the 1570's that the actually existing mosaic of nucleated district and provincial capitals was established in the *high provinces*. Following this initial resettlement program, a small number of additional clustered villages were founded in the region. One of these was Mosocllacta in Acomayo (also known by its Spanish name, Pueblo Nuevo), created in the seventeenth century. In another case, the inhabitants of three *ayllus* of Acopia, a Toledan village in Acomayo, were moved to a new site along with a thousand landless Indians, or *forasteros*, from Pampamarca in Canas/Canchis (Villanueva 1982:167).[2]

The tight clustering mandated by the resettlement program was soon deemed impractical, however. Not infrequently, a whole *ayllu* moved in a block out of a *reducción* village to the countryside to be close to their fields or ancestral lands. These *anexos*, or annexes, of the *reducción* built their own chapel, started to have their own fiestas, and eventually renounced the work obligations owed to the *reducción* village. In Canas, for example, it was this hiving off process that made Layo independent from Langui, Quehue from Checca, and Ocoruro from Yauri. All three later became capitals of their own districts in the colonial province of Canas/Canchis.

Dispersion also took a more individualized form, whereby one, two or several households set themselves up near their fields and pastures. Already in the seventeenth century considerable communally owned grazing land in the *puna* was occupied by Indian herders. For example, at Rondocan, in Acomayo province, six *estancias* (small ranches) totalling 66 people were counted in the nearby *puna* with 147 enumerated in the village (Villanueva 1982:128–138). Papres, Acomayo had eleven *estancias de indios* (Indian houses and corrals) in the *puna*, the farthest of which was one league away from the village (Villanueva 1982:146). At that time and even today, some outdwellers also had a house in the village to which they returned for fiestas.

Four centuries after Toledo's resettlement scheme was instituted, the pattern is quite different than the viceroy must have originally intended. Many more people in the region live dispersed outside the *reducción* villages than within them. This generalization is least applicable in zones where irrigation water is scarce or centrally allocated, and is most true for grazing lands on the *puna*. The latter pattern is evident in the district of Chamaca (Chumbivilcas), which is comprised mostly of *puna* grasslands lying at elevations between 3,600 and 4,400 meters above sea level. These grasslands are suitable only for livestock raising, since agriculture is frequently thwarted by frosts and hail. To adapt themselves to the need for extensive tracts of land of low forage quality, the 5,843 people in Chamaca live in dispersed dwellings. Together their herds total some 10,000 head of cattle, 25,000 sheep, and 2,000 alpacas. Most inhabitants of Chamaca belong to one of the nine peasant communities who collectively own about one half of the land in the district. Because of its historic role as a Toledan *reducción*, and especially following its designation as district capital in 1825, the district capital of Chamaca has received the honorific classification of "city" in Peruvian census and administrative records. This in spite of the fact that Chamaca has never had any urban character. For at least 150 years, Chamaca has been half-abandoned; in 1981, only 165 people still lived there.

Oppression at the hands of Spaniards and *mestizos* became another reason for dispersion outside the *reducción* villages. Spaniards who came as administrators, priests, miners and hacendados sired offspring by Indian women. According to Spanish colonial law, the mixed-blood, or *mestizo*, individuals from these unions were not subject to tribute or *mita* obligations. Although opportunities for *mestizo*-owned commerce and landholding in the *reducción* villages increased as Indians departed for the mines to fulfill their *mita* obligations, the *mestizo* population in the region remained small through the seventeenth century. In 1689, the parish of Yanaoca, for example, had 600 Indians and only ten to twelve *mestizos*; Langui had 800 Indians and eight *mestizos* (Villanueva 1982:245-6). It was not until the eighteenth century that the non-Indian presence increased. In 1786, one census counted 783 Indians and 233 *mestizos* in Langui, and 959 Indians and 125 *mestizos* in Yanaoca (Vollmer 1967:278). Not infrequently, Spaniards and *mestizos* abused their formal or informal power over natives by contriving to steal communal land and irrigation water or by allowing their livestock to invade communal crop fields. Constant aggravation with no recourse for justice in these matters caused the Indians to retreat to areas beyond the reach of Spaniards, *mestizos* and their animals (Villanueva 1982:314). Security seems to have been a major motive. In 1690 in Paruro, for example, Indians from the towns moved to the *punas* to build dwellings from which they might better "guard their potato fields and livestock" (Villanueva 1982:447).

Most *reducción* villages never had a true central place function, because they were not meant to be much more than encampments of Indians. Few towns were wisely sited with regard to water supplies or topographic junctures that would have favored their development as service centers.

FIGURE 1.3   Sunday market in Yauri, Espinar (photograph by Deborah Poole).

But widespread dispersion of population outside the central village was another factor that suppressed the potential for the emergence of a series of regional cities. Drained of people, these villages have not had the dynamism or demographic thresholds to expand functions. Only one *reducción* village in the region, Yauri, has shown potential for evolution into an urban center, this in spite of being one of the colder places in Peru. Its livestock economy, modern slaughterhouse, nearby copper mines, Sunday market, and road access to Arequipa have given Yauri a solid commercial base for expansion, all enhanced by its central location in a vast *puna* from which roads now radiate in several directions. Most other villages in the high provinces, however, have little to attract outlying folk. Weekly markets in small pueblos, if they exist, are increasingly bypassed for those in larger towns such as Yauri and Sicuani (Fig. 1.3). Near roads, traders owning trucks collect wool, hides, mutton, cheese, beef, and young live animals and take them directly to Arequipa—or, less frequently, to Cusco—without the intervention of local markets. Rather than economic revitalization, improvement of the transport system has thus often brought stagnation instead to intermediately located villages.

Communications

Linkages between villages and Cusco have always been difficult to implement and to maintain. In this part of the Andes, valleys, which in most areas facilitate human access, instead form steep canyons that are not easily penetrated. In the face of such barriers, sheer distance is only a secondary isolating factor. For example, the village of Totora in Chumbivilcas is visible from Surimana in Canas across the Apurímac gorge, for they lie less than three kilometers away as the crow flies. When they still functioned, the church bells of each could be heard clearly by people in the cohort village. But to travel between them, a whole day's trip on foot or horseback is required down one canyon side and up the other.

Many foot and llama paths still in use are believed to predate the Spanish conquest. The horses, mules, and donkeys introduced by the Spaniards converted many of these Inca paths into pack trails (*caminos de herradura*). Mule driving was important in the high provinces and annual fairs at Coporaque (Espinar), Tungasuca (Canas) and Pampamarca (Canas) were occasions for extensive mule trading into the 1930s. In the case of Pampamarca, the colonial fair remains today an important rainy season fair where cattle, horses and llamas are sold for fattening or to meat buyers from Arequipa and Cusco (Poole 1982). Mule driving had already begun to decline earlier in the century as a result of competition from the Peruvian Railway which in 1908 reached Cusco from Puno and Arequipa. This new mode of transportation was much easier than the old mule trails which seem to have been in perpetual bad condition. Echoing other contemporary travelers, Antonio Raimondi (1874), the Milanese expatriate geographer who traveled overland in his explorations of Peru over a period of nineteen years, frequently alluded in his field journal to the poor state of these lines of communication. After heavy rains, the sharp hooves and heavy weight of loaded pack animals turned the trails into quagmires.

River crossings have formed a crucial link in the regional transport system of the high provinces, whatever the form of locomotion. In the dry season, the low water and quiet flow often make fording or rafting possible, but during the rainy season, stream beds turn into raging torrents. In this period, the act of crossing a river without a bridge or *oroya* (rope or hanging basket) is to risk drowning. The suspension bridge using strands of woven plant materials, either pliable branches, agave fibers, or tough grass stems, was the major indigenous solution. Fifteen native bridges are recorded in the history of the region as defined here, the longest of which were those hung across the Apurímac gorge to connect Cusco with Cotabambas. Made of agave fibers from wild-growing plants nearby, two of these bridges were over forty meters long. Earlier in the twentieth century, steel cables replaced the plant materials, and until the 1930s tolls were collected. One of these bridges was owned by the Municipality of Paruro even though that town was many kilometers from the crossing site. The bridge keeper charged one *medio* for a person using it, and one *real* for a loaded pack animal, which increased to four *reales* if it carried minerals or alcohol. These suspension bridges could not accommodate truck traffic and their importance as key points in the movement of goods rapidly decreased by 1950. Four stone arch bridges using *"cal y canto"* were constructed in the colonial period, and in this century, several metal beam spans have been built to allow trucks to pass at all seasons. Fording continues to be the means of crossing many unbridged locations, but is impossible at times of high water.

The first vehicle roads into the region were built in 1928, one from Cusco to Paruro, the other from Cusco to Acomayo via the Vilcanota Valley. These early roads were built with forced Indian labor under the *Ley de Conscripción Vial* decreed by President Leguía in 1920 (see Orlove, chapter 3, this volume). In general, provinces closest to Cusco had the first roads. Overall, however, few roads were built in the region. The Apurímac canyon and tributaries enormously complicate the construction of any kind of vehicular road. Only two road building efforts in the region have penetrated the four principal *quebradas* (ravines) to their floors; one from Santo Tomás to Llusco and Quiñota and the other from Cusco to Cotabambas. Roads were and still are often impassable in the December to April diluvial period that brings mud, landslides, and high water. To these factors should be added the episodic nature of road maintenance which can no longer be counted upon as a community *faena*, or communal work party, using volunteer labor. The weight of trucks, which constitute most of the vehicular traffic, causes road surfaces to rapidly deteriorate. Some roads have scarcely improved from the time they were first built. Livitaca, for example, was first reached by vehicles in 1941 on what was little more than a track; that surface remains rudimentary today.

Roads now pass through or to provincial capitals, suggesting that prefectures politically influenced where roads were built within their jurisdictions. Such linkages, however, have not turned those towns into regional marketing centers. Rather than reinforcing politico-administrative centrality, roads in the sierra seem to restructure the commercial hierarchy. Farmers along a road can bypass nearby villages by loading their products on a truck that takes them directly to Cusco, Sicuani, or Arequipa. Moreover, highways have themselves become a magnet for new settlement and several former truckstops—such as El Descanso, which is now a district capital in Canas—have grown into sizeable villages. Elsewhere, when mining ceased at Suyktutambo and Condoroma, the district capitals were moved away from the abandoned mine sites to new market settlements which were in the process of forming near the highway.

Absence of vehicle roads is the prime isolating factor in the late twentieth-century Peruvian sierra. Without trucks to transport surplus agricultural products, commercial farming is hardly viable and self-sufficiency becomes an indication of poverty. The poorest villages today are those typically far off the road. For example, Omacha, which lies some seven hours by horseback from Pillpinto, has no store or market, and artisans no longer live there. Yet fifty years ago, when that degree of isolation was the rule, such inactivity and desolation was less common. Colquemarca in 1938 had no vehicle road and shipments required a three-day mule trip to Combapata on the Cusco-Arequipa railway. Yet Colquemarca did have electric lights on the plaza, a potable water supply, and substantial food surpluses. Today, by comparison, when truck travel has become the standard, Colquemarca's public lighting system is in a state of total disrepair due to both depopulation and to the village's seasonal inaccessability by road.

Today a third of all fifty-two district capitals in the region are still inaccessible to wheeled vehicles. In addition, more than 100 other sizeable communities are still more than three hours walk from a road. More than anything, this lack of roads explains the weakness of ties between the city and the countryside. Places off the road now are at a much greater disadvantage than when the whole region was trackless. Until the twentieth century, for example, Capacmarca (Chumbivilcas Province) and Quiquijana (Quispicanchis Province), two towns that are roughly equidistant from Cusco, had much the same accessibility on pack trails. As muledriving declined and roads reached the Vilcanota valley, however, Capacmarca was thrown into an isolation which has paralyzed the life of the community in ways not apparent today in the Vilcanota valley town of Quiquijana.

Regional Depopulation

Isolation has been severely exacerbated by recurring demographic losses whose cumulative effect has been to devitalize the region. In the fifty year span between Viceroy Toledo's *reducción* program in the 1570s and the next major population census in 1620, population in the region declined by nearly half (Cook 1981:246). For one thing, disease epidemics swept through the clustered settlements, unleashing higher mortality than if the population had remained dispersed. Village-by-village detail of these devastating outbreaks over four centuries of introduced pestilence may never be accurately reconstructed, although local documents have scarcely been tapped. Enough is known to realize that an array of diseases was responsible: measles, scarlet fever, typhoid fever, typhus, influenza, plague, and especially smallpox. Malaria ravaged residents of and visitors to the hot valleys below 2500 meters along the Apurímac.

Another cause of heavy mortality was the *mita*, or enforced conscription to the mines. For two centuries thousands of able-bodied Indians were plucked from their home villages in three of the *corregimientos* in the region; most never returned. Two *corregimientos*, Chumbivilcas and Cotabambas, vere required to send laborers to Huancavelica, the infamous mercury mine far to the north (Poole 1987). Indians from Canas, which then included present-day Espinar, were sent to the mita at Potosí. Less well known is that selected parishes in Chumbivilcas and Cotabambas were sources of *mita* labor for Cailloma, a silver mine in the Department of Arequipa. In addition to those Indians sent to work in the mines and who died there or on the road, others fled the region to become rootless people (*forasteros*) who have broken ties to their home community to avoid this form of slavery (Glave 1988; Poole 1987; Villanueva 1982:36, 464; Wightman 1990). The demographic effects at a local level were devastating. In Chamaca in 1689, the village was described as being in ruins as a result of depopulation from the *mita* (Villanueva 1982:295). In Velille, the heavy and continuous labor exactions destroyed three of the four *ayllus* in the village (Villanueva 1982:314). In the village of San Agustín de Cotabambas, the vacuum left by the *mita* at the end of the seventeenth century forced the total reorganization of property boundaries (Gutierrez 1987:163). Haquira was described as a partial ghost town where the few people who came back from the mercury mines were blackened and spitting out bubbles of blood (Villanueva 1982:36). By 1690, the total population of the seven province region had fallen to only 38,000.

In the modern period, communal life began to decline in the 1940s when permanent outmigration to cities bled the zone of many of its young people. Direct migration from the high provinces to Arequipa and Lima started to occur in the 1950s. The capital city soon became the preferred destination because the number of jobs and the wages were generally higher there than in the sierra. Between 1940 and 1961, massive departures drained off a third of the population of the region, both from the villages and from the surrounding countrysides (Brisseau 1981:336). These losses, as percentages of total provincial populations, varied somewhat: from −42 percent in Acomayo and Grau, −39 percent in Canas, −38 percent in Cotabambas, −36 percent in Paruro, −32 percent in Chumbivilcas, to −26 percent in Espinar. Remarkable in this outmigration is that most of it went to Lima. For example, by the mid-1970s Colca, an isolated village of some 600 people in Acomayo, had sent 250 to 300 migrants to Lima (Skeldon 1974:242).

The unrewarding nature of mountain farming has been one important reason so many people have left the region in recent decades. Prices for domestic farm products have been largely controlled by the Peruvian government. Peasants, here or anywhere in the world, have little incentive to produce surplus if the prices they get provide them no recompense for their efforts. The APRA government price policy of the late 1980s provided very little incentive to stay in farming. Moreover, because of the government's failure to support peasant agriculture in Peru, most of the food now consumed in Peruvian cities is imported. An example of such poor planning is provided by the government's decision in 1990 to suspend the agricultural credit programs upon which peasants relied to purchase the chemical fertilizers and insecticides needed for commercial farming. This policy has not only led many peasants in former potato exporting regions, such as Chumbivilcas, to abandon production of cash crop potato varies, but also exacerbated outmigration from many parts of the high provinces.

During the 1980s and 1990s, political violence or the looming threat of it has also pushed peasants off their land to seek a safer life in cities. During 1991 a temporary state of emergency was declared for most of the high provinces of Cusco. Some regions in the Department of Apurímac have been living under a military state of emergency, with suspended constitutional guarantees, for years. In these regions, the fear and violence perpetrated by both Sendero Luminoso and the military-led counterinsurgency have led to drastic outmigration. Intimidation has left some zones nearly depopulated and their lands in a state of permanent fallow.

Social factors also account for urban migration from the high provinces. After World War II, adolescents in this part of the sierra became aware of coastal *criollo* culture and the accoutrements of modern life. Teachers sent to serve in the government-funded schools now found in most villages invariably expressed dissatisfaction to their students about the social life and cultural level of the villages. The first migrants from remote villages were Spanish-speaking *mestizos*. Gradually peasant children, including those who could barely speak Spanish, also began to move to the cities in search of employment. Although economic need is usually given as the reason for individual departures, the motivations are in reality much more complex (Flores Ochoa 1972).

As migration continues, the overall population of the high provinces region stagnates. Between 1972 and 1981, while Peru grew 2.6 percent and the sierra 1.3 percent, the high provinces grew only 0.3 percent. However, differences exist among provinces (Table 1.1); one district, Acomayo, actually lost people between 1972 and 1981 in spite of a high birth rate.

Regional Impoverishment

This zone of isolation and outmigration is also one of extreme poverty (Peru 1986). In the broad region of the sierra, the southern highland provinces, excluding Cusco, Puno, Arequipa and Juliaca, have a lower standard of living than anywhere else in Peru (Ortíz 1986:25). If a large number of variables involving living standards, economic potential, and the

TABLE 1.1 Demographic Trends of the High Provinces

Province	1961	1972	1981
Chumbivilcas	51,030	58,312	63,603
Espinar	36,982	41,461	44,539
Cotabambas	38,934	40,438	42,539
Canas	28,604	31,546	33,217
Paruro	31,728	31,536	32,385
Acomayo	30,754	29,980	27,556
Grau	28,310	27,776	28,032

SOURCE: Perú 1966, 1974, and 1983.

TABLE 1.2 Economic Situation of the High Provinces and Comparisons with Other Highland Provinces

High Provinces		Others	
Province	Index value	Province	Index value
Espinar	8.65	Arequipa	102.64
Chumbivilcas	−10.88	Cerro de Pasco	61.00
Canas	−11.20	Huancayo	30.14
Acomayo	−20.30	Puno	19.50
Grau	−22.03	Cusco	15.92
Cotabambas	−27.67	Juliaca	9.56
Paruro	−28.42	–	–

SOURCE: Ortiz 1986.

analysis of economic activities are factored together, four (Acomayo, Grau, Cotabambas, and Paruro) of the ten most disadvantaged provinces in Peru are located in the high provinces of Cusco and Apurímac (Ortíz 1986:36–38; see Table 1.2).

An evidence of the regional deprivation is the dilapidation of the built landscape which perennially appears to be at the point of collapse. Indeed, much rural construction has disappeared, and this is not a recent phenomenon.[3] Antonio Raimondi (1874) described Livitaca as ruined and abandoned in the 1880s. In Acopia, he commented on the wretched appearance of the plaza and streets. Yanaoca, in spite of being a provincial capital, had none of its adobe dwellings whitewashed. In Chamaca, Raimondi's observation of the many roofless stone houses with tumbled down walls matched my observations in that same village a century later. The overwhelming dominance of adobe construction attests to its virtue as an economical material. A range of roofing materials are used, however. Grass thatch is still seen in remote areas. Valley towns with suitable clay deposits and tile works, such as Paruro, have houses topped with red Spanish-style tile. Along highways in the higher provinces such as Espinar, Canas, and Chumbivilcas, however, dwellings are now normally covered with sheet metal, the first major signal in the landscape of a divorce between the peasantry and their environment.

The condition of the village church says much about the state of rural poverty. Disrepair has been its chronic state. In the late seventeenth century, reports from village priests to Bishop Mollinedo commented on the dire condition of church buildings and the slim financial support they received (Villanueva 1982). After independence, many villages lost their resident priest and his advocacy role. Starting in 1850, indigenous community members were no longer required to pay fees to support the church. In his 1874 report to Lima, the subprefect of Paruro, for example, commented that most of the churches in his province were in complete ruin. Today, years of neglect have taken their toll. While still the largest building in town, the church does not function very actively in the life of the community. In most places, a priest comes but once a year to hold a mass for the patronal fiesta. Few standing church buildings in the region predate the nineteenth century, although the interior objects are generally older (Gutierrez 1987). Hagiographic canvases of the Cusco school of painting, jewelled saints and silver altars have made them small museums of colonial art. Beginning in the 1960s, the theft or even armed robbery of these increasingly valued objects became cause for alarm. To protect this village patrimony, churches normally remain locked and visiting strangers are scrutinized for their motives.

Natural disasters have contributed to the destruction of the infrastructure. A list of the local catastrophes has never been compiled for the area, but until this century, outside assistance in reconstruction was not provided. In 1650 the *reducción* villages of Paruro, Huanca Huanca, and Yaurisque in the Province of Paruro were destroyed by the same earthquake that devastated the city of Cusco. In 1707, many towns in that same zone were levelled by another earthquake. In 1819, the whole pueblo of Vilcabamba (Cotabambas) slid into the Vilcabamba River, damming up the stream. When the dam later broke, the large quantity of water that surged downstream into the larger Apurímac River destroyed the famous Spanish bridge over it (Raimondi 1899:383). In 1939, Pomacanchi and Santa Lucia were left in shambles by an earthquake, as was Yanaoca in 1942. Floods have also seriously damaged settlements in the Apurímac canyon, notably Pillpinto, Colcha, and Nayhua, all three in the province of Paruro. In addition, several devastating locust invasions have been recorded for the warmer valleys—the most recent one being in 1989.

One of the persistent causes of poverty is a resource base that cannot adequately sustain the population. More than in most parts of the sierra, good soils are rare and are limited to valley bottoms or terraces. The lack of irrigation water precludes full use of some of these alluvial soils. Slope lands that have been cultivated without irrigation during the rainy season have been so eroded that yields are extremely low. Population pressure only partially explains this practice, although densities are high given the

FIGURE 1.4   Tiled two-story building on the plaza of Pillpinto (photograph by Daniel W. Gade).

resource base. Acomayo, primarily agricultural, has thirty people per square kilometer, making it the most dense of the seven provinces and the only one with an overall demographic decline. Acomayo has also had a strong tradition of temporary migration which provides alternative opportunities to farming tiny parcels. Beginning early in the twentieth century, many peasants leading laden mules and llamas left the province for Cusco's semi-tropical La Convención Province to trade their potatoes and *chuño* for coca, coffee, and cane alcohol. Some traders also became agricultural laborers on coca haciendas and were allotted parcels of land on which to grow their own crops. People from Sangarará and Acos in Acomayo Province, and especially Pillpinto in Paruro Province, became known for their role in highland coca trading. All three are communities with severe land shortages. Pillpinto is located on a river terrace some twenty meters above the Apurímac River, pinched between the stream bed and the nearby cliffs (Fig. 1.4). The scarcity of crop land in the community encouraged inhabitants to look beyond the local resource base. When a road was completed to the coca zone, several men from Pillpinto bought trucks and gained control of much of the coca trade for the *provincias altas*. A different kind of migration from Acomayo has been the street cleaners of Cusco, 75 percent of whom have come from Pomacanchi (Skeldon 1974:175).

Some degree of regional poverty can also be attributed to conscious and unevenly conditioned human decisions of the past. Forced to work in distant mines and nearby cloth mills during the colonial period, peasants neglected their home villages which then declined. A land tenure system which persisted until the 1970s enabled the powerful few to appropriate large properties which were not, however, efficiently farmed. While extracting food supplies, mineral wealth, and human talent from the provinces, the city of Cusco has contributed very little in return. As Cusco began to gain the advantages of an urban center, *hacendados* who had lived mostly on their estates settled permanently in the city. The products sold from their *hacienda* benefited Cusco city, but little of the money so earned was returned to the *hacienda* or its district. Likewise, different institutions in the city have owned considerable areas of land in the high provinces. The Colegio de Ciencias, a secondary school in Cusco founded by Simón Bolivar in 1825, has derived rents from properties in Canas, Espinar, and Paruro that at one time totaled more than 5,000 hectares.

Entrepreneurs in Cusco, while never numerous, have not sought to invest in the region. Government entities entrusted with the development of infrastructure have allocated few financial resources to the *provincias altas*. Brisseau (1981:450–451) points out that for psychological and other reasons the managerial class in Cusco has generally avoided the high country. Instead it has been drawn to the lands to the north and east of the capital. The lower and warmer reaches of the Vilcanota or Urubamba valley to the north and west of Cusco have been a favored site for recreation and a source of fruits, vegetables, and staples such as maize. At still lower elevations below 1,500 meters, wealth for Cusco has come from coca growing and the exploitation of cinchona, wood, rubber, and gold. This "El Dorado syndrome" focused on the warm valleys works to the disadvantage of the high provinces.

Tambobamba:
Case Study of Isolation

The isolation that has characterized so much of the high provinces is epitomized by Tambobamba. Its isolation has been both a cause and an effect of its historical *raison d'être*, tenuous communications with the outside world, demographic and economic stagnation, and episodic violence.

The isolation of Tambobamba is highlighted by its relatively important place within the Apurímac area from the colonial period to the present. Founded in the 1570s as a *reducción* named for its patroness image, the Virgin of the Assumption, Tambobamba was considered separate from San Andrés de Palcaro, an adjacent but independent *reducción* lying just on the other side of a small river. A modest centrality was accorded

Tambobamba/Palcaro by its original status as the seat of two parishes, each with a resident priest. After an epidemic nearly wiped out the population of San Agustín de Cotabambas to the north, the capital of the *corregimiento* was shifted to Tambobamba. The discovery of metal deposits at Cochasayhuas and the possibility of acquiring large landholdings brought Europeans to the general area. The original inhabitants of Tambobamba/Palcaro, virtually all Indian farmers, gradually dispersed to outlying settlements, ceding their place in the central village to *mestizos*. Yet the majority of the people within the district of Tambobamba remain peasant.

With Peru's independence in 1821, Tambobamba became the capital of the Province of Cotabambas. Until 1873 when Cotabambas became part of the Department of Apurímac, the province's subprefect was responsible to the prefecture in Cusco. In 1919, the name of the province was changed to Grau and the provincial capital was shifted to Chuquibambilla, a town 75 km closer than Tambobamba to the departmental capital in Abancay. Efforts in the 1930s to return the provincial seat to Tambobamba stalled, but continual agitation led to a compromise solution in 1960 when Grau Province was split to form the province of Cotabambas. Although the new province's areal extent was much truncated compared to the earlier unit with this name, Tambobamba was able to regain the coveted status of provincial capital.

The motor age arrived in the Peruvian highlands in the late 1920s but did not reach Tambobamba until the 1980s. The difficult terrain into and out of the Apurímac gorge was for a long time too much of an engineering challenge to road builders. Although plans for a road were made already in the 1920s, the province had no political leverage to get the central authorities to act. In the 1930s, a landing strip was constructed for airplanes bringing in mining machinery to Cochasayhuas, but this facility did nothing to decrease the isolation of Tambobambinos. Overland movement by pack animals on trails in deplorable condition made travel slow, onerous, and expensive.

By the 1960s, almost all other provincial capitals in the sierra had secured vehicular access, but Tambobamba continued to depend on a form of transport no different from that of 350 years earlier. The psychological isolation was as strong as the geographical isolation. In 1965, a newspaper reporter for *El Comercio* of Cusco called Tambobamba "the most forgotten town in the country," lacking not only an elemental road to the outside world, but also electricity, potable water supply and a functioning post office. By then the town did have a Guardia Civil post, a response to the high incidence of cattle rustling. The presence of gendarmes, however, did not stop miscreants from setting fire in 1969 to a whole barrio of Tambobamba in an act of vengeance, or robbers from assaulting the mail carrier from Cusco and stealing the mail bags. In 1970, the Cusco newspaper claimed that "among the forgotten towns of Peru, Tambobamba occupies the very first place," and went on to assert, rather dubiously, that the absence of electricity encouraged thieves to use the cover of darkness "to rob the townsfolk blind." Municipal taps did not function, forcing residents to draw their water needs from unsanitary irrigation ditches. Telegraph service was paralyzed and, to add insult to injury, the post office had no stamps so mail could not be sent. It was assumed that once a truck road reached the town, all these shortcomings would be rectified.

Tambobamba's status as a classic backwater has gone hand in hand with the strength of its folkloric traditions. The town's fiestas have been known far and wide for the enthusiasm they generate, especially the main one in mid-August honoring the Virgin of the Assumption. Each of the three *ayllus* in the town organized one day of bull fights for that patronal feast. One of them was a bullfight in which a live condor, tied to the back of a bull, used its powerful wings and beak in a vain attempt to gain release from the enraged bovine. Although the tradition was broken and then revived in the 1970s, Tambobamba has been one of the last remaining Andean towns to hold this gruesome, yet compelling, spectacle which many interpret as a symbolic reference to the violence of the colonial period and the ethnic or racial conflicts that have been Peru's colonial heritage (Arguedas 1941; Delgado 1958). Since the nineteenth century, this and other fiestas have been lubricated with abundant cane alcohol (*aguardiente*) transported on mule-back from the sugarcane *haciendas* in the Valley of the Apurímac and its tributaries. The nearest source of *aguardiente* was *hacienda* Uchubamba in the nearby Santo Tomás valley where, as late as the 1970s, cane juice was pressed out between cylinders moved by oxen and distilled in a technologically primitive operation. *Aguardiente* producers there and elsewhere have profited from the connection that greatly expanded after Independence between religious fervor and extravagent ingestion of this crude product.

It took more than a decade to extend the road to Tambobamba from its old rival to the north, the town of San Agustín de Cotabambas. Finally in the early 1980s, Tambobamba was linked by a road to Cusco, 182.5 km away. The trip over this road, however, was a strenuous trial of innumerable ascents and descents. Landslides periodically halted all traffic. Even under the best of conditions, it would not be fair to say that the isolation of Tambobamba has been broken. New demands can be expected for a better road with more frequent service.

Violence and the Remoteness Factor

Outlawry is also related to isolation. Far from centers of justice many acts are perpetrated with impunity and abuses become institutionalized. Historically, the high provinces of Cusco acquired a notoriety for violence as a result of the Tupac Amaru rebellion of the late eighteenth century. Canas, Acomayo, and Chumbivilcas were principal arenas in which José Gabriel Condorcanqui "Tupac Amaru II" led attacks against the royalist establishment for its oppressive *mita* policies as well as against the abuses of *corregidores* and *hacendados* who ruthlessly exploited Indians. Many of the eighteen textile workshops (*obrajes* and *chorrillos*) that had been set up in the region were destroyed by the rebels (Moscoso 1963). Sangarará, Surimana, Pampamarca, Tungasuca and Livitaca were among the towns that witnessed the outbursts of a normally placid people pushed to their limits. Although independence from Spain did not come until four decades later, the rebellion placed the colonial government on notice that its control was in dispute.

A direct link between the legacy of Tupac Amaru II and subsequent rural violence in this region would be hard to prove. Yet the many confrontations over the usurpation of land and livestock, labor disputes, and abuses by the authorities there suggest not only a pattern, but a tradition of violence (Poole 1988; Stavig 1985). In this century, the regional powderkeg exploded over a six year period, starting in 1918 in Paruro, shifting to Espinar in 1921, and culminating in 1923 in a string of bloody skirmishes in Canas, Chumbivilcas, Paruro, Acomayo, and Cotabambas (Piel 1967; Valderrama & Escalante 1981). *Hacendados*, fearing for their lives, alerted authorities and journalists in Cusco of recent or impending jacqueries (Deustua 1981). Most of the many incidents that have transpired over the years have never received outside publicity. Many conflicts have reflected the tensions between peasants and the rural *mestizo* elite.

Between the episodic revolts, a more prosaic yet unrelenting activity— livestock rustling or *abigeato*—has set the overall tone of lawlessness. Its history is still being sorted out, but its virulence may have started after Peruvian Independence. None of the 1689 reports to Bishop Mollinedo refers to it. In Chumbivilcas, rustling goes back more than a century (Velasco 1874:494; see Poole, Chapter 3, this volume). It is in the lonely *puna*s with few people and many animals that it is most common. Theft or robbery of livestock on the hoof is usually accomplished by stealth under the cover of darkness, but sometimes involves as well armed assault against owners or caretakers. Ranches steal animals from peasants who, in turn, steal cattle or sheep from the big spreads. Not surprisingly, law enforcement in the region, such as it is, has long been preoccupied with rustling, because livestock are a highly mobile form of property which can be spirited off the

premises in one fell swoop. The provincial and district jails (if they function) are normally filled with men charged or convicted of rustling.
Abigeato is clearly one of the most important sociological phenomena of
the high provinces. It affects class and ethnic relationships and may determine the choice of land use in areas plagued with the problem. Not infrequently, houses and enclosures are situated to provide maximum security
against intruders. The threat of assault may account for the abandonment
of dwellings in the village in order to guard herds more efficiently in the
distant *puna*. If defense is not possible, people have little recourse but to
leave the land entirely and migrate to the city. Almost all outside observers who have spent time in the region have commented on the preva-
lence of *abigeato* (Orlove 1980; Poole 1988; see also Poole, Gose and
Paponnet-Cantat, this volume).

Quite a different aspect of regional violence in the high provinces is the
recent emergence of ideologically inspired political violence, attributed to
the two guerilla movements, Sendero Luminoso and the MRTA
(Movimiento Revolucionario Tupac Amaru). The more significant of
these two groups, the Peruvian Communist Party "Sendero Luminoso"
(Shining Path), was formed as a splinter Maoist party in the 1970s in Ayacucho, and has since spread elsewhere in the sierra and to the coastal cities. Up to now, the Cusco region has been relatively quiescent, wedged between the states of emergency declared in Ayacucho and Andahauylas to
the north and Puno to the south. Because of their location between Puna
and Apurímac, however, the high provinces have served as a strategic
corridor for Senderista columns moving from Ayacucho and Apurímac
into and out of Puno. (For further discussion of Sendero and recent political violence in the region, see Rénique, Chapter 7, and Poole, Chapter 8,
this volume).

Conclusion

A regional scale of analysis helps us to understand how remoteness from
centers of official decision-making has influenced the society and economy of the high provinces of Cusco. The mark of sequestration is every-
where evident on the cultural landscape of this fragmented expanse of
Peru. Regional isolation must be seen as both a cause and an effect of a cultural and economic configuration in which the past weighs heavily. The
failure of the Spanish conquerors to create a hierarchy of urban centers
which would serve as development magnets for the surrounding countryside resulted in a parasitic relationship with Cusco, which lorded over a
vast territory and drained off resources to that one city. Since the colonial
period to the present, the high provinces have been marginal, subsistence-
oriented appendages, yet the outcome of this economic and social depri-

"endemic violence" → troubling phrase

vation has been the strength of indigenous tradition (Gade 1992). Native practices of land use and technology, have contributed to the resilience of folk to survive from generation to generation in the face of enslavement, natural disasters, and endemic violence.

region of refuge

The *provincias altas* can be considered a region of refuge, a concept elaborated first by the Mexican anthropologist Gonzalo Aguirre Beltran (1967) to describe isolated zones that maintain themselves at subsistence level without much interference from the country of which they form a part. What have been called indigenous survivals are notably strong here. More than 95 per cent of the inhabitants of the high provinces, including peasants, *mestizos* and town dwellers, speak Quechua by preference. Racial mixture in the region has been quite common in Paruro, Grau, Cotabambas, and parts of Chumbivilcas, and is attributed in local folklore to "mixing" with Portuguese miners who supposedly came into the area sometime in the past. In local tradition, fair-haired and even blue-eyed "Indians" do not constitute a contradiction. Other typical ethnic markers,

ethnic markers

such as dress, show more variation than speech. At higher elevations outside the towns, for example, homespun fabric—considered indicative of "Indianness"—predominates. Men's ponchos and women's *llicllas* (woven shawls) are made from locally spun and woven sheeps wool. Manufactured clothing of Western style, on the other hand, is most common in agricultural villages and in the valleys. The habit of going barefoot or, at most, wearing sandals (*ojotas*) originally made from llama hides but now from recycled truck tires, are other practices considered diagnostic of "Indian" status in the region.

The force of native tradition is also expressed by the presence of more than 250 legally recognized peasant communities (*comunidades campesinas*). The largest number of them (55) are in Chumbivilcas which has 64 per cent of its territory owned by peasant communities, by far the highest proportion of any of the seven provinces (Díaz & Pelupessy 1976). While some peasant communities are recent social creations, most have territorial and historical identities that go back to the colonial and precolonial periods (Glave 1988; Poole 1987).

A heterogenous history is also manifested in material culture. *Achira* (*Canna edulis*), a starchy tuber cooked in underground pits, is a pre-Columbian crop plant still grown in the Apurímac valley (Gade 1966). It is sold as a special delicacy at the Corpus Christi festival in Cusco and at other dry-season regional fairs. This tradition may have started with the Inti Raymi, an Inca festival which overlapped during the colonial period with the Catholic imposed Corpus Christi processions. *Quihuicha* (*Amaranthus caudatus*) is still grown in the *provincias altas*, though it is now quite rare in the Peruvian sierra as a whole. The high protein seed crop may have been of considerable historic importance in the region below

3,000 meters where irrigation was not possible. Other folk practices seem to have survived here longer than in other less isolated regions. For example, some *chicha* is still made from the fruits of the wild-growing pepper tree (*Schinus molle*).

Artisan production continues in some areas (Fig. 1.5). Certain communities in Espinar and Chumbivilcas have long made homespun wool yarn and fabric (*bayeta*) in excess of their own needs. Charamoray in the district of Colquemarca has been a center for pottery produced without wheel or kiln. This crude but regionally esteemed earthenware is traded at certain annual fairs in exchange for agricultural products, the most notable of which is at Pampak'ucho (Paruro Province) in mid-August (Poole 1984:240). Several of the last remaining suspension bridges in the Andes made of plant material are also found in the high provinces (Gade 1972) (Fig. 1.6). The best known of these is the bridge of woven grass (*Keswachaka*) which crosses the Apurímac River in Canas at 3,650 meters above sea level.[4]

Aguirre Beltran (1967) asserted that hostile topography has saved populations from extinction by offering geographical isolation. But biophysical constraints are not the real explanatory element in analyzing the creation of a region of refuge. Rather it is the accumulation and historical consequence of human decisions made over time that have set the stage in this particular case. Forced resettlement into *reducciones*, the imposition of *mita* and *reparto*, and abuses by priests who were supposed to protect, all contributed to a tradition of human exploitation that has engendered violence.

Future changes in the infrastructure in the sierra will clarify the fallacy of environmental determinism. Indeed, the unfolding events of this century are proving instructive. While the threat of guerrilla-inspired violence may not ultimately succeed, it could induce major socio-economic change in this and other parts of the highlands. Citing the poverty of the zone, development specialists are likely to applaud any form of modernization, including large-scale mineral exploitation and hydroelectric schemes. In the process, the ethnographic character of this special part of the Andes will continue to undergo rapid permutation.

FIGURE 1.5   Artisan making wool hats in Espinar (photograph by Deborah Poole).

FIGURE 1.6   Repairing a hanging bridge between the communities of Charamoray and Urubamba, Chumbivilcas (photograph by Deborah Poole).

Notes

1. The Province of Canchis is not included in this discussion because most of its inhabitants do not live in the same degree of isolation as do people in the zone to the west of the Vilcanota valley. The provincial capital of Canchis, Sicuani, has substantially diversified its functions since the 1950s and is now the second largest urban center in the Department of Cusco. The expression "high provinces" (or its Spanish equivalent *"provincias altas"*) has a certain arbitrariness in any case, for several provinces—Quispicanchis, Paucartambo, Anta—in the Department of Cusco that are normally excluded from that usage nevertheless have extensive areas of *puna*. On the other hand, the "high province" of Paruro has quite a few people living in temperate valleys below 3,300 meters.

2. The reports published in Villanueva 1982 were part of a church administered study ordered by the bishop of Cusco, Manual de Mollinedo y Angulo, in 1689. As a whole, the assemblage of reports submitted by the parish priests conveys substantial insight into the demographic and economic character of small villages in southern highland Peru in the late seventeenth century. For this reason I have used the reports extensively here as a descriptive source for the colonial period high provinces. The reports vary considerably, however, from parish to parish. Some are cursory summaries on the state of church property, while others provide a detailed census of inhabitants, where they live in the parish, and the problems they faced.

3. In the late colonial period, some Indians apparently believed that hiding livestock, reducing crop acreage, and neglecting property could be an effective ruse to defend themselves against exploitation by greedy *corregidores* and tribute payments (Mörner 1978:110). If the deception worked and was widely adopted by peasants, the built landscape even today may owe something to a practice established before independence.

4. The first known published description and photograph of this rope bridge occurred in Gade (1972: 98–99) and Gade and Escobar (1972: front cover). Later, the *National Geographic* published Loren McIntyre's (1973:781–785) color photographs of the renewal of the bridge, erroneously claiming that he "discovered the only known remaining *keshwa-chaca* ... such discoveries make every issue of National Geographic a reader's delight and a collector's keepsake." Subsequently the public relations conscious Cusco brewery and the Ministerio de Transportes y Comunicaciones promoted the bridsge as a tourist attraction. Most recently, Bruce Weber described the bridge in the March 20, 1988 issue of the *New York Times Magazine*. The international publicity garnered by this ingenious creation of Andean people is its best guarantee of surivval as long as there are comuneros who still know how to make the ropes. However, the bridge is of value only for aesethetic and ethnographic reasons; a modern steel beam structure built in the 1960s is nearby.

Bibliography

Aguirre Beltran, Gonzalo. 1967. *Regiones de refugio*. Mexico City: Instituto Indigenista Interamericano.

Arguedas, José María. 1941. *Yawar Fiesta*. Lima.

Bakewell, Peter. 1984. *Miners in the Red Mountain: Indian Labor in Potosí, 1545–60*. Alburquerque: University of New Mexico Press.

Brisseau Loaiza, Janine. 1981. *Le Cusco dans sa region: étude de l'aire d'influence d'une ville andine*. (Travaux de l'Institut français d'Etudes andines, vol.16; and Travaux et Documents de géographie tropicale, No. 44. Talence/Bordeaux: Centre d'Etudes de géographie tropicale du Centre National de la Recherche scientifique.

Cook, Noble David. 1981. *Demographic collapse, Indian Peru, 1570–1620*. New York: Cambridge University Press.

Custred, Glynn. 1974. "Llameros y comercio interregional." In G. Alberti & E. Mayer (eds.) *Reciprocidad e intercambio en los Andes peruanos*, pp. 252–89. Lima: Instituto de Estudios Peruanos.

Delgado Vivanco, Edmundo. 1958. "El toro en el folklore." *Revista del Instituto Americano de Arte* (Cusco) 8:59–99.

Deustua Carvallo, José. 1981. "Intelectuales y campesinos en el Sur andino." *Allpanchis*, 17/18:41–60.

Díaz Gómez, Jorge and Wim Pelupessy. 1976. *Economía campesina y desarrollo regional del Cusco-Perú*. Lima: TAREA.

Escobar Moscoso, Mario. 1980. "Estudio comparativo de los valles del Urubamba y el Apurímac." In *El hombre y la cultura andina*, T.4, pp. 657–674. Lima: Congreso Peruano de Cultura.

Flores-Galindo, Alberto. 1977. *Arequipa y el sur andino, siglos XVIII–XX*. Lima: Editorial Horizonte.

Flores Ochoa, Jorge A. 1972. "Some of the Other Reasons Why People Migrate." *Papers of the Kroeber Anthropological Society* 45/46:40–54.

Gade, Daniel W. 1966. "Achira, The Edible Canna, Its Cultivation and Use in the Peruvian Andes." *Economic Botany* 20 (4):407–415.

———. 1972. "Bridge types in the Central Andes." *Annals of the Association of American Geographers*, 62: 94–109.

———. 1991. "Reflexiones sobre el asentamiento andino de la época toledana hasta el presente." In S. Moreno Y. and F. Salomon (eds.), pp. 69–90. *Reproducción y transformación de las sociedades andinas siglos XVI–XX*. Quito: Ediciones ABYA-YALA and Movimiento Laicos para América Latina.

———. 1992. "Landscape, System, and Identity in the Post-Conquest Andes." *Annals of the Association of American Geographers* 82 (3): 460–477.

Gade, Daniel W. & Mario Escobar. 1972. "Canyons of the Apurímac." *Explorers Journal* 51 (3):135–140.

———. 1982. "Village Settlement and The Colonial Legacy in Southern Peru." *Geographical Review* 72 (4):430–449.

Glave, Luís Miguel. 1980. "Problemas para el estudio de la historia regional: El caso del Cusco." *Allpanchis*, XIV(16):131–164.

———. 1988. "Demografía y Conflicto Social: historia de las comunidades campesinas en los Andes del sur." Instituto de Estudios Peruanos, Documento de Trabajo No.23. Lima: Instituto de Estudios Peruanos.

Gutierrez, Ramón. 1987. *Arquitectura virreynal en Cusco y su región*. Cusco: Editorial universitaria.

McIntyre, Loren. 1973. "The Lost Empire of the Incas." *National Geographic*, 144 (6): 729–787.

Mörner, Magnus. 1978. "La rebelión de Tupac Amaru en el Cusco desde una perspectiva nueva." *Actes du XLIIe Congrès Internacional des Américanistes*. Paris: Société des Américanistes, 3:109–125.

Moscoso, Maximiliano. 1963. "Apuntes para la historia de la industria textil en el Cusco colonial." *Revista Universitaria* (Cusco) 122-125:67–94.

Orlove, Benjamin S. 1980. "The Position of Rustlers in Regional Society: Social Banditry in The Andes." In B. Orlove and G. Custred (eds.). *Land and power in Latin America*, pp. 179–194. New York: Holmes & Meier Publishers.

_____. 1985. "Relaciones de producción y conflicto de clases en Atalaya, una mina del sur del Perú." *Allpanchis*, 26:213–246.

Ortíz, Alvaro. 1986. "Diagnóstico de la desigualdad y pobreza de las provincias de la Sierra del Perú." In: *Estrategias para el desarrollo de la Sierra*, pp. 15–42. Lima/ Cusco: Universidad Nacional Agraria La Molina & CERA Bartolomé de Las Casas.

Perú. 1966. *Sexto censo nacional de población. Primer censo nacional de vivienda, 2 de Julio de 1961*. Lima: Dirección Nacional de Estadística y Censos.

_____. 1974. *Censos nacionales. VII de población, II de vivienda, 4 de Junio de 1972*. Lima: Oficina Nacional de Estadística y Censos.

_____. 1981. *Programa de desarrollo de la micro-region Espinar-Chumbivilcas: organismo regional de desarrollo del Sur-Oriente*. Cusco: Instituto Nacional de Planificación.

_____. 1983. *Censos nacionales. VIII de poblacion, III de vivienda, 12 de julio de 1981*. Lima: Instituto Nacional de Estadística.

_____. 1986. *Inventario y evaluación de los recursos naturales de la zona alto andina del Perú: Departamento de Cusco*. Lima: ONERN.

Piel, Jean. 1967 . "A propos d'un soulevement rural péruvien au debut de vingtième siècle: Tocroyoc (1921)." *Revue d'histoire moderne et contemporaine* 14:375–405

Poole, Deborah. 1982. "Los santuarios religiosos en la economía regional andina (Cusco)." *Allpanchis* 19:79–116.

_____. 1984. Ritual-economic Calendars in Paruro: The Structure of Representation in Andean Ethnography. Unpublished Ph.D. thesis, University of Illinois at Urbana-Champaign. Ann Arbor: University Microfilms International.

_____. 1987. "Qorilazos, abigeos y comunidades campesinas en la provincia de Chumivilcas." In A. Flores-Galindo (ed.), *Comunidades Campesinas: Cambios y permanencias*, pp. 257-295. Lima & Chiclayo: CONCYTEC & Centro Solidaridad.

_____. 1988. "Landscapes of Power in a Cattle-Rustling Culture of Southern Andean Peru." *Dialectical Anthropology*. XII:333-64.

Raimondi, Antonio. 1874. *El Perú*. Lima: Imprenta del Estado. Vol.I

_____. 1899. "Itinerio de los viajes de Raimondi en el Perú: Cusco, Quispicanchi, Lucre, Pisac, etc., y regreso hasta Abancay." *Boletín de la Sociedad Geográfica de Lima*, 8:361–87.

Skeldon, Ronald. 1974. Migration in a Peasant Society, The Example of Cusco, Peru. Unpublished Ph.D. thesis, University of Toronto. Ottawa: National Library of Canada.

Stavig, Ward. 1985. "Violencia cotidiana de los naturales de Quispicanchis, Canas y Canchis en el siglo XVIII." *Revista Andina* 3: 451–468.

Valderrama Fernández, Ricardo & Carmen Escalante Gutierrez. 1981. *Levantamiento de los indígenas de Haquira y Quiñota 1922–1924).* Lima: Universidad Nacional Mayor de San Marcos, Seminario de Historia Rural Andina.

Velasco, Javier. 1874. "Memoria que presenta el subprefecto de la provincia de Chumbivilcas." *El Peruano* 32 (2):493–494.

Villanueva Urteaga, Horacio (ed.). 1982. *Cusco 1689: economía y sociedad en el surandino: documentos.* Cusco: CERA Bartolomé de Las Casas.

Vollmer, Gunter. 1967. *Bevölkerungspolitik und Bevölkerungsstruktur im Vizekönigreich Peru zu Ende der Kolonialzeit (1741–1821).* Berlin/Zurich: Verlag Gehlen.

Wightman, Ann. 1990. *Indigenous Migration and Social Change: The Forasteros of Cusco, 1570–1720.* Durham, NC: Duke University Press.

2

The Dead Policemen Speak: Power, Fear, and Narrative in the 1931 Molloccahua Killings (Cusco)

Benjamin Orlove

In order to explore the broad topic of violence, this chapter adopts a narrow spatial and temporal focus, a series of attacks and killings which took place in highland Peru in September 1931. The central effort of this chapter is to challenge certain divisions in the study of violence. One such division is the separation between physical acts of violence, such as torture and murder, and representations of violence, such as written narratives; another is the related analytical distinction between instrumental and symbolic intentionalities in violent acts. The approaches which emphasize the physical and instrumental poles may be termed "histories of power," since they underscore the significance of violence in establishing and maintaining material domination. The alternative approaches, which direct attention to the symbolism and representation of violence, may be termed "histories of fear," since they acknowledge the emotional dispositions which accompany violence.

This chapter locates the events of 1931 within a history of fear as well as within a history of power. Phrased somewhat differently, this chapter examines the positions of the Indian peasants, landowners, officials and other people in systems of power, particularly the economic institutions of the *hacienda* and the community and the political institutions of the state. It also examines their positions in systems of fear, particularly narratives of dangerous acts, persons and places.

In the study of violence, and indeed in the study of social life more generally, such histories of power and fear cannot be separated. As Taussig has argued, fear and power are linked in complex ways: in order to exercise control, dominant elements in society often draw upon the fear which subordinate elements feel towards them, but the dominant elements themselves often fear those whom they rule (1987). Lechner offers a general account of the appropriation and creation of society-wide fears by authoritarian states in Latin America; though he focuses on recent military regimes in the Southern Cone, his analysis of "cultures of fear" bears directly on this earlier Peruvian case (1992). Both Taussig and Lechner show, in different ways, that a real, or material, world of power in which individuals have interests cannot be opposed to an imagined, or mental, world of fear in which individuals have emotions. This chapter argues for this unity of power and fear through a close examination of the brutal events in the remote province of Espinar rather than through an analytical consideration of theoretical issues.

The Violence at Molloccahua, 1931

Espinar, the site of the violence, is one of the *provincias altas* of the department of Cusco. It can roughly be divided between a lower zone of mixed agriculture and pastoralism along the Río Salado, and a higher zone which includes pasturelands, mines and barren mountaintops. The capital of the province, Yauri, is located on a set of low hills that rise several tens of meters above the plains.

Despite its function as the center of governmental authority, Yauri was a small village in 1931, with a population somewhere between 1000 and 1500, including some Indians, as well as the *mestizos* who formed the bulk of its inhabitants. The five district capitals in the province, like Yauri, were inhabited predominantly but not exclusively by *mestizos*. They were, however, much smaller in size. None of these hamlets had a population of over 500. The bulk of the population, between 20,000 and 25,000 Indian peasants, resided in the countryside on *haciendas* (privately owned estates) and communities. Aside from a few families of *hacendados* (estate-owners), there were virtually no *mestizos* in the countryside, so there was a very strong association between Indians and rural areas on the one hand, *mestizos* and the more urban villages on the other. One of the rural communities, about 20 kilometers from Yauri, was located at the foot of another one of the hills rising above the plains. This community, this hill, and the pre-Inca fortress located on it were all known by the name Molloccahua.

The events themselves began to unfold on 12 September 1931, when a group of five *mestizo* men, armed with rifles, set off from Yauri on horseback.[1] They included the acting governor of the district, Alberto Meza; his cousin, Genaro Flores, the owner of several *haciendas* in the area; and three policemen, Monzón, Torres and Zanabria, who were not from the province but who were stationed in Yauri. They were carrying an order from Olivares, the subprefect, to arrest Domingo Tarifa, an Indian peasant, against whom Genaro Flores had issued a complaint,[2] and several other Indian peasants, who had been accused of rustling livestock from *haciendas* but who had eluded capture on other occasions.

The group arrived at Molloccahua and found Domingo Tarifa, who ran away in an attempt to escape. They shot and killed him. After loading his body on a horse, they began to ride back to Yauri. They later claimed that they had intended to present the body to officials in Yauri as part of the evidence for a report which they would make. However, they were soon intercepted by a large crowd of Indians, who demanded the return of the body. Meza, Flores and Monzón quickly escaped, though they all had some minor wounds from rocks that had been thrown at them. Torres and Zanabria remained behind, and were later tortured and killed.

The stories which Meza, Flores and Monzón told when they returned to Yauri filled the town with panic. The subprefect sent out a series of telegrams to officials in neighboring provincial capitals, in Cusco and in Lima, requesting that men and arms be sent to put down the rebellion.

On the next day, 13 September, the subprefect called a general meeting in Yauri. He gathered the weapons that were available in town and handed them to the young men, organized in a sort of urban militia. These men took turns surveying the countryside from the towers of the church, located on a hill in town. They also patrolled the town and checked for suspicious meetings. For the first few days, many women in Yauri spent the night in church under heavy guard, because they feared the possibility of rape by Indian rebels. The parish priest began a series of masses which ran on an almost daily basis for the rest of the month and well into October, in which he exhorted the Indians who were present in Yauri to obey authority.

The first of the reinforcements which the subprefect had requested also arrived on 13 September, a group of ten men headed by a police sergeant. They rode from Ayaviri, the capital of a neighboring province in the Department of Puno, and immediately set out to patrol the province. They arrested Francisco Arbuez Alvarez, an *hacendado* who was suspected of being involved with the uprising, and took him back to Ayaviri. Genaro Flores accompanied them on this trip, in order to provide details about the events. Like the other groups that would travel through the province in the next week, these men did not report encountering any opposition from Indian peasants. Nor were there reports of efforts by the Indian peasants to intercept the trucks that traveled in the province.

During the following week, the subprefect sent out a number of telegrams to officials in Cusco and Lima, in which he implored them to send policemen to reinforce the few who were in Yauri. His concerns were echoed by the reports of turmoil in Espinar which newspapers in Cusco published almost every day. The reinforcements did arrive, mostly on horseback, though one set came from Ayaviri in a truck which the provincial office of the British commercial firm Gibson and Company had lent them. Another of these groups, composed of thirty men from Chumbivilcas under the command of a police lieutenant, traveled out to Molloccahua on 15 September for a brief reconnaissance trip. They found the mutilated corpses of Torres and Zanabria next to one of the terraces at the foot of the fortress, but left them there, rather than bringing them back to Yauri.

The most dramatic events took place on 19 September, exactly one week after Tarifa's killing. The police and other men from Espinar and the neighboring provinces traveled to Molloccahua. They retrieved the bodies and took several dozen prisoners. Before leaving, they set fire to the village. In September, several months after the end of the rainy season, the pastures were very dry. Winds spread the flames across a number of hectares. Although the adobe walls of the houses could not burn, the thatch roofs and wooden beams caught fire. Many houses burned, and a number of Indian peasants were killed. Before the conflagration had ended, the policemen rode off, taking Zanabria's and Torres' bodies back to Yauri, where the parish priest held a service for them.

At this point, the story breaks into two halves. Groups of policemen, landowners and local townspeople from Yauri raided Indian settlements through the province for the next six weeks or so and took a number of prisoners. Many of the prisoners remained in the Yauri jail, but at least three separate sets of prisoners were sent to police stations in the departmental capital of Cusco. The Indian peasants seem to have been less active. The subprefectural archives and the newspaper articles refer to "threats" of Indian attacks, but not to any specific attacks themselves. This disparity suggests either that the Indian attacks did not materialize or that the victims of such attacks did not seek any redress from the courts or police. By December, the *mestizo* raids came to an end, and the province began to return to a calmer state.

The second half of the story involves the bodies of the dead policemen, which were taken under heavy guard on a three-day trip to the city of Cusco, along with a number of Indian prisoners. The first stage of the trip, from Yauri to Ayaviri, was made on the Gibson truck. From there, the group continued by train, stopping at several points to put the corpses of the policemen on display. A wake was held for the policemen when the group arrived in Cusco on 22 September. Their burial took place on the following day after a large funeral, at which many officials made speeches, a number of which were published in the Cusco newspapers.

The prisoners were held in a police station, rather than being transferred to jail, where they would have been under the jurisdiction of civil authorities. Despite complaints in newspapers about the harsh treatment which they received, they remained in the police station at least until 2 October, the time of their last appearance in the documentary record. I found no mention made of them after that date.

A group of twenty-two additional prisoners was sent to Cusco on 5 October. They were held in jail, though without formal judicial procedures to establish their innocence or guilt, on the basis of police testimony that these prisoners were the principal suspects in the murder of Zanabria and Torres, and that they had voluntarily turned themselves in. The last set of prisoners connected with the Molloccahua events, a group of ten, was sent from Yauri to Cusco on 22 November. As with the former groups of prisoners, I found no official record either of their sentencing or of their release.

Despite the brutal killings, these events do not, to my mind, constitute an instance of familiar form of political action in the Andes, the "Indian uprising,"[3] since the Indian challenge to authority was essentially limited to a single afternoon. Although the inhabitants of Molloccahua did kill and disfigure two policemen, these acts seem so brief, spontaneous and limited that they lack the sustained and purposive qualities usually associated with movements termed "uprisings" (Merriam 1984:665–666). In a later section, I will examine the notion of "Indian uprising" as presented in the documents of the period. The following section describes the period itself.

Violence Within a History of Power

One means of understanding this episode in Molloccahua is to seek the material antecedents and intended consequences of acts of physical violence. Such a history of power locates the events within the major economic systems and political institutions of the region and the nation. Even a cursory examination of Espinar shows a great inequality in power within the province, similar to patterns elsewhere in the *provincias altas* and many other portions of highland Peru. The key economic issue was the division between a small *mestizo* landholding elite and a large Indian peasantry, with conflicts between the two over the control of land and labor. The tensions created by this division were exacerbated by commercial expansion in the 1920s, which led *hacendados* and peasants alike to seek control of land. The shifting political context also heightened the atmosphere of conflict, since the growth of the central government opened the scope of Indian peasant challenges to *mestizo* domination by eroding the provincial *mestizos'* earlier monopoly over local forms of state power, and by giving some room for Indian peasant participation in formal national politics. The creation of the province of Espinar in 1917 also contributed to increased political competition between the Indian peasants and the *mestizo* townspeople and *hacendados*.

Livestock-raising was the principal economic activity of Espinar, supplemented by some agriculture and, in a few areas, mining. The organization of labor in livestock-raising was dominated by the harsh and strongly seasonal climate. During most of the year, each herder could oversee a herd of a few dozen or hundred animals, making sure that they moved from their corrals to their pastures each morning and that they returned at night. The *haciendas* had some permanent peon workers who performed the routine work of the herds, and in exchange received rights to pasture animals of their own on *hacienda* lands, much as the *comuneros* (community members) drew on household labor to graze individually owned animals on pastures controlled by communities or by small kin groups. Larger work groups assembled twice a year: to shear the wool from the sheep and alpacas at the beginning of the rainy season, so that the animals' fleece could grow back during a period of milder temperatures and more abundant pastures, and to slaughter animals at the beginning of the dry season, so that herds could be reduced just when the cold dry weather would reduce the availability of pasture and facilitate the preservation of meat. The *comuneros* organized these large work parties through a variety of forms of reciprocal exchange. The *hacendados* drew temporary labor from the communities by offering them wages in the form of wool, crops, or cash, or by granting them rights to use *hacienda* pasture. Participation in these large seasonal work parties was one of the key forms in which *comuneros* directly experienced the presence of *haciendas* in their economic lives.

The demand for wool from the *provincias altas* grew during the early decades of the twentieth century. British-based wool export firms, established in southern Peru in the nineteenth century, had consolidated a dense network of suppliers. Despite this increase in demand, there was relatively little capital investment in production, due partly to the difficulties of controlling improved pastures and herds in this unfenced region (Orlove 1977). This made the competition for pasture all the more intense, since individuals could increase their income primarily by taking away pasture from others. Though Indian communities and kin groups often were involved in disputes over pastures to which they both laid claim, the most severe tensions involved *hacendados*, who sought to control the pastures belonging to neighboring communities and to reduce the herds which their peons grazed on *hacienda* lands. In these disputes, the power of the *hacendados* rested not only on their control of land but also on their monopoly over political office. As district governors, they could demand that Indians within their jurisdiction perform unpaid labor; as justices of the peace, they could resolve disputes to favor themselves, their kin and their close associates. The immediate antecedents of the killings at Molloccahua—the claims of an *hacendado* to a peasant's land, the use of kinship ties between *hacendados* and political authorities—are characteristic of the province and of *gamonalismo* throughout the *provincias altas* in this period.

When the province of Espinar was separated from the province of Canas in 1917, a number of additional offices were created, notably a subprefecture and a higher-order court. With the increase in official business, a notary public office was also opened. These new positions favored the *hacendados* even further. It is in this context of the increase of offices, and of tensions, that the new programs of the second Leguía government (1919–1930) must be seen. Among these programs was an act, promulgated in 1920, which required adult men to perform a number of days' unpaid labor in the construction and maintenance of roads. Most *mestizos*, and very few Indians, could afford to pay the fine for failure to participate. The *hacendados* in Espinar controlled the provincial commission and were able to have roads built, without any expense to themselves, to connect their properties to national transportation networks. However beneficial this program was to the *hacendados,* it also demonstrated their increasing reliance on central authorities. This tendency was also clear in the new police force created in 1922 on the model of the Spanish Civil Guard. Though the police force was concentrated in Yauri, and though the police backed up the *hacendados* in their claims against peasants (as was shown in Molloccahua), the presence of this potentially autonomous agency was another sign that the *hacendados'* power monopoly was declining.

Not all of Leguía's programs favored the *hacendados*. In particular, the government undertook a number of measures to garner some support from the *indigenistas* who had been gathering strength in previous decades (see Poole, Chapter 3, this volume, for a fuller discussion of *indigenismo*). It created an official registry of recognized Indian communities (*comunidades indígenas reconocidas*) which protected the lands of recognized communities. The government also encouraged the opening of rural schoolhouses. *Indigenista* leaders in Cusco helped to appoint an *indigenista* subprefect and parish priest to Yauri, creating a context in which as many as thirty-one communities were recognized in Espinar by 1929, one of the largest number in any province in Peru. In 1930, individuals directly opposed to *indigenismo* replaced this subprefect and priest, and no additional communities received recognition for several years.[4] About fifty delegates from communities throughout the province attended an Indian Congress (*Congreso Indígena*) in Yauri in 1930, where they requested the opening of additional rural schools and issued a number of complaints against abusive authorities.

Tensions within the province were exacerbated by national politics. The 1929 crash created a severe fiscal crisis for Leguía, who was deposed in 1930 by a military coup with some populist overtones. The leader of the coup, Sánchez Cerro, resigned in March 1931. A provisional government established an electoral commission which set 11 October 1931 as the date for presidential elections. The intervening period witnessed the most massive demonstrations in Peruvian history (Stein 1980). The only party whose participation was prohibited by the electoral commission was the Communist Party, active in many parts of the Department of Cusco, including the *provincias altas*. The atmosphere within the department and the country as a whole was tense. Rallies were disrupted, riots broke out, and there were a number of political assassinations, setting the stage for disputes following Sánchez Cerro's claims to victory (Stein 1980).

An explanation of the violence at Molloccahua in terms of a history of power would focus on this combination of regional and national forces which led groups to fight over material resources and state power. The conflicts over the control of land and labor had long set Indian peasants and *mestizo* landowners against one another. The formation of the province of Espinar in 1917, the commercial expansion of the 1920s, and the policies of the Leguía government all increased these tensions. In such a view, the likelihood of violence in the province of Espinar was high and steadily increasing. The events of Molloccahua can be recast in such terms as a set of stages: some *hacendados* draw on state power to seek control of some land, but some peasants resist these efforts, and the state then represses them. Such an account offers a view which is not so much inaccurate as limited, since it fails to give adequate consideration to the underlying ethnic tensions which existed well before the 1920s. In other words, such a view places unbalanced emphasis on the class basis of identity, rather than including ethnic dimensions as well. It also overemphasizes the dilemmas of capitalist conflict in shaping state action, while ignoring the difficulties of constructing nationhood in Peru, a nation in which one ethnic group dominates another. This history of power can be complemented by a history of fear, that is, an examination of the images which each side held of each other. Such an effort can render more comprehensible otherwise puzzling features of the killings: the panic which gripped many of the individuals who were involved and the brutality of their acts.

Constructing Terror:
A Captain Speaks to a Reporter

A long newspaper article will serve to introduce the discussion of the history of fear. I would like to suggest that this article not merely reflects two related *mestizo* emotions (fear of Indians, trust in the state) which surfaced around the events of Molloccahua, but that it expressed these emotions powerfully and presented them to the readers in such a manner that they became more enduring than they otherwise would be. It appeared in one of Cusco's leading newspapers, *El Comercio,* on 5 October 1931, more than three weeks after the killing of the two policemen and more than two weeks after the burning of the village of Molloccahua and the funerals of the dead policemen. This date gives it more narrative closure than earlier accounts, which were written before the repression was complete. My translation retains certain odd features of the original: the lack of agreement in number between subject and verb; the lack of clear objects of prepositions; the lack of clear antecedents of relative clauses; dangling participles; inconsistent capitalizations and spelling.[5] I have placed within square brackets pieces of information which the author of the article could have assumed that the readers knew. For reasons which I will explain later on, I use the English word "Indian" for the Spanish word *indígena,* and render the Spanish *indio* as "Indio."

The events of Mollockahua. Communist propaganda and the Indian uprising. … Horrifying and Dantesque scenes in which the furious Indians attack two policemen. … The director of the tortures and of the uprising is a corporal who was discharged from Army Battalion No. 9 [based in Cusco]. … Several Communist agitators are now among the Indian masses of Espinar and Canas. … Other important declarations of Captain Briolo.

"EL COMERCIO," which has wished to provide full coverage about the bloody events which took place in Mollockahua—Province of Espinar—sent a special reporter so that he could interview the Police Captain, Señor Carlos Briolo, and obtain from this Leader facts about the origins, development, and especially about the activities and agitation which in this moment is overcoming the Indian communities of Espinar, and is turning the normal calm into anxiety, offering a grave threat to the peaceful inhabitants and property-owners of that important Province.

Captain Briolo, the cultured and distinguished Leader of our police institution, has supplied our special reporter with interesting and excitingly up-to-date information which he personally gathered and checked in the places which were the theater of the mournful and horrifying events, facts which, because they are connected to matters which have worried the public, we are now delivering by means of this article.

History of the Inkaik fort of Mollockahua. Mollockahua is an Inkaik military fort, located on the banks of the Río Salado, a major tributary of the Apurímac, which forms the boundary between the districts of Pichigua and Yauri, around which a large number of Indian families live, the plains of which were the theater of Dantesque and hair-raising acts, last September 12. The fortress of Mollockahua is surrounded by four concentric irregularly curved walls, with large towers and doorways in Inkaic style, on whose sides are found the ruins of two ancient towns: Antamarka and Ckanamarca, the latter of which was the seat and capital of the Ckana Nation. The military fort has received a new baptism in blood, by the very same ferocious, rebellious and indomitable Ckanas, who always agitated and provoked insurrections against the authority of the Emperor of the Inkas, in the times of their greatest glory, and, as history states, the conquest of the Ckanas was completed (*se consumó*) only on the condition that one of the Emperors of Tahuantinsuyo would take the daughter of the CKANA CHIEF as a legitimate wife, forming an alliance, and converting the Ckanas ever after in a reigning aillu and a royal lineage.

Captain Briolo heads for Espinar. Carrying out the orders which the Head Commander Major Flores Hidalgo had given him, Captain Briolo headed for Espinar, leading a detachment [of policemen], with the goal of clarifying and obtaining, in the theater of the events, facts which would shed light on the origin and development of the events, and his trip particularly had the aim of finding out about the internal behavior of the permanent garrison of the Civil Guard based in Espinar, in relation with the recent events.

Antecedents of the tragedy. The policemen Zanabria, Torres and Monzón headed for Mollockahua within the jurisdiction of Pichigua, complying with orders which emanated from political authorities and with the object of capturing three individuals demanded (*individuos pedidos*) by justice, and while they were near the domicile of one Tarifa, one of the individuals demanded by justice, a multitude of Indios, men and women, who received the policemen who were under orders, with protests and shouts, armed with sticks, stones and slingshots, and as the Indian avalanche seemed serious, they fired in the air, with the aims of frightening them off, however, the Indians determinedly attacked the policemen in order to corner and disarm them, setting off a struggle, and, as the shots were more frequent, someone among the ranks of the rioters happened to be wounded. The crowd which saw one of their own fall precipitously abandoned the field, leaving the three policemen and the wounded Indian alone.

The wounded man dies. The policemen approached the wounded man and found out that he was nobody less than Tarifa, one of the individuals demanded by justice, but, as the wound had been mortal, he died a few instants later.

The policemen set off towards Espinar with the cadaver. Alone and with Tarifa's cadaver at their side, the policemen resolved to carry the dead man on horseback in order to present him to the authorities in Espinar and to inform them about the events.

A surprise attack. The policemen had gone more than a kilometer back towards Yauri when, in a surprising and violent manner, a mob (*turba*) of Indios attacked the three policemen, and as the avalanche was formidable and determined, the policeman Zanabria fell to the ground in the first attack as the consequence of a strong blow from a slingshot which hit him in the head. Torres, who was walking almost next to the fallen one, was completely disoriented, only shot his rifle in an effort at defense, but did not hit his mark. The furious and demon-possessed (*endemoniados*) Indios easily dominated Torres with rocks and slingshots, capturing and disarming him.

The flight of Policeman Monzón. Policeman Monzón had remained about one hundred meters from his companions at the time of the attack and because of the fury and the form in which Zanabria had been wounded, he began to flee, confused and nervous, pursued by the rioting Indios for nearly two kilometers, and, thanks to the fact that he intercepted a horse which he found on the road, he succeeded in escaping from his pursuers.

Policeman Zanabria dies. Policeman Zanabria being mortally wounded, as the result of a ferocious slingshot blow to the head, in the hands of his executioners, he was finished off with the rifle which moments earlier the unfortunate Zanabria had held, being beaten with its butt and stabbed with its bayonet.

A Dantesque and horrifying scene. Policeman Torres, the prisoner of the epileptic (*epilépticos*) Indios, was subjected to chilling torture and martyrdom, obliged to undress, was made to carry the cadaver of his companion Zanabria on his back, countermarching towards the fortress of Mollockahua rather than following the road to Yauri, on this path the tortures which Torres received are indescribable (*inenarrables*), not being able to tolerate the weight of the cadaver, he fell down and got up several times and, no longer being able to remain standing with his macabre burden, Torres is tortured with red-hot irons and advances a few more steps with this mortifying stimulus.

Martyrdom and death of Torres. Like infernal furies and with a profusion of the most terrible and atrocious forms of torture, the bestialized Indios conceived of the idea of cutting out his tongue and putting out his eyes, and having completed these barbarous mutilations, the wretched Torres, near death, is forced, drowning in his own blood, blind, to continue forward with the cadaver on his back.

Exhausted and faint, and since the human organism is not able to resist so enormous and agonizing a martyrdom, he expires, like a martyr in the Roman Circus.

Such a horror and such barbarism, not even the peoples (*pueblos*) of Greece and Rome nor any other people had been able to conceive of tortures like these, nor Dante, in his Divine Comedy, makes his worst enemy march past such monsters in Hell.

The head of the torturers. The Indios in their frenetic insanity (*locura*), bitterness, hatred and delirium, obeyed Damián Nuñoaka, a Corporal of Battalion No. 9 [based in Cusco] and treated him as their leader.

The Indian movement in Espinar obeys Communist instigators. The documents which Captain Briolo found clearly indict the agitators who have overcome the communities of Espinar so that they obey an intense Communist propaganda campaign, and that they are very determined, in particular two members had gone from this city [Cusco], charged with the proclamation, instruction and formation of cells of the Communist International among the Indian masses.

Major Indian leaders. The most important Indians who lead and instigate the masses are known by the names of Santiago Huacarpuma, Quintín Mogrovejo, Agustín Huacho, Pablo Mogrovejo and others.

The current state of the province. With the presence of twenty men from the
Civil Guard, apparently it has been possible to dominate the situation, and
tranquility is renewed once more, and, on the other hand, they will pursue
the apprehension of the principal leaders at any price, and with this object
groups composed of five policemen each are scouring the province, pursuing
the authors of the horrendous crime of Mollockahua and, at the same time, locate the creole (*criollo* [that is, from coastal Peru]) Communist agitators.

Finally Captain Briolo pointed out that it is necessary to think seriously of
uprooting these Communist movements which are the work of two or three
agitators who, taking advantage of the ignorance of the Indios, try to commit
outrages, and, what is worse, the pacific residents, citizens and property-
owners are in imminent danger, since it would not be strange to contemplate
a Communist demonstration of more far-reaching proportions.

This article depicts the fear which the *mestizos* felt and creates fear
within the reader. It does so through a number of means, notably the selective inclusion and exclusion of events (for example, it makes no mention of the burning of the community of Molloccahua, an event in which
the Indians would appear as the victims rather than the perpetrators of violence). The savagery of the Indians is opposed to the civilization of the
state, firstly in the discussion of the fortress (the present-day rural inhabitants of Espinar are equated with the pre-Inca Canas, a savage, violent, and
rebellious people, while the Incas and their capital city of Cusco are
equated with civilized state rule) and secondly through the extended image of Torres as Christ, opposed to the demonic Indians. The article uses
the word martyrdom, and makes direct comparisons between the Indians
and the pagan Romans. The other resemblances, though unstated, are numerous, and likely to have had some effect on the readers: Torres' wounds
are like Christ's; Zanabria is the cross he carries; Torres' stumblings are
like the stations of the cross; and the hill of Molloccahua is like Calvary.
These themes of barbarism and Christianity are neatly spatialized in the
suggestion that the policemen moved back and forth along a line which
ran from Molloccahua to Yauri.

Despite the richness of such themes, however, I would like to focus on
another dimension of the article: the contrast between its great implausibility on the one hand and its presumed acceptability to the reader on the
other. There are several aspects to this implausibility. Firstly, the article
describes some physical acts which would be difficult to perform: how
could Torres, once his body had been burned with red-hot irons, his
tongue cut out, and his eyes put out, have continued to carry Zanabria?
Secondly, it presents unusual coincidences. One might well believe that
the policemen, having been surrounded, would have shot into the air and
then hit an Indian, who would then fall to the ground, and one might even
accept that the sight of his falling would have led the other Indians (previ-

ously described as an "avalanche") to "precipitously abandon" the area, leaving the policemen free to approach the man whom they had just shot. However, it strains the norms of believability to discover, first, that the fallen Indian was one of the individuals whom they were seeking and, second, that this Indian happened to die "a few instants later." The final, and most striking, feature of the implausibility of these events is not their improbability but their unknowability, since there were no trustworthy eyewitnesses. The surviving policeman, Monzón, had fled the scene as quickly as possible, after Zanabria had been wounded but before he died. Even if Monzón could have anticipated Zanabria's death, he could not have known what happened to Torres. The two men from Yauri, Meza and Flores, were not mentioned in the article. A reader who knew of them, though, might have thought that they also left as fast as they were able. Nor could the Indians, described as "epileptic," "demon-possessed," "in frenetic ... insanity," have been reliable sources. The basis of the story, therefore, must be Zanabria and Torres. The reader might imagine that officials could somehow have reconstructed the events on the basis of the mutilated corpses, perhaps in conjunction with visits to the terrifying fort of Molloccahua.[6] Captain Briolo could make the dead policemen speak. They told him of their tortures, a key element in the account since the repeated accusations that the Indians were barbarians rested on the fact that they had tortured the policemen, not that they had killed them or disfigured their corpses.

The fact that the newspaper published this article does not mean that all the readers believed every detail without question. However, it does suggest that the article had a fair degree of acceptability to many, if not most, of the readers. There are several possible overlapping sources for this acceptability, in addition to the considerable weight which stems from the fact of publication in a newspaper, which, as Walter Benjamin has shown, can transform a particular account of events into information which has a "claim to ... verifiability" and therefore to being believed (1968[1936]:89–90). First, the article confirmed, rather than altered, many of the details which had been published in the previous weeks in Cusco newspapers and which circulated in the form of rumors. Secondly, this account is also framed in a credible fashion, opening with a familiar and appealing reference to Cusco's glorious history as the Inca capital, and closing with the comforting notion that the police are acting to prevent such uprisings in the future. Thirdly, this article may have tapped the readers' very deep fear of the Indians. There is a steady progress of terror, since each new phase of the Indians' treatment of the policemen presents greater harm than the previous ones. The Indians charge towards them, they surround them, they disarm one and undress the other, they torture them, they kill them.[7] Finally, and in part as a corollary of this fear, the article may have tapped into the readers' wish to put their trust in the state. The article claimed that its single source was a high police official, Captain Briolo, who was in turn ordered by an even higher official, Major Flores, to travel to Molloccahua to obtain "facts." These orders imply the existence, and therefore the discoverability, of these facts. The readers may have placed a good deal of faith in the ability of the state to carry out its will and to see everything for which it searches. Whatever the details, the state ordered the facts to be known, and the word of the police captain became, if not the truth, at least a story that could be told in an unchallengeable fashion. The article takes the violence out of history. The barbarous acts are ones that Indians commit because of their essential nature.

The Construction of an Indian Uprising: Narrative and Identity

Although the newspaper article is longer and more lurid than the other documents connected with the violence at Molloccahua, it shares with them a reliance on the contrast between Indian and *mestizo*. There is, however, a major difference between the newspaper article and the other documents. Rather than appearing after the major events were over, these documents were written and read as the other events unfolded. They thus demonstrate the links which can exist between texts and actions in a more immediate fashion than the retrospective newspaper article.

Before I begin a detailed examination of the texts, however, it is important to consider their nature as sources. I rely principally on two distinct sets of documents found in separate archives. The first is a series of *oficios* (official communications) dating from 12 September 1931 to 25 February 1932, located in the subprefectural archive in Yauri, the capital of the province of Espinar; I use the abbreviation DA to refer to these documents, since the volume in which the copies of the *oficios* were located is labeled *Diversas Autoridades* (Diverse Authorities—the different officials to whom the messages were directed). The second is a set of articles found in the archival collections of two newspapers in Cusco, *El Sol* (ES) and *El Comercio* (EC). The fourteen articles in these newspapers which describe the events date from 15 September to 24 November 1931.

Many of the articles take some pains to construct the authority and truth of their accounts of events. They emphasize the spatial and temporal proximity of their sources to the events which they described. In the first few days after the events in Molloccahua, the newspaper articles comment that rumors were circulating in Cusco about the events, and repeatedly express regrets at being unable to inform their readers about the situation. These early articles state that they lack facts (*datos*) which are true (*verídico*). Later articles describe their sources, notably provincial correspondents and interviews with eyewitnesses, and contrast the trustworthy information (*información fidedigna*) which they contain with the rumors which were still circulating. The newspaper articles may also acquire a tone of veracity from the formal style in which they are written.

The sources all present the events in Espinar in terms of a narrative which, in its most basic form, consists of a sequence of two stages: first, Indians engage in an uprising; second, the state ends the uprising, and, in so doing, restores order. These stages may be divided into sub-stages. In the first stage of the uprising, some leaders incite the Indians to begin the uprising, and other Indians join the uprising. In the second stage, the state discovers the uprising, the state recruits civilians into the group which seeks the arrest of the Indians, and the state patrols the area of the uprising to prevent new outbreaks. This narrative of uprising fits into a more general sort of narrative of crime, in which the state has, and fulfills, the responsibility to protect its citizens and to enforce its laws.

Recent work shows the importance of the multiplicity of narratives in shaping the different positionalities within cultures of violence (Taussig 1987, Feldman 1991). In the case of Molloccahua, this narrative of Indian uprising is only one of the many that could be constructed. I have analyzed elsewhere the accounts which the Indian peasants told me in 1972 (Orlove 1991a). To summarize them briefly, they offer a very different story, composed of three stages: the inhabitants of Molloccahua were the innocent victims of an unexpected attack by the abusive *hacendados* and their allies, the political authorities; the inhabitants of Molloccahua made some minimal efforts to defend themselves; the landlords and authorities returned with more reinforcements, killing some of them and taking many more of them off to prison. It could be argued that the image of massacre is central to these accounts, and that they fit into a more general type of narrative of abuse. However, these accounts differ from the *mestizo* accounts discussed in this chapter not only because they are told by the opposite side, but also because they were not contemporaneous, and because they were told to an outsider, rather than to potential participants in the events themselves. Because of these differences, I do not treat these accounts at length in this chapter, though I do consider them elsewhere (Orlove 1991a), and I examine Indian narratives of violence in my other chapter in this volume.

Stated most simply, my argument is this: the written *mestizo* sources constructed their narratives around the terms *indígena* ("Indian," both as noun and as adjective) and *sublevación* ("uprising," from *sublevar*, "to rise up"). These terms were central to ordinary *mestizo* conversation in Cusco, as is shown by a recent analysis of personal correspondence in the 1920s and 1930s from that city (de la Cadena 1993). These words might appear odd ones on which to base narratives of crime. It was not illegal to be an

Indian, and neither the word *sublevación,* nor its close, though less frequent used, synonym *levantamiento,* ever appeared in sources written in
administrative style. They invariably replaced in these texts by legal
terms, usually *motín y asonada* (riot and disturbance), but occasionally by
other words such as *rebelión* (rebellion) and *sedición* (sedition). However,
the authors of the accounts drew on images of the Indian and the uprising,
directly suggesting to these notions, even when they used administrative
alternatives. In this way, the authors built narratives of Indian crimes and
state intervention that were not only coherent but also apparently convincing, in that these stories succeeded in generating passive consent and
in mobilizing active support for the repression. It seems likely that these
terms were persuasive precisely because they derived from everyday discourse rather than from a terminology, which, if more official, was also
more remote. It seems virtually certain that, without these terms, the narratives would have been descriptions of specific crimes committed by
people who happened to be Indians; with them, they became discussions
of Indian criminality.

The words *indígena* and *indio* have long co-existed in the vocabulary
and conversation of Spanish-speaking Peruvians as the two principal
terms which refer to Indians. Both terms appear in the titles of books and
articles published in Cusco in the 1920s, for example. It is, of course, more
difficult to reconstruct the usage and connotation of terms in the informal
style of daily spoken conversation than in official published texts, although the usages and connotations in these two contexts influence one
another. However, the word *indígena* seems to have had a tone that was
more official and more modern (de la Cadena 1993). It had been used relatively little in the nineteenth century, and it was bound up with
indigenismo, the movement which supported the rights of Indians and
sought to improve their conditions (see Poole, Chapter 3 of this volume).
Indio, by contrast, was more informal and more pejorative. The sources
make no use whatsoever of the class-based term *campesino* (peasant),
which came to be the official replacement of *indígena* in Bolivia in the
1950s and in Peru in the 1960s.

The subprefect relied exclusively on the word *indígena* in his *oficios,*
probably avoiding the use of *indio* because he was writing to other government authorities in an official capacity. The newspaper accounts also
used the term *indígena* extensively, casually employing it in simple descriptive phrases such as "the *indígena* uprising" (ES 15.9.31), "a large
group of *indígenas*" (ES 17.9.31), "the *indígenas* who were recently arrested" (EC 30.9.31). They reserved the word *indio* for occasional longer
phrases which are more complex, rhetorical, and invariably negative: "in
warlike fashion two thousand *indios* took control of the fortress of
Molloccahua located near the town [of Yauri], inhumanly assassinating

the two policemen" (EC 19.9.31). The word is sometimes used to refer to a general typological Indian rather than to specific Indian persons: "the thoughtless cruelty of the *indio*" (EC 26.9.31). The coexistence of two words for Indian, among its other consequences, creates a difficulty in translation from Spanish into English. As was previously mentioned, "Indian" will be used only to translate *indígena,* and the word "Indio" will appear in English texts where *indio* is used in the original Spanish.[8] In a few documents, some individuals are presented as Indians, not by the use of the word Indian, but by the inclusion of Quechua surnames (Huillca, Huayhua, Hancocallo) and by the omission of the honorific "don" which was used when landowners and townspeople were arrested.[9]

The authors of these sources employed the word Indian in consistent ways. Indians are often presented as a mass or horde: "a mob" (DA 13.9.31), "a mass of Indians" (EC 17.9.31), "Indians [from] other hamlets are continuing to gather together, forming an enormous mass" (DA 16.9.31). Their individuality is played down. The sources mention the names of particular Indians only in the context of the arrest of leaders, but they repeatedly focus on specific large numbers. One *oficio* referred to "more than five hundred rioting Indians" (DA 12.9.31), and another reported that

> today we will continue investigations and explorations in order to establish the exact number of the rioting Indians, who are now reconcentrating themselves in the fortress of Molloccahua; the approximate number of the rioting Indians is more than a thousand. ...(DA 17.9.31)

In sharp contrast to the varied ways in which these sources write about Indians is the complete absence of the word *mestizo,* the term most often used by social scientists and historians to contrast with Indian. The category of non-Indian is usually left unmarked. On occasion it is indicated by very general and categories, most often an "us" which includes the authors and the audiences of the texts but which excludes the Indians. In delivering a eulogy, one policeman spoke of the "compassionate confidence which we have all fatally deposited in the Indio" (EC 26.9.31). His "we" presumably included his entire audience: the two cadavers, the other policemen who were present, and a large crowd of townspeople from Cusco. Other sources were slightly more indirect. They distinguished Indians from a "public" (*público*), at times a public which newspaper articles would inform about Indians, at others a public which had opinions about the events, at still others of a public whose order and tranquility had been disturbed by the uprising.

What most clearly opposes the "us" of the authors and the audience of the sources from the Indian "them" is the civilization of the former and

the savagery or barbarism of the latter: "our Indians, whose cultural level
is far below that of a civilized being" (EC 19.9.31). The tortures and murders of the policemen were termed "savage acts" (ES 22.9.31; EC 23.9.31).
The policeman who delivered the just-cited eulogy spoke of the manner in
which policemen "travel to the most remote hut where they live, bringing
them civilization" (EC 26.9.31).

The barbarism of the Indians was manifested in several ways. They
were prone to violent emotions, especially fury and ferocity, and they
lacked "rational" qualities (DA 15.10.31). Their acts were destructive:
"their threat of invading this [provincial] capital [of Yauri] and the districts of Ocoruro and Condoroma, to complete their devastations" (DA
15.10.31). This barbarism was also spatialized in the accounts. Indians
were associated with uncivilized natural regions, such as "unpopulated
areas" (DA 13.9.31), "open countryside" (DA 31.10.31) and "mountain
ranges" (EC 26.9.31), and with uncivilized places, such as the previously
mentioned remote huts and the "gloomy (*tétrico*) fort" of Molloccahua
(DA 24.9.31). The labeling of the rebels as an "avalanche" was also a
spatialization, since it linked Indians with high mountains (and with other
features as well: massiveness, surprise, movement, uncontrollability, destruction). Such spatialization served to distinguish the authors of the
texts from the Indians, since the sources without exception adopted an urban viewpoint. The *oficios* stated that they were written in Yauri, the town
where the subprefect had his office, much as each newspaper article included the name of the town where the reporter who wrote them was
based, usually Cusco but occasionally a provincial capital. The sources
also addressed an urban audience, explicitly in the case of the *oficios*, written to other authorities based in towns, and implicitly in the case of the
newspapers. This urban emphasis also appears in the fear, cited above,
that the Indian masses would invade towns and in the word *vecino*, which
refers to town dwellers, and its derivatives such as *vecindario* (DA 6.10.31),
used to describe the intended victims of the Indians.

One sign of Indian barbarism which the sources emphasized again and
again was their excessively violent treatment of the human body. The
subprefect provided elaborate descriptions of the mutilated corpses.

> Zanabria, with his eye-sockets entirely emptied out, with immense gashes all
> across his face, especially in the forehead, his cheeks cut into slits, mutilations
> on his lips and genital organs, the thoracic and abdominal cavities burned
> with a red-hot iron shovel. [The body of] Torres revealed the same unforget-
> table deformities. …(DA 24.9.31)

One eulogist recounted the acts of mutilation themselves, offering (perhaps because the bodies themselves were in front of him) a less elaborate,
and more plausible, account than the long newspaper article.

> The mass of Indians killed these two servants [policemen] with sticks and
> stones, after applying red-hot iron to them; the bodies were dragged and in-
> humanly stabbed with their own bayonets. (EC 26.9.31)

Another eulogist began by speaking of the dead policemen's
"wounded, disfigured faces." Rather than continuing by discussing the
rest of their bodies, he emphasized instead the prematurity of their death,
stating that the murdered policemen were "as young as beautiful flower-
petals that have just opened themselves to the nourishing rays of the
sun." He elaborated on his difficulty in expressing himself ("I feel my
heart fill with emotion, my eyes fill with tears, my tongue and lips stutter,
and my soul trembles"), and concluded by pointing out that the police
force is "the safeguard of all the social institutions that exist and live under the rule of law in civilized countries" (EC 26.9.31).

At times this emphasis on Indian barbarism even comes to denying
their "humanity," through the use of the words such as "inhumanly" (EC
26.9.31) and "bestialized" (EC 5.10.31) and through the use of the centu-
ries-old association of Indians with devils, as well as through more elaborate constructions. One journalist invented the notion of *lèse* humanity
(*lesa humanidad*) from the idea of *lèse majesté* (*lesa majestad*), a crime committed against a sovereign power:

> ... some Indio prisoners, who had taken part in the consummation of this hor-
> rible crime of *lèse* humanity, which we must describe as a barbarous act,
> which reveals an incipient level of culture and appropriate only to savage
> tribes, with an absolute lack of understanding of the most basic principles of
> humanity. (EC 23.9.31)

These sources, then, center on a specific sort of actor, the Indian horde,
composed of barbarians who are prone to a particularly uncivilized and
anti-civilized type of act, the uprising.[10] The accounts do not represent uprising simply as a series of violent *acts* committed by the rebels against authorities, but rather as a *state* in which the rebels remain until they are arrested. In an early telegram, the subprefect indicated both his certainty
that the Indians continued to be rebels and his uncertainty about their specific activities: he described the attack of the rebels on the policemen and
asked the subprefect of the province of Canchis "to send machine guns in
order to arrest the Indian rebels, who continue to grow in number, who
knows, perhaps so that they can attack this town [Yauri]." (DA 13.9.31)
The *oficios* and newspaper accounts present this state of uprising as a single event with a beginning and with the possibility of ending. It is clear
that the uprising began at one moment, with a specific challenge to authority. One newspaper account states:

In the capital of Espinar province, an Indian uprising broke out on Saturday afternoon. ... A large crowd of Indians attacked the policemen ... who had captured escaped Indian criminals. (ES 17.9.31)

It is equally clear that the uprising could be brought to an end by arresting the rebels and by convincing potential rebels not to join the uprising:

We know that a few days ago a large detachment left this city [Cusco] in order to combat the rebels, and it is hoped that this situation, which could have had serious consequences, has been definitively resolved by now. (EC 19.9.31)

The notion of the uprising as a single event is also contained in the phrase *sanción ejemplarizadora,* which could be translated directly as "example-setting sanction" and more loosely as "teaching them a lesson." In an early telegram to the Minister of Government in Lima, the subprefect stated:

I request you send definitive orders Subprefects Ayaviri Juliaca [nearby provincial capitals in the Department of Puno] aid repressive force commit example-setting sanction assassins policemen succumbed completion duty (DA 12.9.31)

A later newspaper account, unconstrained by limits on the number of words, used this phrase in its description of the reception of the two cadavers upon their entry into the city of Cusco:

public opinion passionately comments on the way in which these servants of the nation had been assassinated, while they were carrying out their duty and at a young age, when their efficient services would have brought great benefits to the collectivity, requesting a severe example-settling sanction to the parties who are guilty of this savage crime. (EC 23.9.31)

This phrase "example-setting sanction" establishes a narrative in that it links two events, the policemen's deaths and subsequent punishments. It extends the range of individuals in the narrative beyond the criminals and punishers by broadening the audience for whom the "example" is set. The arrest and punishment of the rebels do not merely bring to justice individuals who have committed one or more crimes; these acts offer to a larger population of potential criminals, victims and punishers an example of how the state will respond to any similar crime. The phrase carries a number of connotations: that the state's punishments go beyond the narrow limits of the sanctions which the state is legally required to perform; that these punishments have an informative function; that these punishments notify a broad set of people that the state may repeat such punishments again; that the state will claim, on future occasions, that such punishments are motivated by transgressions; that the state reserves the right to decide which transgressions merit such punishments. In short, the phrase implies that the state is simultaneously announcing the arbitrary nature of its power and proclaiming that the exercise of such power is entirely the consequence of the actions of those who violated the previously unstated code.

Corresponding to the state of rebellion on the part of the Indians is the state of fear of the townspeople. One of the first *oficios*, a telegram, reads "inhabitants this capital [Yauri] have great anxiety invasion rebels" (DA 12.9.31). This anxiety continued well after many Indians were killed in Molloccahua, and others were arrested and taken off. Nearly a month later the subprefect wrote of

> the current dangerous situation … the burdensome circumstances which weigh on the inhabitants of the villages [of Yauri, Ocoruro and Condoroma] and … the stormy situation which a part of this province is going through. (DA 15.10.31)

The relation between the narratives and fear is a complex one. Insofar as the narratives rest on explicit images of "Indians" and "uprisings," they implicitly create an image of non-Indian victims, whose fear of the violent Indian hordes is entirely reasonable. These narratives, then, like many other narratives, lead the audience to accept that certain actors within the narrative experience fear. Like some narratives, they present this fear in a way which might frighten the audience itself, much as an effectively told ghost story, a well-written spy novel, or a Hitchcock film, might. These narratives go much further than the ghost story, the spy novel and the Hitchcock film, however, in the degree and manner with which they lead their audiences to identify themselves with characters in the narratives, especially the inhabitants of Yauri and the policemen. The narratives present "Indians" in a fashion that makes them identical to the Indians with whom their audience interacted on a daily basis. The narratives thus conjoin an element of everyday *mestizo* life, "the Indian," with a less common narrative figure, "the uprising," tied to memories of uprisings of previous decades and centuries. This link rests on the ease with which the authors of the texts could convince their readers that "uprisings" were a kind of act which Indians were prone to do. The narratives thus induced fear in their readers, not merely by a general empathy which connected audience and characters, but by a more specific and immediate identification. They implanted, or reinforced, the notion that the Indians whom the newspaper readers saw as porters in the streets, as vendors in markets, as servants in their homes, were the same as the Indians who tortured and killed *mestizos* in Espinar.

There was, however, one issue which created a serious lack of fit between "Indian" and "uprising," the two key elements of the narratives. If Indians are fully barbaric, then they would be so spontaneous and emotional, so lacking in rationality and indeed in the human capacity for thought, that they would be incapable of the sustained action implied by the unitary nature of uprisings. Since an uprising is a coherent series of events, it must have participants who are more intelligent than the Indians. This point is particularly important in the *oficios* written in administrative style. In these documents, *motín y asonada*, the legal variant of "uprising," was on occasion modified by the phrase "with a elaborated criminal plan" (DA 13.9.31), and the charge made against the Indians who met at night in Molloccahua was that they "were hatching their criminal plans" (DA 31.10.31). Even in documents in the formal style, though, the Indians were said to have "sinister plans" (DA 16.9.31).

The feature in the narratives which prevents this potential conceptual difficulty from surfacing is the portrayal of the Indians as being gullible and easily led. This quality of the Indians manifests itself in a number of different ways in the sources. Firstly, the Indians are shown as very willing to follow the directions of their *cabecillas* (headmen). The *oficios* and the newspaper accounts both reiterated the need to locate these seditious headmen. These headmen were often mentioned by name rather than forming part of a horde. Some of them were particularly dangerous because they were army veterans, and as such not only had learned to use firearms, but also had been exposed to many new ideas.

Secondly, the Indians were very susceptible to outside agitators and their propaganda, of which the prime example was Communism, that threat to society and to order not only in Espinar but throughout Peru and the world:

> the presence of the so-called Communists, who under this title do nothing but stir up the Indian masses with lies … sowing the seed of dissociative and fraudulent ideas, which constitute a serious danger to the collectivities. (EC 19.9.31)

The only evidence which the sources presented that the Indians were Communists was the statement that they "proclaimed" [*proclamaban*] Communism (DA 12.9.31). Otherwise, it was taken for granted that they could be Communists, and *comunista* was used as a synonym for *sublevado*. The categories of Indian, Communist and rebel overlapped considerably. For example, the phrase *cabecillas comunistas* (DA 31.10.31), referring to men with Quechua surnames, could have denoted either Indian headmen who are also Communists or Indian heads of Communist cells. The sources present three major aspects of the Communist threat: Communist agitators enter the province from outside, some local Communist headmen emerge, and the entire Indian mass becomes Communist. Taken together, these three aspects, which resemble three phases of an epidemic, constitute a coherent narrative of Communist infiltration.

The credulity of the Indians, though, had a third, positive aspect: if properly taught, they could be led back from uprisings and Communism. The previously mentioned notion of "example-setting sanction" suggests that the Indians could be impressed, particularly by direct physical violence. An *oficio* which the subprefect sent to Bishop Farfán of Cusco suggests another, less violent, means of instructing the Indians. The subprefect justified his request that the bishop extend the parish priest's stay in Yauri in the following manner:

> Representative elements of local society in general, as well as from the districts of Ocoruro and Condoroma, have come to my office, asking that I direct myself to you, most illustrious señor, informing you, that in relation to the bloody events of "Molloccahua," provoked by some Communist Indians, the insurrectionists continue to threaten to invade provincial capital and the above-mentioned districts, in order to complete their destructive aims, and granted the urgent necessity of warding off this danger in its early phases, by means of the priestly and profoundly persuasive word of the current parish priest ... who, on diverse occasions and in dangerous moments had been able to bring Indian ferocity back to rational order and composure, with exhortations of faith and Christianity. (DA 15.10.31)

More generally, these questions of leadership are another facet of the *mestizo* feelings of vulnerability. The provincial elites did not believe that they could control the Indian masses, either by themselves or through the local Indian headmen. The danger always existed that leaders such as Indian army veterans or Communist agitators could direct the inherently violent Indians to rise up. Faced with this possibility, the provincial *mestizos* recognized that they alone could not be sure of maintaining order, but needed other intermediaries to assure their control of the Indian masses, whether parish priests, who had been a presence in the province for centuries, or the police force, a much more recent creation.

Fear and Power:
The Consequences of Narratives

A good deal of the recent literature on violence has emphasized its nature as a distinct social and cultural phenomenon. A recent account of terror in Northern Ireland may be taken as representative (Feldman 1991). Rather

than treating violence as a consequence of some temporally and epistemo-
logically prior conflict between social groups, it presents as violence as a
phenomenon with a certain degree of autonomy, since the identities of social actors are constituted in part through violent acts. Feldman's book
also points to the inseparability of two aspects of violence: the physical
acts, in which some individuals inflict physical harm on the bodies of
other individuals, and the representational acts, especially narratives, in
which images of these individuals are constructed and received. The
events in Molloccahua also demonstrate this inseparability. I would like to
argue that the authors of these sources influenced the actions of their
readers by shaping their perceptions of these events. I support this claim
with two sorts of evidence, first by reexamining the events in
Molloccahua, Espinar and Cusco in 1931, and second by placing these
events in the broader context of power, fear, violence and repression in
twentieth-century Peru.

In the hours and days after the *mestizos* were attacked at Molloccahua,
state officials and *hacendados* were able to draw support for the repression
of the Indians by appealing to the familiar image of the Indian uprising.
Formally established procedures for calling on state power would have
been less effective. The subprefect in Yauri is probably the individual who
made most effective use of this image. If he had had to present the fragmentary and uncertain information which he had on 12 September, he
might not have received so many reinforcements so quickly, and the repression in Molloccahua might have been less violent. More generally, the
notions of "Indian" and "uprising" were central to the urgent pleas which
the subprefect sent to authorities during the second half of September and
all of October. The subprefect's basis for making these appeals would
have been much weaker if he had listed as a unconnected series the specific acts which he alleged: (1) the Indians kidnapped and beat the governor who had ridden out from Yauri with the policemen; (2) they dis-
armed, stripped, mutilated and killed the policemen; (3) they formed a
large mass; (4) they threatened to invade *haciendas* and towns, where they
might destroy property, rape women, and kill men, women and children;
(5) they created a state of great agitation in the province. By placing these
disparate acts within the single extra-legal category of "uprising," he unified them, rendered them as crimes (*delitos*), and made massive immediate
repression a necessity, since the state of uprising could be ended only by
direct state intervention. His narratives also erased any autonomous *mestizo* violence and focussed on Indian violence. By turning all the repression into a response to the Indian uprising, he avoided mentioning the fact
that armed civilians—landowners and townspeople—nearly always accompanied the policemen. The narratives underscore the linkage between
uprisings and Indians, both by a nearly automatic modification of the

noun "uprising" by the adjective "Indian" and by the overlap in attributes between rebels, Indians, Communists and savages.

The subprefect was not the only individual to make such effective use of the image. The Cusco newspapers recorded two disputes in which certain parties used the language of "Indians" and "uprisings" to obtain support for certain views and to reject alternative claims. The first dispute involves what would now be called issues of "human rights." J. Francisco Ibérico, a government attorney (*agente fiscal*), provided a newspaper with a copy of an *oficio* which he sent to a trial judge (*juez instructor*) in which he stated:

> My office has just been informed that the Indians who were recently arrested, after the shameful tragedy of Yauri (Espinar), are now in the local police station, men and women, and that they are being tortured by their custodians. (EC 30.9.31)

He went on to say that the prisoners should await trial in government prisons rather than in a police station. The newspaper supported this claim, stating that "laws should always be applied with the impartiality and justice which they demand, without distinction of race (*raza*) or social position" (EC 30.9.31). The reply, by Humberto Florez Hidalgo, a major in the police force, was published three days later. He stated that the government attorney should not have lent support to the rebels in this fashion, that the men and women prisoners had never been tortured, and, moreover, that the prisoners came under military, rather than civilian jurisdiction, having been involved in the crimes of *"rebelión, sedición o motín contra la tranquilidad y seguridad pública"* (EC 2.10.31) (rebellion, sedition and riot against tranquility and public security). This use of an imprecise element in Peruvian law which could justify repression in many circumstances is likely to have been successful because earlier articles had led the readers of Cusco newspapers to accept as a matter of fact the absence of tranquility and security in Espinar. They made it difficult to imagine alternative versions of the story, such as the peasants' "massacre" accounts which I heard in 1972. This application of this particular law turns the townspeople's fear and their sense of their own vulnerability into a crime which the "rebels" have committed, adding grounds for widespread police action in the province. The major further stated that the police who

> carry out their service in rural and unpopulated areas are considered to be field sentries (*centinelas de campaña*) and attacks on them are included and punished under article 257 of the Military Code. (EC 2.10.31)

This shifting of the allegiance of the police from their civilian superiors to the military again makes use of what had become the standard understanding of the situation, the extra-legal category of "uprising." It rests on the notion of the police as victims, rather than perpetrators, of attacks, and places them, and their prisoners, outside civilian view.

The second of the two disputes involved Francisco Arbuez Alvarez, a landowner from Espinar. The sources first mention him as having been arrested on 13 September by the first group of policemen to enter the province. As the subprefect wrote to the prefect in Cusco, these policemen

> informed themselves about the situation in the province, and after having made preliminary investigations, returned to the city of Ayaviri, taking with them don Francisco Arbuez Alvarez, the owner of *hacienda* Canllipampa, charged by his own brother don Adrián N. Alvarez as a longstanding and fearless *indigenista,* that he surely was the author of this recent movement. (DA 24.9.31)

About a week later, a Cusco newspaper printed an article with the headline "About an untrue piece of information in a new newspaper: 'La Unión Popular' in the unfortunate events in Espinar" and the subhead "A certificate which broadly proves the innocence of the honorable citizen señor Francisco Arbuez Alvarez." The article does not directly quote the prior newspaper article, but simply notes that "we are pleased to publish this important document, which vindicates a citizen who did not participate at all in the Indian uprising in Yauri." The certificate, signed by the principal authorities and *vecinos* of Yauri, states:

> the citizen señor Arbuez Alvarez is a person of honorable record who has never been a Communist, who is an active member of the Decentralist Party, in whose public and private life honesty and correctness are supreme, without having participated in any form in the Indian Communist movement of the whole province. (EC 30.9.31)

It seems reasonable to juxtapose the *oficio* and the newspaper article, since part of the scandal surrounding Arbuez must have had to do, not merely with private gossip linking him with the uprising, but with the public fact that he had been arrested after the policemen were killed. He was cleared not only of having led the movement but having participated in it at all. The evidence which was presented is telling. Despite the fact that *indigenismo* was not illegal, Arbuez was first believed guilty because his own brother accused him of being a committed *indigenista.* He was later proved innocent because he was clearly not a Communist (he was a member of a party other than the Communist Party, and a fairly conservative one at that), and, moreover, because he was well-known as a respectable person. The equations of *indigenismo* with Communism, and Indians

with Communists, are striking, as is the sense of how sharply drawn lines
were in Yauri: the individuals who supported *indigenismo* ran the risk of
social ostracism and detainment by the police. Arbuez had his name
cleared in a manner which served notice to *indigenistas* that they could be
charged with an extra-legal offense, that of betraying their fellows, which
was punishable by exclusion from respectable society.

The image of "Indian uprising" thus had great power. It lay at the center of acts of re-naming. This image allowed the subprefect to make facile
accusations that Indians were rebels, and therefore in need of "example-
setting sanctions"; it allowed the major to declare that policemen were
field sentries, and therefore beyond the jurisdiction of civilian agencies; it
allowed provincial *mestizos* to decide that a member of a leading *hacendado*
family was an *indigenista* and therefore someone to be ostracized. However, the power of the image exceeds these instances of its tactical use in
immediate circumstances. The events of Molloccahua can be seen, not
only as a moment in which concrete individuals utilized these narratives
of Indian uprisings for their particular ends, but also as a moment in
which these narratives were confirmed as part of the *mestizo* common-
sense understanding of their world. These re-namings did not merely
draw upon the established narratives; they adapted the narratives to
changing circumstances while reinforcing their core injunctions: fear the
Indian, trust the state. In short, these re-namings were one of the points
where histories of power and histories of fear intersect.

Although these narratives functioned at times in benign ways (we have
seen how the state, with its civilizing mission, gave title to Indian communities and opened rural schoolhouses in Espinar in the late 1920s), at other
times they formed part of what Taussig has called "a culture of terror"
(1987). Indeed, the imaginings of the documents resemble some of the
gruesome fantasies, recounted by Taussig, which *mestizos* created about
savage Indians and wild places in lowland Colombia. These Andean and
Amazonian cases share other attributes: the fears which obsess the *mestizos* when they face the limits to their power, the enactment of torture by
these terrified bearers of civilization. To take only one example of such
terror, the newspaper reporter, drawing on his interview with Captain
Briolo, offered a detailed account of the "martyrdom and death" of Torres, the second of the policemen to be killed in his account. One of the last
of the "indescribable ... tortures" which he received was to have his
tongue cut out before his eyes were put out. Thus, one instance of the
"horror" and "barbarism" which he suffers, for some moments at least,
was that he could see his tormentors while he was unable to speak to them
or about them. This condition was precisely that of the other policemen
who burned the village of Molloccahua. As the reconstruction of the
events has shown, the policemen were the tormentors at this point, rather

than the tormented, but they were in reality what the journalist had imagined them to be: silent witnesses of tortures. They saw, not Indians hordes torturing policemen, but policemen and other *mestizos* bringing suffering and death on Indians; they saw fire spread across the pastures that surrounded the village, they saw roof after roof burst into flame, but they did not speak—or at least they left no written record of what they saw. They were silenced, though they did not, of course, have their tongues cut out. Any witnesses who might have been moved to speak publicly would have been aware of the dangers of such acts. They were familiar with the case of Arbuez Alvarez, the hacendado who had barely been able to salvage his honor and social position after he was accused of being an indigenista, and they knew of the public chastisement of the government attorney who complained that Indian prisoners held in Cusco police stations were being tortured. It seems appropriate to consider the treatment which the hacendado and the attorney received as instances of what the subprefect termed "example-setting sanctions." These examples were set before a wide public. For the people who witnessed the wakes for the dead policemen and for the readers of the newspaper accounts of the events of Molloccahua, an elemental truth was not merely repeated, but confirmed and strengthened: the state, the all-seeing state, is the only protection against the savage Indians who threaten to overwhelm society. An important corollary was also established: the state will seek out and attack mestizo allies of the Indians as well.

Conclusion

The events of Espinar in 1931 show the difficulty of keeping separate the commonly opposed notions of the instrumental and symbolic dimensions of violence. They also demonstrate the interconnections between physical acts in which some individuals inflict bodily harm on others and representational acts in which images of harmful acts and dangerous individuals are created. The case of Molloccahua may appear to offer a particularly bleak prospect for the future of Peru in this regard. It is important to keep in mind that the images discussed in this chapter coexist with other discourses of power and identity. To mention just a few, I have briefly referred to the Indian counternarratives of Molloccahua as a massacre. More generally, peasant autonomy can be strengthened by the selective appropriation of elements of the image of wildness—spatial fixity in the countryside, resistance to externally imposed change, unpredictability, and a willingness to fight, as in the current revival of the K'ana identity in Espinar, described by Poole in the introduction to the volume, and as in other forms of Indian peasant opposition to state intervention, whether in ritual matters (Chapter 4, this volume) or in the control of territory (Orlove 1991b).

Nonetheless, this belief in Indian savagery and rebelliousness has retained its great potency through its long history. It is linked to the notions of civilization and Christianity, longstanding central elements of narratives of mestizo identity. Other writers in this volume, including Poole in Chapters 3 and 8 and Gose in Chapter 5, trace this belief back to European conquest of the Americas and even earlier to other expansionisms within Europe, and follow it forward to the current violence in Peru. The instance of Molloccahua, though, serves to underscore not only the durability of this belief but its ability to continue despite the accretion of new specific elements or the loss of old ones. In this sense, some terms which are central to the Molloccahua documents were nearing the end of the period in which they were widely used. The notion of "uprising" was little used after the 1930s.[11] Other terms, particularly indígena, were only beginning to come into usage.

Elements of the national political language of the 1960s and 1970s show the continuity of these images as well as their capacity for being reworked. The term campesino came to replace the word *indígena,* which in 1931 had begun to displace the older indio in official discourse. This effort to substitute a class-based term for a racial category did not, however, eliminate the image of the highland Indian. Rather than the old *sublevación,* the terms *invasión* (land invasion) and *toma de tierra* (land takeover) were used for the notion of "uprising." These words echo the fears of the mestizos of Espinar and Cusco in the 1930s that Indians would occupy their lands and towns, and extend these notions to all Peruvian estates and even to squatter settlements outside major cities, primarily on the coast. In this sense, these terms acknowledge the increasing migration of highland peasants to colonization areas in the eastern lowlands and to urban areas. Even invasiones of coastal haciendas could took on a racial component, as in the labelling of the invaders in cotton haciendas in Piura as cholos (Yambert 1989).[12] These peasant invaders threatened Peru's movement towards development and democracy, much as the Indian rebels of earlier decades challenged Peru's place among civilized and Christian nations. The formation of squatter settlements is also perceived in Lima as a process in which Indians have surrounded the civilized *mestizo* city.

> Today Lima is a city of *cholos,* that is, it has been cholified. ... Thousands of indigenous peasants live in so-called *barriadas* or marginal neighborhoods. In effect, ... these districts ..., like mushrooms, have arisen in the outskirts of Lima as if to enclose it in a ring of misery and social promiscuity. ... It is this invasion of the capital by the highlanders ... that is the revolution that hum-

bly arrives at the gates of Lima … and continues to transform the republican
and *mestizo* capital. (Varallanos 1962, cited in Lobo 1982:xvi)

The significance of these images in the 1980s and 1990s is even more
chilling. I refer to the continuities in the discourse as well as in the actions
of state officials—the close collaboration between police and local elites,
the mass arrests, the mass extrajudicial executions, the military authority
over prisoners held before trial, the notion of the *sanción ejemplarizadora*.
The language of Lima as "a city of *cholos*" and the victim of "invasion" an-
ticipates the military patrols in the same *barriadas*. Rénique's account
(Chapter 7, this volume) of the failure of the present-day military to distinguish between Sendero Luminoso and legal left-wing parties is very reminiscent of the sweeping accusations in which many people in 1931 were
labelled as Communists and *indigenistas*, much as the burning of the village of Molloccahua resembles the killings in the neighboring province of
Chumbivilcas in 1990, as described by Poole (Chapter 8, this volume). As
that chapter demonstrates, the present repression draws its legitimacy
from a rhetoric which justifies killings and disappearances in the name of
attacking terrorism. This rhetoric depicts the Indian and the countryside
as animal, savage and violent, and attributes rationality and justice to the
state. It draws powerfully on images of the struggle between barbarism
and civilization and of the besieged city.

Another resemblance links the Peru of 1931 and the Peru of the 1980s
and the 1990s: a severe economic contraction which followed a period of
economic expansion linked to the growth of raw material exports and industrial production. Such circumstances demonstrate limitations of the
state's ability to mediate tensions between classes. These circumstances
also bring forward the difficulties of discourses of the nation-state to mediate tensions between ethnic groups. The challenges for the social scien-
tist and historian which are raised both by the violence at Molloccahua
and by the violence in present-day Peru are to link immediate economic
crises with enduring cultural oppositions: that is, to connect the instrumental and symbolic dimensions of violence. The lessons of Molloccahua
for these challenges are the intertwinings of the history of power and the
history of fear. This case shows how the rifle, the telegraph and the newspaper were complementary instruments of violence in 1931. It directs us
to look for other such complementarities in the present, and to remember
that the body and the mind are inseparable sites of violence.

Notes

1. To reconstruct the events in Espinar in 1931, I have relied not only on the
Spanish-language texts of that year, but several other sources as well. The notarial

archives in Yauri contain documents in which individuals involved in these events have recorded land sales, wills, and acts of recognition of paternity of illegitimate children. In addition, in 1972 I recorded oral histories of the events from peasants and townspeople in Espinar. Although these sources disagree on a number of points, they permit a detailed account of the events. I have published longer accounts of the events in earlier articles (Orlove 1980, 1990, 1991a).

2. Despite my thorough review of relevant portions of archives in the subprefecture of Espinar and of the notaries public in Yauri, I found no record of the basis of the complaint, that Tarifa had sold a plot of land to Flores but refused to deliver it to him.

3. In making this claim, I do not wish to call into question either the long and significant history of entirely genuine uprisings in the Andes in the colonial and republican periods or the importance of the discussion of such uprisings, and other forms of resistance, within national scholarship and politics; it appears to me that a careful examination of events for which the status of "uprising" has been presented, rather than an unquestioning acceptance of such a categorization, is the proper response to the fact that many people have denied the importance and, in some cases, the existence, of other uprisings.

4. The rate dropped elsewhere in Peru, but not as sharply. The rate at which communities were recognized was lower for 1930–1932 (21.7 communities per year) than for 1926–1929 (72.8 per year), but such recognition did continue (Orlove 1990a:154).

5. These inconsistencies in spelling merit particular attention, because in this period spelling had become a site in which *indigenista* issues were debated. Some writers began to recognize the very genuine difficulty of distinguishing among Quechua phonemes while remaining within the orthographic conventions of modern Spanish. They sought to render visible in the written text both the distinctiveness of the Indian language and their commitment to the depiction of this distinctiveness. These efforts were often expressed inconsistently, even within single texts. Molloccahua alternates with Mollockahua, and even entirely Spanish morphemes were given new spellings. I have sought to depict these efforts. For example, I have used Inkaic to translate the word *inkaico* in this newspaper article, and Inkaik for *inkaiko*. The author, or perhaps an editor, sometimes replaced the Spanish suffix -ico with a more Indian-appearing -iko.

6. Regular readers of Cusco newspapers would not even have imagined that there was any forensic evidence to support these claims, since the eulogies published in the newspapers, and the other accounts by individuals who saw the two dead policemen, emphasized the similarities of the wounds on the bodies, rather than differences between them from which an account of deaths in different manners and at different times could be constructed. A telegram sent by the subprefect (which the newspaper readers would not have seen, though newspaper reporters and editors might have) is the only account by someone who saw the bodies which singles out one of the policemen. He describes the mutilations of Zanabria's body in detail, and then says that Torres "revealed the same unforgettable deformities" (DA 24.9.31). This telegram would suggest that they received the same treatment, and makes it especially difficult to believe that Torres was the one who had been more extensively tortured while still living, as the reporter claims Briolo told him.

7. This article omits a detail of the tortures—the mutilation of the policemen's testicles—which some readers were likely to have known, since the subprefect had reported it and since *mestizo* oral accounts in 1972 mentioned it (Orlove 1991a); this possible hint of restraint may have also rendered the story more credible.

8. In one of the eulogies, the suffix -ada, which connotes large size or number and forward motion, was applied twice to *indio* to make *indiada* (crowd of Indians): "These two policemen, designated by their superior officers to capture three prisoners who had escaped from jail, on the 12th of this month, were assaulted by a strong *indiada* in the place called Molloccahua, and without understanding the blind cruelty of a misguided *indiada*, the policemen hoped to convince it [the *indiada*], without reaching the fatal epilogue that their brave prudence would bring them." (EC 26.9.31)

9. One *oficio* indicates the Indian nature of a prisoner in a different and gender-specific fashion: "I also communicate to you that the detainee Andrea Huamanchoque has a seriously ill female child" (DA 5.10.31). A phrase more refined than *"tiene una criatura enferma de gravedad"* would have been used for a *mestiza*.

10. In choosing a translation for these terms, I have wavered between the English words "rebellion" and "uprising," both of which refer to violent or warlike opposition to a government or to legal authorities. "Uprising" seems the preferable of the two, not only because *rebelión* might be the Spanish counterpart of the English "rebellion," but also because "uprising" comes close to the Spanish terms. "Uprising" carries a greater tone than "rebellion" of sheer defiance for its own sake, and a lesser sense of a political program. A rebellion has a goal; an uprising may not. The title of the film "Rebel Without a Cause" indicates the understanding that rebels ordinarily have causes; this understanding does not necessarily extend to those who engage in *sublevaciones*. By favoring "uprising," though, I create the problem of translating *sublevado*, a participant in a *sublevación*; "rebel" is an ordinary English word, but "upriser" is not. I therefore have chosen, on stylistic rather than analytical grounds, to use the words "uprising" for the event (*sublevación*) and "rebel" for the participants (*sublevados*).

11. Other archaic usages in these documents include the term *conjura* (conspiracy), a commonplace label for political opposition in the nineteenth century but rare by the 1920s. Another somewhat archaic element is the fullness with which the image of Torres as Christ is developed in the long newspaper article, an analogy that strikes readers more accustomed to the texts of the 1940s and later as dated.

12. The term *cholo*, particularly when used as a general descriptive label, refers to individuals who occupy a racial, social and cultural position between Indians and *mestizos*.

Bibliography

Benjamin, Walter. 1968 [1936]. The Storyteller. *In* Benjamin, Walter. *Illuminations: Essays and Reflections.* Edited and with an introduction by Hannah Arendt. Pp. 83–109. New York: Schocken.

de la Cadena, Marisol. 1993. *De-Indianizing the Culture: Elite and Plebeian Intellectuals in Cusco, Peru, 1900–1992.* Unpublished manuscript, Department of Anthropology, University of Wisconsin.

Feldman, Allen. 1991. *Formations of Violence: The Narrative of the Body and Political Terror in Northern Ireland.* Chicago: University of Chicago Press.

Lechner, Norbert. 1992. Some People Die of Fear: Fear as a Political Problem. *In* Juan E. Corradi, Patricia Weiss Fagen and Manuel Antonio Corradi, eds. *Fear at the Edge: State Terror and Resistance in Latin America.* Pp. 26-35. Berkeley: University of California Press.

Lobo, Susan. 1982. *A House of My Own: Social Organization in the Squatter Settlements of Lima, Peru.* Tucson: University of Arizona Press.

Merriam Webster Inc. 1984. *Webster's New Dictionary of Synonyms.* Springfield, Massachusetts: Merriam Webster Inc.

Orlove, Benjamin. 1977. *Alpacas, Sheep and Men: The Wool Export Economy and Regional Society in Southern Peru.* New York: Academic Press.

———. 1980. Molloccahua 1931: un levantamiento campesino en el sur del Perú. *In* Jorge Flores and Abraham Valencia, eds., *Rebeliones indígenas quechuas y aymaras: Homenaje al bicentenario de la rebelión campesina de Thupa Amaro 1780–1980.* Pp. 133–154. Cuzco: Centro de Estudios Andinos Cuzco.

———. 1990. Rebels and Theorists: An Examination of Peasant Uprisings in Southern Peru. *Research in Social Movements, Conflicts and Change* 12:137–185.

———. 1991a. La violencia vista desde arriba y desde abajo: Narrativas oficiales y campesinas de encuentros conflictivos en la sierra sur del Perú. *In* Henrique Urbano, ed. *Poder y violencia en los Andes.* Pp. 237–259. Cusco: Centro de Estudios Regionales Andinos.

———. 1991b. Mapping Reeds and Reading Maps: The Politics of Representation in Lake Titicaca, Peru. *American Ethnologist.* 18(1):3–38.

Stein, Steve. 1980. *Populism in Peru: The Emergence of the Masses and the Politics of Social Control.* Madison: University of Wisconsin Press.

Taussig, Michael. 1987. *Shamanism, Colonialism and the Wild Man: A Study in Terror and Healing.* Chicago: University of Chicago Press.

Varallanos, José. 1962. *El cholo y el Perú. Introducción al estudio sociológico de un hombre y un pueblo mestizo y su destino cultural.* Buenos Aires: Imprenta López.

Yambert, Karl. 1989. The Peasant Community of Catacaos and the Peruvian Agrarian Reform. *In* Benjamin Orlove, Michael Foley and Thomas Love, eds. *State, Capital and Rural Society: Anthropological Perspectives on Political Economy in Mexico and the Andes.* Boulder: Westview Press. Pp. 182–209.

3

Performance, Domination, and Identity in the *Tierras Bravas* of Chumbivilcas (Cusco)

Deborah Poole

Más donde un
"ccorilaso" pasa,
ni las moscas se le arriman,
ni los fantasmas le espantan,
nadie le pone el pie encima.
—"Amuvar," 1960[1]

Today throughout Cusco and much of southern Peru, the province of Chumbivilcas is romantically referred to as the *tierra brava*—the brave, untamed or wild land. The inhabitants of this mythologized landscape are, in turn, known as the *qorilazos*, or "golden lassos," a term whose double linguistic roots in Quechua (*qori*) and Spanish (*lazo*) speak for the cultural contours of a province where the boundaries between "Indian" and "*mestizo*" have been thoroughly redrawn. As Cusco's own "wild land," Chumbivilcas fulfills a double role in the Cusqueño social imagination. On the one hand, like other frontiers, it is the dangerous fringe that defies Cusco's civilized center. On the other, it is the symbol of what Cusqueños like to think of as their irrepressibly romantic spirit. In accordance with this image, the province's inhabitants are considered to be indominable, vaguely criminal people who nevertheless have an altogether admirable penchant for fine horses, romance, and the sad, nostalgic poetry of traditional Andean *huayno* music. Living on the edge of civilization, they are considered to be independent, strong willed, erratic, and incorrigibly unruly—the very essence of Cusco's collective spirit of *rebeldía*, or rebelliousness.

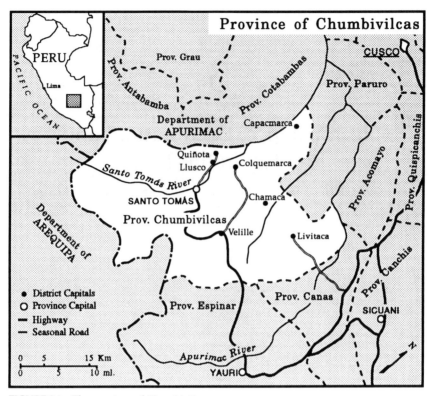

FIGURE 3.1   The province of Chumbivilcas.

This recalcitrant streak of *rebeldía* is attributed to Chumbivilcas for several very good reasons. In the first place, Chumbivilcas, like the other high provinces described by Gade in Chapter 1 of this volume, is a land of extreme geographic isolation. Its capital, the old *reducción* town of Santo Tomás, is a twenty-four hour ride from Cusco or Arequipa on buses and trucks which make the trip, at best, only once a week. To reach the other district capitals of Chumbivilcas, one usually must then travel between four hours and several days, on foot or horseback from Santo Tomás.[2]

A second reason contributing to Chumbivilcas's legendary status as the *tierra brava*, is its history of banditry and its economic grounding in the traditional agrarian estates owned for generations by a handful of sometimes notoriously powerful families. Although such estates were once common throughout the Peruvian highlands, Chumbivilcas is today one of the few areas of Peru where descendents of the land-owning families continue to rule as local strongmen and political bosses, or *gamonales*, despite the fact that the 1970 agrarian reform took away much of the property which had supposedly sustained them in power (see Paponent-Cantat, Chapter 6, this volume). Violent beatings and robberies of peasants by *abigeos* (livestock rustlers), who sometimes work with or for the *gamonales*, are also much more common in Chumbivilcas than in other provinces, where *abigeato* (rustling)—although frequent—is not practiced with nearly the same degree of violence as in Chumbivilcas.[3] It is in large part due to the combined efforts of the *abigeo* and the *gamonal*, that Chumbivilcas continues today to be Cusco's poorest and least developed province (see Table I.1 in the Introduction to this volume).

Finally, and in counterpoint to the continuing *gamonal* rule, the Chumbivilcano peasantry has gained its own reputation for rebelliousness through its insistent demands for social justice and land. As Paponnet-Cantat points out in her chapter in this volume, Chumbivilcano peasants played a vanguard role in land invasions of the 1960s, and were active in founding Cusco's departmental peasant federation. More recently, during the national peasant strikes of the 1980s, Chumbivilcas has been the scene of militant and sometimes violent confrontations between peasant unions and the *gamonal* authorities responsible for implementing government policy in the province. Following a 1990 massacre of Chumbivilcano peasants by Peruvian army personnel, the provincial peasant league launched a national campaign to investigate the massacre and to denounce other human rights abuses in the *provincias altas* of Cusco and nearby Apurímac (see Chapter 8, this volume).

The folkloric fame of the *tierra brava* thus speaks in many ways for the reality of the province's history and people. It is a land where frontier images and resurgent violence are not only mythologized and imagined, but are in fact very real. At the same time, however, cultural boundaries are never easily drawn. Indeed, it might well be argued that almost any of these traits could be applied to other high provinces subject historically to *gamonal* rule. In particular one thinks of Canas with its *gamonales*, Espinar with its history of peasant uprisings and militant provincial peasant league, and Antabamba with its history of *abigeato* and peasant revolts. Nevertheless, of these provinces, it is Chumbivilcas alone which today occupies the special *symbolic* role of the Cusco Frontier; Chumbivilcas alone to which Cusqueños will unanimously refer when discussing banditry and rustling; and Chumbivilcas alone which is said to have its own recognizable folkloric type known fondly throughout Cusco as the *qorilazo*. In short, of all the *provincias altas*, it is Chumbivilcas which has most successfully enshrined its history of violence and *gamonal* brutality within the regenerative nostalgia of a frontier myth.

This chapter will explore what it is about Chumbivilcas and the *qorilazo* which has given the province and its people this special aura or fame in Cusco's cultural identity and lore. Specifically, I will look at the role of performative violence in the historical construction of tradition and folklore in Chumbivilcas. In examining this construction of tradition, I will consider Chumbivilcano folklore an extreme or radical expression of a constellation of traits characterizing *provincias altas* culture in general.[4] I suggest that Chumbivilcano cultural tradition, as an essentialized expression of this larger regional identity, has been shaped by the mythology surrounding the folkloric figure of the *qorilazo*. The admired qualities of this folkloric figure are in turn grounded in both gender ideologies and the theatrical (or performance) idioms of Chumbivilcano *gamonalismo*.

In the first section of the chapter, I trace the origins of *gamonal* culture in Chumbivilcas to the *pandillas*, or mounted bands, and livestock rustling of the mid to late nineteenth century. I suggest that, as practiced in Chumbivilcas, livestock theft has historically been motivated not only by economic factors (for example, the sale or accumulation of livestock), but also by the *gamonales'* need to generate symbolic capital in the form of a highly theatricalized and violent masculinity. This "symbolic capital" was of equal importance in explaining the *gamonales'* ability to accrue and hold onto local power, as was the economic wealth they accumulated in landholdings and herds.

In the second section of the chapter, I then explore the ways in which the idioms of masculinity and violence that permeated nineteenth and early twentieth century *gamonal* culture are today reproduced in bullfights, horsemanship contests, and the idealized figure of the *qorilazo*. As folkloric traditions these expressions of Chumbivilcano cultural identity were canonized as "custom" in the 1920s and 1930s by a Cusco intelligentsia known as the *indigenistas* with close ties to the *provincias altas* elite. The folkloric customs celebrated—and at times invented—by the *indigenistas* of the 1920s and 1930s in turn provided the basis for state sponsored folklore programs taught in recent decades by Chumbivilcano schoolteachers, many of whom are themselves descendents of local *gamonal* families. This official folklore, which celebrates a masculine *rebeldía* grounded in the theatricalized violence characteristic of *gamonal* political culture, today forms an important part of the *qorilazo* identity shared by Chumbivilcanos of both sexes and all social classes.

The Origins of *Gamonalismo* in Chumbivilcas

As in other parts of Latin America, independence from Spanish colonial rule brought with it decidedly ambivalent results for the indigenous communities of highland Peru. In conformance with the liberal ideology of the Latin American *criollo* elite who had fought for independence from Spain, Indians were declared equal citizens of the state, their communal landholdings were abolished, and, for the first time, lands which the Spanish crown had protected as *ayllu* or community lands were declared legally alienable. Such legislation paved the way for a massive transfer of land from indigenous *ayllus* to the *mestizos* who would eventually form Peru's highland landholding elite. This process, which would take place over the course of the nineteenth century, was not immediate, but rather unfolded at different periods and through diverse combinations of legal and illegal manoeuvres in different regions of the Peruvian highlands (Burga & Flores-Galindo 1987; Deere 1990; Gootenberg 1991; Mallon 1983; Manrique 1988; Piel 1982). The specific rhythm and dynamic of land transfers reflected differing patterns of regional articulation to the capitalist labor market, the differing productive strategies of both the *mestizos* and Indian communities who inhabited a given region, and the differing involvement of regional *mestizo* elites with the central government in Lima. Unlike the neighboring department of Puno, where processes of nineteenth century land consolidation have been relatively well documented (Jacobsen 1982), the process remains relatively unstudied for much of the *provincias altas* of Cusco and Apurímac. What is clear, however, is that—as in the neighboring high provinces of Arequipa (Manrique 1986 & 1991)—the formation of large landholdings took place relatively late in the nineteenth century, under the direct stimulus of the wool export market. Up until that time, *mestizo* landholdings in the province seem to have remained relatively small (Poole 1987). Isolated from urban markets and trade routes, existing haciendas relied—as in other areas of Cusco (Glave & Remy 1983)—on a subsistence strategy combining agriculture and high altitude herding.

Politically, as well, Chumbivilcas and the neighboring high provinces remained isolated from the influence of a nascent Peruvian state more concerned with resolving the factional rivalries and wars between Lima's elite and the series of regional *caudillos* who contested Lima's hold on power, than with consolidating its hold on the vast national territory (Gootenberg 1989). As a result, for at least the first fifty years of independence, state presence was remarkably weak in that area of the southern highlands stretching between the cities of Arequipa and Cusco. Such provinces as Canas (which then included Espinar) and Chumbivilcas were comprised of factionalized territorial domains controlled by local bosses or small *mestizo* landholders whose power often ostensibly came from their positions as office-holders and, hence, as representatives of the state. Within these domains, numerous free-holding Indian communities or *ayllus* served as the labor pool without which the small haciendas—and their *mestizo* owners—could not exist. Having retained control over at least portions of their ancestral lands, these *ayllus* responded to the initial economic crisis (i.e, from approximately 1820 to 1850) by retreating into the regional economies of local production, traditional trade, and the unsalaried labor-for-land arrangements with local haciendas, upon which their region had depended for centuries.[5]

This situation was to change, however, after approximately 1850 when the demand for alpaca wool on the international market began to rise. Agents from the English-backed Arequipeño commercial houses toured Chumbivilcas and its neighboring provinces, buying wool from the Indians who owned the vast majority of the region's camelid herds. In Chumbivilcas, where the *mestizo* haciendas produced primarily cattle and sheep, the new export market produced a seemingly contradictory situation in which *mestizo* producers maintained a very low level of market activity, while "traditional" Quechua-speaking Indians entered full force into southern Peru's fledgling capitalist economy.[6] This situation directly contrasted with that of neighboring Puno, where *hacendados* effectively monopolized both the production and commercialization of wool (Jacobsen 1982). Instead, in Chumbivilcas, it was outside merchants and middlemen—many from the provinces of Arequipa—who assumed the role of market agents for both *hacendados* and Indians.

Even as the wool economy extended its hold on the southern highlands, the central state in Lima—which had been newly enriched and strengthened by the booming *guano* market—continued to ignore the highlands and its representatives there (Gootenberg 1991). Isolated from state sanction and aggravated by their loss of power over the Indians in the regional wool economy, local strongmen, or *gamonales*, set about to fashion new modes of consolidating power and asserting their claims to superiority over the Indians. These notions of superiority were based on a racial discourse promoted by the liberal state. Within this discourse, Indians were portrayed as constitutively (or biologically) inferior and, as such, as obstacles to progress and the nation. In Chumbivilcas and other areas of the southern highlands, however, the easy polarities of such racial thinking were challenged by the all too visible economic ascendancy and independence of the wool-producing Indians, as well as by the fact that the provincial *mestizos*—who self-identified as "whites"—shared most cultural traits, including language, with the Indians around them. In other words, whether thought of as phenotypical or cultural, no clear "racial" lines existed in nineteenth century Chumbivilcas. Instead, these lines had to be forcefully and emphatically drawn if the traditional systems of domination were to prevail. In Chumbivilcas, the idiom through which these lines would be graphically—and somewhat theatrically—drawn would be livestock rustling, or *abigeato*.

In previous research, I have traced the history of livestock rustling in Chumbivilcas in three overlapping historical periods stretching from approximately 1830 to 1930 (Poole 1988). These three periods were characterized by progressively elaborate forms of theatricalized violence and by the differing ways in which violence is recognized as an attribute of the *gamonal's* personal power. This assignation of violent power to the person of the *gamonal* is critical, as we will see, to the ways in which Chumbivilcano folklore later comes to incorporate performative displays of violence into bullfights and other folkloric traditions. Here I will summarize only briefly these three periods in order then to discuss the ways in which rustling has contributed to a culturally specific understanding of the nature and limits of personal power in Chumbivilcas.

1830–1870

Criminal documents from this period show a high percentage of cases involving the use of physical, one-on-one violence by state-appointed office-holders. In these cases violence appears as a legitimating idiom for authority in areas of weak state support for appointed office-holders. Livestock thefts reported from this period occur within the context of these other, more inclusive, crimes committed by appointed authorities of the state such as governors, mayors, municipal council members, and sub-prefects. The criminal activities of these men were directed to the building of personal power in the form of a monopoly over claims to state office, and not necessarily to the accumulation of material goods.[7]

The consolidation of local power which these acts afforded was further reinforced by its placement within wide networks of personal relations. These networks of friendship and *compadrazgo* (ritual kinship) replaced the largely non-functional geography of state bureaucracy and market in Chumbivilcas in the early Republican period. Thus, as in other areas of Peru, local authorities often relied on cousins, uncles, *compadres* ("co-parents," or ritual kin), and nephews who held strategic offices in neighboring provinces. This alternative, or personal, geography was useful in that whenever a complaint did surface against an authority, that authority would manipulate the judicial system in such a way that the plaintiff had to travel long distances to a different jurisdiction to seek justice.

In summary, during this period of weak state sanction for provincial or district authorities, local office holders consolidated their domain of authority around two types of social relations: violent physical relations (between the two immediate parties in an act of physical violence) and the social relations constitutive of "justice" as an act of accomodation or negotiation. Through this latter type of relations, the authorities constructed a geography wherein local residents' dialogues with the state and its law were mediated through the person and geographic network of a particular authority figure. Both physical violence and judicial procedure (law) thus came to be identified as forms of social relations intrinsic to, or centered on, the person who not only embodies state authority, but who also controls the territory or landscape of judicial procedure. In court records from this period, witnesses often explain the violence of murders, whippings, beatings, persecutions, and tortures as activities coherent with the personality of a particular authority, or as one witness expressed it, of "his natural malignity" (ADC, CSJC, Leg.114, 1854: f.9). Physical violence *per se* is not considered by any of the plaintiffs or witnesses as something inherent to the *activities* in which the authorities practiced such forms of violence as livestock theft. Rather, violence as a personality trait and as a repeated mode of social interaction is associated with the cumulative acts, including cattle theft and the administration of "justice," through which state authorities constructed both their personal and jurisdictional (or territorial) legitimacy.

1870–1900

During the following stage of livestock-rustling history, the one-on-one physical violence practiced by local authorities was extended to incorporate a more highly theatrical form. This new theatrical form was the *pandilla*, a band of from five to sixty armed and mounted men working under the orders of a particular *patrón*, or boss. These *pandillas*, which begin to be prominent in Chumbivilcas around 1860 or 1870, built upon those equations of legal jurisdiction with the personal territories of powerful men developed during the preceding period. During the 1880s and 1890s, they emerge as the controlling force in the political and economic life of Cusco's *provincias altas* (Burga & Flores-Galindo 1987; Piel 1982).

An example of how these *pandillas* operated in Chumbivilcas is provided by an incident in November 1880 in the town of Livitaca (ADC, Prefectura, Contensiosos y Admins., Leg.5, 1861–9). Some months earlier, a group of local landowners had joined together under the umbrella of *Civilismo* to protest taxes on rural and commercial properties.[8] Having stockpiled "forty precision firearms with 4000 cartridges and eighty rifles with the same amount of ammunition" (ibid.f.8), and led by their governor and tax collector (*recaudador*), Francisco Salas, a band of "eighty armed men" went to the community of Tocroyo in the neighboring district of Chamaca. Standing on the bridge in Tocroyo, Salas twice shouted "long live the gang (*argolla*)," in an audacious challenge to the provincial subprefect, Mariano Rodríguez, a Pierolista from Chamaca.[9] Salas finished his challenge to the state for whom he supposedly worked, by "expressing that he was a *huapo peleador* ['brave or handsome fighter'] and that he had confidence in his men who only moved for him" (ibid. f.8v). In response to his audacious challenge, the *"huapo peleador"* was arrested and put in jail in Santo Tomás charged with "forty seven pending criminal offenses" (ibid. f.10). Among these charges were those of "repugnance for the present government," refusal to send conscripts to Lima, forming a *"junta* for rebellion," and pocketing part of the "praedial, industrial and eclesiastic taxes for the semester of San Juan" (ibid. f.8). Undaunted, Salas's gang immediately set about preparing a jail break for their leader.

Meanwhile, the subprefect, Rodríguez, left his provincial office in Santo Tomás for the town of Colquemarca, where he could better organize his own *pandilla* of thirty armed and mounted men. As Rodríguez and company set out from Colquemarca, Salas' men "closed off the streets (*boca calles*) and made trenches" in Livitaca (ibid. f.10). As the subprefect's men rode in the village, "they opened heavy fire [which lasted] until dawn" (ibid. f.10v). After twenty four hours of combat, the subprefect finally ran out of ammunition and raised a white flag. Surrender, however, would prove insufficient recompense for Salas's men, who greeted Rodríguez's capitulation with yet more violence.

> [I]n this state, [Rodríguez and] the six Colquemarquino martyrs who accompanied him were killed by garroting and beating; all of them were stripped of their clothing and the subprefect's cadaver was tied to a ladder and carried in triumph on the shoulders [of Salas' men], who went in procession around the plaza [of Livitaca] to the derision and jeers of the rabble. The following day they buried the destroyed body, with no shroud other than its own skin, in the door of the church, mocking the sanctity of the cadaver because the place was apparently [chosen] with the idea that his tomb be trod on by all the residents of the town, that they might know that there rested a subprefect (ibid. f.10v).

Meanwhile Salas' cadaver was buried in Santo Tomás

> with a tolling of the bells, in a lined and fringed coffin, in a mass with the body present, wake and funeral ceremonies, accompanied by all of the National Guard, a muscial band, and buried with pomp in one of the chapels of the church in the center of the town (ibid. f.10v).[10]

Salas' audacious entry into Chamaca, jail break in Santo Tomás, battle in Livitaca, and barbarous burial of the subprefect, clearly speak for the theatrical qualities of the *pandillas* that had begun to operate throughout the province as the arms of powerful authorities and landowners. As political theater, however, the activities of *pandillas* like those of Salas and Rodríguez also required an audience who understood the idioms of power inscribed in their outbursts of masculine bravado and brutality. As spectators of the *pandillas'* activities, this audience would be receptive to (and therefore complicitous in) the scenario and script presented by men such as Rodríguez and Salas. In the case just discussed, for example, there is evidence that Salas' rebellion—though not, perhaps, his alleged misuse of the taxes already collected—was both supported and viewed by a broad cross sector of social classes dissatisfied with the burdens of taxation. In fact, four days prior to Salas's fiscal rebellion and public *desafío* (challenge) to the subprefect, the *"indiada"* of Chamaca had attempted to assassinate Francisco Pacheco, the governor of Chamaca, over this very issue of taxes (ibid. f.9). Salas' decision to launch his rebellion from a bridge on the border between Rodríguez's hometown of Chamaca and that of his *pandilla* members from Colquemarca symbolically reinforced his verbal challenge to Rodríguez. Equally important, however, was the fact that the bridge was also in full view of Chamaca itself where an already existing undercurrent of popular fiscal unrest, and even violence, on the part of the Indian masses lent poignancy to the *"guapo peleador's"* gesture of anti-state *rebeldía*. His anti-state posturing is then consolidated by his *pandilla* (or *argolla*) who, upon capturing and killing the subprefect, make a public mockery of the state representative's burial in Salas's hometown of Livitaca.

Further indication of the Chumbivilcano *gamonales'* peculiarly marginalized identity with respect to the very laws and state they were supposed to represent is the fact that the local factional disputes and power struggles inspiring Salas' and Rodríguez's *pandillas* borrowed the affiliations (Civilista and Pierolista), though by no means the allegiances or purposes, of the two sides in a national civil war. These symbolic factions used the language of national political discourse to reinforce forms of local power which ran contrary to effective state presence at the local level. Salas, although nominally both a civilista and tax collector, led a rebellion against the taxes implemented by the Civilista party's own leader, Manuel Pardo. Rodríguez, though an employee of the state, could not count on the protection of the state. Nor could the state rely on him for the efficient implementation of the technologies of regulation and control inscribed in such practices as censuses and taxation—the very practices which supposedly defined and implemented the networks (or "effects") of power constitutive of a liberal bourgeois state. Rather, in the local systems of power which both the tax collector Salas and the subprefect Rodríguez helped to form, the reproduction and legitimation of power still directly depended on the visibility and corporeality of a public or theatrical display of violence that was conceptually dissonant with the civil institutions, liberal ideology, and legal discourse underlying *the ideal* of the Peruvian republican state.[11]

The fact that so many of the Chumbivilcano *gamonal* rebellions during this period occurred around issues of taxation, registration, and other forms of attempted state regulation and control reflects the importance of this discrepancy between discourses of power appropriate to, on the one hand, the liberal republican state, and, on the other, the personal power of the *gamonal*. *Gamonales*, who rarely paid taxes due to the corruption of local authorities, certainly were not rebelling against the fiscal burden of taxation, as were perhaps the Chamaca Indians, whose rebellion against war levies and conscription anticipated Salas's own tax revolt. Rather, they were rebelling against a state whose presence was actualized through such competing practices or technologies of power as *matrículas* (population registries), censuses, regulated taxation, and paper currency.[12] In opposition to this more subtle inscription of power in the public sphere, *gamonales* held up the masculine (or "monarchical") icon of the *guapo peleador* as the rallying point for their anti-tax rebellion.

Although originally formed for the purposes of political infighting between factions of the *gamonal* or landowning elite, *pandillas* such as Salas' later provided the organizational model for the gangs of rustlers and livestock thieves who surface with increasing frequency in the criminal records of the 1890s and early 1900s. These *pandillas* stole livestock from both Indians and *mestizos*. Land too was frequently stolen under the pretext of "charging pasture fees." In fact, the use of legal and economic discourse to legitimize violent appropriations comes to be a distinguishing trait of *pandilla* activity during the latter part of this period. (Other *pandillas* claimed to be "buying" the animals they stole [Poole 1988:377].) Through such repeated usage in the context of theatricalized violent force, the *gamonal*-rustler appropriated the judicial and economic rhetoric of the State, and turned it into a theatrical convention establishing the fictional space, stage, or *landscape*, within which his *pandilla's* spectacle of violence was to be viewed and interpreted.[13]

The *pandillas* also usurped legal power by creating an economic and political geography in which the centers of administrative and economic activity came to be located not in the district or provincial capitals, but in the haciendas belonging to those families with the most powerful *pandillas*. It was from these haciendas that the *gamonales*, aided by the dramatic presence of their armed *pandillas*, directed the political life of their province, forcing state authorities to travel to them to conduct official business (ADC, CSJC, Leg.41–4, 1909; ADC, CSJC, Leg.255, 1890). To control this territory, the Peruvian government frequently had recourse to "exceptional measures," such as the company of army sharpshooters sent to Chumbivilcas in 1894 in an attempt to control *pandillas* and *bandoleros* (bandits) (BN, D6258, 1894, ff.5–6). Similar measures were taken in the repeated, unsuccessful attempts to create rural commissaries in Chumbivilcas (BN, E52, 1906), or simply to collect taxes from the Chumbivilcas landowners, an activity which frequently required army intervention (ADC, Admin. del Tesoro Público, Comunicaciones, Leg.183, 1892–93). This physical and conceptual distancing of state authorities from political and economic power contributed to the association of *pandillas* with a spirit of *rebeldía* that came to be considered characteristic of Chumbivilcas as a whole. As such, these late nineteenth century *pandillas* built upon the tradition of men like Salas, as well as upon the tradition of violent rule by state authorities developed during the previous period (1830–70).

1900–1930

During the early stages of *pandilla* activity, men like Salas and Rodríguez rode with and actively participated in both political and rustling *pandillas*. Documents from the subsequent stage of *abigeato* history are, by comparison, dominated by accounts of *cuadrillas* (mounted gangs) acting under orders of a *patrón* who nonetheless does *not* personally join them in their raids.[14] Although in these cases it is clear to whom the *cuadrillas* belong, no witness is able to say, as was so commonly the case a decade before, that the *gamonal* himself inflicted physical harm, raided the *estancia*, or stole a cow. This shift in role for the *gamonal* corresponds precisely with those years—1900 to 1930—when the sheep wool produced on haciendas began, for the first time, to compete successfully with the alpaca produced primarily by Indians. In light of this new found economic legitimacy in the national market system, the *gamonal* withdrew from the personally illegitimate role he had formerly played as participant in the *pandilla*. His position as "owner" (*patrón* or *dueño*) of the rustling gang, however, remained intact.

One example of this is the case of Waraqo, an Indian community of Colquemarca whose lands and animals were continually attacked by *cuadrillas* belonging to "Doctor" Ugarte, the national deputy of Chumbivilcas to the Peruvian congress (MAA, Waraqo, 1924). Faced with this situation, the community members in 1924 sent a letter to the President of Peru, stating that

> the *gamonales* [Ugarte and Aguirre] form numerous gangs of assailants and lackey thieves from their haciendas, armed to the hilt with rifles and other imposing arms and headed by those bandits [the *mayordomos* (foremen) of the haciendas] who are the scourge and final desperation of our families (ibid. f.3)

These *cuadrillas*, which included between twenty and forty men armed with "revolvers, carbines and other arms of the State" (ibid. f.2v), not only stole cattle. They also evicted Indians from their homes and burned pasture lands to force the Indians to work on Ugarte's haciendas. As a result of these "patrols" (*patrullas*) by Ugarte and Aguirre's "boys," the community of Waraqo lost in the course of two years "416 sheep, 149 cows, 190 horses, 24 mules, 16 houses and one breeding donkey" (ibid. f.2). In their letters, the Indians clearly identify the men responsible for orchestrating these attacks. Yet they cannot say the *gamonales* themselves attacked them.

Criminal or legal responsiblity for the production of violence and the stealing of property had instead passed to the *"muchachos"* (boys) who worked for the *gamonal*.

In other contemporary cases, this transferral of legal responsibility is complemented by the new legal role of the *gamonal* himself. In these cases, the *gamonal* appears in two apparently conflicting roles. In the eyes of the local populace, the *gamonal* was the "owner" of the *cuadrilla*. In the eyes of the State, however, the *gamonal* appeared in the role of lawyer, "protector," or "legal defender" of the largly Indian *abigeos* (Poole 1988).

Abigeos of the 1920s often employed extreme methods to dissuade their victims from following them into their patron's hacienda lands, or, alternatively, from entering the jurisdictions of unfriendly district or departmental authorities. One tactic was to place those victims who dared to complain in jail under the conjured-up charge of being themselves "inveterate and habitual rustlers" (ADC, CSJC, Leg.196, 1926, f.1). In other cases, *gamonales* used their personal ties of *compadrazgo* and kinship with the provincial authorites to discourage the functioning of justice (e.g., ADC, CSJC, Leg.197, 1927, fs.76; ADC, CSJC, Leg. 197, fs. 4; AMI, 1919, Abancay, fs.7; AMI, 1926, Grau, fs.27; ADC, Leg.196, 1925, fs.2; see Poole 1988). Building upon the traditions of territorial autonomy and physical coercion developed by the state authorities and *pandilla* leaders who preceded them, these *gamonales* from the 1920s and 1930s succeeded in consolidating Chumbivilcas's *tierras bravas* as a stage for the theatrical production of their own violent personal power.

The *Qorilazo* Tradition

This history makes clear the extent to which the special frontier character and aura of isolation which today cling to the *tierras bravas* of Chumbivilcas, have been constructed around the ideological and economic interests of a *gamonal* elite. *Cuadrillas* of *abigeos* working for known *gamonales* served, on the one hand, to increase the visibile association of physical violence with both the person and the personal authority of the *gamonal*, and on the other, to facilitate the flow of livestock into the *gamonales'* haciendas. The *gamonal* sold (stolen) livestock into the capitalist market and returned with the money earned to his hacienda in Chumbivilcas. There the money was re-"invested" not in capital improvements for the production of more capital (i.e., livestock), as was the case elsewhere in Peru (Burga & Reátegui 1981; Deere 1990; Jacobsen 1982; Orlove 1977). Rather, in Chumbivilcas, the money returned was converted into symbolic capital in the form of gold and silver, fancy horses, saddlery, fighting cocks, and pedigree fighting bulls.

An example of how this form of accumulated wealth was employed to construct the stage of *gamonal* power is provided by the Alvarez family of Colquemarca. Today Qolquemarquinos talk of how Luciano Alvarez, the grandfather of this still powerful clan, would sit prominently in the *punas* of his hacienda surrounded by his animals, his trunks of gold and silver coin, and his ever present and well-armed bodyguards. As a member of the most powerful family of Colquemarca, this man is also rumored to have been responsible for a mass grave supposedly uncovered on his hacienda after its appropriation in the agrarian reform. His family, moreover, is attributed with control of recognized rustling territories in Chamaca and Colquemarca. During Luciano's days, the maintenance of these territories was the responsibility of his Indian "*muchachos.*" Thanks in part to the work of these *muchachos*, by 1930, Luciano Alvarez had accumulated on his five haciendas in Colquemarca, 2510 horses, 7800 cows, 750 bulls, 39 donkeys, 4100 head of sheep, and 680 mules (de la Barrerra 1930). According to the same source, Washington Ugarte, Chumbivilcas's deputy to the national congress and scourge of the community of Waraqo, owned over 4000 camelids, 850 head of cattle, and roughly 1300 head of sheep.

But it was not only the spectacle of the *gamonal* as ostentious spendthrift, coercive employer, and, occasionally, corrupt state official which determined the special "frontier" quality Chumbivilcas holds today, for this is a pattern found throughout many other parts of highland Peru (cf, Arguedas 1980; Favre 1964; Mariátegui 1925; Manrique 1988). Rather it was the manner in which the *gamonal's* personal involvement in rustling and other forms of violence was subsequently developed into a folkloric tradition centered on certain widely accepted idioms of masculinity, "bravery" (*bravura*), and pastoral or frontier nostalgia. To understand how this tradition, which is shared by all members of Chumbivilcano society, developed out of a history of criminal violence that benefitted directly only one small provincial elite, it is necessary to examine the role of the two social groups responsible for constructing the institution of contemporary Chumbivilcano folklore. These are the *indigenista* intellectuals and the local schoolteachers, both of whom are related in class and ethnic terms to the *gamonal* elites of the *provincias altas.*

Indigenistas

To look at the first of these two figures, it is necessary to move our scenario away from Chumbivilcas itself, and to consider the image of Chumbivilcas in the eyes of the Cusco intelligentsia. During the same years in which Washington Urgarte was directing his *cuadrilla* of *abigeos* in Waraqo and Luciano Alvarez was counting his cows in Colquemarca, a circle of intellectuals in Cusco was busily developing a movement that became known as *"indigenismo." Indigenismo* was a culturalist and nationalist movement dedicated to defending the legal rights and cultural authenticity of the Andean Indian. From their highland base in Cusco, the *indigenistas* argued that it was Andean culture—and not the *criollo* or Spanish culture of Lima and the coast—which constituted the true basis of Peruvian national culture. Implicit within the Cusco *indigenistas'* writing was a critique of both modernity and the Lima-centered policies of the Peruvian state. This critique resonated with both Peruvian highland regionalist sentiments of autonomy and a broader pan-Latin American movement towards nationalist redefinition (Deustua & Rénique 1984; Poole 1992; Rénique 1991; Tamayo H. 1980). During the administration of President Augusto Leguía (1919–1930) known as the "Patria Nueva," or "New Fatherland," many *indigenistas* became active in redefining state policies towards Peru's indigenous communities and developing cultural and educational programs (Valcárcel 1981). Their involvement with Leguía's Lima-centered state reflected not so much an abandonment of their regionalist ideals, as the appeals of their nationalist discourse to the new Peruvian middle-class that emerged along with Leguía's modernizing state (Burga & Flores-Galindo 1987:125–142; Parker 1992).

One of the most influential statements of *indigenista* philosophy was *El Nuevo Indio*, published in 1930 by the Cusqueño writer José Uriel García (García 1986). In *El Nuevo Indio*, García proposed that it was colonial art and *mestizo* culture—and not a pure "Indian" or Inca culture—which was the authentic form of Cusqueño social identity.[15] As such, he saw the mission of the *indigenista* intellectual vanguard as that of constructing a "New Indian" whose roots in the Andean landscape would transcend the racial and class dichotomies of Inca versus Spanish, Indian versus white.

In his search for the New Indian, García looked to the south of Cusco towards the ancient Inca province of Cuntisuyu.[16] Within Cuntisuyu, he argued, it was the province of Chumbivilcas where the rugged *punas* and harsh climate had bred an especially vigorous race of *mestizos*. Upon the arrival of Spaniards to Cusco, the Indians retreated in a cowardly manner to the *punas* of Cuntisuyu where, García claimed, "the civilizing work of the Incas had not arrived, much less the conquering flood of the Spaniards" (García 1986:43). As a result, during the colonial period, the inhabitants of the Chumbivilcano *punas* acquired a peculiarly ambivalent character. At once the "timid and pathological soul ... of simple indianity" and the "absolute master of his environs," the Cuntisuyu Indian represented, for García, "the entrails of our nationality and of all original culture extracted from the land" (ibid., 47).

García's image of the Chumbivilcano puna, then, combined two characteristics: an autonomous, and hence potentially redemptive, millenarian tradition; and an emasculated Indian race which had turned pathological due to its cowardly retreat from Spanish and *mestizo* civilization. This unseeming state of wimpish stagnation, however, was not in accord with the Chumbivilcanos' fame for *rebeldía* and bravery (*bravura*). These qualities, García argued, originated instead in a historical transformation introduced to Chumbivilcas

> with the aid of the bovine, the horse and the sheep, animals which gave more movement and drama to the grasslands … . These [animals] were vital elements for the conquest of these empty spaces which the Incas, for lack of these animals, could not dominate well. With the aid of the bull and the horse, the Cuntisuyu man, especially the Chumbivilcano and the Cotabambino, who are the representatives of this zone … advanced their life immensely in relation to their prior state of inactivity. The *toro bravo* [brave bull] and the wild stallion came to be their contenders along with nature. Since then, in constant interaction with these [contenders], he has continued to refine his instincts and to unleash his energies. The horse breakings and bullfights, the lassoing and corraling of herds of wild steers … constitute excercises in a virile and barbarous education which sharpens the will. (ibid., p.44-5; translation mine)

With the introduction of bulls and horses, Chumbivilcas's Indians were thus transformed into a more masculine and vigorous race. Yet this remasculazation of the puna Indian—and with him, his jealously guarded millenarian traditions—was still not sufficient to form the prototype of García's "*nuevo indio.*" The other, Spanish, half of the *mestizo* racial equation had to be similarly remasculated by leaving behind the feminine comforts of their valley houses and haciendas, to penetrate (and be penetrated by) the rugged *puna* landscape:

> This space is vertical rather than horizontal. In order to conquer it, it is necessary to climb the mountain, ascend rugged slopes, conquer abysses, surpass peaks, better one's self, leaving behind the swollen curves of hillocks and hills, like one who retreats from the morbid feminine temptations and the accusing weakness of a blandness of the soul. (ibid., 43; translation mine)

Once in the dramatic and tragically silent punas all ambivalence of character and sexual identity were destined, García argued, to disappear:

> On these implacable lands there is only one dilemma for a man: perish or dominate. Nature obliges forceful and emminent action. No compromise [*términos medios*], no parasites, nor bland souls as in the sweet landscape of the valley … . On this stage, luck and danger are the unavoidable elements of this vital drama. (*ibid.*, 44; translation mine)

From this historic racial and cultural mixture emerged the Chumbivilcano *mestizo*, "master of distances, tamer of the void" (ibid. 48). Yet as prototype for García's *Nuevo Indio*, the masculine qualities of the *mestizo qorilazo* run perilously out of control, due to his intimate relationship with the landscape in which he lives. Autonomy and *rebeldía*—healthy characteristics of the *nuevo indio*—merge into a criminal behavior which, more than a symptom of masculine bravery, is also regenerative and playful. Thus, for García, the Chumbivilcano becomes "an essentially sporting and youthful spirit. Who knows whether homicide and robbery are, in many cases, no more than sports in this atrociously tragic countryside" (ibid., 45).

Other *indigenistas* concurred with García in their romanticization of the Qorilazos. Like García, they attributed the Chumbivilcanos' penchant for delinquency to the same forces of increasing velocity by which, according to García, the Andean landscape had been transformed by Spanish animals and transportation:

> With the [Spanish] conquest, the [Andean] landscape suffered a transformation; as J. Uriel García has well observed, it has become *mestizo* [*amestizado*]. The new contribution of European crops like wheat and barley has given it a new physiognomy, and the presence of the horse, the ox, the sheep, etc., has influenced the economy and served also to transform the landscape and its inhabitant. The consequence [of this transformation] is the Ccarabotas ["leather-booted"] Chumbivilcano, who rides on his small colt, challenging with the speed of his mount the most vast distances of the *puna*. But this runner whose blood burns with his victory over the slopes of the plain, soon becomes a sportsman of danger, his colt no longer serves to challenge the prairie wind, but rather is used for banditry and rustling. (Yepez Miranda, 1940:35; translation mine).

These *indigenista* intellectuals' vision of Chumbivilcano culture both drew on and exaggerated a real tendency towards violence and *rebeldía* in Chumbivilcano society. By the late nineteenth century the Chumbivilcano *gamonales'* fame for violent reprisal had become notorious throughout the Cusco region. Recurring incidents like that between Salas and Rodríguez had come to characterize the province, lending it a certain reputation for delinquency, rustling, violence, and crime. This reputation of the Chumbivilcano *gamonal* increased as the state extended its reach into the public life of Cusco. As republican forms of civil society came more and more to regulate Cusqueño social and political identity, the iconic qualities of the anti-state Chumbivilcano grew in the Cusqueño imagination.

Particularly effected by such romanticizing imagery were those *indigenista* intellectuals who sought to construct autonomous forms of regional culture at the precise moment when they themselves were becom-

ing increasingly involved with the central state. Such a reading can easily
be ascribed, for example, to the *indigenista* Luís Valcárcel's recounting of
his experiences as candidate for the province of Chumbivilcas in 1919.[17]
After describing the *"nefasto"* (ominous) and violent nature of electoral
politics in Chumbivilcas, Valcárcel (1981:201–202) describes how he was
forced to conduct his campaign through a skillful handling of fissions
within and between the province's most powerful families. Valcárcel reasoned that such maneuvering would still not prove sufficient to win an
electoral campaign, however, because "the people of Chumbivilcas were
wild people (*gente brava*), accustomed to ride around all day on horseback.
In order to win their sympathies I had to organize a journey to that province taking them many gifts."

For Valcárcel, the Chumbivilcano elite represented a pre-political society governed by such forces as kinship, violence, and the gift. As we have
seen, in the writings of Valcárcel's *indigenista* contemporaries Uriel García, Atilio Sivirichi, and Alfredo Yepez Miranda, Chumbivilcas was similarly invoked as allegory for the anti-state and anti-coastal roots of an indigenous *mestizo* Andean culture. Their choice of Chumbivilcas as the site
in which to inscribe this idea of a naturally rebellious Andean spirit had,
however, as much to do with their own status as middle-class provincial
intellectuals, as with the actual forms of rebellion and violence present in
Chumbivilcas itself. During the 1920s, forms of civil and state regulation
became increasingly entrenched in the Cusco countryside due to President Leguía's registration of indigenous communities and *conscripción vial*
(forced conscription for road construction), as well as to the organizing activities of Lima based groups such as the Tahuantinsuyu Committee,
named for the "Four Suyus" of the Inca Empire (Davies 1974; Deustua &
Rénique 1984; Kapsoli 1984). Subject for the first time to the surveillance of
both state institutions and outsiders such as the Tahuantinsuyu Committee, *gamonales* who, like Salas, Rodríguez, and Ugarte, had once played off
both local and state spheres of political legitimation were placed in newly
contradictory situations. Some, as we have seen, pulled out of the personal roles they had previously played in illegal activities, while retaining
control (or ownership) of their *pandillas*. Others withdrew to their isolated
haciendas. Still others—particularly those from Canas and Puno—became
indigenista intellectuals dedicated to defending the Indian and to defining
an authentic Andean tradition.

For such provincial intellectuals, the Chumbivilcano *hacendado* stood
out as a form of "pure" *gamonal*. As we have seen, state institutions were
still relatively weak in the more remote stretches of Chumbivilcas, and,
though by no means all of the province's landowners engaged in such activities, certain Chumbivilcanos attained a certain notoriety in Cusco for
their complicity in *abigeato* and *cuadrillas*. For their neighbors in provinces

such as Canas—where *pandilla* and rustling activities had once rivaled those of Chumbivilcas in the later part of the nineteenth century [18]—these men came to represent a form of nostalgia for "the good old days" when personal power had brought with it the benefits of loyalty, autonomy, and wealth. In my conversations with older *indigenistas* from Canas I was often struck by the extent to which they both glorified and reviled notorious figures from Colquemarca's Alvarez clan. When speaking of these men, the two qualities most often noted were those of authenticity and *rebeldía*. This latter was, in turn, broken down into the admirable "manly" qualities which the Canas intellectuals saw as inherent to the *provincias altas* as a whole, and a reactionary violence which they were careful to specify as something peculiar to Chumbivilcas. By thus circumscribing the *gamonal*'s violent side—which, of course, ran contrary to the *indigenistas*' stated political and social identity as defenders of the Indian—the Canas *indigenistas* could both salvage his image as a manly adventurer and bohemian like themselves, *and* distinguish themselves from his less desirable traits.

This intellectualized nostalgia for the authenticity, manly adventure, and instinctive *rebeldía* of the Chumbivilcano *gamonal*, speaks for the *indigenistas*' social dilemma as landowners, as members of Cusco's *mestizo* elite, and as intellectuals interested in revindicating regional claims for political autonomy and cultural revitalization. The *indigenistas* were impressed by the examples set for them in the Indian rebellions of 1921–24 in Haquira, Colquemarca, Yauri, Tocroyuh, and other places in Cusco's *provincias altas* (Burga & Flores-Galindo 1987; Piel 1967; Valderrama & Escalante 1981). They astutely perceived in these rebellions both an eventual end to their privileged social status and the need to redefine Cusco's social and cultural agenda so as to include the Indian masses as part of an *indigenista* vanguard movement led by the *mestizo* intelligentsia (Deustua & Rénique 1984:69-96; Rénique 1991). In this respect, the *indigenistas*' discourse of liberal reform ressembled very closely that of *gamonales* such as Rodríguez and Salas. In the face of both market competition with independent Indian wool producers and rising Indian discontent with local forms of exploitation and governance, the nineteenth century *gamonal* molded a spectacle of personal power which would, on the one hand, bridge the "separate" worlds of Indian and *mestizo*, and on the other, present these newly united worlds as part of a unified front of anti-state *rebeldía*. The *indigenistas* molded a similarly structured discourse of cultural authenticity intended to represent Indian and *mestizo* as part of a single Andean culture under the leadership of an *indigenista* vanguard of artists and intellectuals (Poole 1992).

In both cases, the idiom or rhetoric chosen to bridge the "gap" of ethnicity and class was that of masculinity. For the *gamonal*, it was a masculine rhetoric of violence that would cut across the critical ethnic/class divide separating Indian peasant and *mestizo* landowning males. It also provided a theatrical idiom which focused on the male body as a source of violent coercion. This focus highlighted the necessarily personal nature of local power in what were emerging as the *tierras bravas* of Chumbivilcas. For their part, García, Valcárcel, and other Cusco *indigenistas*—in examples too numerous to cite here—also relied heavily on tropes of fecundity, fertilization, and penetration in their description of the Andean landscape. Most drew on a scenario like that outlined by García, in which the stagnant and effeminate Indian becomes enmasculated with the arrival of horses, bulls, and Spaniards. As the different effects of state power and progress intervened in the *indigenistas'* world, however, the *qorilazo's* form of power came to acquire a delinquent quality in the eyes of the *indigenistas*. From this split between a positively valued masculine *rebeldía* and an atavistic criminality emerges the *indigenistas'* romance of the Chumbivilcano *abigeo* as icon for what we might think of as masculinity run amok. The *indigenista* vanguard in Cusco took it as their task to set this masculine energy and *rebeldía* in order again.

One of the routes chosen for this reordering was the establishment of authentic folklores for Chumbivilcas and other Cusco regions. This was done through a variety of institutions. On a national level, Luís Valcárcel was able to implement his theories as Minister of Education and director of the national museum (Valcárcel 1981). On a local level, Atilio Sivirichi and other disciples of Uriel García actively sponsored folklore programs in Cusco and its provinces. Sivirichi, for example, introduced and sponsored the famous Chumbivilcano musician Francisco "Pancho" Gómez Negrón. Pancho Gómez—whom the *indigenista* historian José Tamayo Herrera (1980:273) calls "the living incarnation of the small town bohemian and adventurous cowboy"—was from the notorious Negrón family of Colquemarca (one time enemies of the Alvarez clan). He died performing an equestrian stunt in 1950 for a Cusco public in the Inca fortress of Saqsahuaman, and was posthumously crowned by Uriel García's Institute for Interamerican Art as "Precursor of the Emancipation of American Popular Art." Today one of the most popular Chumbivilcano bands—with some three or four commercial record albums—is called "Conjunto Pancho Gómez Negrón." The *indigenista* photographer, Martín Chambi, immortalized the *qorilazo* costume and attitude made famous by Pancho Gómez in his portrait of a group of *qorilazos* in Cusco.[19]

Folklore

It is largely as a result of such *indigenista* cultural projects that the *qorilazo* is celebrated throughout the Department of Cusco as a "typical," pictur-

FIGURE 3.2   *Qorilazos* (photograph by Martín Chambi, c. 1930).

esque folkloric figure. Today, dance groups of "*qorilazos*" are a favorite part of all Cusco folklore shows, and civic and religious parades. Their costume is that of the Chumbivilcano *mestizo* rancher: *qarawatanas* (leather chaps), a red poncho, white hat, boots, spurs, and *liwi* (bolas). In oral tradition, the *qorilazo* is assigned the personality of a bohemian romantic, steadfast in his solitude, loyal only to his horse, and well-versed in the romantic *huaynos* with which he courts his many women. Finally, he is a master bullfighter, fearless in the face of death, intrepid in his solitude. In these attributes, the *qorilazo* holds much in common with other popular frontier types including the more well-known Argentine gaucho, American cowboy, and Mexican *bandido*.[20]

Within Chumbivilcas itself, these characteristics of the *qorilazo* have been mythologized in a large repertoire of *huaynos* immortalizing the province and its uniquely masculine charms.[21] These songs tell of the exploits and sadness of the *qorilazo* as he rides alone over the hostile Chumbivilcano punas. Their invocation of the viril puna landscape, masculine virtue, and "*sentimiento andino*" (Andean sentiment) all mimic themes from the *indigenista* philosophy outlined above.

The most important public forum for the *qorilazo* mystique, however, occurs in the fiestas of Santo Tomás, the provincial capital. The principal feasts of Santo Tomás take place on June 21 (the anniversary of the creation of the Province of Chumbivilcas), September 8 (the feast day of the Virgin of the Nativity), and on Christmas Day when Chumbivilcanos celebrate the *takanakuy,* a ritualized fist-fight in which men take vengeance on those who have done them wrong or insulted them over the last year. Since the participants are all masked, and therefore presumably unrecognizable, each man's vengeance is spent on an anonymous victim symbolizing the real or desired object of vengeance. Unlike the ritual battles performed in other regions of *provincias altas,* where distinct communities face off against each other (see Orlove, Chapter 4 this volume), the Chumbivilcano *takanakuy* is a strictly individual and internal affair: the point being to exact vengeance from individuals who have harmed you during the year. As ritual performance, the *takanakuy* functions as a public forum for displays of manliness and *bravura,* since the participants, although supposedly in disguise, are in fact recognizable to nearly all members of the relatively small communities.

On the other two feast days, the focal point of *qorilazo* display is the bullfight or *corrida.* The *corrida* which I attended in 1986 was held on June 21, the anniversary of the province of Chumbivilcas. As in other Santo Tomás bullfights, events began the evening before, when the bull is "seen off" in the *toro kacharpariy* (farewell to the bull). This event consists of an equestrian contest performed in the plaza of Santo Tomás. Riders and mounts are judged in two categories: *caballo de paso* (gaited horse) and *caballo chumbivilcano* (Chumbivilcano horse). In 1986, the year in which I attended the *toro kacharpariy,* the judges were the school teacher Alvarez and the accountant Gómez, eldest sons of prominent *gamonal* families from Colquemarca and Chamaca, respectively. (Both were also reputed to be experienced *abigeos.*) They took their job quite seriously, even going so far as to suspend drinking until after the responsibility of choosing the best Chumbivilcano man and horse had been successfully accomplished. The winner of the Chumbivilcano category is judged as the rider who best captures the qualities of the *qorilazo.* This rider must have a proper costume including *qarawatana, liwi,* poncho, *ch'ullu* (knitted cap with earflaps), wool felt hat with leather chinstrap, spurs, boots, and "correct" harness for the horse. The horse should be one of the province's own small *puna* horses, noted for their small size, thick hair, endurance, and stubbornness. In the riding contest itself, the equestrian ideal for both categories is the precise opposite of that for the coastal *caballo de paso* for whom pace, refinement and responsiveness are judged desirable features. Instead, in Santo Tomás, the winners are those men who prove most successful in spurring their mounts into increasingly wild behavior, such that the end result resembles the dialogue between a Western-style horsebreaker and an untrained, wild horse.

FIGURE 3.3 *Gamonales* and horses in the Toro Kacharpariy, Santo Tomás, Chumbivilcas, 1986 (photograph by Deborah Poole).

In the bullfight for which this ritual acts as *entrada* or prelude, these qualities of indominability and endurance are transferred from the *puna*-horse to the men who enter the ring. The *plaza de toros* (bullring) which will house this transference of animal qualities sits on the outskirts of the town.[22] By early afternoon, organized groups of *vecinos notables* (prominent *mestizos* from the town) had begun to parade toward the bullring in a raucous and sentimental prolongation of the serenades and fiestas which had continued throughout the night of the *toro kacharipariy*. Upon arriving to the bullring each family (or clan) group files into a booth prepared for them in the row of draped and decorated grandstand boxes which form half of the circle enclosing the bullring. Crowded along the other half of the curving walls, were hundreds of *campesinos* from the peasant communities of Santo Tomás. The opposing sides of the ring were accentuated by the division of the bullfights into two fighting styles: the *misti toro* (*mestizo* bull) and the *yawar mayu* (river of blood).[23]

Misti toro, with which the *corrida* begins, differs from the classic Spanish bullfight, on which it is in other ways patterned, in that the Chumbivilcano spectacle is designed to slay not the bull, but the man. Accordingly, the ratio of men to bulls is reversed, so that one man enters the ring to face three or more bulls simultaneously. Given such odds—plus the important fact that the aspiring *toreador* (bullfighter), who can be of either *misti* or *campesino* origins, is usually drunk—the Chumbivilcano bullfight is often tantamount to so much drunken carnage. Such carnage is considered not only normal but desirable. As indicated by one man who explained the custom (i.e., the standard or normative ideal) of the bullfight to me:

> The man enters to fight the bull with his poncho—the ponchos are also special, you see. He is always half drunk and the bull, the most daring there is, catches him and throws him over, [and] at times he desembowels him and the woman comes up to the man and gathers up his guts.

After the final bull, the crowd files out of the bullring singing the song "*Chiqchischay paraschay*" (little hail and little rain) in which improvised verses play with themes of luck and destiny. The repeated refrain of "little hail, little rain" contrasts the fertility or goodness brought by rain, with the accompanying evil of destructive hail.

Hakuraqchu manaraqchu	Still we go or still we don't
Chiqchischay paraschay	Little hail, little rain
Icha ima ninkiraqchu	Or what yet do you say?
Chiqchischay paraschay	Little hail, little rain.
Qayna wata kunan hina	Next year like today
Chiqchischay paraschay	Little hail, little rain
Ichas kashun ichas mana	Maybe here maybe not.
Chiqchischay paraschay	Little hail, little rain
Que bonito es mi toro	How pretty is my bull.
Chiqchischay paraschay	Little hail, little rain
Con cachito conchayperla	With horns of mother of pearl
Chiqchischay paraschay	Little hail, little rain
Torito phiña turito	Little bull, mean little bull
Chiqchischay paraschay	Little hail, little rain
Puka razo enjalmantin	With an all red harness
Chiqchischay paraschay	Little hail, little rain
Noqallataq qatimuyku	I alone have led you
Chiqchischay paraschay	Little hail, little rain
Qanllarataq waqrawanki	You alone have gored me
Chiqchischay paraschay	Little hail, little rain
Maytan hamuranchis chayta	Where did we go then?
Chiqchischay paraschay	Little hail, little rain
Hakuraqchu manaraqchu	Still we go or still we don't
Chiqchischay paraschay	Little hail, little rain

> *Maytan hamuranchis chayta*   Where did we go then?
> *Chiqchischay paraschay*   Little hail, little rain.[24]

In the 1986 *corrida*, however, the crowd singing "*Chiqchischaylla paraschaylla*" returned disappointed to their homes. Little blood had been shed and only one man disemboweled. No women were forced to jump into the ring and, amidst the dust raised by charging bulls, publicly gather up the guts of her valiant hero. In short, the province's manhood—and hence luck—had been severely questioned. On my return visit in 1988, friends in Santo Tomás were careful to point out to me that things were nonetheless improving, since the bullfight that year in Quiñota had been "*bien buena*," resulting, they claimed, in seven disembowelings and three deaths.

Such carnage, however, pales in comparison with the glorious past when, as I was often told, up to forty or fifty bulls were brought in for every bullfight from Colquemarca's Hacienda Lacaya. Famed for his *toros de lidia* (fighting bulls), the owner of Lacaya, Mariano Alvarez—who was the son of Luciano Alvarez and the uncle of the schoolteacher who served as *toro kacharpariy* judge in 1986—is frequently spoken of today as a colorful and exemplary *qorilazo*. Integral to this identity, were his apparently manly qualities of solitude and autonomy, and his lack of restrictive family ties. A true bohemian, Mariano, like other Chumbivilcano *gamonales*, maintained not only a stable of horses, but, until his move to urban Cusco, one of women as well. As one of his contemporaries described him to me, "He was a confirmed bachelor [*solterón*] and later would get hold of any woman. He married in Cusco [where he had moved after losing Lacaya and his other haciendas in the agrarian reform], but in Chumbivilcas he lived with girls, with many girls." Like other Chumbivilcanos, Mariano's manhood as well as economy suffered the consequences of the agrarian reform.

Another notable hero of Chumbivilcano lore is the intrepid *abigeo* Vicente Cruz whose performance on the other end of the bullfighting circuit is held up still today as an example of manly self-sufficiency.

> This guy from Velille, Vicente Cruz, one who is a famous *abigeo*, once it happened that the bull had ripped out all of his guts and his woman put back in all of his guts, along with some other women, right in the middle of the bullfight; and there was a big needle like the muleteers use, some five centimeters long, and then and there with that sheepwool thread which one can get around here, the stomach of the man was sewn up and the man, Vicente Cruz of the *abigeos*, recovered. He is still around today; he was easily healed. No medic or doctor went. [It was done] with home medicines only and just like that the man was healed.

FIGURE 3.4 "Indians" in the Yawar Mayu, Santo Tomás, Chumbivilcas, 1986 (photograph by Deborah Poole).

The counterpart to this ballet of men and bulls, and of guts and women, is the shortlived *yawar mayu*.[25] In this segment of the bullfight, four peasants dressed in the black *bayeta* (homespun wool) traditionally associated with Indians, face a single bull. Gracefully choreographing the bull's charges as he crisscrosses the ring, the "Indians" perform for twenty minutes or so, after which the bull is set loose. No Indian women are called for to stitch up their wounds.

Conclusion

Today's bullfight incorporates not only many of the performative aspects and masculine displays of the nineteenth century *pandilla* and its successor, the "traditional" Chumbivilcano *abigeo*. It also plays on many of the same forms of nostalgia, gender opposition, and masculine violence at work in *indigenista* philosophy. Most obviously we might think of the woman scraping up her husband's bloody bowels, the crazed *qorilazo* spurring his horse into a bloody froth, the drunken *misti* confronting four wild bulls, and the four sober Indians who together face a single bull. If in colonial Spanish courts, the testimony of two Indians was considered equivalent to that of a single Spaniard, in Chumbivilcas today it takes the manhood of four Indians to equal that of one *mestizo* "*qorilazo*."

Although the symbolism of such public displays of masculine *bravura* may appear all too easy to decipher and deconstruct, it is important not to naturalize the sphere of cultural representation. We must instead inquire who were the architects of these popular traditions, and look for the sources of their imagery in such diverse sites as history, literature, legal discourse, and gender ideologies.[26] Just as the *indigenistas'* fascination for the Chumbivilcano *qorilazo* could be traced to their ambivalent status as traditional intellectuals caught between their defense of the Indian and their historical class ties to Cusco's landholding elites, the premium placed on folklore and *costumbre* (custom) in 1980s Chumbivilcas may well be related to the new intellectual status of the *gamonal* descendant as provincial schoolteacher. As described by Paponnet-Cantat and Gose in their contributions to this volume, the role of schoolteacher has become one of the most important activities through which *gamonal* families in the *provincias altas* have retained both their hold on local power and their claims to superior social and cultural status. Whereas remote teaching posts go unfilled in many of Cusco's other rural provinces, in Chumbivilcas and other parts of the *provincias altas* teaching posts are actively solicited by the sons and daughters of local *misti*, or *gamonal*, families. Although by no means all these teachers choose to continue the more overtly abusive or violent forms of power that characterized their fathers' and grandfathers' local rule, the coveted teaching posts serve to distinguish them both culturally and socially from the peasants or "Indians" who attend the schools. An important element in the construction of this ideology of distinction is the teaching of proper tradition and custom in the folklore programs featured in all Peruvian primary and secondary school curricula. In Chumbivilcas, this curriculum has effectively excluded traditional indigenous instruments and dances from the region (for example, the *pinguillo* flute and the distinctive Carnival dances and songs of Chumbivilcas) in favor of the singular figure of the *mestizo qorilazo*. Through the parades, school plays, and dance presentations in which peasants are shown that their practices do not constitute part of the province's authentic cultural tradition, Chumbivilcano teachers have successfully utilized the disciplinary technology of state-sponsored folklore programs to generalize an idealized image of the masculine accoutrements of *gamonal* violence.

Although the bullfights, the *toro kacharpariy*, and to a lesser extent, the schoolchildren's folklore programs might well be construed as a simple continuation of the public spectacles of coercive superiority characterizing the political culture of the 1920s *gamonal*, they in fact constitute a strategic move away from the traditional *gamonal* conception of power as in-

FIGURE 3.5 Schoolchildren presenting *Qorilazo* dance on national Teachers Day, Charamoray, Colquemarca, 1986 (photograph by Deborah Poole).

volving brute physical force. Although both repressive physical violence and *abigeato* are certainly still practiced by some *gamonales*—including the *toro kacharpariy* judge who now works as a schoolteacher—the effects of *gamonal* power in the bullfight and in folklore are no longer strictly repressive. Instead, in this era after the agrarian reform and the subsequent penetration of such state apparatuses as development agencies, banks, and schools into Chumbivilcas, what makes *gamonal* power hold is their ability to control the productive force of those technologies of power which shape the identities of Chumbivilcanos of all social classes.

   Which brings us back to the 1986 *corrida* I attended with descendents of the famous Luciano Alvarez, the "bohemian" Pancho Gómez Negrón, and other of the Colquemarca *gamonales* whom Chambi had photographed in the 1930s. I sat in the grandstand with these *gamonales*. I listened to their songs and drank their beer. I remembered the horror stories I had been told by *campesinos* about these men. Notorious as thieves, rapists, *abigeos*, even as murderers, these *gamonales* maintained the public persona of schoolteacher, accountant, or merchant. Some were members of the national teachers' union (SUTEP); others claimed allegiance to national leftist parties (Izquierda Unida) or to the ruling government party (APRA). It was their other persona, however, which was now in center stage. In the *corrida*, their ideals of masculinity and self were displayed as

icons of Chumbivilcas itself, of what it meant to be a "Chumbivilcano."
And I wondered why the hundreds of *campesinos*—many of them members of the militant provincial peasant league—who lined the other side of
the bullring had come to watch these men. When I later asked them, I
heard stories very much like those I have printed here. They came, in
short, to admire horses and bulls which they would never own, and hope-
fully to witness a disemboweling, which I for one was relieved to have
missed. For them as for the *gamonales*, it was the *caballos de paso*,
qarawatanas, bulls, and guts which formed the stuff of Chumbivilcano culture—or, as the peasants themselves explained it, the essence of "nuestra
costumbre" (our customs). In an otherwise complexly negotiated world of
shifting ethnic and class identities, the bullfight revealed the success of an
intellectual project which had sought, through its definitions of folklore
and custom, to impose a singular form to the notion of Chumbivilcano
culture. As a hegemonic project mounted by intellectuals with ties to the
gamonal class, the bullfight and its attendant folkloric practices had successfully enshrined the icons, attitudes, gestures, and symbols of an otherwise reviled and abusive elite as the identity of an entire province.

At the core of this fragile consensus among *gamonales*, *indigenistas*, and
peasants about the nature of Chumbivilcano culture, reside the twin concepts of violence and gender. At its most basic level, violence involves the
physical confrontation of opposing forces whose inequalities are constructed as a gendered opposition. Man versus animal, masculine *mestizo*
versus effeminate Indian, wounded man versus healing woman: these are
just some of the more simple oppositions that emerge from the particular
playing out of violence in the Chumbivilcano bullfight. What is of particular importance in understanding the dynamics of Chumbivilcano culture,
however, is the gendered nature of the *ethnic* identities that emerge from
such a series of symbolic oppositions. In a region where the phenotypical,
cultural, and linguistic distinctions supposedly separating Indian from
mestizo are effectively blurred in the course of daily life, such gendered oppositions provide a value-laden reference point for restoring the dualities
of a dominant racial discourse in which "Indians" are pitted against
"Spanish" or "mestizos." It is not enough, however, to say simply that the
bullfight somehow either "reproduces" or engenders this already existing
set of ethnic or racial oppositions. Rather, it is important to consider carefully the range of social agents responsible for the historical progression
which occurs from the theatre of violence mounted by the nineteenth-century *gamonal*, to the folkloric performances mounted by twentieth-century
indigenistas, the *qorilazos* they invented, and the primary school teachers
who carry on the banner of "tradition." The intimate historical relations
and dependencies existing between the overlapping discourses, activities,
and beliefs of these landlords, rustlers, intellectuals, and teachers explain

the complex process through which violence and gender have been inscribed into the heart of Chumbivilcano culture and folklore.

Notes

1. From the poem "Chumbivilcano," by 'Amuvar,' in *LIWI*, August 1960, p. 11. LIWI is a newsletter published on an irregular basis by Chumbivilcano schoolteachers during the 1960s and early 1970s.

2. Velille and Livitaca can both be reached by truck, although Livitaca is not on a main road. Chamaca, though connected to Livitaca by a trunk road, only has regular truck traffic for its annual fair on Corpus Christi (see Gade, Chapter 1, this volume). Colquemarca has a seasonal road connecting it to Velille. Quiñota and Llusco are both located on the road to Haquira and do not have regular truck connections to either Santo Tomás or Cusco. Capacmarca can be reached only by foot or horseback from either Colquemarca, Santo Tomás or Paruro (see Paponnet-Cantat, Chapter 6, this volume). During the rainy season, there are often no trucks or buses at all from Cusco to Santo Tomás due to the extremely perilous condition of the roads.

3. In other areas of the Andes (Orlove 1980; Langer 1987; Valderrama & Escalante 1981), the "social banditry" model of cattle-rustling seems to hold to a much greater extent than in Chumbivilcas itself, where *abigeato* was dominated by the *gamonales* and by the values brought to it by *gamonal* culture (Poole 1988).

4. I prefer "construction" over "invention" of tradition since the latter implies a greater degree of conscious manipulation and even fabrication on the part of a dominant elite (Hobsbawm & Ranger 1983). While useful in understanding the motives of ruling elites who attempt to control or fabricate traditions, "invention" fails to acccount for the process by which traditions must then be accepted by a broad cross section of social classes in order to become effective components of the dominant or hegemonic culture. In referring to the "construction" of tradition, then, I am referring to the complicitous process whereby traditions emerge from specific class histories and are manipulated—and accepted—by both the dominant elites and popular classes.

5. Regarding the relatively flexible ability (or tendency) of Indians in the colonial and early republican periods to withdraw from and enter into the market economy, see Glave 1980. Gootenberg (1991:146) has suggested that the Indian economy's flexibility, or ability to withdraw, was more marked in areas such as Chumbivilcas which were characterized by low population densities.

6. This access to monetary income did not necessarily signify significant wealth (Miller 1982:301–3). Indians were, of course, cheated roundly by the wily middlemen and commercial agents to whom they sold their wool (Flores-Galindo 1977:64–77; Jacobsen 1982:103–11; cf., for a slightly later period, Burga & Reategui 1981:74–110). The point is that at least they did have access to both the market and a source of income independent of the hacienda economy *per se*. This was an option many of the *mestizo* hacendados in Chumbivilcas did not share at this time. Regarding price curves for these years and general structure of the wool market,

see Miller 1982, Jacobsen 1982:271–340; Spalding 1977, Burga & Flores-Galindo 1987:33–45, and Flores-Galindo 1977.

7. Relative frequencies of types of crimes are extracted from the "Libros de Resoluciones Verbales" and "Relaciones de Causas Civiles y Criminales" kept for each province. For a more detailed analysis of this type of early violent crime by state office-holders, see Poole 1988:374–6.

8. Civilismo was the party associated with Manuel Pardo. As Minister of Hacienda during the government of President Mariano Ignacio Prado (1865–67), Pardo was responsible for re-introducing personal taxes which had been abolished by the early Republican government.

9. Pierolistas were followers of Nicolás de Pierola, a populist leader during the War with Chile. They were opposed to the Civilistas led by Manual Pardo.

10. The events surrounding Salas's assassination, which was apparently done in reprisal for Rodríguez's death, are not mentioned in the document.

11. This confrontation between the diffuse power of the state and the masculine iconic power of the *gamonal* or local strongman, suggests an opposition between the forms of power which Foucault (1979) refers to as "monarchical" and "modern," thus implying that they occur in a historical sequence. That such forms of power coexisted throughout the history of Chumbivilcas, suggests that a sequential or chronological opposition between types of repressive power does not hold in the context of states such as Peru where both forms of power must be considered part of the "modern" state (cf., Coronil & Skurski 1991).

12. Local authorities and *gamonales* rebelled against the implementation of paper currency because paper money could not as easily be accumulated and recirculated as the gold or silver coin from which provincial tax collectors had profited for decades (Hunefeldt 1991).

13. For a detailed description of how one such rustling pandilla constructed their theatrical crimes, see Poole 1988:376–8.

14. *Pandilla*, which is derived from *pando*, meaning curved or twisted (such as cards which are marked by cardsharks) refers to a group which is formed with the intention of tricking or damaging. *Cuadrilla*, on the other hand, derives from *cuatro*, or four, and is used to designate "a division of an army's followers into four parts to distribute the booty." The shift in usage from "*pandilla*" to "*cuadrilla*" to refer to the armed bands of Chumbivilcas, occurs in the 1910s. As such, it corresponds closely to the shift from the *pandilla* as a politically intentioned group headed by the *gamonal*, to the *cuadrilla* as a group working for the *gamonal*, and existing so as to literally divide up the (four-footed) animals they steal.

15. *El Nuevo Indio* was written as a rebuttal to Luís Valcárcel's treatise on neo-inca indigenismo, *Tempestad en Los Andes* (1927). In Valcárcel's vision, the authentic Andean Indian was defined as the one who had retained the most features of Inca society and culture. García's celebration of the *mestizo* was meant to counter Valcárcel's romantic vision of Indian purity with a cultural agenda based on Cusco's popular *mestizo* working and peasant classes.

16. Cuntisuyu was one of the four provinces or "*suyus*" into which the Inca Empire was divided. It covered the south west quadrant of territory extending out from the city of Cusco and included the present-day provinces of Paruro and Chumbivilcas, as well as all of the Department of Arequipa.

17. Valcárcel, who was not from Chumbivilcas, was a leading Cusco intellectual and founder of the *indigenista* movement. At that time it was common for representatives of isolated provinces such as Chumbivilcas not to be from the districts they represented in congress.

18. For descriptions of some of these nineteenth century Canas *pandillas*, see Poole 1988.

19. Chambi's photograph is today commonly captioned as a portrait of a *gamonal* surrounded by his Indians. In fact, the photograph is of the diputado Washington Ugarte surrounded by a group of Qolquemarquino *mestizos*, including Pancho Gómez Negrón.

20. Villena (1977;66–7, *passim*) attributes the *liwi* and other elements of *qorilazo* costume to the colonial trade in mules with Tucumán, Argentina. Such contacts with Argentine gaucho culture were not, however, exclusive to Chumbivilcas since Tucumán was the principal source of mules for all of southern and central Peru throughout the colonial period. The colonial mule trade does not, therefore, explain the development of the notion of a *qorilazo* culture in Chumbivilcas as opposed to the many other areas through which Tucuman muleteers passed.

21. For examples, see the journal *Liwi*, as well as Poole 1988 and Villena 1987.

22. Before the construction of this bullring in the 1970s, all bullfights took place in the central plaza of Santo Tomás, where the *toro kacharpariy* takes places still today.

23. The bullfight for the patronal fiesta on September 8 (Virgin of the Nativity) is divided into *alqo toro* ("dog bull") for the mestizos of the town and *runa toro* ("people bull") for the peasants from surrounding communities. I did not hear the term "alqo toro" used for the June 21 bullfight, nor am I aware of the *yawar mayu* taking place in the September festivities. For a description of the September bullfight, see Roca W. 1960 and Villena 1987:141–50.

24. The song continues on for many verses, which can change or be improvised. The version given here is from Villena (1987:150–1); English translation and Quechua orthography mine.

25. The name "*yawar mayu*" invokes ritual battles such as those described by Orlove in Chapter 4 of this volume. In these battles women sing songs describing a "river of blood" in order to inspire the men who are fighting. "*Yawar mayu*" is also the name of a dance in which costumed dancers whip each other about the legs.

26. For an analysis of Peruvian criminology and legal discourse, see Poole 1988 and Poole 1990.

Documents Cited

Archivo Departamental del Cusco (ADC)

Sección Corte Superior de Justicia del Cusco (CSJC)

Leg.114, 1854. Denuncia y causa criminal interpuesta por el yndígena Valeriano Quispe del ayllu Pataqueña de Livitaca y en nombre de otros yndígenas del mismo ayllu, contra el recaudador Don Antonio Salas, 1854, fs.82.

Leg.255, 1890. Libro de Actas de la Visita general practicada por el Señor Juez de Primera Instancia de la Provincia de Chumbivilcas D.D. Manuel E. Vizcarra en 1890, fs.26.

Leg.41–44, 1909. Carta del Juez de Primera Instancia de Canas al Presidente de la Corte Superior del Cusco, Yanaocca, 19.V.09; fs.4.

Leg. 196, 1926. Carta de Mateo Mosqueira vecino del pueblo de Huayllati, provincia Grau, al Presidente del Tribunal Correcional (del) Cuzco, 18 de octubre 1926, f.1.

Ibid. Queja ynterpuesta por Hipólito Quispe, Julian Cusihuaman, Julian Pacco, Mariano Perez, Matias Huamani, Gregorio Choqque, Faustino Mendoza, Amos Villalobo, i Tomotea Ramos viuda de Vargas, al Presidente del Tribunal Correccional del Cuzco; 19 de octubre del 1925, fs.2.

Leg. 197, 1927. Ynstruccion criminal contra Eulogio Cáceres, marcial Cabrero, Agustín Caballero, Domingo Ccahuana, … y dos gendarmes, por asalto y robo de ganado 1927, fs. 76.

Ibid. Denuncia del delito del robo de ganado vacuno, ovejuno, y cabruno ynterpuesta por Nicolás Cruz, vecino de Coyllurqui, de la provincia de Grau, de la estancia de Patahuasi, robo perpetrado por Don Rufino Montesinos, Hacendado, 27 de enero 1927, fs.4.

Sección Prefectura

Contensiosos y Administrativos, Leg.5, 1861–91. Expediente del Ex-Subprefecto de la Provincia de Chumbivilcas D. Mariano E. Rodríguez, Cuzco, 1887, fs.20.

Sección Administración del Tesoro Público

Comunicaciones, Leg. 183, 1892–3. Carta del Juan Cancio Berrio, subprefecto de la Provincia de Chumbivilcas al Señor Tesorero Departamental del Cusco, Santo Tomás, 13 de octubre 1892, fs.1.

Ministerio de Agricultura y Alimentacion, Sicuani (MAA)

Expediente de reconocimiento y títulos de la comunidad campesina de Waraqo, Ccolquemarca, Chumbivilcas, 1924.

Biblioteca Nacional (Lima) (BN)

E-52, 1906, Memoria elevada a la prefectura del Departamento del Cusco por el Subprefecto de la Provincia de Chumbivilcas, Autura Gutierrez García, fs.5.

D-6258, 1894, Documentos relativos a la represión del bandolerismo en el Departamento del Cuzco, por el Prefecto Don Pedro Mas, 26 agosto, 1894, fs.16.

Archivo del Ministerio del Interior, Lima (AMI)

Comunicaciones entre la Prefectura de Apurímac, y el Señor Supprefecto de la Provincia de Cotabambas, D. Camilo Astete, sobre agentes subversivos encabezados por los agentes de Montesinos, y Pazos Varela, Abancay, 1919, fs.7.

Queja de abusos de autoridad y abigeato contra el subprefecto de Grau, Don Luís Granadino, ynterpuesta por los yndígenas de Pichibamba, Grau, 1926, fs.27.

Bibliography

Arguedas, José María. 1980. *Yawar Fiesta*. Lima: Editorial Horizonte.

Burga, Manuel y Alberto Flores Galindo. 1987. *Apogeo y crisis de la república aristocrática*. 4a edición. Lima: Ed. Rikchay Perú.

Burga, Manuel y Wilson Reátegui. 1981. *Lanas y capital mercantil en el sur. La Casa Ricketts, 1895–1935*. Lima: Instituto de Estudios Peruanos.

Coronil, Fernando & Julie Skurski. 1991. "Dismembering and Remembering the Nation: The Semantics of Political Violence in Venezuela," *Comparative Studies in Society and History*, 33(2):288–337.

Davies, Keith. 1974. *Indian Integration in Peru*. Lincoln: University of Nebraska Press.

de la Barrera, Emilio. 1930. *Los Equinos, auquenidos y estadística ganadera de la Provincia de Chumbivilcas*. Lima.

Deere, Carmen Diana. 1990. *Household and Class Relations. Peasants and Landlords in Northern Peru*. Berkeley: University of California Press.

Deustua, José & José Luis Rénique. 1984. *Intelectuales, indigenismo y descentralismo en el Perú, 1897–1931*. Cusco: CERA Bartolomé de Las Casas.

Flores-Galindo, Alberto. 1977. *Arequipa y el sur-andino, siglos XVIII–XX*. Lima: Editorial Horizonte.

Foucault, Michel. 1979. *Discipline and Punish*. New York: Vintage.

García, José Uriel. 1986. *El Nuevo Indio* (1930). Cusco: Municipalidad del Cusco.

Glave, Luis Miguel. 1980. "Problemas para el estudio de la historia regional: El caso del Cusco," *Allpanchis*, XIV:131–66.

Glave, Luis Miguel & María isabel Remy. 1983. *Estructura agraria y vida rural en una region andina. Ollantaytambo entre lso siglos XVI y XIX*. Cusco: CERA Bartolomé de Las Casas.

Gootenberg, Paul. 1989. *Between Silver and Guano. Commercial Policy and the State in Postindependence Peru*. Princeton: Princeton University Press.

———. 1991. "Population and Ethnicity in Early Republican Peru," *Latin American Research Review*, 26(3):109–157.

Hobsbawm, Eric & Terence Ranger. 1983. *The Invention of Tradition*. New York & Cambridge: Cambridge University Press.

Hunefeldt, Christine. 1991. "Circulación y estructura tributaria: Puno 1840–1890." In H. Urbano (ed.), *Violencia y Poder en Los Andes*, pp. 189–210. Cusco: CERA Bartolomé de Las Casas.

Jacobsen, Nils. 1982. *Land Tenure and Society in the Peruvian Altiplano: Azángaro Province 1770–1920*. Ph.D. dissertation. University of California, Berkeley

Kapsoli, Wilfredo. 1984. *Ayllus Del Sol*. Lima: Tarea.

Langer, Erick D. 1987. "Andean Banditry and Peasant Community Organization, 1882–1930." In R. W. Slatta (ed.), *Bandidos: The Varieties of Latin American Banditry*, pp. 113–130. New York: Greenwood Press.

LIWI. 1960. *Liwi. Edición extraordinaria dedicada al magisterio chumbivilcano*. Cusco, set. de 1960 (mimeo)

Mallon, Florencia. 1983. *The Defense of Community in Peru's Central Highlands. Peasant Struggle and Capitalist Transition 1860–1940*. Princeton: Princeton University Press.

Manrique, Nelson. 1986. *Colonialismo y pobreza campesina. Caylloma y el Valle del Colca Siglos XVI–XX*. Lima: DESCO

_____. 1988. *Yawar Mayu. Sociedades terratenientes serranas, 1879–1910*. Lima: DESCO.

_____. 1991. "Gamonalismo, lanas y violencia en los Andes." In H. Urbano (ed.), *Violencia y Poder en Los Andes*, pp. 211–223. Cusco: CERA Bartolomé de Las Casas.

Mariátegui, José Carlos. 1925. "El Proceso del gamonalismo," *Amauta* 25(julio-agosto):69–80.

Miller, Rory. 1982. "The Wool Trade of Southern Peru, 1850–1915," *Ibero Amerikanisches Archiv, N.F.*, VIII(3):297–311.

Orlove, Benjamin S. 1977. *Alpacas, Sheep and Men. The Wool Export Economy and Regional Society in Southern Peru*. New York: Academic Press.

_____. 1980. "The Position of Rustlers in Regional Society: Social Banditry in the Andes." In B.S.Orlove & G.Custred (eds.), *Land and Power in Latin America: Agrarian Economies and Social Processes in the Andes*, pp. 179–194. New York: Holmes & Meier.

Parker, David. 1992. "White Collar Lima, 1910–1929: Commercial Employees and the Rise of the Peruvian Middle Class," *Hispanic American Historical Review*, 72(1):47–72.

Piel, Jean. 1967. "Un soulevement rural péruvien: Tocroyoc (1921)," *Révue d'histoire moderne et contemporaine*, XIV.

_____. 1982. *Crise agraire et conscience créole au pérou*. Paris: Editions du CNRS.

Poole, Deborah A. 1988. "Landscapes of Power in a Cattle Rustling Culture of Southern Andean Peru," *Dialectical Anthropology*, 12:367–98.

_____. 1990. "Ciencia, peligrosidad y represión en la criminología indigenista Peruana." In C. Walker & C. Aguerre (eds.), *Bandolerismo, Criminalidad y Sociedad en Peru y Bolivia, siglos XVIII–XX*, pp. 335–367. Lima: Instituto de Apoyo Agrario.

_____. 1992. "Figueroa Aznar and the Cusco Indigenistas: Photography and Modernism in Early Twentieth-Century Peru," *Representations*, 38:39–75.

Rénique, José Luis. 1991. *Los Sueños de La Sierra*. Cusco en el Siglo XX. Lima:CEPES.

Roca W., Demetrio. 1960. "Fiesta de la Virgen de la Natividad," *Liwi*, 7:17–26.

Sivirichi, Atilio. 1937. "El contenido espiritual del movimiento indigenista," *Revista Universitaria del Cusco*, 72 (lra semestre 1937):1–23.

Spalding, Karen. 1977. "Estructura de clases en la sierra peruana, 1750–1920," *Análisis* I:25–35.

Tamayo Herrera, José. 1980. *Historia del indigenismo cusqueño siglos XVI–XX*. Lima: Instituto Nacional de Cultura.

Valcárcel, Luis. 1972. *Tempestad en los Andes* (1927). Lima: Editorial Universal.

_____. 1981. *Memorias*. Lima: Instituto de Estudios Peruanos.

Valderrama F., Ricardo & Carmen Escalante G. 1981. *Levantamiento de los indígenas de Haquira y Quiñota (1922–24/Apurímac, Cuzco)*. Lima: Seminario de Historia Rural Andina, Univ. Nacl. Mayor de San Marcos.

Villena Aguirre, Arturo. 1987. *Qorilazo y Region de Refugio en el Contexto Andino*. Cusco: Papelería Peñarol.

Yepez Miranda, Alfredo. 1940. "El Proceso Cultural del Perú: La Unidad geográfica y cultural de la costa," *Revista Universitaria del Cuzco*, I(78):3–52.

4

Sticks and Stones: Ritual Battles and Play in the Southern Peruvian Andes

Benjamin Orlove

The English term "ritual battle" and its Spanish equivalent *batalla ritual* appear with some frequency in the anthropological literature on the Andes. At first glance, the phrase seems to be an appropriate label for certain occasions. These events are called "battles" because two opposed groups of men (and, much less frequently, women) fight with one another, often quite violently. They are called "ritual" because they take place only on certain important dates in the ceremonial calendar, because the nature of the fighting is so fixed and elaborate, and because they lack the usual stakes of war: the winners do not take territory or tribute from the losers, and they do not even demand subordination or obedience in political contexts.

Drawn by the enthusiasm of the participants and by the sheer drama and apparently exotic nature of these events, a number of ethnographers and folklorists have described these ritual battles. This chapter describes two such events which I observed in the early 1970s in the *provincias altas* of Cusco. The first is Ch'iaraje, named for the *puna* (high grassland zone) site where groups of men fight with slingshots and whips, sometimes taking captives and, on occasion, killing them. The second is *ch'iwka*, a game resembling hockey which is played in squares in district capitals and villages in the Río Vilcanota valley. This chapter seeks to account for the presence of these events in the *provincias altas*, and to compare them to similar events in another Andean region, the northern portion of the department of Potosí, Bolivia. In comparing ritual battles in these two areas, the chapter also reflects on perceptions of these events by both local people and anthropologists. It compares the Western term "ritual battle" with the Quechua words *tinkuy* (to meet, to join forces) and *pukllay* (to play) used to describe these events. It discusses the difficulties of an analysis that rests either on such general Western concepts as "ritual" and "battle" or on the local Andean concepts for these events. Because these events are so violent and because they seem to differ so sharply from Western practices, they manifest with particular clarity a general issue in the study of human society—the fact that human action cannot be described in an entirely neutral language, but rather only through categories of action which in turn derive from a variety of often unexamined sources. In particular, an analysis of these events and the stories and conversations about them reveals that the participants seem to categorize violent acts somewhat differently than Western social scientists often do. The final sections of the chapter argue for a historical understanding of these events, in two related senses: firstly, that the patterning of these events has been influenced by changing relations between peasants, elites and the state, and secondly, that the participants and audiences of these events understand the events and the identities which they portray in explicitly historical terms.

Ch'iaraje

A number of sources have described the fights at Ch'iaraje, a spot roughly near the center of the province of Canas (Alencastre and Dumézil 1953; Gilt Contreras 1955; Gorbak, Lischetti and Muñóz 1962; Barrionuevo 1971). I had read some of these reports when I witnessed one such fight in 1973, and found it to be virtually identical with the accounts from the 1950s and 1960s. The most recent account which I have located indicates that the events continue to take place essentially without change (Mendoza 1993).

On the morning of 20 January 1973, the feast of Saint Sebastian, I took a truck to Yuraccancha and climbed with two other anthropologists, Abraham Valencia and George Primov, to a hill in the *punas* of Canas about 4660 meters above sea level. At this place, the site of Ch'iaraje, several hundred peasants had been gathering. There were about ten women from Sicuani and Langui selling beer, cane alcohol, and smaller quantities of bread and soft drinks. The peasants came mostly from the communities and *haciendas* of the district of Quehue, with some from Langui and a few from the provincial capital of Yanaoca. About a kilometer and a half away, on the other side of the plain was another hill with a similar number of people, mostly from Checca. Smaller numbers of people went there from El Descanso and Yanaoca. The local people could recognize each others' districts of origin.

The full contingent of people had assembled by 9 A.M. They drank for another hour or so and then descended to the plain, where they fought with the Checca side for about an hour. They returned to the peak where they ate and rested until 1 P.M. A group of women from Quehue joined hands and walked in a circle, occasionally reversing direction. My notes record in English the words of the song which they sang in falsetto as they walked: "Don't be afraid, brother; the stones will come down like hail, there will be rivers of blood."

A larger battle took place until 3 P.M., when the last prisoner was taken by the Quehue side. During the fighting, about one-third of the men were on horseback. The others were on foot. They used slings to hurl rocks at each other. They also had whips, some with large pieces of metal attached to them. Many men had wounds on their ankles, apparently the result of efforts to lame them.

The fighting took place between teams of about fifty men each. The teams, which did not seem to have leaders, sometimes stood a few tens of meters apart, but at times the individual fighters were barely able to use slings because the teams had moved so close that they could not swing them. As they drew to within earshot, they shouted insults at each other. In both morning and afternoon, a number of small groups who had been observing the fighting from other nearby peaks and flanks of hills came down to take part in the fighting, apparently without premeditation; several individuals commented that they had not planned to fight, but suddenly felt the impulse to join in. For about an hour in the afternoon, two sets of teams, separated by about 200 meters, fought at the same time, while other people were scattered around the plains on the edge of the main fights.

The goal of the fighting was to take prisoners, for whom the Spanish term *prisionero* was used both in Spanish and Quechua. In most of the recent previous years, there had been several such prisoners, who had been taken to the lands of the other side, stripped, beaten and killed. The prisoners' corpses, sometimes decapitated, were abandoned for their families to retrieve in remote areas on the border between the districts. The captors retained the prisoners' clothes (and their horses as well, if they had been mounted when captured) thus preventing their relatives from carrying out an important part of the local funeral customs, the ritual washing of the deceased person's clothes.

On the day that I witnessed the events, no prisoners were taken in the morning, although two or three were captured in the afternoon. The first one was taken by the Quehue side, held at the peak, and, I believe, released. The second one, a man from Checca, was surrounded by a large group, also from the Quehue side. His captors stripped off his poncho and shirt, bound his hands, and took him, on his horse, close to the main hill of the Quehue side but not to its peak, where he was badly punched, struck and kicked (see Figure 4.1). I overheard a dispute between groups of men

FIGURE 4.1   Prisoner taken at Ch'iaraje, 20 January 1973 (photograph by Benjamin Orlove).

from Quehue and Langui, both of whom wanted to take him to their own lands. The former outnumbered the latter, but the latter claimed to have captured him. The men from Langui argued that since Quehue already had a prisoner, it was now their turn to take one. Those from Quehue countered that the people from Langui had already taken a prisoner but had carried him off without much notice. In the end, the prisoner was taken to Quehue. The men from Quehue said that he had killed one of their side in the past and cut his head off, so that they had to capture and kill him in revenge.

A policeman from the police force, the Civil Guard, was present. This policeman told the peasants that they could take the prisoner to Quehue, but that he would accompany them to make sure that there would be no killing. He did set off with them, though the peasants did not seem to take seriously his claim that he would prevent the death. Several peasants told me how policemen and even the subprefect from Yanaoca had come in previous years to break up the fighting, but both sides had united to drive them away.

One other group of outsiders was present: a film crew of eight men and women, who appear in my notes as "assorted long-hairs, US, Brazilian, German, Spanish." They had a good deal of expensive camera and sound equipment. Walking across the plain and up both hills, aiming large tele-photo lenses at participants, they seem to have offended both sides. The

film-makers left around noon after several explicit threats of physical violence to them and their cameras.

Several people assured me that such battles take place at that location
not only on 20 January, the Feast of Saint Sebastian, but also once in December, on 1 January, and on the Day of Comadres before Carnival. Several peasants from Quehue also said that battles are fought on the same
day in Toqto, where peasants from Quehue and Checca join against others
from Livitaca, whom they refer to as *chhuchu*, a Quechua term meaning
"hard, leathery."[1] The violence is restricted to these times and places;
members of opposing sides meet and interact without any acrimony on
other occasions.

I will quote verbatim a paragraph of my field notes to suggest how ex-
traordinary these events seemed to me:

> It's difficult to convey the character of the place, the two teams spread out on
> the flanks of a hill, the cries and shouts continuous, "¡*Carajo!*" [Damn!] from
> both sides, the *waraq'a* [sling] cracking, occasionally two groups of
> footsoldiers coming closer for *cuerpo a cuerpo* [single combat] fighting, and
> then a knot forming around the prisoner when one is taken, afraid of a sur-
> prise attack to get him back.

Ch'iwka

The game of *ch'iwka* has received much less attention in the ethnographic
literature than the fighting at Ch'iaraje. I therefore offer a fuller account of
the events which I witnessed on 1 January 1973, and conversations which I
had with townspeople and peasants in January, 1973.

The game of *ch'iwka* that I saw was played in the uphill or eastern portion of the Plaza de Pampacucho in Sicuani, the capital of the province of
Canchis and the largest town in the *provincias altas*. This location placed it
at the foot of the steps leading up to the chapel of Pampacucho a few tens
of meters above the plaza on a low hill. Teams came from the lower *barrio*
(neighborhood) of *uray calle* (*uray* [lower, Quechua] and *calle* [street, Span-
ish]) and the upper *barrio* of *wichay calle* (*wichay* [upper, Quechua]). The di-
viding line between the two *barrios* crosses the Río Vilcanota where a
bridge once stood at a spot called *chakapata* (on the bridge, Quechua) and
continues, more or less perpendicular to the river along Calle Bolivar and
Calle Castilla. The *ch'iwka* site is entirely within *uray calle*, while the Plaza
de Armas and the cathedral are in *wichay calle,* as shown in Figure 4.2.
These locations are unusual, because in most highland towns and villages
the line which separates upper and lower *barrios* runs directly through the
main square.

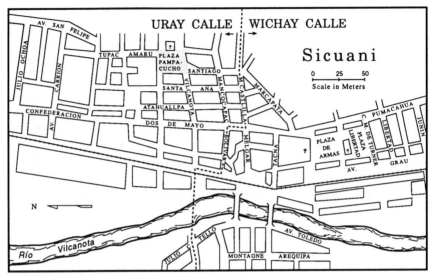

FIGURE 4.2   Sicuani.

Before the game of *ch'iwka* itself, some young boys from the two sides were playing soccer in the square, their faces blackened and each boy in uniform. Those from *uray calle* wore the cream-colored sweaters of Peru's national league Universitario team. Those from *wichay calle* wore the blue-and-white striped ones of Universitario's competitor, Alianza. Several vendors sold mangoes, candy, soft drinks and *salteñas* (baked pastries filled with meat and vegetables).

A larger crowd began to assemble after 2 P.M. The players, spectators and several people called *neutrales* (neutral ones; that is, unaffiliated with either side) assembled at a table. The *neutrales* have several responsibilities: storing the equipment from year to year, refereeing the game, and trying (with only partial success) to keep spectators off the field during the game itself. There are two major items of equipment. The first is an agricultural tool, made of eucalyptus wood, commonly called *maruna,* although in the context of the game it is referred to as *ch'iwka* or *ch'iwkana.* This tool is ordinarily used for smashing large clods of earth after plowing or preparing fields for planting. It is a long stick, shaped like a club or a cane, with a handle about one and a half meters long and a large head or hook at one end. The second, specific to the game, is a wooden ball about 30 centimeters in diameter made from the wood of *lloq'e,* a tree (*Kageneckia lanceolata*) native to the highlands.

The captain (*jefe*) of the *uray calle* team was chosen more or less by consensus. The captain of the *wichay calle* team had held this position the previous year as well. He is well-known and well-liked throughout Sicuani.

A worker in the wool trade, he lives in the upper *barrio*, but comes from the city of Juliaca in the department of Puno. His nickname, Waliki, means "okay" in Aymara, indicating both that his birthplace was in one of the Aymara-speaking provinces relatively far from Sicuani and that he is known for his amiable personality. My curiosity was awakened by the fact that a non-local held a key role in a traditional activity. He might have had strong ties with local people, I thought, or perhaps he triggered in some people's minds the thought that the department of Puno stands as *wichay* in relation to the entire Vilcanota valley as *uray*.

The *neutrales* kept an eye on the selection of players and the distribution of equipment. The name *wallpascha* (little chickens) was used for the team from *uray calle*, and *qowischa* (little guinea pigs) for the one from *wichay calle*, although several spectators suggested that some players on each team resided in the opposite *barrio*. (One neighbor of mine stated that a coin was flipped to choose names for the teams, with *cara* [heads] corresponding to *qowischa* and *sello* [tails] to *wallpascha*.) Each of the prospective players chose a *ch'iwkana* from the large number which the *neutrales* had stored from the previous year. They made this selection with much care, because each *ch'iwkana* is different. The better ones have larger heads or have handles which are longer, thicker or straighter. The captains seemed to be the first to pick a *ch'iwkana*. Some individuals seemed quite assured of their spot on their team, but at several points individuals were selected for teams by a kind of game of chance played with the hands. Each team was composed of four players, including the captain. All players seemed to be drunk.

The game was divided into two *tiempos*, the term used for the halves of a soccer match, each of which lasted about 45 minutes. There was a half-hour break in between, so that the whole game lasted from 3 P.M. to 5 P.M. The participants and audience seemed to agree that the object of the game was to score points by making *goles* (goals). In the first half, the *wallpascha* team from the lower *barrio* attempted to score goals on the upper half of the square, and the other team on the opposite side. As in soccer, the sides were reversed in the second half. However, these goals are different from ones in other games such as soccer and hockey, because a team that had crossed the line to make a goal would continue to knock the ball far off the playing field, as shown in Figure 4.3. At times they would go a block or more away, before allowing the ball to be returned to the field. There did not seem to be any effort to have the ball returned precisely to the middle of the field after a goal.

When the game began, the ball was wrapped in red metallic foil, which was soon knocked off as the players struck the ball with their *ch'iwkanas*. The players usually stayed close to one another, all near the ball. Occasionally one or two players would fall behind as others chased the ball.

FIGURE 4.3   Church and *ch'iwka* playing field in Pampacucho Plaza, Sicuani (photograph by Benjamin Orlove).

Nobody played the role of goalie, I think not merely to avoid the risk of being struck, but also from a desire to remain in the thick of things.

At several points, two players would lock their *ch'iwkanas* and a third player would get the ball. On a number of occasions players would hit each other, often quite hard. After one man was hit in the leg with a *ch'iwkana*, I heard a spectator comment, "*¡Es juego de hombres, carajo!*" (This is a game for real men, damn it!). On two occasions, players dropped out and were replaced by men in the crowd who had previously expressed a desire to play. However, there was no area that corresponded to a dugout. These replacement players entered without any formal selection process or, as far as I could see, any signal from the captain. They just went up to a player who was leaving the game, took his *ch'iwkana,* and began to play. The interjected comment in my field notes is quite different from that in the Ch'iaraje notes. I wrote that there "doesn't seem to be much strategy involved."

The crowd was composed of about 400 or 500 people, mostly townspeople. I saw few people who were obviously well-off and few who seemed to be peasants. Many couples were present with their children, and at times two or three couples and their children all sat together. Many spectators sat on the steps of the church. Well over half, but not all, of them were sitting on the side of the square corresponding to their *barrio.* In ad-

FIGURE 4.4   *Ch'iwka* players on Pampacucho Plaza, 1 January 1973 (photograph by Benjamin Orlove).

dition, many of the children and adults were also on the field, and on numerous occasions entered into conversations with one or another of the players. The spectators usually got away in time as the players came after the ball, but on four or five occasions they blocked the players' access to the ball. None of the spectators was hit, although on three separate occasions children fell down as they ran away from the players, causing considerable laughter from the audience. After the game was over, the *neutrales* gathered up the ball and the *ch'iwkanas* and the crowd gradually dispersed. There was no lingering atmosphere of violence; the members of the two *barrios* mixed easily on the following days.

When I spoke with him after the game, one of the *neutrales,* a man named Tuero, commented that *ch'iwka* in Sicuani used to be played on the Calle Dos de Mayo, a street also oriented parallel to the river, from *chakapata* down to the current site of the hospital. On January 1, the newly inaugurated community authorities would attend mass. They served food and *chicha* (home-brewed maize beer) to the peasants, who would then play *ch'iwka*. The game was much more "*bravo*" (fierce), Tuero said, with many players hitting each other on the head or leg (cf. Poole, Chapter 3, this volume, on the term *bravo*). Around the middle or later 1940s the game was moved to the Plaza de Pampacucho. This date would place the shift several years after the opening of the large annual fair at that site. The game was first played at the lower, western side of the square but is now played at the upper, eastern side. The orientation of the axis of the field was in both instances parallel to the river. In earlier years, *qowischas* and *wallpaschas* were teams with more or less fixed membership within *uray calle*, who played earlier in the day than the game between the two *barrios*. The former game has since disappeared. Boys used to play with smaller *ch'iwkanas*. Tuero said that the ball currently in use is made of eucalyptus wood, although *lloq'e* wood is more appropriate. The current ball has been getting smaller over the years, because of being hit so often. He mentioned that it is always wrapped in metal foil, though sometimes of gold or silver color rather than red.

He also mentioned that the game was brought into the region during the time of the Incas. Tuero told me that it was important to keep such customs going and that he has played a part in its expansion, having lent a ball and *ch'iwkanas* to members of the communities of Trapiche and San Felipe, who had just begun playing *ch'iwka* this year. He showed me five trophies which bore plaques stating that he and Pedro Macsi, another important *neutral*, had the responsibility of keeping the game from disappearing.

In addition to these observations and this long conversation with Tuero, I also heard a number of briefer stories about *ch'iwka* and its history, which I group here under related themes:

1. *Purpose of the game in Sicuani.* It used to be played for territory, which one *barrio* would win from another.
2. *The game as omen in Sicuani.* It used to be believed that the winning team would have a good year and the losing team a bad year.
3. *Injuries and deaths in the game in Sicuani.* In the 1960s, there had been some deaths of players. In 1971 several players sustained fractures.
4. *Local variants of the game in the district of Sicuani.* Ch'iwka is played between teams of six players in four locations: San Felipe, the peasant community immediately downriver from Sicuani; Trapiche, the community immediately upriver; and Huitacca and Uscapata, two communities near Trapiche. The teams are organized with captains as in Sicuani and also bore the names *wallpascha* and *qowischa*, corresponding to *uray* and *wichay* divisions. The game in Trapiche was reputed to be very violent, resulting in many injuries.

5. *Local variants of the game in the province of Canchis.* In Checacupe, up-per and lower *barrios* play *ch'iwka* in just the same fashion as in Sicuani. However, the game is played only on 1 November, All Saint's Day, and the ball is smaller.

6. *Local variants of the game in the province of Acomayo. Ch'iwka* is played in the province of Acomayo in the towns of Acopía, Pomacanchi, Sangarará and Rondocán, and possibly in other smaller communi-ties as well. It is organized along similar *uray/wichay* divisions. *Ch'iwkanas* like those in Sicuani are used there as well, although the ball is smaller. *Ch'iwka* is played on All Saints' Day and on Christ-mas, although occasionally unscheduled games are also held.

Anthropological Categories: Ritual Battles

The two events show a number of similarities in terms of the location, tim-ing and manner of the action. Not only are both of them restricted to cer-tain dates in the religious calendar, but their timing corresponds to the middle of the rainy season, from All Saints' Day (1 November) to Carnival (February–March). Two groups of men drawn from specific areas come with many of their supporters to a field. Each group has its own edge of the field, while spectators, also divided by their place of origin, watch from high ground nearby. Eager to inflict wounds, the participants pursue each other back and forth across the field while their supporters look down from higher ground or join them in the field itself. One group de-feats the other, by taking a captive in Ch'iaraje or by knocking the ball through the other's side in *ch'iwka*. The victorious group continues to hammer on the other, by carrying the captive away in Ch'iaraje and by knocking the ball past the end of the field in *ch'iwka*. These encounters are divided into two halves of roughly equal length, but the timing is far from precise. Both groups can agree on what could be called the "score" (pris-oners in Ch'iaraje, goals in *ch'iwka*). But the participants, all of whom have drunk a good deal of alcohol, seem as much involved in the thrill and vio-lence of the game as in the final outcome (Saignes 1989). It is not only the *presence* of this violence, but the *centrality* of the violence, that leads me to include both within the category of ritual battle. For example, a player may be deemed successful even without scoring "points" if he breaks an opponent's bones or makes him bleed. Nonetheless, the two events differ in important details such as the location and the nature of the action, the ethnic and class background of the participants, and the degree of vio-lence.

One approach which could account for the presence of the two in the *provincias altas* and for the differences between them can be found in the works of the Mexican anthropologist Gonzalo Aguirre Beltrán, whose concept of region of refuge has been suggested as appropriate to the *provincias altas* of Cusco (see Gade, Chapter 1, this volume). Within regions of refuge, culturally encapsulated Indian minorities continue their distinctive ways, including, one may presume, ritual battles. As applied to the *provincias altas*, the theory goes on to suggest that those groups who are highest in elevation and furthest from roads and towns are most distinctive (van den Berghe and Primov 1977:251). The reports of recent change in *ch'iwka* support the view that the "rate of sociocultural change" is rapid in the valleys, and the greater cultural distinctiveness of Ch'iaraje accords with the view of indigenous culture as the "predominant cultural influence" in the *puna* (van den Berghe and Primov 1977:251).

A quite distinct approach involves a structuralist model based on the concept of dual organization. One of the strengths of such an approach is its ability to account for many features of ritual battles, such as the timing, location, composition and use of certain symbols, through references to the logic of Andean culture within the context of specific groups. Its corresponding weakness, as will be discussed later, is its inability to account for the presence of such battles among some groups and their absence elsewhere.

According to structuralists, ritual fights are an expression of the way in which Andean people think of encounters between paired elements, as linked and opposed (Platt 1986). It seems consistent with the dualism inherent in Andean thought (Zuidema 1964; Isbell 1985; Palomino 1971; Urton 1990:76–93; Fioravanti 1986) that *tinkus* or encounters between sections of ethnic groups take place in the squares of the towns and villages that are their ceremonial centers, while *ch'ajwas*, or encounters between ethnic groups, are held on the boundaries between the lands of the groups (Platt 1987; Abercrombie 1986; Harris 1982). The ethnic groups quite literally have no common ground.

The case of *ch'iwka* would present a simple and straightforward example of an encounter of two halves at the central point of meeting and division, or, more specifically, of confrontations, held in plazas, between upper and lower *barrios*, whether in Sicuani or in the other valley towns and villages. Ch'iaraje could be seen, in parallel terms, as the encounter at the boundaries of groups at a higher order—major divisions within the province of Canas, or, in the case of Toqto, between the provinces, and pre-Columbian ethnic groups, of Canas and Chumbivilcas. One could present the people of the province of Canas as "the K'anas," a pre-Inca society famed for its warriors and bravery (see Orlove, Chapter 2, this volume). The arguments between people from Quehue and Langui could then be seen as a dispute over their position in their half of the K'anas, with those from Quehue claiming structural superiority over those from Langui, and the latter arguing for structural equality and an alternation of turns.[2] In this view, the opponents of "the K'anas" at Toqto become "the Chumbivilcas."

It is even possible to construct an overarching dualistic framework which accounts for the differences between *ch'iwka* and Ch'iaraje. One would need to conceive of "the Canas" and "the Canchis" (alluded to in Valencia's discussion of *ch'iwka*) as the *puna* and valley segments of what was once a single unit, possibly corresponding to the colonial administrative unit known as Canas y Canchis. The two ritual battles could then be seen as taking on the contrasting and complementary attributes of the *puna* and the valleys, so richly described for other areas of the Andes by Isbell (1976), Bouysse-Cassagne (1987), Harris (1978, 1982) and Platt (1986, 1987), as well as by Gose (Chapter 5, this volume). Many features may be noted. For example, the combatants at Ch'iaraje ride animals and fight with pastoral tools (whips and slings), while the opponents at *ch'iwka*, who fight on foot, use agricultural tools. The teams at *ch'iwka* bear names, *qowischa* and *wallpascha*, which reflect the nature of the valley, not only because guinea pigs and chickens are raised there in closer association with agriculture, but because they are kept near the house, rather than let to graze on fallow fields or open range as are sheep, cattle, llamas and alpacas in the *punas*. From a structuralist perspective, such domesticity could be equated with women, with valleys, and the small size of the Plaza de Pampacucho, much as the greater wildness, or violence, of Ch'iaraje refers to maleness, the *puna*, and the large size of the pampa on which the fighting occurs.[3]

An examination of other ritual battles can further the analysis of Ch'iaraje and *ch'iwka*. Examples may be drawn from virtually the entire Andean region.[4] The cases all share a number of features: opposed groups, regular scheduling within a ritual calendar, occurrence within the rainy season, and emphasis on bloodshed. Many authors list specific features of such dualistic oppositions: encounters between upper and lower moieties, exchange of sexual partners and of foodstuffs, and the linkage between the mediation of such oppositions on the one hand and the fertility of humans, fields and flocks on the other (Hopkins 1982; Platt 1987).

Rather than continuing to expand the list of cases of ritual battles, it is worth pausing to consider the category of ritual battle altogether. The phrase "ritual battle" conjoins two terms, both of which refer to attributes of action (repetition and symbolic elaboration in the first, violent conflict and competition in the second) that can be found to varying degrees in many sorts of activity on a variety of social, temporal and spatial scales. This broad extension has several consequences. First, each term denotes a somewhat poorly delimited range of activities. For some portion of this range, few, if any, anthropologists would disagree over the correctness of applying the term; for other portions, the debates over the appropriateness of its use would be more extensive. Secondly, these terms, particularly "ritual" but also "battle" (and its associated concepts of "war" and "violence"), have major theoretical importance, because of their ubiquity and their interconnections with other attributes of human action. Each term, then, tends to be not only ambiguous, but to have an ambiguity that different people would seek to resolve in different ways. It would be difficult to deny that *ch'iwka* and the events at Ch'iaraje were rituals (since participants gather on religious festivals, move in highly patterned ways, and so forth) or that they were battles (since armed men fight, injure and sometimes kill one another).

The word ritual also implies a contrast with practical activity. For example, ritual plowing, described for many parts of the Andes, refers to, and contrasts with everyday plowing: pebbles, rather than seeds, are placed on, rather than in, the earth's surface, in village squares, rather than in fields (cf. Platt 1986:240). In a similar fashion, the phrase "ritual battle" suggests an activity that is ritualized and like a battle, though lacking a material purpose such as the conquest of territory or the taking of booty. It is, however, more difficult to establish this ritualized, non-instrumental equivalent for battles than for planting. One problem is that sowing is a common activity in the Andes while battles, at least in the most basic sense of large-scale encounters between armed forces such as armies and navies, are not. A more general problem, for Andean anthropologists at least, is finding non-instrumental gestures or acts that can represent or symbolize the violence that defines real battles. If these gestures or acts do not cause actual harm, then they might not be taken as standing for violence at all, but for some more diffuse category of "conflict" or "opposition". If they do cause such harm, then they tend to become real, rather than ritual violence, with the instrumental ends being, not territory or booty but the equally material injuries—the spilled blood, the broken bones, the killed prisoners. For an event to be recognizable as a ritual battle, then, it must be violent enough to resemble a real battle, without being so violent that it becomes a real battle.

This uneasy conjunction makes classification difficult. Indeed, there is some anthropological debate regarding the division of such events in highland Bolivia into *ch'ajwas*, which anthropologists consider to be "real battles", and *tinkuys*, termed "ritual battles" (Harris 1978:36–7; Godoy 1985; Abercrombie 1986:258–9). *Ch'ajwas* are classified as "real battles," primarily because in some instances one group takes territory from another, while *tinkuys*, without such ends, are "ritual battles". Instrumental violence—violents acts whose purposes are not restricted to harming opponents corporally, but include other sorts of material or communicative consequences—leads anthropologists to remove events from the category of ritual battle, presumably because the purpose of the violent acts is something other than ritual representation of battles.

Events may also fall out of the category of ritual battles for the opposite reason that anthropologists consider them insufficiently violent to be taken as representing violence at all. They are thus described as rituals, but not as ritual battles. The criteria by which anthropologists distinguish ritual battles from other encounters are often not very explicit or clear. Elsewhere in the department of Cusco, Carnival celebrations include stylized dances in which two groups confront each other, often insulting each other and, in some instances, whipping or striking each other and drawing blood (Poole 1984: 378–92; Allen 1988:182–9). The participants in these Carnival events often speak of an association between the dances and human fertility. Even though the participants in these events depict violence, and sometimes cause genuine injury, ethnographers have tended to label these events as "dances" rather than "ritual battles", perhaps because there is much singing, the spilling of blood is limited, and no one is killed. Similarly, confrontation between groups from different communities in village squares are common throughout the Andes during Carnival. They might argue or fight with slingshots, using fruit such as guavas and quinces as ammunition. Anthropologists have not used the word "ritual battle" to describe such events: acts which are not themselves violent are not taken as representing violence (Collins 1981, Allen 1988). Like the term "Indian uprising" which I discuss in Chapter 2 of this volume, the notion of "ritual battle" has a fuzzy, constructed quality; more generally, these two terms illustrate the difficulty of fitting violence into social scientific categories (cf. Poole, Introduction, this volume).

Andean Categories: *Pukllay* and *Tinkuy*

Faced with the difficulties of establishing firm criteria to distinguish "ritual battles" from other events, one might attempt to dispense with the term altogether and replace it with the native terms used to describe Ch'iaraje, *ch'iwka*, and similar events. The word *tinkuy* is widely used for ritual battles not only in Cusco, but also in Potosí (Harris 1982; Platt 1986, 1987), Ayacucho (Isbell 1985:113) and Pasco (Mayer 1977:76). *Tinkuy* is often translated simply as "to meet" but sometimes rendered more elaborately: e.g., "an encounter or meeting between two like persons or substances" (Cusihuamán 1976:146; Lira 1982:285; cf. Allen 1988:206; Sallnow 1987:136–40; Casaverde, Sánchez Farfán and Cevallos V. 1966). Mayer defines it as "the harmonious meeting of opposite forces," such as the place in which two rivers meet to form one (1977:76). It could be claimed that the notion of "harmony," thought incompatible with that of violence in

Western culture, might be an appropriate label for fighting to the death in the Andes.

An example of another event frequently describe as a *tinkuy* is the walking of community boundaries at Carnival. Peasants from neighboring communities meet at a rock or pile of rocks (*mojón*) which marks a point on their common border. They walk slowly from one point to the next, inspecting them and discussing whether they have been moved. In some instances, the walkers are accompanied by musicians. These events, which are simultaneously festive and tense, can lead to exchanges of insults and, on occasion, blows, though most of them are quite amicable. Anthropologists who use the Quechua term *tinkuy* to describe ritual battles imply that the unity of the overarching category which links Ch'iaraje and *ch'iwka* with these other events and with the most common sense of the term—two individuals simply meeting each other on a road or in a field—is more important than the differences which separate them.

The term which local people use most often for Ch'iaraje, however, is *pukllay* ("to play").[5] The word *pukllay* has a broad schematic range, and can be used to refer to such things as children's games and adolescent flirtation. Though most English-speakers would agree that the former is certainly a kind of "play" and that the latter may be as well, in the Andes both activities often take on a kind of physical violence that English-speakers would not associate with play. Allen describes how "[a] teenage girl can actually become violent, hitting the object of her admiration in the arms and face, calling him an ugly dog." At Carnival, this sort of attention becomes more extreme: "a boy dances up to his girl seductively, but their dance soon turns into a contest as they whip each other's legs in a growing frenzy." Even under ordinary circumstances, though, "an affectionate couple tease each other with mild insults and pelt each other with small sticks and stones" (1988:78–79). In some valley communities in Canchis, potatoes—the larger, the better—are thrown during the harvest, either by a man or a woman, to express affection. On one occasion, when I joined in a work party in the community of Trapiche which a peasant family had assembled to harvest a field, I was surprised to feel a potato strike me on the back as I was bent over digging in the earth. Quickly standing up and looking around, I saw several young women with their hands in front of their mouths, only partially concealing their laughter. The humor lay in some combination of the secretive audacity of the thrower, the complicity of her friends, and the incongruity of the presence in a work group of a foreigner such as myself. These forms of *pukllay* suggests that peasants such as those Allen describes would not make the radical distinction between insulting someone and striking someone implied in the proverb quoted in the title of this paper: "Sticks and stones will break my bones, but names will never harm me." An implicit recognition in Western folklore of the Andean lack of distinction between the two could be found in another, perhaps more sophisticated, retort of insulted children: "I'm rubber, you're glue, whatever you say goes back to you."

There are still other examples of *pukllay:* the songs and dances at Carnival, which have been studied in detail elsewhere in the department of Cusco, though not in the *provincias altas* (Poole 1984:355–405; Allen 1988:182–89; Radcliffe 1990), and soccer, which has been received with great popularity in the *provincias altas* as elsewhere in Peru. The notion that teams draw their members from neighborhoods or communities is found throughout Latin America and is not restricted to the Andes. However, there may well be some modifications of the game of soccer to meet Andean cultural notions. I recall several such features—a preference for playing on dates of traditional ritual significance such as 1 January, an imprecision about the length of the game, and a tendency for players to cluster near one another rather than to spread themselves across the field as a tactical concern for placing and blocking goals would dictate. A future researcher, more familiar with the sport than I, might well find in highland soccer an Andean parallel to the Melanesian reworking of an English game depicted in the well-known film "Trobriand Cricket: An Indigenous Response to Colonialism".[6]

In conclusion, the phrase "ritual battles" underscores the distinctiveness of these events from Western patterns of behavior and violence. It marks discontinuities with other practices in the Andes. Although the native words *tinkuy* and *pukllay* imply a difference from Western patterns of behavior, they may also suggest other, distinct associations as well. Since the basic meanings of these words (to meet, to play) are general, and neutral to positive in tone, they emphasize continuities between these events and other practices in the Andes. The words *tinkuy* and *pukllay* suggest that participants perceive similarities between these events and others (between soccer and Ch'iaraje, for example, which strike most anthropologists as very different), although these words do not indicate that all these events so named are equivalent to one another. The phrase "ritual battles," on the other hand, suggests a separation between these events and others.

My own field notes reveal the difficulties of these issues of terminology. Although there are some terms that I used for both *ch'iwka* and Ch'iaraje, most notably "sides" and "teams," there are some that I restricted to the one or the other. I do not think that I strayed far from objectivity in referring to the round wooden object in the former as a "ball," or the dead body of the *prisionero* in the latter as a "corpse." But the equation of the former with sport, the latter with war, and the contrast between the two, appears in several pairs of terms which I used consistently in my notes ("game"/"battle"; "play"/"fight"; "equipment"/"weapons").

Once again, then, we are faced with a dilemma. The Western term "ritual battle" is too slippery and too exclusive, since by defining only the middle portion of a range of events it leaves as ambiguous the criteria by which cases may be judged either excessively or insufficiently violent. The Quechua terms *tinkuy* and *pukllay*, by contrast, are too inclusive. They place a very large number of forms of action under the same rubric as the violent encounters in the Plaza de Pampacucho and the high *punas* of Canas.

The difficulty so far, then, lies in the problem of locating these events within broader categories of events. One resolution is to move beyond systems of lexical classification altogether to examine discourse more broadly. In particular, the two events may not only be compared by studying the specific terms which describe them, but also by looking at the stories which participants and their audiences tell about them. I will divide these stories, perhaps arbitrarily, into two categories, which I will term "accounts of revenge" and "internal accounts," reserving a third term, "external accounts," for later discussion. The revenge accounts connect individual events through their outcomes. For example, Ch'iaraje participants with whom I spoke stated that they hoped that their side would take prisoners and kill them, because they wanted to revenge the deaths that were inflicted on them at recent battles. In *ch'iwka*, the participants repeated the scores of previous encounters, suggesting that they were keeping track of which side was ahead. In both cases, there are specific violent acts which are noted—deaths or goals—and the participants display a concern in preventing the other side from gaining ascendancy over them. They come to these events, not merely because attendance is deemed appropriate or customary, but because each event is a link in a chain of such events. These revenge accounts contain a well-described theme in Andean culture, the importance of *ayni*, ongoing reciprocal exchanges in which like is repaid with like. Much as two households might exchange labor, returning one day's work for a day received, *barrios* or groups of districts exchange goals or deaths. The partners maintain a relationship through this exchange.[7]

I use the term "internal accounts" to refer to the narratives which the participants themselves give about the events. These internal accounts do not focus as sharply on outcomes as the revenge accounts; instead, they generalize about them and discuss the ways in which these events have or have not changed. These accounts look back over the decades that are within living memory and refer to even earlier times, for example, the distant era of the Incas. These internal accounts also emphasize violence, though in a different fashion than in the accounts of revenge. For Ch'iaraje, the internal accounts emphasize the unity of the combatants against outsiders and their opposition to change. They have driven away the police and even the subprefect, much as they limit the intrusions of gringo filmmakers. In 1952, Alencastre and Dumézil (1953:22) were told that "many times" the police and subprefect attempted to stop the violence at Ch'iaraje, once even with machine guns, but that on all occasions the peasants chased them away, and were able to maintain the same kind of activity as before. That this continuity is important is suggested by anthropological accounts of *tinkuys* in another portion of the department of Cusco to the north of the *provincias altas*, where the participants could not prevent such outside intervention. These accounts convey the local people's sense of a fundamental change in the ritual battles in the early 1950s when the police put an end to the killings, even though events before and after that shift could both be classified as *tinkuy* (Allen 1988; Sallnow 1987).

Where the emphasis on the internal accounts of Ch'iaraje is on the maintenance of earlier practices, the stress in *ch'iwka* is on how practices differed in the past. The internal accounts describe the ways that practices were different in the past. I heard many individuals comment on specific changes: the site was moved; traditional authorities now play a less important role; the ball is made of different wood; people do not fight as fiercely as they once did; peasant communities have begun to play the game which formerly had been limited to towns. Others offered a more general discussion of change. Some spoke of *ch'iwka* as an ancient tradition, one which the Incas brought to the native inhabitants of the region, but has now become diminished. Others told of its revival, due to the persistent effort of a few devoted individuals. This tradition has become diminished, perhaps radically altered, but some essential core of manly violence does survive.

Some additional notes on violence may be made at this point by looking closely at the ways in which the revenge accounts specify which actions constitute a reciprocation of other actions, and at the descriptions in the internal accounts of the maintenance or reduction in levels of violence. In both Western and Andean understandings, a continuum may be drawn from (1) insults to (2) blows which do not break the skin to (3) blows which make blood flow to (4) killing. This continuum classifies acts by the degree of harm which they inflict, rather than by other possible criteria, such as the intentions of the persons who carried them out or the weapons that were used. Both Western and Andean systems separate the first three from the fourth. Western accounts, however, tend to mark the break between non-violence and violence as occurring between the first and the second. The Andean version locates a less sharp discontinuity at a different location, between the second and the third. This difference reflect the greater emphasis on the boundedness of the person in Western accounts, and hence a greater emphasis on the surface of the human body as the location of this boundary. In Andean accounts, an insult—an injury to an individual's social person—is not as radically different from injuries to an individual's biological person as in Western accounts.

Through a comparison of these events with the *mestizo* accounts of the events in Molloccahua (Orlove, Chapter 2, this volume), two additional categories can be added: (5) dismembering corpses and (6) preventing kin from burying corpses. As far as I am able to reconstruct from the *mestizo* accounts of these events in 1931, the Indian peasants saw the greater gap lying between the fifth and sixth categories, while the *mestizos* emphasized the separation of the fourth and fifth. These accounts furthermore suggest that the forced stripping of clothes was considered a violent act by both Indians and *mestizos*, lying somewhere between the third and fourth categories.[8] Closer examination of accounts of the various forms of detention, interrogation, torture and killings in the 1980s and 1990s (cf. Poole, Chapter 8, this volume) might reveal additional categories, as well as a more complex system of ranking than a single ordinal scale.

History, Narrative, and Violence

Since temporality is so important in Western social science as well as in the revenge accounts and the internal accounts, it is possible to link the two into a third type of narrative, which I shall call "external accounts," because they compare particular events with other places and periods, and because they seek to explain these events in term of external institutional contexts rather than internal cultural categories. These external accounts would draw simultaneously on two apparently incompatible vocabularies: that of social scientists, derived in part from a Western attempt to explain experience and history based on notions of "violence" and "symbol," and that of Andean Indian peasants, who categorize experience and social events according to a different set of criteria (*tinkuy, pukllay, ayni*). To ask why the *tinkuys* in one region are more violent than those in another raises questions about time as well as about space: why have these encounters developed differently in one region than another? Why did peasants in one place and time respond to pressure from the police by eliminating the most violent aspects of ritual battles and in another place and time by driving the police away?

Such efforts at synthesis may be seen in the rich literature on the northern portion of Potosí, a region where two types of ritual battles, *tinkuy* and *ch'ajwa*, continue to have a great deal of importance, corresponding closely to the *ch'iwka* and Ch'iaraje in the *provincias altas*. There are many features of the subsistence agriculture and the cultural concepts in the region that are similar to those elsewhere in the Andes. One can trace the history of the region far into the past—to the pre-Inca Charka and

Qaraqara federations, to the relatively brief incorporation of the region into the Inca Empire, to its reorganization under the Spanish Empire and its close links with the colonial silver mines of Potosí, only 150 kilometers away. These different political systems all reinforced the identification of Indian peasants with ethnic groups and *ayllus*.

The political history of the region since Independence has been complex. The Indian peasants of northern Potosí, though they retain elaborate forms of ayllu organization, have not simply been bypassed by history. They actively fought the Bolivian state's efforts to shift from a system of land rights which reside in the *ayllus* to a system of private property. Because such a shift would have caused much of their lands to pass to *mestizo* and criollo owners, the Indians sought to maintain reciprocal obligations which they saw as linking them with the state (Platt 1982).

The ritual battles can be understood in this regional context. The ethnic groups have considerable strength as political units which administer local affairs, negotiate with the state, and defend Indian peasant lands against outsiders. They also form an arena in which Andean political ideologies are presented, utilized and reformulated (Rivera Cusicanqui 1986). In some instances, the ritual battles become directly intertwined with national politics as the state intervenes to control land fought over in "traditional" *ch'ajwas* (Harris and Albó 1984:90–9). Regional history does not shape ritual battles, however, only in such cases of direct government involvement. The unusually wide scope of exclusively Indian peasant politics in northern Potosí has also influenced the development and persistence of ritual battles in the region. The revenge accounts which Platt (1986, 1987) offers are quite similar to the ones which I include from the *provincias altas.* It seems plausible that the reciprocity of violence featured in ritual battles forms part of a commitment by members of particular ethnic groups and *ayllus* to manage their internal affairs. I have not seen counterparts for this Bolivian region to the internal accounts outlined above for Cusco's provincias altas; it seems plausible, however, that the Indian peasants' reputation for violence would also serve to keep local *mestizos* and state agencies from taking control of their lands.

The case of northern Potosí can assist in sketching an explanation for the importance of ritual battles in Cusco's *provincias altas*. Although some elements of dual *ayllu* or moiety structures like the ones in northern Potosí are also found in Cusco's *provincias altas*, these structures are less elaborate in the Cusco area (Poole 1987; Glave 1989). The *provincias altas*, for example, do not have analogues to such practices as the continued payment of tribute (*tasa*) to the state.[9] Moreover, in part as a result of Peruvian state policy, the traditional Indian authorities who participate in *ayllu* ritual have been largely displaced by modern authorities who hold office in a system organized by national government decree. Finally, the system of ethnic groups and *ayllus* is today much weaker in general in the *provincias altas* than in northern Potosí. However much all forms of *tinkuy* and *pukllay* can be presented as structural equivalents, if we choose to follow a structuralist explanation, it might at first glance seem puzzling that full-scale ritual battles would be found both in northern Potosí, with more elaborate dual structures, and in the *provincias altas,* with less elaborate ones. Similarly, if we invoke the other approach described earlier, northern Potosí might appear to be an even clearer instance of "region of refuge" than the *provincias altas,* and hence should have retained a wider array of ritual battles.

A more promising avenue of explanation lies in the contrasting histories of the two regions. The factors which have shaped the ritual battles in Potosí suggest what other influences might operate in the Cusco area. One can point to a series of parallels in the two regions. In both regions, Aymara federations were incorporated into the Inca Empire and later into the colonial labor tribute system (Bouysse-Cassagne 1978; Glave 1989). The distance from the *provincias altas* to Cusco is roughly equal to the distance of northern Potosí to the city and mines. Both regions saw the emergence of export economies in the nineteenth and twentieth centuries, and both had agrarian reform programs.

The differences, however, stand out as sharply as the similarities. The structure of ethnic groups and *ayllus* in northern Potosí has been strongly influenced by colonial policy and republican tribute collection, quite unlike the more recent Peruvian government policies of recognition of communities (Gootenberg 1991). Although many features of communal land use and tenure are similar in the two regions (Orlove and Godoy 1986), *haciendas* have controlled a greater amount of land in the *provincias altas,* both in the colonial and in the republican period. The export economies are also quite different. The large-scale silver and tin mines which predominated in northern Potosí drew few of their workers and little of their foodstuffs from the immediate region (Bakewell 1984). In the wool export economy of the *provincias altas,* by contrast, many peasants raise sheep and alpacas whose wool they sell, or produce agricultural products which are sold or bartered with herders involved in the export economy (Orlove 1977a).

The ritual battles in both regions bear a complex relation to the ongoing Indian peasant resistance to claims to control their lands and labor. For northern Potosí, there are documented instances of direct state involvement in a *ch'ajwa*. There is also a more general tie between the ritual battles, on the one hand, and the strength of *ayllus* and indigenous political authorities, on the other. In both regions, the active political role of peasants accounts in part for the development and patterning of the ritual battles. In the *provincias altas,* peasant political efforts have been directed against landlords more often than in northern Potosí, and in recent years peasants have entered extensively into close political dealings with government agencies. Thus, *ayllu* structures in the provincias altas have been reduced by market economic activity and links to the state, unlike northern Potosí, but peasant resistance has been strong in both regions, though it has taken different forms. As other chapters in this volume make clear, the history of the *provincias altas* has been marked by periods of great violence. In this century, the expansion of the wool export economy and the Peruvian state have provided a context in which *haciendas* and communities have fought, often bitterly, among themselves and with each other. More concretely, there is a close spatial association between Ch'iaraje and nearby Indian peasant rebellions, both in Canas, particularly in Langui in 1921, and in nearby sections of the province of Espinar in 1921 and 1931 (Orlove 1980, 1990). Both the actual killings in Ch'iaraje, and the participants' and local observers' sense of Ch'iaraje as unchanging, maintain the reputation for violence of the peasants who have fought on repeated occasions in this century to retain their lands. By contrast, where peasants elsewhere in the Department of Cusco have been less active politically, police have succeeded in eliminating such killings at *tinkuys* (Allen 1988, Sallnow 1987).

Looking more closely at internal accounts about Ch'iaraje, we can examine the moments when the opposed sides are seen as uniting. They do so on several occasions: against Indian peasants from Chumbivilcas at Toqto, an instance which fits most easily with a structuralist account; against the police and the subprefect at Ch'iaraje; against filmmakers, also at Ch'iaraje. In the minds of the participants, or at least in their words, the lack of change in Ch'iaraje is due to the unflagging resolution of the peasants of Canas to prevent such change by directing their weapons, not at each other, but at powerful outsiders. Because of this linkage, statements that the two opposed sides join as allies in the face of a higher-order invader, whether police or cinematographers, cannot be taken as the working of structural dualisms. Rather, these statements suggest a kind of historical awareness, intentionality and agency that is difficult to reconcile with structuralism. It is interesting to note that this battle is the most striking case of a *costumbre* (custom) which the police attempt to prohibit and which the participants succeed in maintaining.[10] The authorities phrased their opposition in terms of national culture (they view the ritual battles as barbaric and uncivilized) and in terms of violence; for the Indian peasants, the ritual battles mark their distinctiveness and confirm their reputation as fighters.

The opposition of the participants at Ch'iaraje to the filmmakers is also of interest. They resented the filmmakers' lack of courtesy and unwillingness to offer them anything in exchange for being photographed, and their violence may simply have spilled over towards all outsiders. They also may have had other motives: a dislike of being treated as an object of touristic curiosity, a suspicion that the filmmakers were informers or spies, or a distrust of the long zoom lenses of the movie cameras. They may also have had a more sophisticated awareness of the importance of media and representations, and wanted control of the terms under which outsiders would come to see pictures of this event. This last possibility is supported by the fact that some Indian peasants were willing to present the ritual battles as an item of folkloric interest in a context in which they had some control and received some political recognition. A version of the fighting at Ch'iaraje, without much bloodshed, was presented, for example, at a folk dance festival near Sicuani on 16 June 1973. By holding the festival at Raqchi, the site of the most widely known Inca ruin in the *provincias altas,* the sponsors created a strong sense of a link between the festival, current Indian peasant populations, and a pre-Hispanic past.[11] Such performances of stylized versions of Ch'iaraje at dance festivals have continued to the present (Mendoza 1993).

Ch'iwka also lends itself to this sort of reexamination of internal accounts. All people with whom I talked spoke of *ch'iwka* as changing and all mentioned valley settlements as the locations in which it is played. No *puna* communities, even those quite close to Sicuani, have adopted the game. *Ch'iwka* was once restricted to a fairly narrow range of settlements—district capitals and the provincial capitals of Sicuani and Acomayo. The game is now found in a wider range of settlements. It has been retained in Sicuani, despite the growth in population and urban functions, and it is spreading to peasant communities, which are smaller in size and lack certain features found in the district capitals such as central squares and weekly markets. In Sicuani, its continued existence and its transformation are the product of the efforts of specific individuals and of the interest of many local dwellers. As in the case of Ch'iaraje, participants have some involvement in controlling the ways in which *ch'iwka* is represented more widely in Peruvian society, notably through the selective establishment of friendships and collaborative ties with anthropologists.

Playing and watching *ch'iwka* affirm several sorts of ties. One set of connections links Sicuani to its past, when the town was smaller and had a more rustic ambience. The second set affirms commonalities which link the provincial capital of Sicuani to district capitals in the valley and to other communities near Sicuani. These ties may reflect the high social, occupational and geographic mobility in the region. Many of the inhabitants of district capitals had lived in peasant communities or still maintain lands and houses there. Their adoption of a game which had been restricted to town dwellers suggests their claim to a new urban status, much as the extension of the game to the communities nearest to Sicuani suggests a claim of commonality with Sicuani which inhabitants in the communities would not have made in previous decades. In this sense, the game of *ch'iwka* represents a kind of levelling of distinctions among settlements and social groups that had formerly been important in the valley. This levelling is connected with a decline of the local *mestizo* elites who formally dominated the district capitals and their replacement by Indian peasants (Orlove 1977b). It is also linked with the increase of commercial and artisanal activity in the countryside (Orlove 1974, 1977a). One might have expected, though, that the adoption of *ch'iwka* in peasant communities would lead people in Sicuani to drop rather than to maintain the game. Its retention suggests a continued identification with the peasant populations of the valley as a whole. The regionalist sentiment to the game is reflected in its spatial distribution, restricted to the provinces of Canchis and Acomayo, and a few nearby districts of Quispicanchis.

It is difficult to give a simple ethnic reading to this identification, whether in the sense of the opposition between Indians and *mestizos*, or in the sense noted in Potosí of the differences among distinct indigenous ethnic groups or *ayllus*. It is not simply that some urban *mestizos* in Sicuani are playing at being Indians, or that the inhabitants of some Indian peasant communities aspire to *mestizo* status by adopting an urban game (de la Cadena 1990). The identification does seem to be with a region (the *provincias altas*) and a zone (the valleys), expressed at times through perceived continuities with the past of an ethnic group called the Kanchis and the enactment of this continuity through performances of male violence. There are striking parallels with the evocations of a K'ana ethnic identity in the case of Ch'iaraje and Molloccahua.[12]

Conclusions:
Narrative, Performance, and Agency

Several impulses lead people to gather at the plains of Ch'iaraje or the Plaza de Pampacucho at the appropriate days of the year. In the most immediate terms, they can play (*pukllay*) in a particularly thrilling kind of exhibition of masculine bravery, while also defending the honor of their district or neighborhood against that of the opponents with whom they meet (*tinkuy*). Once they arrive, they are not disappointed. There is a great excitement to these events for both participants and observers. Indeed, the line is difficult to draw between these two sets of individuals. It often happens that someone who came merely to observe gets caught up in the spirit of the moment, picks up a sling or *maruna*, and joins in the fray. Even those who do not "play" themselves mingle with the "players" in the plaza or plain while stones or wooden *ch'iwka* balls fly through the air, and eat and drink with them in the long break halfway through.

Most of them quite drunk, the participants and local observers head home late in the afternoon, where they will return to their everyday lives, in which the ritual opponents interact without any hostility. Riding across the high *punas* of Canas or walking down the streets of Sicuani and other valley towns, they talk among themselves, reviewing the "meeting" which has just taken place. How do they understand their own broken bones and bloody limbs, these wounds which their kin and neighbors also bear, the occasional corpse? We may examine some answers to this question which has fascinated social scientists at least since the 1950s and which is of central importance to this volume. The structuralists are partially correct in suggesting that the wounds and deaths manifest the identities of the participants as men and as members of spatially defined communities, much as the "region of refuge" model accurately underscores the importance of locating the *provincias altas* as a remote portion of a larger social order where such ethnically distinct practices are maintained. The participants in these events and their audiences, though, offer a more detailed interpretation of these corporal signs and a more active view of this relation to a wider order.

The local narratives—both revenge accounts and internal accounts—of these events place a great deal of emphasis on violence. Each event is an opportunity for groups to avenge themselves against their opponents; the historical continuity of the events consists of a maintenance of their essential core, the public display of the willingness of males to shed blood and to give and receive blows. These local narratives suggest an implicit continuum along which violent acts can be ranked: (1) insults, (2) blows which do not break the skin, (3) blows which make blood flow, (4) killing, (5) dismembering corpses, and (6) preventing the burial of corpses. As discussed earlier in this chapter and in Chapter 2 (this volume), this categorization differs in significant ways from the implicit categorizations of violence among *mestizos* in the region and among Western social scientists. Within these narratives, moreover, the participants do not only define themselves in relation to spatially defined communities, such as *barrios* like *uray calle* in Sicuani, or districts like Quehue in Canas. They also present themselves in terms of wider identities, variants of the regional Indian peasantries discussed in the external accounts. *Ch'iwka* and Ch'iaraje are powerful means of affirming and instantiating certain claims—that *puna* peasants are autonomous and rebellious, that valley dwellers in town and country alike share a way of life and a distinctive regional identity, and that both, in their particular ways, are tough, impressive fighters. On the one hand, these events are genuine enactments of violence within highly structured ritual contexts; on the other hand, they are also representations of a more general potential for violence that might be expressed outside the limits of these contexts. By showing their commitments to fighting among themselves, the participants also express, with great effectiveness, their willingness to fight other people on other occasions (cf. Poole, Chapter 3, this volume).

These identities—perhaps identifications would be a better term for such explicit claims to identity—form part of the understandings which the inhabitants of the *provincias altas* have of their own history. They see themselves neither as isolated from the wider world nor as subordinate to it, but rather as capable of influencing their relations with it. Ch'iaraje and *ch'iwka* present these understandings to participants and local audiences, as well as to outsiders, some of whom oppose them and offer different conceptions of identity. Moreover, through the revival of *ch'iwka* and the presentation of Ch'iaraje at dance festivals, these events create opportunities for local people to collaborate with intellectuals and officials in their own self-presentation. In showing themselves to be perfectly balanced opponents when they contend with each other on regular occasions, the participants announce that they are formidable opponents to those against whom they might choose to fight at other times as well. Ch'iaraje and *ch'iwka* demonstrate to local audiences and outsiders alike a strength that has often been challenged, but never wholly subdued.

Notes

I would like to thank the following individuals for the helpful comments on previous versions of this paper: Stephen Brush, William Hamilton III, Zoila Mendoza, George Primov, Michael Sallnow, Ward Stavig, John Treacy, Thomas Turrentine and Pierre van den Berghe. I owe special thanks to Thomas Abercrombie and Deborah Poole for their generosity in providing me with unusually thorough and insightful comments. Field research in the Department of Cusco was funded by the Foreign Area Fellowship Program. This article was completed during my residence as a Fellow at the Humanities Institute of the University of California, Davis.

1. A derogatory term, *chhuchu* is not used exclusively to refer to Chumbivilcanos. Chumbivilcanos also use it to refer to Cotabambinos, as Cotabambinos to refer to Antabambinos. (cf. Poole 1987).

2. To account for the presence of people from Yanaoca on both sides of the fighting, I could then point out that, as the capital of "the K'anas," it would have portions allocated to both of the halves or moieties.

3. Harris (1978) explores with great subtlety the interrelations of the ways in which Andean people speak of genders and ecological zones. Though both are composed of pairs (male/female and *puna*/valley), in which the elements have characteristics both of complementarity and of inequality, they are not simply equated.

4. Other authors report cases from Ecuador (Hartmann 1972, 1978; Brownrigg 1972), Bolivia (Abercrombie 1986:258–9; Harris 1982; Platt 1986; Rasnake 1988:188), and Cusco (Sallnow 1987:136–46; Allen 1988:182–189) Both Allen and

Sallnow describe a battle resembling Ch'iaraje, except that the bodies of the victims, rather than being returned to their fellows, were buried, either "where [the corpse] fell" (Allen 1988:183) or "in a deep ditch near by at a place called Tallikuyoq ... a spot regarded with dread, for the mutilated corpses are said to be still moist and will remain so forever, perpetually oozing blood into the earth" (Sallnow 1987:138). Gorbak, Lischetti and Muñoz (1962) list twenty-two such cases from Peru and six from Bolivia. Although most of their descriptions are quite brief, a few are detailed, and their bibliography refers to a number of sources, such as Bandelier (1910), who describes some "regular engagements" (88) resembling Ch'iaraje at the border between communities on the Isla del Sol in Lake Titicaca (88,96) and others ("combat" [115]) like the *tinkus* of Potosí in the square at Copacabana. Hopkins (1982) offers a rich account of a ritual battle in Langui in 1772. This battle was held at a spot quite close to Ch'iaraje, and resembled it in a number of points.

5. Another Quechua term for Ch'iaraje is *tupay*, which also means "to meet" (Alencastre and Dumézil 1953:12). *Tupay*, however, has a broader set of referents than *tinkuy*.

6. This film, released in 1976, is now distributed in the United States through the University of California Extension Media Center.

7. Abercrombie, for example, notes that "[w]hether in *tinku* or *ch'axwa*, vengeance for previous losses plays a crucial role in the motivation of fights. ... the term for vengeance (*ayni*) is the same as is used to describe the exchange of labor prestations. In addition, it is used to refer to the exchange of sponsorship which takes place during the fiesta." (1986:259).

→ 8. The act of stripping clothes off someone against their will may be subject to differing interpretations. In Western accounts, the skin appears the natural boundary of the human body, so that acts such as insults or stripping clothes would be construed as acts of humiliation rather than as violence. The consequences of stripping the clothes are understood principally in terms of shame, of rendering visible the parts of the body that are ordinarily kept covered. (It is possible, though, that the gaze itself is physicalized, as the English metaphor "a cutting glance" suggests, so that uncovering and looking is itself a kind of physical injury.) Andean accounts, by contrast, seem to treat cloth and clothing as constitutive of the social person, so that removal of a person's clothing resembles wounding a person's body. Though issues of shame are present in these accounts as well, the consequences of stripping also involve the loss of the clothing itself. The act of injury seems to end in Western terms when the stripped individual is once again decently dressed, in Andean terms when the person's clothing is returned to its owners (including, if need be, the deceased person's heirs).

9. The closest equivalent is the offering of animals and first fruits to district officials at Carnival by some communities (Orlove 1977a), but that is not as generalized, and does not have the same close links to the internal organization of the communities as tribute does in northern Potosí.

10. Abercrombie (1986:258–9) also notes the somewhat more successful efforts of the police and military to suppress *ch'ajwa* in Oruro.

11. The festival was billed as an *homenaje al campesino peruano* (homage to the Peruvian peasant) and as a *gran desfile folklórico* (great folkloric parade). It was spon-

sored by the Canchis branch of the National Instituto of Culture, at that time linked to left-wing parties, and by the Permanent Central Commission of the Raqchi Folklore Festival. Eleven groups performed, nine of which were social clubs, schools or semi-official folkdance groups from Puno, the neighboring department famed for its elaborate dances. The other two were both listed as delegations from districts in the *provincias altas*: the "liwi dance" presented by the delegation from Livitaca in Chumbivilcas. This dance also has links to ritual battles, since it is associated with *yawar mayu* (Poole 1990; Allen 1988:184, 188). Interestingly enough, the Ch'iaraje performance was the only event listed as an *estampa costumbrista* ('traditional image'), rather than as a *danza* ('dance'). The participants may well have sought a measure of political recognition or support from the government, because of the sponsorship of the festival and its timing, close to 24 June, a date of significance in both the ritual calendar and the national political calendar (it had been the *Día del Indio* since the 1920s and became the *Día del Campesino* when the agrarian reform act was proclaimed on that date in 1969).

12. The issue of indigenous ethnic identity is one that surfaces in a comparison of the *provincias altas* and northern Potosí. Such identities seem quite weak in the former region, but not entirely absent. There are repeated references in stories, songs and jokes which suggest some level of identification with a province of origin; a urban troupe of folkdancers in Sicuani, for example, named themselves the Centro Qanchi de Arte Vernacular. In reviewing my field notes from the *provincias altas*, I came across several uses of the word *chhuchu*. For example, it was the nickname of a man from Chumbivilcas who worked as an employee in the Sicuani post office. And once, when a neighbor of mine in Sicuani and I were preparing to ride our bicycles to the local hot springs of Uyurmire, several kilometers way, the term was applied to me. I had tied a towel around my waist, and my neighbor, quite amused, called me by that term, explaining that peasants from Chumbivilcas and parts of Espinar carry ponchos that way, rather than in the more widespread fashion of tying a carrying cloth, blanket or poncho over one or both shoulders. The most striking use of such ethnic labels, though, came on 8 January 1973, when I visited the community of Uscapata in a narrow side-valley of the Vilcanota within the district of Sicuani. Hot on the trail of variants of *ch'iwka*, I ran across a peasant whom I knew. He was planting one of his non-irrigated fields, and said that it would rain from January through March in the entire "*nashun*," a word which I take to be his pronunciation of the Spanish *nación* ('nation'). His first example of another place in this *nashun* was Tinta, the former capital of all of Canas, Canchis and Espinar in the colonial period. He then included other places, among them Pampamarca, one of the *puna* districts in Canas closest to Tinta.

Bibliography

Abercrombie, Thomas. 1986. *The Politics of Sacrifice: An Aymara Cosmology in Action.* Ph.D. dissertation, Department of Anthropology, University of Chicago.

Alencastre, Andrés and Dumézil, Georges. 1953. Fêtes et usages des indiens de Langui (province de Canas, département du Cuzco). *Journal de la Société des Américanistes* (N.S.) 42: 1–118.

Allen, Catherine J. 1988. *The Hold Life Has: Coca and Cultural Identity in an Andean Community.* Washington and London: Smithsonian Institution Press.

Bandelier, Adolph F. 1910. *The Islands of Titicaca and Koati.* New York: The Hispanic Society of America.

Barrionuevo, Alfonsina. 1971. Chiaraqe. *Allpanchis Phuturinqa* 3: 79–84. (Cusco.)

Bouysse-Cassagne, Thérèse, Harris, Olivia, Platt, Tristan and Cereceda, Verónica. 1987. *Tres reflexiones sobre el pensamiento andino.* La Paz: Hisbol.

Brownrigg, Leslie. 1972. El papel de los ritos de pasaje en la integración social de los Cañaris Quichuas del austral Ecuatoriano. *Actas del XXXIX Congreso Internacional de Americanistas.* 6: 92–99. (Lima.)

Casaverde, Juvenal. 1969. El mundo sobrenatural tradicional de los Quechuas. *Wayka* 1:6–17. (Cusco.)

Collins, Jane. 1981. *Kinship and Seasonal Migration among the Aymara of Southern Peru: Human Adaptation to Energy Scarcity.* Ph.D. dissertation, Department of Anthropology, University of Florida.

de la Cadena, Marisol. 1990. De utopías y contrahegemonías: el proceso de la cultura popular. *Revista Andina* 15:65–76.

———. 1992. De-indianizing the Culture: Elite and Plebeyan Intellectuals in Cusco, 1900–1992. Unpublished manuscript, Department of Anthropology, University of Wisconsin.

Fioravanti-Molinié, Antoinette. 1986. El simbolismo de frontera en los Andes. *Revista del Museo National.* 48:251–86. (Lima.)

Gilt Contreras, Mario Alberto. 1955. Las guerrillas indígenas de Chiyaraqe y Toqto. *Archivos Peruanos de Folklore* 1:110–119. (Cusco.)

Glave, Luís Miguel. 1989. *Trajinantes. Caminos indígenas en la sociedad colonial, siglos XVI/XVII.* Lima: Instituto de Apoyo Agrario.

Godoy, Ricardo. 1985. *Peasant Mining: Small-scale Mining in the Jukumani Ayllu, Northern Potosí, Bolivia.* Cambridge, MA: Harvard Institute for International Development.

Gootenberg, Paul. 1991. Population and Ethnicity in Early Republican Peru: Some Revisions. *Latin American Research Review* 26(3):109–158.

Gorbak, Celina, Lischetti, Mirtha, and Múñoz, Carmen Paula. 1962. Batallas rituales del Chiaraje y del Tocto de la Provincia de Kanas (Cuzco–Perú). *Revista del Museo Nacional* 31: 293–304. (Lima.)

Harris, Olivia. 1978. Complementarity and conflict: an Andean view of women and men. *In* LaFontaine, Jean S., ed. *Sex and Age as Principles of Social Differentiation.* Pp. 21–40. London and New York: Academic Press.

———. 1982. From asymmetry to triangle: symbolic transformations in Northern Potosí. *In* Murra, John V., Wachtel, Nathan and Revel, Jacques, eds. *The Historical Anthropology of Andean Polities.* Pp. 60–79. Cambridge: Cambridge University Press.

Harris, Olivia and Albó, Xavier. 1984. *Monteras y quardatojos: campesinos y mineros en el Norte de Potosí.* (segunda edición revisada). La Paz: CIPCA.

Hartmann, Roswith. 1972. Otros datos sobre las llamadas "batallas rituales". *Actas y Memorias del XXXIX Congreso Internacional de Americanistas.* 6:125–135. (Lima)

———. 1978. Más noticias sobre el "juego del pucara". *Amerikanistiche Studien* 20: 202–218. (Bonn)

Hopkins, Diane. 1982. Juego de enemigos. *Allpanchis* 20:167–187. (Cusco)

Isbell, Billie Jean. 1976. La otra mitad esencial: un estudio de complementariedad sexual andina. *Estudios Andinos* 12:37–56.

_____. 1985. *To Defend Ourselves: Ecology and Ritual in an Andean Village.* Second Edition. Prospect Heights, IL: Waveland Press.

Lira, Jorge A. 1953. Puhllay, fiesta india. *Perú Indígena* 4(9): 125–134.

Mayer, Enrique. 1977. Beyond the nuclear family. *In* Ralph Bolton and Enrique Mayer, eds. *Andean Kinship and Marriage.* Pp. 60–80. Washington, DC: American Anthropological Association.

Mendoza, Zoila. 1993. *Shaping Society Through Dance: Mestizo Ritual Performance in the Southern Peruvian Andes.* Ph. D. Dissertation, Department of Anthropology, University of Chicago.

Orlove, Benjamin S. 1974. Urban and rural artisans in southern Peru. *International Journal of Comparative Sociology* 15(3–4):193–211.

_____. 1977a. *Alpacas, Sheep and Men: The Wool Export Economy and Regional Society in Southern Peru.* New York: Academic Press.

_____. 1977b. The decline of local elites: Canchis in southern Peru. *In* Adams, Richard and Fogelson, Raymond, eds., *The Ethnography of Power.* Pp. 337–348. New York: Academic Press.

_____. 1979. Two rituals and three hypotheses: an examination of solstice divination in southern highland Peru. *Anthropological Quarterly* 52(2):86–98.

_____. 1980. Molloccahua 1931: un levantamiento campesino en el sur del Perú. *In* Flores, Jorge and Valencia, Abraham, eds., *Rebeliones indígenas quechuas y aymaras: Homenaje as bicentenario de la rebelión campesina de Thupa Amaro 1780–1980.* Pp. 133–154. Cusco: Centro de Estudios Andinos Cusco.

_____. 1990. Rebels and theorists: An analysis of peasant uprisings in southern Peru. *Research in Social Movements, Conflicts and Change.* 12:137–185.

Orlove, Benjamin S. and Godoy, Ricardo. 1986. Sectoral fallowing systems in the central Andes. *Journal of Ethnobiology* 6(1):169–204.

Orlove, Benjamin S. and Guillet, David. 1985. Theoretical and methodological considerations on the study of mountain peoples: Reflections on the idea of subsistence type and the role of history in human ecology. *Mountain Research and Development* 5(1):3–18.

Palomino, Salvador. 1971. Duality in the social organization of several Andean populations. *Folk* 13:65–68.

Paredes Candia, Antonio. 1966. *Juegos, juguetes y devertimientos del folklore de Bolivia.* La Paz: Ediciones Isla.

Platt, Tristan. 1982. *Estado boliviano y ayllu andino: Tierra y tributo en el norte de Potosí.* Lima: Instituto de Estudios Peruanos.

_____. 1986. Mirrors and maize: the concept of *yanantin* among the Macha of Bolivia. *In* Murra, John V., Wachtel, Nathan and Revel, Jacques, eds., *Anthropological History of Andean Polities.* Pp. 228–259. Cambridge: Cambridge University Press.

_____. 1987. Entre ch'axwa y muxsa. Para una historia del pensamiento político aymara. *In* Bouysse-Cassagne, Thérèse, Harris, Olivia, Platt, Tristan and Cereceda, Verónica. *Tres reflexiones sobre el pensamiento andino.* Pp. 62–132. La Paz: Hisbol.

Poole, Deborah. 1984. *Ritual Economic Calendars in Paruro: The Structure of Representation in Andean Ethnography.* Ph.D. dissertation, Department of Anthropology, University of Illinois.

————. 1987. Qorilazos, abigeos y comunidades campesinas en la Provincia de Chumbivilcas (Cusco). *In* Flores-Galindo, Alberto, ed., *Comunidades campesinas: cambios y permanencias,* Pp. 257–295. Chiclayo y Lima: Centro de Estudios 'Solidaridad' y CONCYTEC.

————. 1990. Accomodation and resistance in Andean ritual dance. *TDR.* 34(2):98–126.

— Radcliffe, Sarah A. 1990. Marking the boundaries between the comunity, the state and history in the Andes. *Journal of Latin American Studies* 22:575–594.

— Rasnake, Roger. 1988. *Domination and Resistance: Authority and Power among an Andean People.* Durham, NC: Duke University Press.

Rivera Cusicanqui, Silvia. 1986. *"Oprimidos pero novencidos" Luchas del campesinado aymara y quechwa 1900–1980.* La Paz: Hisbol.

Saignes, Thierry. 1989. Borracheras andinas: Por qué los indios ebrios hablan en español? *Revista Andina* 13:83–128.

Sallnow, Michael J. 1987. *Pilgrims of the Andes: Regional Cults in Cusco.* Washington, D.C., and London: Smithsonian Institution Press.

Urton, Gary. 1990. *The History of a Myth: Pacariqtambo and the Origin of the Inkas.* Austin: University of Texas Press.

Valencia, Abraham. 1970. *Cultura i platería en San Pablo.* Tesis de doctorado, Programa Académico de Antropología, Universidad Nacional San Antonio Abad del Cuzco.

van den Berghe, Pierre and Primov, George. 1977. *Inequality in the Peruvian Andes: Class and Ethnicity in Cuzco.* Columbia: University of Missouri Press.

Zuidema, R. Tom. 1964. *The Ceque System of Cusco.* Leiden: E. J. Brill.

5

Embodied Violence: Racial Identity and the Semiotics of Property in Huaquirca, Antabamba (Apurímac)

Peter Gose

For decades, anthropologists have argued that Andean racial concepts are problematic, and that they actually refer to more mutable distinctions of class and ethnicity.[1] Yet in their rush to demonstrate the non-racial referents of racial discourse, anthropologists have sometimes forgotten that notions of race are ubiquitous in rural Andean society, and that they have long marked individual and group identities within it. One need only listen to Andean people discuss their society for a short while to discover that they believe it to be composed of "Indians," "*Mestizos*" and to a lesser extent, "Whites." Each "race" is thought to be defined by a substance, "blood," which is common to all its members, creates a solidarity among them, and specifies their conduct.[2] For example, I was once told by a self-identified *mestizo*: "we have two bloods that run in our veins, one which is Indian, noble and hard-working, another which is Spanish, lazy and overbearing." This clearly expresses the idea that working and ruling are racially determined activities. It is therefore absurd to pretend that Andean people "have very little racial consciousness" (van den Berghe and Primov 1977: 118), or that anthropologists are the ones who essentialize "the fluid and often ambiguous quality of Andean personal identity" (Starn 1991: 70). Racist discourse exists in Andean society, and it attempts to impose bounded, essentialist identities.

However, it is true that there are no clear-cut phenotypical divisions to which these "racial" terms could correspond, and that their biological reference is necessarily suspended in use. Furthermore, they are even less adequate as a way of characterizing modern cultural or linguistic differentiation (Fuenzalida 1970a: 25–6, 63, 72). Anthropologists have had little choice but to conclude that these "racial" terms provide imaginary vehicles for the apprehension of power relations in society. What they have not really explored are the implications of representing power relations in this totemistic manner.

As a first step, we must realize that racist discourse does not necessarily aim to describe Andean society accurately. Rather, it may seek to alter social interactions performatively, to impute and impose boundaries which otherwise might not exist. For example, these "racial" terms treat modern Andean society as the product of an ongoing encounter between the Indian and the Hispanic that was initiated by the Spanish conquest. By evoking a moment when it was theoretically possible to draw clear-cut biological and cultural boundaries and applying it in the present, these terms brutally simplify 450 years of history, during which both parties to that original encounter transformed each other in their subsequent interaction. Thus, racist discourse reinvents a largely imaginary biocultural dichotomy under the sign of an historically transcendent act of conquest. This is a phenomenon I join Gow (1991) in calling "the myth of the conquest."

Like all myths, the myth of the conquest has a partial but important truth. What it expresses, in a way that no academic analysis of class and ethnicity ever could, is the violent nature of *gamonalismo*, an extra-legal form of domination that emerged from the collapse of the colonial state in nineteenth century Peru, and which still exists in some of its provinces. The general outlines of *gamonalismo* have been summarized by Poole (Chapter 3) in this volume: a fusion of local economic and political power in the person of a small resident landowner (*gamonal*), whose intimate familiarity with "Indian" culture, on the one hand, and systematic violation of it on the other, upheld a servile social order in isolated agrarian settings. Although the *gamonales* typically monopolized local state offices, their power as a class derived, paradoxically, from the institutional weakness of the Peruvian state in its rural hinterlands. Precisely because the republican state was too weak to enforce tributary relations reliably in the countryside, the *gamonales* took it upon themselves to do so. They developed a style of personal domination based on spectacular acts of violence, which became their trademark. Thus the sovereignty of the *gamonal* was in permanent conflict with the state and the rule of law, even though it was notionally connected to them (Poole 1988). What the violence of the *gamonal* did enact directly, however, was the myth of the conquest, a cultural construction of power that was reaffirmed every time society was understood in terms of "race."

Racially essentialized notions of personhood were central to the personal domination that *gamonales* strove to establish. Their idea of "race" codified the tributary relations that existed between Indian and Spanish estates during the colonial period, but it did so within the individualist and scientific discourses of a republic that was known to proclaim the formal equality of its citizens periodically (see Davies 1974). In particular *gamonal* ideas of "race" made the judicial enforcament of colonial tribute relations obsolete and redundant, because they were now held to be natural. The *gamonales* saw servility as an inherent, racially-inscribed aspect of "Indian" personhood, and expected to elicit it in face to face interaction by virtue of their more powerful personalities, derived from their "overbearing" Spanish blood. Thus the *gamonales* proceeded to validate the "Hispanic" component of their identity by violating "Indian" others in an endless "reconquest" of specific localities. Of course these racial attributions were problematic, and that was one of the reasons they were applied with such force. Once applied, however, they had a profoundly rigidifying effect on rural Andean society, one that has often been underestimated.

Even the *gamonales* who were most committed to this racist folk model typically understood themselves as *mestizos*, that is, as people with a "mixed" identity that was neither wholly Hispanic or Indian. It was this very indeterminacy and relativity of identity that made the *gamonales* such volatile characters, whose behavior toward the "Indian" could oscillate from a sympathetic and sincere participation in agrarian ritual at one moment, to an intimidating destruction of their livelihood in the next (cf. Poole 1988). These dual impulses of attraction and violation are very precisely codified in the idea expressed to me by several self-identified *mestizos* that the origins of *mestizaje* go back to the forced consummation of the lust of the Spanish conquistador for the beautiful Inka princess (*ñusta*). This image of primordial rape is a central element of the myth of the conquest as a whole.

Andean racist discourse could provide endless variations on the basic theme of violently induced differentiation and dominance. To repeat them all would be to buy into the myth of the conquest itself, namely that violence is the "truth" of colonialism. Rather than follow Taussig (1987) into this new foundationalism and its attendant revelations, I prefer to discuss the relatively impure and mediated forms of violence I encountered while doing fieldwork in Huaquirca during 1981–3. This town of 800 people is located in the Province of Antabamba, Department of Apurímac, and has only begun to emerge from *gamonal* domination over the last forty years, according to local accounts. Yet apart from witnessing two acts of assault by *gamonal* families, everything I learned about violence in Huaquirca was from people's recollections of the town, the land, and local politics. There was also speculation about whether the war between Sendero Luminoso and the Peruvian army would reach Huaquirca, and how it would affect life there. In short, only rarely was violence an immediate reality for anyone during my time in Huaquirca, but it shaped people's lives profoundly nonetheless, as both memory and expectation.

In Huaquirca, there is a pronounced social differentiation between people who call themselves commoners (*comuneros*) and other people who call themselves notables (*vecinos notables*). Although these groups correspond to the "Indians" and "*mestizos*" of the myth of the conquest, they have always been differentiated by more than just violence, which makes them rather more complex and interesting to study. Perhaps the single most important criterion that differentiates these two groups is the egalitarian mutual aid relation of *ayni*, which is practiced exclusively by commoners, and characterizes most of the work done on their land during the growing season.[3] Commoners also work the land of the notables, but through asymmetric relations of wage labor or *mink'a*, that is, work for a day's food and drink, with no obligation for the host to reciprocate his or her own labor.[4] Notables may work their own land along with the commoners they recruit, but consider it shameful to reciprocate, and only do so in the most desperate of circumstances. Many notables prefer to avoid field labor altogether.[5] Instead, they pursue commerce, schoolteaching careers, and above all, local political office, which they virtually monopolize as a group. As local rulers, notables solicit and supervise public works projects that are carried by the tributary labor (*faena*) of commoners. Finally, commoners and notables only rarely intermarry. The resulting group endogamy may contribute to a sense that the difference between notables and commoners is somehow a matter of "race."

In this chapter, I will discuss the legacy of *gamonal* violence in these social relations, not only as it has become embodied in local racist discourse, but also in the physical layout of Huaquirca and its fields. Rather than treat violence as something separate from the material and social organization of everyday life in Huaquirca, I will focus instead on how it informs and enforces a variety of aesthetic distinctions that are ultimately about class (cf. Bourdieu 1984). It was for these distinctions that the *gamonales* fought, and it is through them that their violence lives on, and continues to structure social relations.

Race and Space
in the Town of Huaquirca

Huaquirca lies at the end of a secondary road that departs from the Lima-Cusco highway near Chalhuanca, and picks its way over the alpine zone (*puna*) and down into the Antabamba Valley (Fig. 5.1). An average of two trucks per week cover the sixty kilometers to the town of Antabamba, the capital of Antabamba Province. The trip generally takes between six and ten hours. About twice per month, a truck will continue on across the val-

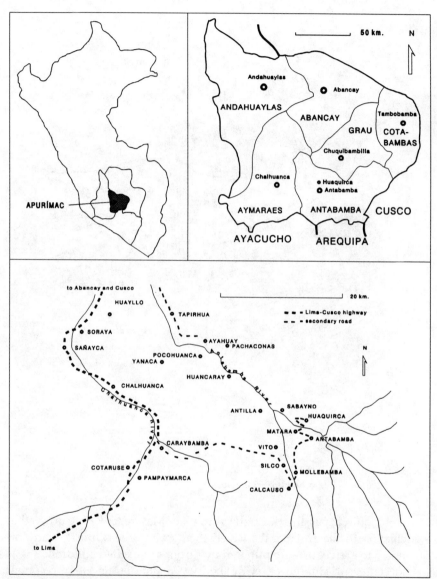

FIGURE 5.1   Location of the study.

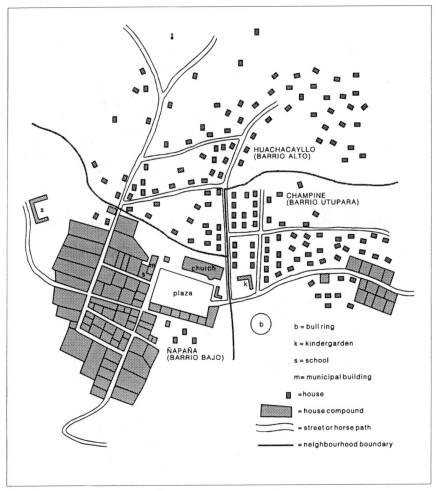

FIGURE 5.2   The neighborhoods of Huaquirca.

ley to Huaquirca, passing through the town of Matara, creeping down the switchbacks to the Antabamba River, then scaling the opposite flank of the valley to arrive, usually pursued by throngs of excited children.

The center of Huaquirca is defined by a ponderous early colonial church that dwarfs all other buildings with its immense bulk. The three neighborhoods (*barrios*) of which Huaquirca is composed all border on the church and the plaza in front of it (Fig. 5.2). There are good historical reasons for the visual centrality of this church. In the 1570s, three pre-existing settlements (one of which corresponds approximately to one of the modern neighborhoods) were consolidated to form Huaquirca as it is now

known, through the colonial policy of *reducción* (see Gade, this volume).
Many residents think that the church's massive walls incorporate squared
stones from the abandoned precolumbian dwellings that can still be seen
in the neighborhood of Champine. There is thus a sense in which this
church symbolizes the social order that took form during the colonial
period. Indeed, the ecclesiastical Parish of Huaquirca was the *de facto* local
presence of the state well into the 18th century. With the declaration of the
republic in 1821 and the withdrawal of state subsidies to the clergy, the
church found itself in crisis throughout the Province of Aymaraes (of
which the Antabamba Valley was then still a part).[6] With time, the clergy
left the area, and the church building itself began to decompose, and continues to do so into the present. No priest has lived in the town since the
mid-nineteenth century, and now only four or five masses per year are
celebrated in the church by the priest from Antabamba.

The church's main entrance faces onto the plaza, which is about the size
of a soccer field, and is occasionally used as such. There are three shops
open on a regular basis in the plaza. These are owned by people who were
once itinerant salesmen from the Departments of Puno and Cusco. The
rest of the houses on the plaza are either occupied by families, or abandoned. Next to the church are several public buildings, a telephone office
that is occasionally open, the two-story municipal offices of the District of
Huaquirca, and one of the town's two elementary schools.

In the early morning, notable men holding or aspiring to hold political
power in the district will meet in the plaza to chat informally or argue in
Spanish before breakfast. Commoners with a matter to raise stand pa-
tiently a few paces away, waiting for a lull in the conversation to address
the appropriate official, usually in Quechua. Other notable men may
comb the streets around the plaza during the growing season, seeking to
recruit commoners to work in their fields. Older commoners dressed in
ragged coats held together in a loose patchwork may give way to an ap-
proaching notable on the narrow sidewalks, stepping into the muddy
street, even doffing their misshapen felt hats. Women and children pass
into the plaza to see if any of the shops baked bread the night before, and
to buy cane alcohol and coca leaves for work parties they may be sponsor-
ing that day. By 9:00 in the morning, most activity in the plaza ceases, as
children go to school, and adults begin to prepare for the day's work. During the day, the only people likely to be seen in the plaza are small children playing or men getting conspicuously drunk in the shops. In the late
afternoon, children return from school, adults from the fields, and another
round of errands brings people to the plaza before dinner. Thus the plaza
is only occasionally anything more than a zone of transit. If the church and
plaza were once the founding pillar of Huaquirca, they have now become

a kind of no-man's land, and to know this town is to know its three outlying neighborhoods, their reputations, and interrelations.

Behind the church, going uphill, is the neighborhood traditionally
called Huachacayllo, now called the Barrio Alto (Upper Neighborhood).
This neighborhood is characterized by loose, rambling clusters of houses
placed almost randomly on the hillside, and connected by myriad paths.
Interspersed with the clusters of houses are areas of unoccupied hillslope,
covered with low undergrowth and eucalyptus trees, which gradually
take over completely in the upper reaches of the neighborhood.

The houses themselves are rectangular, rarely more than five by ten meters in floor area or one story, and have mud brick walls broken only by a
low framed wooden door, secured with a padlock when the residents are
not in. Of the seventy five houses in this neighborhood, there were equal
numbers with thatch, tile, and tin roofs during the period 1981–3. Of these
roof materials, thatch, which is locally available, is the cheapest and least
prestigious, followed by tile, which comes from the neighboring town of
Matara, and then tin, which can only be obtained from the city, and at
greater cost, but also with greater prestige. The privacy of the house relative to the exterior world is not generally carried over into further internal
partitioning: most houses in this neighborhood consist of one large open
room. The only public building in Huachacayllo is a small, tin-roofed chapel used in the Christmas rituals. The two shops that sell cane alcohol and
coca leaves are rarely open, since their owners are primarily agriculturalists.

Only commoners live in Huachacayllo, and it is unusual to hear Spanish
spoken in the neighborhood. As a result, it is commonly presented as the
"most Indian" of Huaquirca's three neighborhoods by those who live in
the other two. Since Huachaca is one of the dominant surnames in the
neighborhood, people often speculate that in the precolumbian past, there
was an elder *kuraka* named Huachaca who led his people (*ayllu*) to the site
in question and settled them there, thus creating Huachacayllo. There is
every reason to believe that this neighborhood, and particularly its name,
are considerably more recent than this, and prevailing local notions to the
contrary serve only to posit the precolumbian, and hence "Indian" ances-
try of its inhabitants.[7]

Huachacayllo residents have also been described as *"punáticos"* (residents of the alpine zone, herders) by a native of Huaquirca (Centeno Zela
1949: 5). There is a grain of truth in this, since people from the *puna* have,
in a few cases, come down to live in this neighborhood. Nonetheless, the
residents of Huachacayllo, and the vast majority of their ancestors, have
never been anything other than agriculturalists. Since most valley people
consider those who live in the *puna* to be less civilized and more "Indian"
than themselves, the attribution of a pastoral background to the residents

of Huachacayllo is little more than another way of asserting their "Indianness." The modern alternative designation of the area as the Upper Neighborhood also promotes this association with the *puna* by singling out elevation as its most salient feature.

The neighborhood of Champine borders on both the plaza and Huachacayllo, but is much less sprawling than the latter, even though it has the same number of houses. The density of settlement in Champine is much greater than in Huachacayllo, and leaves few open areas of natural vegetation. In some areas, houses are even oriented parallel to each other in a semi-grid pattern. Approximately forty of the houses in Champine have tin roofs, with the remaining thirty five split equally between tile and thatch. There are several two story houses, and many more that are divided into two or more rooms. Most houses still share a common yard with others, but in contrast to Huachacayllo, most of these yards are at least partly enclosed by dry stone or mud brick walls. Champine has no shops, but does include the town's graveyard, its bull ring, kindergarten, and a medical post which has never been opened, because the state has been unable to persuade competent personnel to work there.

Champine is also inhabited exclusively by commoners, but is not as poor a neighborhood as Huachacayllo, as the greater proportion of tin roofs and two story houses suggests. This difference is further reflected in the clothes of its inhabitants, which are predominantly store-bought, not homespun or endlessly repaired cast-offs. Once again, Quechua is spoken in the home, and only rarely is Spanish heard on the street, even though most inhabitants are quite able to speak it. The same pattern of daily activity found in Huachacayllo also prevails in Champine, since its residents are all agriculturalists. Yet the neighborhood has a significantly different feel to it. In part, this is due to the concentration of the Aiquipa family in Champine. The Aiquipas appear to have been precolumbian rulers (*kurakas*) in the area, and were retained in this capacity by the Spaniards throughout the colonial period, for which they were granted title to a large extension of terraced land just upstream from Champine by an official named Zola y Castillo in the 18th century (Tamayo 1947: 58). Modern inhabitants of Huaquirca universally consider Champine to be the oldest of the town's three neighborhoods. This is because it contains the archaeological remains from which the church is said to have been constructed, and because it is home to the Aiquipa family, with their illustrious past.[8]

Ñapaña, or the Lower Neighborhood, is the only one of Huaquirca's three barrios to be laid out on a grid pattern. Its parallel and perpendicular streets are usually accompanied by cement sidewalks, drainage ditches, and streetlights, and form an orderly public matrix into which rectangular house compounds, separated from the street by high mud brick walls or two story buildings, aggregate in blocks. Ñapaña is generally thought of as the neighborhood of the notables or *mistis*, even though they account for only twenty of its sixty households. In fact some of the town's poorest commoners also live in this neighborhood. But because it has been so thoroughly shaped by the fortress-like house compounds of the notables, and because the latter refuse to live anywhere else in town, Ñapaña effectively is a *misti* neighborhood. There can be little doubt that this grid pattern is a physical reflection of notable dominance, whether or not we join Flores (1973:46; 1974:184) and Brush (1977:26) in seeing such grid patterning more abstractly as one of the cultural traits that defines the "ethnic" identity of the Andean *mestizo*.

The heightened formal separation of public from private space in Ñapaña gives the streets over to a restricted but regular set of activities. Children play in the dirt and on the sidewalks. It is here that notable children now learn Quechua, since Spanish has become the language of the home in the past two or three generations. Groups of notable men congregate on the corners to talk in the morning, while commoners willing to work for a day's food and drink stand by with their tools. Notable women wearing single-layered skirts or pants bustle by in straw hats that cover their short, unbraided hair. Since Huaquirca's two schools are located in Ñapaña, there is also a routine movement of children and teachers through the neighborhood during the day. The teachers can be distinguished from other notables and well dressed commoners by the fact that they do not wear hats to work.

The portals (*puertas de calle*) through which one passes from the street into a house compound in Ñapaña are made of heavy eucalyptus wood that can be bolted shut from the inside, or padlocked from the outside: people who wish to enter knock or call out first. From the portal, the compound opens out onto a yard (*kancha*) that is usually covered with flagstones, and equipped with a deep cement sink and tap with running water. Here clothes may dry on lines, relatively safe from theft. The yard is also a general work area and zone of transit among the various rooms or semi-independent outbuildings arranged along the periphery of the compound's four walls. None of these rooms are directly connected to each other by means of internal doors; to pass from one to the other means to pass through the yard onto which all doors face, with their respective padlocks. The walls which separate one compound from another include niches for chickens to roost and lay eggs in, safe from theft. During my stay in Ñapaña, one of the few remaining yards still shared by more than one household was partitioned when one family decided that it was losing animals due to the existing arrangement. The protection of property therefore does appear to be an important factor in the enclosed, four square layout of Ñapaña, and this is partly confirmed by the breakdown of the grid pattern on certain peripheral areas of the neighborhood inhab-

ited by commoners. Some poor commoners who dress as raggedly as anyone in Huachacayllo, and who have very little property to protect, nonetheless inhabit the enclosed interstices between notable compounds.
Conversely, there are some relatively wealthy commoners living in
Champine, where no real compounds exist. What most distinguishes the
notables is not their property consciousness (since everybody at least
locks the door to their house) but their almost fanatical spatial segregation
of activities within the compound (cf. Stein 1961: 70).

The multiplicity of functionally specialized rooms in the notable house
compound effectively sorts life into an implicit folk dichotomy of the instrumental and the expressive. The kitchen, larder, storerooms, and yard
are where one deals with the necessities of life such as cooking, washing,
preparing for work in the fields and mending tools. This is also the sphere
in the notable house compound within which commoners move, either as
day laborers or more permanent domestic servants. An even more de-
graded space is the yard, where the dung of assorted animals sadly accu-
mulates, and must be walked through. It is here that commoners are
served their meal after a day's work on the notables' land. The bedrooms
are the only rooms used on a daily basis that begin to transcend such in-
strumentality. Here pictures of the national soccer team, naked blond
women, and far away places adorn the walls, and old newspapers and
magazines acquired in a lifetime of trips to Abancay, Cusco, Arequipa, or
Lima are stored.

Only on special occasions are the dining rooms and salons used. Like
the bedrooms, they usually have plank floors. They also feature the added
refinement of plaster walls that are painted in pastel colors, and sparsely
decorated with family portraits, calendars, religious and political iconog-
raphy. These rooms exist to stage banquets in honor of a fiesta or the visit
of a relative from the city. In order to acknowledge the significance of
these gatherings, the assembled notables may engage in their characteristically florid style of formal public speaking, but the success of the function is measured by whether people forget their mundane cares and
squabbles with each other in the struggle for local power, by getting
drunk, making music, and telling stories of bygone days. The banquet is
in many ways the quintessential expression of what it means to be *gente
culta* (a refined person) in Huaquirca. Conversation takes place in Spanish, but Quechua is used in occasional witticisms, and to convey orders to
the servants who, as a rule, are the only commoners allowed to enter these
rooms.

Once again, it is not so much raw quantity of wealth that separates notables from commoners as the aesthetic of segregation and refinement
through which they enjoy it. What makes a banquet in Ñapaña different
from the drunken aftermath of a work party in a single room, all purpose

dwelling of Huachacayllo is above all the meticulousness with which it is isolated from other moments of life. These contrasting emphases on separation and integration inform the sense of motivated opposition that exists between Ñapaña and Huachacayllo, and was expressed when they were renamed as Lower Neighborhood and Upper Neighborhood, respectively. In other Andean towns, notables tend to gravitate toward the "civilized center" of church and plaza in concentric opposition to a periphery of commoners.[9] But in Huaquirca, class opposition is spatially expressed through a contrast of civilized valley life to the barbarity of the *puna*. For notables, the contrast between low and high is a simple matter of racial opposition between the *mestizo* and the Indian, whereas for commoners, what makes valley life civilized is the intensive agricultural cooperation of *ayni*, which they find so deplorably lacking in the social life of alpine herders. While residents of Huachacayllo still manage to distinguish themselves from the *"punáticos"* they are sometimes identified with, and can be particularly vociferous in berating the notables of Ñapaña as *q'ala mistis* (naked *mestizos*) for their externality to the moral universe of agricultural cooperation, their neighborhood is inescapably stigmatized, even in their own eyes.

The domestic economies of notables and commoners link these residential areas to various kinds of agrarian property that I will now describe. We will see that the fields and pastures of Huaquirca are also marked by the contrasting emphases on segregation and integration just described, and that these class-laden spatial aesthetics continue to underwrite local notions of race. *spatiality & stigma*

Enclosures Real and Imagined

All of the households whose living space has just been described depend on access to fields and pastures. Not only are there different tenures and modes of transmitting them for different zones of the mountainside, but there are alternative and even contradictory definitions of property in each zone. Local notions of property regularly conflict because they are elaborated through two different frameworks of meaning, one of which is grounded in the class position of the notables, and the other in that of the commoners (cf. Thompson 1975: 261).

Land holdings in the terraced valley or *qheshwa* zone below town are crucial to the independent existence of a household not only because they provide maize and beans as staples, but also the raw material for corn beer, without which it would be impossible for a household to sponsor the work parties that are so basic to interaction as a social unit. All but a few of the viable households in Huaquirca possess between 0.67 and 0.75 ha. of valley land, usually distributed among two to five parcels in different locations. Whether the produce from this land in a normal year is adequate for domestic consumption depends on the success of the complementary potato harvest, monetary income, and of course, family size. Thus there is a considerable range in the standard of living of households owning comparable amounts of valley land. Only two households in Huaquirca own more (but in both cases, only slightly more) than one hectare of valley land. Notables have little difficulty in acquiring sufficient valley land for a viable household, whereas for many commoners it is a struggle. The fact that land is not accumulated beyond these minimal levels in Huaquirca indicates that we are dealing with only one threshold of social differentiation, effectively that between servitude and the formation of an independent household.

Rights to terraced valley land are mainly acquired through inheritance, purchase, or rental. On marriage, a couple generally receives a kind of inheritance called a *dote* or *dotación* from each parental household. When both parental households contribute property of equal value, the young couple lives neolocally, and forms a separate household. But because terraced land is rarely accumulated in excess of domestic needs, the parental households can never part with enough to establish the young couple in this regard. Thus inheritance must always be supplemented by some other mode of access to valley land, usually rental or purchase. As a result, poorer young commoners may seek servile incorporation as herders for a notable or wealthy commoner household. A particular period of service is set before the Justice of the Peace in Huaquirca. The terms include a token cash payment and a monthly supply of provisions (*qhoqaw*) to supplement whatever staples the herder may be able to produce (cf. Concha Contreras 1971: 65).[10] Several widowers and a few landless families perennially exist on the margins of the community in this condition, the latter with their older children affiliated to notable households as domestic servants. As herders, it is very difficult for a young couple to accumulate additional property to form a household of their own, and petty theft from their patrons is virtually institutionalized (cf. Stein 1961: 42, 229).[11] When notables address their herders as "*hijito*" and "*hijita*" (little son; little daughter), they accurately express the paternalistic subsumption of these servants into their domestic economy. Other commoners, who have barely enough land to form their own household, have to work in *mink'a* (that is, for a day's food and drink) for the notables in order to make provisions last. Widowers and the recently married form a disproportionate number of this group. Even in this relatively mild form, servitude thrives on the frustration of the developmental cycle of commoner domestic groups.

Although the only major use of terraced valley land in Huaquirca today is to provide a household with enough maize to exist as an independent economic unit, such land is nevertheless divided into two folk categories: land which is "private" and that which is "of the community." In local custom, individual units of "private" property are defined by stone fences which enclose them along their outer perimeter. By contrast, lands "of the community" are not individually fenced, but form large blocks of hundreds of units which share a common outer fence where they border on roads, paths, and other points of access. The distinction between these two categories of land does not pertain to agricultural use rights, in which they are identical. Both involve exclusive household rights to the produce of a given parcel of land, and both are subject to collective regulation of the timing of the harvest and sale. However these forms of enclosure do define different grazing rights to the stubble left in the fields after the harvest: "private" lands involve exclusive right, whereas lands "of the community" allow every owner's animals free range within the collective enclosure. These rights and restrictions are wholly without foundation in national law, but represent instead the outcome of struggle and negotiation over "customary" practice.

Notables were the driving force behind the creation of "private" land on the terraces, and this imparts a class significance to these folk categories of property. "Private" land is concentrated in the areas known as Pomache and Qochawaña, where most notable holdings are located, and also characterizes Lucrepampa, owned in its entirety by various Aiquipa households. However, it may occur in an isolated fashion anywhere a notable owns property in sectors of communally enclosed land. There appears to be no restriction on the enclosure of land: several notables told me that one simply builds a fence around one's parcel and calls it "private."

It seems that the aesthetic of separation that governs the notable house compound is also at work in the fields. But in the context of the fields, commoners find these statements of separation much more threatening, and several told me of how their older relatives had been forcibly dispossessed of particularly choice parcels of valley land by notables, who proceeded to enclose them on a "private" basis. It is as if these fences were a particularly sharp reminder of the injustices by which the land was taken, and an ongoing threat of further attacks. Commoners find enclosure threatening because it negates reciprocal labor (*ayni*) as a method of recognizing property rights. On unenclosed parcels of land that are "of the community" the proprietary rights of individual households are every bit as strong as they are on enclosed "private" lands, but they are recognized through the conventions of the agricultural work party. To sponsor such a work party, and distribute food and drink to guest workers, is to assume the role of proprietor. Conversely, to attend such a work party as a laborer, and accept food and drink from the hosts, is to recognize them as

proprietors. Therefore the institution of the work party constantly recon-
firms the property rights of individual households, and for commoners,
no further public statement of ownership is required. To claim ownership
through enclosure, then, is to deny that the work party is an adequate vehicle for claiming and recognizing property rights. "Private" enclosure ig-
nores and even negates an entire quasi-legal framework of meaning and
right that is built up by commoners through the culture of the work party.
Commoners therefore describe enclosure as a kind of aggression, something which is tantamount to lawlessness, and an integral part of the theft
of their lands. As we move out of the valley into the alpine zone (*puna*), the
link between enclosure and dispossession, familiar to us from European
history, comes to the fore, and reflects back on the significance of the entire notable aesthetic of spatial use.

All of Huaquirca's households also have access to land in the rotating
fallow fields, or *laymis*, which serve for the cultivation of potatoes, *quinua*,
wheat and barley, and are located above the town, between 3800 and 4200
m. above sea level. There are four *laymi* systems within the territory of
Huaquirca, one large one immediately above town, and three small ones
that are used mainly by the pastoralists in the lower reaches of the *puna*
(Fig. 5.3). For both valley agriculturalists and alpine pastoralists, cultivation of these fields supplements their main source of livelihood. Each
household is entitled to a plot (*chaqmana*) in every *laymi* sector. Once assigned, plots are generally used by a household until its dissolution, at
which point they will be reassigned by the president of the Peasant Community of Huaquirca. At current population levels, land is not scarce in
the *laymis* (cf. Skar 1982: 157), and any given sector under cultivation has
less than half of its total area open. This situation has probably prevailed
only since the 1950's, when a grass with a tough creeping root known as
grama or *kikuyu* was introduced as a miracle fodder. Among its many di-
sastrous consequences for Andean agriculture, this grass has made increasingly difficult the opening of new plots in fallow sectors (see
Montoya, Silveira and Lindoso 1979: 41; Montoya 1980: 305–7; Skar 1982:
155–6). As a result, there is now extra land available in the *laymis* for anyone willing to put in the extra effort to cultivate it. The fact that in both
years that I spent in Huaquirca, people ran out of products from this zone
four months before the harvest was due, and were missing them severely,
is perhaps the best indication of how this grass has reduced the agricultural use of the lower *puna*.

The *kikuyu* grass disaster was the unintended result of certain *hacendados*' preoccupation with cattle raising in the departments of Apurímac and
Cusco (Montoya 1980: 305). Its devastating effect on *laymi* cultivation is
part of a larger conflict between agricultural and pastoral uses of the
lower *puna*, one which constantly pits notables against commoners. As

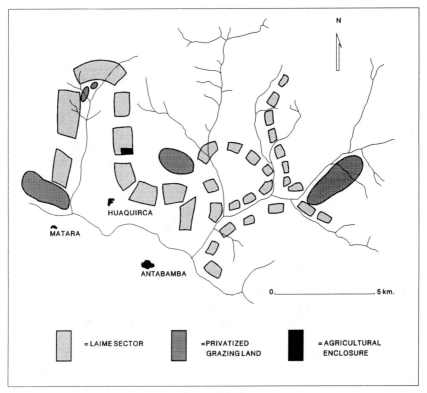

FIGURE 5.3   Agricultural and pastoral uses of the lower puna.

one commoner ruefully remarked to me, "this grass is the worst *gamonal*
we have here." Another area of conflict is the encroachment of cattle on
the unenclosed *laymis* from adjacent fallow sectors. To prevent this,
guardians (*kamayoq*) for each sector under cultivation are appointed from
within the community each year. They live in a hut among the fields from
December to June, keeping cattle out. Animals caught grazing in plots under crop are impounded until their owners pay a fine. However necessary
and reasonable such a system may seem, owners of impounded cattle
rarely pay without a struggle. During my stay in Huaquirca, a notable of
the old school, then in his seventies, even went so far as to attack the
kamayoq with a machete for impounding his cattle. While the fine was well
within the notable's means, he was furious that others' crops should take
precedence over his animals.

Between 1920 and 1940, notables with similar attitudes appropriated
large tracts of land for grazing in some smaller and more distant *laymis* in
the alpine zone (see Figure 5.3). The three notable households in
Huaquirca with the most cattle (two with over one hundred head, one

with over eighty) all appropriated estates of twenty to fifty hectares from what had previously been *laymi* land subject to communal tenure. Commoners still tell of how these lands used to be cultivated, and of the cruelty with which particular notables seized land that was under crop, and put their cattle out to feed on it. In one such case, the commoner family most affected by this dispossession began to steal livestock from other people in the vicinity as its preferred means of livelihood. Many speculate that the notable family who took their land is now their partner in crime, selling the animals which they so artfully pilfer from their neighbors. In this way, notables' seizure of *laymi* land was more than an isolated act of aggression against communal right. Rather, it was the prelude to a more constant and enduring pattern of theft.

Other notable families carved relatively small grazing territories—sufficient to sustain only fifteen cattle—out of *laymi* land.[12] In one case, they partially enclosed their privatized estate, but appear to have lost enthusiasm for the task before it was completed. Once again we see that enclosure is less a functional correlate of wealth than it is a particular strategy for pursuing it, one that is based on a violation of that which is "of the community." Some less aggressive notables have herds as large as sixty head, but still use temporary grazing sites on *laymi* land and respect communal tenure there.

Yet another pattern of land use prevails in the high *puna* above the *laymis*, where pastoralists herd llamas, alpacas, and sheep from dispersed settlements. These people form a separate group from the commoners of the valley, who will not intermarry with them out of a feeling that they are "more Indian" (Concha Contreras 1971: 22, 27). Each household of pastoralists is centered on a principal residence called an *estancia* (ranch) or *hatun wasi* (large house), which includes several corrals and exclusive right to a grazing territory around it, usually including a swamp. The tendency for clusters of adjacent *estancias* to be owned by people of the same surname is due to the predominance of virilocality tied to a transmission of rights to this land through the male line (Palacios Ríos 1977: 77), although uxorilocal and neolocal residence may occur in conjunction with different forms of transmission (Concha Contreras 1971: 23). In addition, each household must have access to a supplementary grazing area that is generally used in the rainy season, when natural pasture is most abundant. These supplementary territories are marked by smaller houses known as *cabañas* or *hastanas*, and access to them is generally regulated in a more flexible, bilateral manner than the principal estates.

Valley people say that pastoralists are "more Indian" than themselves because they lack nucleated settlements and have a propensity to become curers, oracles, or rainmakers. This stereotype also includes the widely held notion that pastoralists are so far removed from mainstream Peru that they have little need or understanding of money, and bury it under the floors of their huts out of pure avarice or ignorance. The reality is that the pastoral economy is far more completely monetized than is that of the valley. Pastoralists receive a significant income from the sale of alpaca and sheep wool, and have long used their llamas as pack animals for a share of the maize harvest in valley towns, and in very profitable combinations of trade and barter over long distances (Concha Contreras 1971 & 1975; Custred 1974). This did not escape the notice of notables in Huaquirca and other towns of the upper Antabamba Valley, who began to acquire *estancias* in the high *puna* from the 1920s onward. The wool that they sheared from their animals in February, along with any they managed to seize from neighboring commoners, underwrote a whole cycle of mule- teer commerce that was almost certainly inspired by the llama herders of the *puna*. In April, they set out with their wool on the month-long return trip to Arequipa, coming home with their mules laden with books, wines, hardware, and even sewing machines: the commodities that defined the civilized life. Any remaining cash would be used to initiate a new round of commerce after the harvest in June. Apples and chili peppers would be obtained in a trip to the coastal valleys and brought back to the Antabamba Valley, along with the finest wines from foreign lands, which the notables were proud to serve each other in those days. The journey continued to Cusco where the chili peppers were sold. The profits were used to buy coca leaves in the high jungle of the Province of La Concep- ción in Cusco. The muleteers would then take the coca back to the Antabamba Valley, or, in some cases, continue on to the town of Coracora in Parinacochas (Department of Ayacucho). By the 1950's, wool-buyers had arrived in the Antabamba Valley as a result of the completion of the Lima-Cusco highway in 1942. This sent the commercial activities of the notables into decline, since there was now a more convenient means of selling their wool, and obtaining the commodities they desired. Nonethe- less, there is considerable nostalgia among the notables for the passing of muleteer commerce, for in it they actively immersed themselves in both metropolitan refinement and the myths and rituals of the *puna*. This al- lowed them to be at once more "White" *and* more authentically "Indian" than valley commoners, and to portray themselves as the bearers of a dis- tinctively "*mestizo*" subculture that made them privileged mediators be- tween two worlds.

Such nostalgia aside, the high *puna* land associated with Huaquirca was, by all accounts, the scene of some brutal dispossessions and enclo- sures during the 1940s and 1950s. Not only were notables from town in- volved, but those from other towns in the upper Antabamba Valley were also trying to acquire some of the excellent grazing land there. One con- temporary account (Tamayo 1947: 58–63) portrays the enclosure of small estates in the *puna* as a precedent for the creation of "private" enclosure of terraced valley land, in a generalized scramble for rights to grazing land of any sort. In the early 1940s, the neighboring town of Sabayno began to press a claim to some land in the principal *laymi* circuit above Huaquirca, putting additional pressure on a collective resource already being eroded from within. In those days, Huaquirca was still an annex of the District of Sabayno, and somewhat subordinate to it politically. By incorporating themselves as a *Comunidad Indígena* (an institution to be described below), the residents of Sabayno hoped to extend the traditional boundaries of their land at Huaquirca's expense. In order to meet this threat, both commoners and notables took to their horses and staged a highly theatrical tour of Huaquirca's boundaries, confronting a similar party from Sabayno in the process. This spurred the residents of Huaquirca to break away from the administrative jurisdiction of the District of Sabayno, and form a separate District of Huaquirca in 1945. The process of *distritalización* has rightly been linked to the notable quest for power at the local level, since it involves the creation of new political posts and patronage opportunities (Orlove 1980: 120). In this case, however, it had the additional effect of settling the boundary dispute with Sabayno in favour of Huaquirca, and halted the expropriation of pasture land within its territory by notables living in other towns of the valley.[13]

When the creation of a separate District of Huaquirca proved insufficient to curb the landgrabbing of the notables still residing in Huaquirca during the 1950s, commoners organized to register the entire territory as a *Comunidad Indígena* in 1957, under legislation meant to curb the illicit appropriation of land. Legally this made all but a small proportion of land with title predating 1920 (mainly that held by the Aiquipas) corporate property of the *Comunidad Indígena de Huaquirca*, and should, in theory, have ended the inheritance, sale, and rental of such land. In reality, it was and still is impossible to enforce this law.[14] Yet the commoners' demonstrated ability to recur to the law stopped the notables from expropriating any more land, and thus stabilized local communal tenure without in any way jeopardizing the exclusive and alienable right to the most central resources of both valley and alpine economies.

A final burst of political activity occurred in 1960, when many of Huaquirca's commoners joined in the land occupation movement that was sweeping all of southern Peru. Elsewhere, these land occupations aimed to recuperate lands illegally appropriated by neighboring *haciendas*. In Huaquirca, however, the occupations were directed at the "private" terraced valley holdings of the Aiquipa family in Lucrepampa, which were apparently being enclosed and possibly enlarged at the time. By enclosing their land, the Aiquipas violated the notion of "communal" property that was sacrosanct to other commoners, and reiterated their claim to be something of a native aristocracy. This, along with the fact that land scarcity was reaching a peak in the late 1950's, made the Aiquipas, and not the local notables, the primary targets of the movement. It seems that some of their lands were not being cultivated, and were occupied by needy commoner families. I came to know the principal leader of that movement, the only commoner who held political office (as a United Left alderman) during my stay in Huaquirca. He told me how the police had come in, and took him to jail in Abancay for two months. This intimidated other commoners, and the movement quickly fell apart.

From the foregoing, it is clear that agrarian property rights in Huaquirca have been continuously renegotiated in an atmosphere of struggle and legal pluralism, in which no one perspective has been entirely dominant. However I do not join Smith (1989) in his contention that such struggles amount to a series of opportunistic economic claims advanced through arbitrary and ephemeral cultural vehicles. In Huaquirca, the basic issue was whether property rights were to be recognized through work parties on unenclosed land, according to commoner practice of *ayni*, or whether they would be proclaimed through enclosure, as the notables and Aiquipas did. Both work parties and the folk classification of land based on enclosure have a long genealogy in Andean culture, and cannot be dismissed as *ad hoc* constructs. They are the focus of moral and legal sensibilities that have built up over time, and to deny this is to deny the tenacity of commoner resistance, among other things.

Perhaps the surest indication that property concepts in Huaquirca are categorical, and not improvisational, is that they occasionally override empirical observation. There can be no doubt, for example, that the alpine pastoralists above Huaquirca have exclusive and alienable right to their grazing territories. Yet valley commoners would regularly insist to me that these lands are "of the community," presumably because they were unfenced, and because (in their experience) only notables would attempt to assert exclusive rights to grazing land. Similarly, when discussing the notables' dispossession of certain pastoralists, or their appropriation of *laymi* land, valley commoners would insist that the notables proceeded to enclose the land in question, although often I later discovered that it remained unfenced. Once again, it appears that we are dealing with a categorical imperative: land that is somehow no longer "of the community" is by definition enclosed.

Spanish customary land tenure is the source of the folk distinction between "private" and "communal" land in Huaquirca. Identical categories of land are defined by enclosure and grazing rights to the harvest stubble in the Province of Zamorra, from which many of the *conquistadores* came (Arguedas 1968: 33–9). In the New World it was colonial policy to promote communal grazing rights to agricultural stubble and uncultivated areas, and to forbid enclosure of the latter, according to ancient Castilian practice (Chevalier 1963: 86–8). Iberian land tenure patterns took hold and persisted in Huaquirca, perhaps because of the unusually high number of poor Spaniards who settled the area as peasants during the colonial period (see Mörner 1978: 29). However there is fragmentary evidence to suggest that similar patterns are widespread throughout the southern Peruvian Andes.[15] It is ironic that the commoners of Huaquirca are so faithful to Spanish land tenure customs, despite the "Indian" ethnicity that is attributed to them.[16]

More significant still, however, are the notables' deviations from these property customs. While they undoubtedly gained considerable economic benefits from appropriating large areas of pasture land, these benefits alone are insufficient to explain enclosure, particularly in the valley. As Arguedas (1968: 38, 258) argues, generalized access to pastures favors those with the most livestock. Therefore it was economically irrational of the notables to enclose their terraced valley land to gain exclusive grazing rights to its stubble. The same could also be said of the enormous effort it would take to enclose a large grazing territory to protect it from the insignificant amounts of fodder that might be lost through the occasional encroachment of other peoples' animals in a zone where exclusive right is recognized. These costs are why, despite prevailing notions to the contrary, most notables have not in fact bothered to enclose their alpine lands. In short, enclosure does not make sense except as a costly statement of separation from that which is "of the community," or in the case of appropriated *laymi* land, as wilful public violation of communal right, both of which define notable identity in a negative and transgressive manner. Thus, enclosure could be seen as a continuation of the notables' refusal of *ayni*, the generalized exchange of labor, food, and drink across household boundaries, by which commoners implicitly affirm each other's property rights. To proclaim one's property rights through enclosure is to deny the efficacy of this labor theory of property, and thus to threaten the rights claimed through it. By their own testimony, the notables frequently made good on this threat. Notable property holdings presuppose servitude not simply because they are too extensive to be attended solely by the labor of their owners, but primarily because they are claimed through a kind of semiotic aggression against the framework of meaning and right which inheres to all that is "of the community."

The Local State and the Domestication
of the *Gamonales*

The notables of Huaquirca carried out all of the expropriations and enclosures described above as acts of personal force, and did not resort to the courts or police to enforce their will. No self-respecting *gamonal* would call the police in to clear his land of a few commoners, as the Aiquipas did in 1960. Notable class power was not dependent on the institutional power of the state, but rather its absence. For example, Huaquirca commoners who ran afoul of a prominent notable could expect incarceration, a public flogging, or an informally administered beating, with little chance of recourse to a higher level of justice, much as certain *hacendados* in other areas of Peru would mutilate peasants who failed to kneel before them (Arguedas 1968: 336; Favre 1970: 130). Other "abuses" for which the notables of Huaquirca were famous included outright seizures of wool, animals, and land, and the forced recruitment of domestic servants and day laborers to work their personal holdings. To be sure, it was as governor, mayor, or justice of the peace that the most "abusive" of Huaquirca's notables committed their most notorious acts of *gamonalismo*. However in occupying these offices, Huaquirca's *gamonales* expected little institutional support for their illegal activities, only a safeguard against prosecution for them. By strengthening the local state, and creating direct links to the central state that evaded notable mediation, the commoner political mobilizations of 1945–60 sent the *gamonales* of Huaquirca into decline.

Yet the fact that I could witness some of these "abuses" still taking place in 1981–3 demonstrates that *gamonalismo* is not an entirely spent force. That it has little to do with holding office became clear to me when I asked a commoner why he was working in *mink'a* for a notable who had just been defeated in elections for mayor, when he knew full well that the favor would never be reciprocated. The reply was: "We work for don Julio because he is a boss." This statement expresses precisely the kind of power that the *gamonales* tried to establish, a power that was inherent to their personal identities, and would make them bosses even when not holding office. While notables continue to monopolize the district level of government throughout the southern highlands, this is a result of their informally constituted power as a class, and not its cause, as some have claimed (e.g. Orlove 1980: 113, 125).

This sort of local rule was in many ways parallel to the existence of the *hacienda*: sometimes its source, sometimes a necessary condition of its existence, and other times, its direct competitor. Certainly the fact that so many *haciendas* were founded or enlarged upon the illegal appropriation of land can only be understood against the background of such a weak state, which in turn was promoted by the lawlessness of the powerful (cf. Hobsbawm 1974: 124–6; Mariátegui 1971: 23). It may be technically correct to insist on the distinction between local "elites" and *hacendados* (Orlove 1980: 113, 126), but to do so implies an overly rigid separation of property from sovereignty in a situation in which *haciendas* were run like fiefdoms beyond the law, and the local state was run like an *hacienda* (Mariátegui

1971: 62–3). Much more fundamental is how the unity of property and sovereignty under *gamonalismo* was constituted by the violation of that which is "of the community" and "Indian," in a constant reenactment of the myth of the conquest.

Gamonal violence has long been an embarrassment to metropolitan Peru, and several governments have tried to curb it. In 1920, the Leguía regime offered legal recognition (and in 1925, registration) of communal land to protect it from the sort of *gamonal* predation described above. This legislation was part of a constitutional package which also introduced *conscripción vial*, a labor draft for road construction which was intended to modernize the Andean highlands (Grondín 1978: 54–5). Although road conscription was supposed to be a universal civic obligation, it in fact applied only to "Indians" and was widely perceived as a revival of the colonial labor draft (*mita*) (Chevalier 1970: 195; Davies 1974: 82–4). This perception was accurate since, for most of the colonial period, there existed a "pact of reciprocity" whereby the state recognized communal land tenure in return for the tributary labor of commoners, then called *indios tributarios* (Fuenzalida 1970b: 224, 230–1; Grondín 1978: 21–2; Platt 1982: 40–1). While the *mita* was officially abolished in 1810, only to be reinstated and again dropped in a bewildering succession of legal forms, it never disappeared in practice.[17] Leguía's only real innovation was to link tributary labor to notions of progress and modernization. This linkage was to prove surprisingly influential and enduring. Although Leguía himself fell in 1930, and *conscripción vial* was officially discontinued after it provoked rioting and burning of files, the same practices were surreptitiously revived in order to complete the major highways through the southern Peruvian Andes during the period 1935–42 (see Montoya et. al. 1979: 36). Every subsequent government has had its own agencies and programs based on communal labor tribute. The formula, however, remains the same: the state provides materials and technical expertise, while the district officials provide the labor of commoners.

The irony of this "modernization" strategy is that it confirms commoners in a tributary status that is essentially colonial and servile. Far from undermining the working assumptions of *gamonalismo*, this "reform" effectively entrenched them. Even as the state struck out at the *gamonales*, it made use of the tributary labor they had struggled so long to preserve, and for such little thanks. But as an old *gamonal* once remarked to me: "the current sweeps away the shrimp who doesn't know how to swim." In their role as political authorities, notables adapted by renting out the tributary labor of "their" commoners to private individuals (Flores 1974: 190; Davies 1974: 13). This sort of "abuse" is arguably just an extension of the civic norm that is supposedly being transgressed, since both modern *indígenista* reformism and old fashioned *gamonalismo* regard "Indians" as providers of unpaid communal labor.

Within this basic tributary framework, a number of nuanced but important changes nonetheless occurred. Prior to the formation of the *Comunidad Campesina de Huaquirca* in 1957, there had been a colonial tradition of communal government based on eight staff-holding authorites (*varayoq*), all commoners, who recruited other commoners for communal labor parties (*faenas*), and enforced prevailing definitions of public order as an informal police. These eight functionaries were placed at the disposal of notable authorities in the following proportions: five to the governor, two to the mayor, and one to the justice of the peace. These *varayoq* recruited labor for the agricultural tasks of their notable overlords, which were included in the definition of *faena* at the time. Notable authorities were also famous for their tours through the alpine zone, during which they seized alpaca wool from each *estancia*, and sometimes commandeered domestic servants, always accompanied by their corresponding *varayoq* (cf. Montoya 1980: 258–62). In short, this system of communal authority was fully implicated in *gamonalismo*, and there are graphic accounts of the frustration that some commoners in other areas of Peru felt in being accomplices to it (e.g. Arguedas 1968: 334). With the passage of the Law of Yanaconaje in 1947, which was designed to abolish unpaid labor, the commoners of Huaquirca found a pretext to discontinue the *varayoq* system, a political triumph that can only be measured by the continuing existence of this system in areas where notables were not subject to pressure from below. Not surprisingly, older notables of Huaquirca still look back with nostalgia on the *varayoq* as a symbol of the time when commoners "still had respect."

Yet not every traditional aspect of communal government was thrown out. One post that was retained was that of the *kamayoq* who, as we have seen, guards the *laymi* sectors under cultivation from grazing cattle. Given the strategic importance of the land they guard, and the conflicts that the *kamayoqs* have had with "abusive" notables over their animals, it is clear that they serve an important collective interest. Every commoner is obliged to serve as *kamayoq* for one agricultural season at some point in his life. Another post that has been retained is that of water judge (Quechua: *unu kamayoq*; Spanish: *juez de aguas*) on each of Huaquirca's seven irrigation canals. These officials are nominated from among each canal's users annually, when they gather for the *yarqa faena* (irrigation ditch cleaning) in the second half of August. In the early 1970s, an attempt was made by a government agency to abolish this system, and replace it with one in which users would pay for irrigation water with money that would constitute wages for those who maintain the canals. This plan was vigorously and effectively resisted by the commoners of Huaquirca, who had neither the money to make such payments, nor were willing to let control of the canals pass out of their hands. The experience of other areas suggests that they were wise to refuse this proposal (e.g. Grondín 1978: 119; Montoya et. al. 1979: 77–80; Montoya 1980: 111), and that there really is an element of self-determination at stake in communal organization (Montoya 1980: 263), even if it is also enmeshed in oppression and servitude (Stein 1961: 233).

Despite pushing several commoners on the subject, I never heard one complaint about *faena* obligations. Perhaps this is because they were only amounting to about ten days per year during my stay. What seems more likely, however, is that labor tribute remains a way of maintaining, or when necessary, asserting a "pact of reciprocity" with the state concerning communal tenure (Platt 1982: 139, 145; Isbell 1978: 171). Since the state is still tacitly dependent on this tribute, it cannot completely disregard the claims made through it, even if these stop well short of those made in the traditional moral economy in which food, drink and music for the workers were part of the bargain. The main issue is the land, and the political mobilizations of the period 1945–60 show that not only did the commoners of Huaquirca perceive the state as a potential ally in the struggle to curb *gamonalismo*, but that they were actually able to make it work as such. We may therefore appreciate how the commoners of towns like Huaquirca see in *faena* something more than their institutionalized subordination to district notables (Stein 1961: 96, 188–9), or their "calculated exploitation" (Grondín 1978). Namely, they see instead an affirmation of a different kind of property and a different kind of sovereignty than that resulting from the endless depredations of the *gamonales*.

The various projects realized through *faena* in Huaquirca reflect the enhanced presence of the central state and the corresponding decline of *gamonal* domination. Schools and municipal buildings were among the first products of the central state's renewed presence in Huaquirca. Although notables controlled virtually all of the positions in the local state and education system, the strengthening of these institutions slowly eroded the personal nature of notable power as it existed in the era of unbridled *gamonalismo*. For instance, the very fact that the mayor governed from the municipal building, and not his salon, already implied a modified notion of power. Furthermore, it was in the schools that commoners first became both fluent in Spanish and literate. Everyone agrees that it was commoners with these new skills who transformed Huaquirca's political structure during the period 1945–60. While it is also true that education led many young commoners to reject the life they had known in Huaquirca and migrate to Peruvian cities, this too was an integral part of the break with *gamonalismo* (cf. Montoya 1982: 296). From the completion of the Lima-Cusco highway in 1942 to the arrival of the road in Huaquirca in 1978, local labor tribute was also used to open the hinterlands to motor transport. Although these roads have steadily drained Antabamba of its people and its wealth, they also ended its days as a "region of refuge" for *gamonales*. More recent priorities have included the installation of running water and electricity, and the construction of cement reservoirs and irrigation canals. Only the water system has actually worked, and the rest have simply absorbed materials and commoner labor without transforming local life.

Of all the changes that took place in Huaquirca since the 1940's, it was the expansion of the local education system which most transformed the nature of notable rule. Education was always highly valued as a mode of personal empowerment by notables in small Andean towns, perhaps even more so in the earlier part of this century than now (cf. Arguedas 1968: 337; Montoya et. al. 1979: 40; Montoya 1980: 304). But only since 1940 has education provided the possibility of a career in the countryside. The notables of Huaquirca were quick to capitalize on this opportunity, and proudly point to a deaf old man in their number who is the first university student ever to have come from the Province of Antabamba. Many others soon followed, and Huaquirca produced enough doctors, lawyers, judges, colonels and academics to fancy itself "the intellectual capital of the Province of Antabamba." Of course these people pursued their careers in the cities, and many lost interest in even visiting the town where they were born. Even the original university student used to insist that "Huaquirca is a garbage dump." Leaving the countryside became little short of an ideology among those who followed him into higher education, to the extent that those who return to teach school are sometimes regarded as failures.

Nonetheless, the demand for teaching posts in Huaquirca is extremely high, and it can take years to be transferred there from another town. Some speculate that it is easier to get a post in the departmental capital of Abancay than it is in Huaquirca. In contrast to many other areas, eleven of the town's thirteen teachers were born locally, and the other two married into notable families, had children, and are long-time residents. Of those notables under the age of forty at the time of my fieldwork in Huaquirca, eleven of sixteen were teachers, and every notable household of this generation included at least one teacher in its focal couple. The status of notable and occupation of teacher have all but converged, and this creates a powerful lobby for the expansion of education (cf. Primov 1980: 153; see also Paponnet-Cantat and Poole, Chapter 3, this volume). With a maximum of 220 students divided among two elementary schools, a kindergarten, and thirteen teachers (for a student/teacher ratio of no more than 17:1), the process is already well advanced. As I left Huaquirca, negotiations for a secondary school seemed to have been successfully completed. None of the notables would consider sending their own children there, despite the considerable cost of maintaining and educating them in the city, but there was great interest in who would get the teaching posts.

One important reason why the only notables left in Huaquirca are all becoming teachers is that this occupation allows them to take advantage of the significant holdings of land and livestock that they inherited from their *gamonal* parents, while also enjoying the benefits of a wage. These wages have widened the economic gap between notables and commoners considerably, but with little visible effect, since most of the money that the teachers earn goes into the education of their own children, which is often facilitated by the purchase of a home in the city. Nonetheless, refinement of the inner sanctums of the notable house compound continues. My stay in Huaquirca coincided with that of an itinerant carpenter from Abancay, who had planned to stay in the area for only six months, but decided after sixteen that he had to disappoint the still escalating notable demand for more cultivated surroundings by leaving.

A schoolteaching career provides notables with more than just the means to continue the pursuit of refinement: it also embodies in praxis the ideal of being a cultivated person. Previous generations of *gamonales* certainly aspired to this cultivation, as shown not only by the homes they built and the products they consumed, but also in their almost slavish veneration of formal education. Yet their pursuit of this goal, through a strategy of violating "the communal," ultimately gave them more notoriety than it did distinction, and thus became self-defeating. Nowadays, even older notables who did not go to university sneer at the "ignorant" *gamonales* of their parents' generation who "barely completed primary school" and therefore "governed by pure abuse." Simply put, *gamonal* violence did not embody the ideal of refinement in the way that schoolteaching now does. It is perhaps for this reason that some of my best informants on the topic of *gamonalismo* were teachers: they not only grew up with it, and lived its repudiation in a particularly intense form (which for many still involves left politics), but found other means to realize the same goals.

By the time of my fieldwork in Huaquirca, condemnation of the *gamonales* was universal and mandatory. In 1982, even the more conservative notables were outraged when the sons and nephews of an old *gamonal* publicly assaulted a wealthy commoner for allowing his prancing horse to make the old man stumble on a sidewalk in Ñapaña. Three of the offenders served sentences of a few days each in the jail of Antabamba, which would have been unthinkable in the past. However the same families, and sometimes the same individuals, were in power as before the struggles of 1945–60. The *gamonales* had been re-educated and absorbed by state reform, but not eliminated. Rather, a *modus vivendi* was reached whereby the notables renounced overt violence in return for an officially sanctioned revival of tribute in the name of progress. On balance, the only thing the *gamonales* lost in their struggle of a century and a half against local commoners and the central state was the right to proclaim their victory. However they could afford to be self-critical, or to silently drop their violent assertion of "racial" difference, since it had already been consolidated in local relations of property, tribute, employment and political power. If there has been a decline in "racial" discourse in the southern Peruvian highlands over the past few decades, it has been partial at best, and it does not mean that group boundaries and identities are breaking down, but on the contrary, that their maintenance has become less problematic.

Conclusion

Gamonal domination took a personalistic form because it was an attempt to re-impose and consolidate colonial notions of personhood in a republican context where the state was not always able or willing to enforce the old legal distinction between Indian and Spanish estates. In the countryside, notables and *hacendados* knew that their class/ethnic privileges depended on the maintenance and expansion of colonial tributary relations. Without neglecting the state, they strove above all to enforce servility in face to face interaction, through the characteristically violent style of the *gamonal*. This violence constantly recreated the bounded group identities upon which tributary relations were based, in a context where they otherwise might have disappeared. As I have argued throughout, this violence amounted to a constant imposition of a conquest model of social differentiation on local society, whereby *gamonales* endlessly rediscovered their Hispanic identity by violating "Indians." The aim of this racist discourse was not to describe existing biological, linguistic, or cultural differences, but to impose simplified tributary notions of personhood on people whose experiences and identities were far more complex. It was a transformative exercise, one whose success is to be measured by the embodied disappearance of the categories in question.

Ironically, it was in their ostensible defeat by an alliance of commoners and the central state that the *gamonales* achieved their most definitive victory: the consolidation of the tributary bond between community and state. That this tributary bond was renovated to bring civilization and order to the hinterlands was better still. Within less than a generation, notables transformed themselves from retrograde *gamonales* to progressive schoolteachers and political authorities in the struggle for modernization. In the process, they not only held the material gains of the *gamonal* past, they also secured the cultivation and distinction which had previously eluded them. However their greatest triumph lay not in this personal transformation, but in the redefinition of "modernization" to incorporate colonial servitude. As a result, we may never know if the *gamonal* era is really over.

Notes

1. See Fuenzalida (1970a), Mayer (1970), Ossio (1978), and van den Berghe and Primov (1977).

2. A woman from Antabamba told me a fairy tale that illustrates these points about race. It seems that a European refugee couple arrived in Lima after the Second World War, and the man found employment with a wealthy Limeño family. The woman was pregnant, and gave birth in the Hospital del Empleado, in the same ward as a black woman. The father of the black woman's child said that he would marry her if she gave birth to a son, but it turned out to be a daughter. Meanwhile, the European woman gave birth to a son, so the black woman bribed a nurse to switch babies. The European couple were despondent, and appealed to their wealthy employer, who agreed to retrieve the son provided he could keep him. So they had a doctor perform a blood test. The blood of the black parents and child was dark and thick, and would not mix with the Europeans' blood, which was thin and red. Within races, however, the blood of parents and their children mixed freely, thus proving relations of kinship. So the little blond boy went to the wealthy family, who in return gave the European couple a beautiful house, and the man a cushy job in the state bureaucracy.

3. For discussions of *ayni* in other regions of the Peruvian Andes, see Stein (1961: 227), Nuñez del Prado and Bonino Nievez (1969: 59–60), Flores (1974: 189), Isbell (1978: 73), Ossio (1978: 17), Montoya (1980: 202–3).

4. Fonseca (1974: 88) notes the asymmetric nature of *mink'a*, and its potentially exploitative character has been mentioned by Fonseca (1974: 91), Mayer (1974: 47), Carter (1964: 49) Malengreau (1980: 515), and Orlove (1980: 118).

5. See Stein (1961: 232), Arguedas (1968: 335), Mayer (1970: 120), Montoya Silviera and Lindoso (1979: 170), and Montoya (1980: 202).

6. See the "Expediente Sobre la Completa Desmoralización Eclesiástica en Aymaraes," 1841, Archivo Arzobispal del Cusco, and Raimondi's description of ruined churches in Totora-Oropeza (1874: 226).

7. This neighborhood is marked by a fierce rivalry between two surname groups, the Huachacas and the Pumacayllos. Perhaps the most important reason for the emergence of Barrio Alto as an alternative name for the neighborhood was that the Pumacayllos could not stand it bearing the name of their foes. A colonial census from 1689 does indeed mention an *ayllu* named after D. Martin Vachaca, a *kuraka*, but it contained only a few Huachacas within it (see Villanueva 1982: 407–8), while many others were scattered throughout the remaining 6 *ayllus* that existed in Huaquirca at that time. As late as 1826, there were no males bearing the surname Pumacayllo in Huaquirca (see "Aymaraes de Indígenas 1826," Fondo de Tesorería Fiscal, Aymaraes Doc. 1, Archivo Departamental del Cusco). In all probability, then, this rivalry whose origins many people in Huaquirca would place in time immemorial, is a development of the 19th century.

8. In the 1689 census, an Ayllo Chambini is mentioned, but did not include any Aiquipas (Villanueva 1982: 409–11), while the latter were concentrated in an *ayllu* bearing the Spanish name Guzman (Villanueva 1982: 399–401).

9. This pattern has been reported by Fuenzalida (1970a: 53), Isbell (1978: 71) Ossio (1978: 10), and Fioravanti Molinié (1978: 1188).

10. Terms varied from between S/10,000 to S/40,000 per year during my residence in Huaquirca.

11. This theft does not necessarily work against the notables in the long run, and could even be seen as part of a structural pattern that keeps herders dependent on their patrons. A particularly revealing example concerns a herder who stole and butchered a cow belonging to the mother-in-law of his patron's brother. She discovered him trying to bury the hide, and went immediately to her son-in-law's brother, who had no choice but to repay the damage. The amount, however, was used to extend the herder's period of servitude for another few years, which would in turn aggravate the motivation to steal further. Since herders are tied to a particular locality by their responsibilities, and are not professional rustlers with networks of *compadres* spanning several valleys, they cannot easily get rid of stolen animals, and are very likely to get caught. Another example concerns a young commoner who broke into a store in Huachacayllo and made off with a large tin of cane alcohol, only to pass out in the street still clutching the incriminating evidence shortly afterwards. After a few days in jail, the justice of the peace offered to pay the cost of the alcohol to the shopkeeper in return for a year of the commoner's service on his estate in the *puna*, an offer that the latter effectively could not refuse. Theft could therefore be seen as a recruitment mechanism for debt peonage. In discussing theft in this light, however, I would not want to deny notable involvement in animal rustling, which seems quite probable in certain cases in the Antabamba region, and has been reported elsewhere as a part of the overall complex of *gamonalismo* (Skar 1982: 246; Poole and Paponnet-Cantat, this volume).

12. This property is named Huaylla Huaylla, and consists of 5.15 ha. It is enclosed and irrigated by the canal bearing the same name as the estate, a highly anomalous practice on land of this altitude (4,000 m.). This estate was owned by a notable, but was part of the only expropriation of land that took place in Huaquirca during the agrarian reform of 1969–75. The land had been bought in 1944 from seven individuals, all of whom must have sold their *laymi* holdings in the sector from which the estate was carved. On being returned to communal tenure by the expropriation of 1975, this land was not reintegrated into the *laymi* system, but lay fallow until 1982, when it was effectively parcelized, each commoner receiving a minute amount of land to cultivate.

13. Huaquirca's rich pasture lands have always been coveted by notables from Antabamba in particular. Not only do a few of them still have *estancias* in the remote *puna* of Huaquirca around Mt. Supayco, but some will even turn their cattle loose in Huaquirca's communal grazing lands, and claim the right to pay the *Comunidad Campesina de Huaquirca* for access to them. While the *Comunidad* seemed to feel that this was an infringement, neither did it refuse this forced rental of its pastures, so this practice may have some customary legitimacy.

14. The most important reason why the law cannot be applied is that it assumes the existence of a communal authority with a mandate to redistribute all land un-

der its jurisdiction as if it were *laymi* land. While there are persistent rumours of communities that still have annual redistributions of land, or did until recently (e.g. Arguedas 1968: 331; Fuenzalida 1970b: 238–9; Malengreau 1980: 533–4), what is never specified is what sort of land. There are no reports which specify a communal redistribution of valley land, and without such an arrangement, rental and sale become virtually the only way of coordinating the developmental cycles of the ensemble of domestic groups in the community. To suppress the sale and rental of land in Huaquirca would also be to suppress the developmental cycle of its domestic groups, and thus, nobody has ever attempted to apply the law.

15. The general pattern of privatized valley land and communal access to the grazing lands of the *puna* has been reported by Malengreau (1974: 179) and Isbell (1978: 38), while Matos Mar (1964: 73, 119) and Ossio (1983: 46) speak of private agricultural use right in general, without distinguishing between valley and *laymi* tenure. Nonetheless, Ossio reports a similar use of enclosure to define traditional "private" property and notes that its absence in the fallow potato fields is taken as an indication of communal control (1983: 47).

16. In this regard, Fuenzalida is entirely right to argue that the archaism of the "Indian" is in fact largely an Hispanic archaism (1970a: 71). Furthermore, one could suggest that modern Andean "Indians" are in this sense closer to the Iberian peasantry than to their precolumbian ancestors (Stein 1961: 12), a point developed at length by Arguedas (1968) in a provocative study that subsequent "ethnicity" theory has been compelled to ignore.

17. See Davies (1974), Stein (1961: 189–90), Fuenzalida (1970b: 230), and Isbell (1978: 171).

Bibliography

Arguedas, J.M. 1968. *Las Comunidades de España y del Perú*. Lima: Universidad Nacional Mayor de San Marcos.

Bourdieu, P. 1984. *Distinction: A Social Critique of the Judgement of Taste*. Cambridge Mass.: Harvard University Press.

Bourricaud, F. 1970. "Choloficación?" In Fuenzalida, F. et al. *El Indio y el Poder en el Perú*, pp. 183–198. Lima: Instituto de Estudios Peruanos.

Brush, S. 1977. *Mountain, Field and Family*. Pittsburgh: University of Pennsylvania Press.

Carter, W. 1964. *Aymara Communities and the Bolivian Agrarian Reform*. Gainesville: University of Florida Press.

Centeno Zela, A. 1949. "El Servicio del Varayoq en el Distrito de Huaquirca." Monografías de Geografía Humana 12: 31. Cusco: Archivo Departmental del Cusco.

Chevalier, F. l963. *Land and Society in Colonial Mexico*. Berkeley: University of California Press.

_____. 1970. "Official Indigenismo in Peru in 1920: Origins, Significance, and Socioeconomic Scope." In M. Mörner (ed.), *Race and Class in Latin America*, pp. 184–196. New York: Columbia University Press.

Concha Contreras, J. 1971. Los Pueblos Pastores del Sur del Perú (y las Relaciones Económicas con los Agricultores) unpublished Bachelor's thesis in Anthropology, Universidad Nacional Mayor San Antonio de Abad, Cusco.

_____. 1975. "Relación entre Pastores y Agricultores." *Allpanchis* 8: 67–101.

Custred, G. 1974. "Llameros y Comercio Interregional." In G. Alberti and E. Mayer (eds.), *Reciprocidad e Intercambio en los Andes Peruanos*, pp. 252–289. Lima: Instituto de Estudios Peruanos.

Davies, T. 1974. *Indian Integration in Peru: A Half Century of Experience, 1900–1948.* Lincoln: University of Nebraska Press.

Earls, J. 1970. "The Structure of Modern Andean Social Categories," *Steward Journal of Anthropology* 2: 69–106.

Favre, H. 1970. "Evolución y Situación de la Hacienda Tradicional de la Región de Huancavelica." In J. Matos Mar (ed.), *Hacienda, Comunidad y Campesinado en el Perú*, pp. 105–138. Lima: Instituto de Estudios Peruanos.

Fioravanti-Molinié, A. 1978. "La Communauté Aujourd'hui." *Annales ESC* 33(5-6): 1182–1196.

Flores Ochoa, J. 1973. "La Viuda y el Hijo del Soq'a Machu." *Allpanchis* 5: 45–55.

_____. 1974. "Mistis and Indians: Their Relations in a Micro-Region of Cusco." *International Journal of Comparative Sociology* 15(3-4): 182–192.

Fonseca, C. 1974. "Modalidades de la Minka." In G. Alberti and E. Mayer (eds.), *Reciprocidad e Intercambio en los Andes Peruanos*, pp. 86–109. Lima: Instituto de Estudios Peruanos.

Fuenzalida, F. 1970a. "Poder, Raza y Etnía en el Perú Contemporáneo." In Fuenzalida et. al. *El Indio y el Poder en el Perú*, pp. 15–87. Lima: Instituto de Estudios Peruanos.

_____. 1970b. "Estructura de la Comunidad de Indígenas Tradicional. Un Hipótesis de Trabajo." In J. Matos Mar (ed.), *Hacienda, Comunidad y Campesinado en el Perú*, pp. 219–263. Lima: Instituto de Estudios Peruanos.

Gow, P. 1991. *Of Mixed Blood: Kinship and History in Peruvian Amazonia.* Oxford: Oxford University Press.

Grondín, M. 1978. *Comunidad Andina: Explotación Calculada.* Santo Domingo: Unidad de Divulgación Técnica, Secretaria de Estado de Agricultura, Republica Dominicana.

Hobsbawm, E. 1974. "Peasant Land Occupations." *Past and Present* 62: 120–152.

Isbell, B.J. 1978. *To Defend Ourselves: Ecology and Ritual in an Andean Village.* Austin: University of Texas Press.

Malengreau, J. 1974. "Comuneros y Empresarios en el Intercambio." In G. Alberti and E. Mayer (eds.), *Reciprocidad e Intercambio en los Andes Peruanos*, pp. 171–205. Lima: Instituto de Estudios Peruanos.

_____. 1980. "Parientes, Compadres y Comuneros en Cusipata (Perú)." In E. Mayer and R. Bolton (eds.), *Parentesco y Matrimonio en los Andes*, pp. 493–536. Lima: Pontificia Universidad Católica del Perú, Fondo Editorial.

Mariátegui, J.C. 1971. *Seven Interpretive Essays on Peruvian Reality.* Austin: University of Texas Press.

Matos Mar, J. 1964. "La Propiedad en la Isla de Taquile." In J.M. Arguedas (ed.), *Estudios sobre la Cultura Actual del Perú*, pp. 64–142. Lima: Universidad Nacional Mayor de San Marcos.

Mayer, E. 1970. "Mestizo e Indio: El Contexto Social de las Relaciones Interétnicas." In Fuenzalida et al. *El Indio y el Poder en el Perú*, pp. 87–152. Lima: Instituto de Estudios Peruanos.

_____. 1974. "Las Reglas del Juego en la Reciprocidad Andina." In G. Alberti and E. Mayer (eds.), *Reciprocidad e Intercambio en los Andes Peruanos*, pp. 37–65. Lima: Instituto de Estudios Peruanos.

Montoya, R. 1980. *Capitalismo y No Capitalismo en el Perú: Un Estudio Histórico de su Articulación en un Eje Regional*. Lima: Mosca Azul Editores.

_____. 1982. "Identités Ethniques et Luttes Agraires dans les Andes Péruviennes." In L. Briggs et. al. *De l'Empriente à l'Emprise: Identités Andines et Logiques Paysannes*, pp. 267–300. Paris: Presses Universitaires de France/Institut Universitaire d'études du Developpement.

Montoya, R., J. Silveira and F. Lindoso. 1979. *Producción Parcelaria y Universo Ideológico: El Caso de Puquio*. Lima: Mosca Azul Editores.

Mörner, M. 1978. *Perfil de la Sociedad Rural del Cuzco a Fines de la Colonia*. Lima: Universidad del Pacífico.

Núñez del Prado, J. and M. Bonino Nievez. 1969. "Una Celebración Mestiza del Cruz-Velakuy en el Cusco." *Allpanchis* 1: 43–60.

Orlove, B. 1980. "Landlords and Officials: The Sources of Domination in Surimana and Quehue." In B. Orlove and G. Custred (eds.), *Land and Power in Latin America: Agrarian Economics and Social Process in the Andes*, pp. 113–127. New York: Holmes and Meier.

Ossio, J. 1978. "Relaciones Interétnicas y Verticalidad en los Andes." *Debates en Antropología* 2: 1–23.

_____. 1983. "La Propiedad en las Comunidades Andinas." *Allpanchis* 22: 35–59.

Palacios Ríos, F. 1977. *Hiwasaha Uywa Uywatana, Uka Uywaha Hiwasaru Uyusitu: Los Pastores Aymaras de Chichillapi*. Unpublished magisterial thesis in Social Sciences, Specialty in Anthropology, Pontificia Universidad Católica del Perú, Lima.

Platt, T. 1982. *Estado Boliviano y Ayllu Andino: Tierra y Tributo en el Norte de Potosí*. Lima: Instituto de Estudios Peruanos.

Poole, D. 1988. "Landscapes of Power in a Cattle-Rustling Culture of Southern Andean Peru." *Dialectical Anthropology* 12(3): 367–398.

Primov, G. 1980. "The Political Role of Mestizo Schoolteachers in Indian Communities." In B. Orlove and G. Custred (eds.), *Land and Power in Latin America: Agrarian Economics and Social Process in the Andes*, pp. 153–163. New York: Holmes and Meier.

Raimondi, A. 1874. *El Perú*, vol. 1. Lima: Imprenta del Estado.

Skar, H. 1982. *The Warm Valley People: Duality and Land Reform among the Quechua Indians of Highland Peru*. Oslo: Universitetsforlaget.

Starn, O. 1991. "Missing the Revolution: Anthropologists and the War in Peru." *Cultural Anthropology* 6(2): 63–91.

Stein, W. 1961. *Hualcán: Life in the Highlands of Peru*. Ithaca: Cornell University Press.

Taussig, M. 1987. *Shamanism, Colonialism, and the Wild Man. A Study in Terror and Healing*. Chicago: University of Chicago Press.

Thompson, E.P. 1975. *Whigs and Hunters*. Harmondsworth: Peregrine.

Van den Berghe, P. and G. Primov. 1977. *Inequality in the Peruvian Andes: Class and Ethnicity in Cusco*. Columbia: University of Missouri Press.

Villanueva, H. 1982. *Cuzco 1689: Economía y Sociedad en el Sur Andino*. Cusco: Centro de Estudios Rurales Andinos "Bartolomé de las Casas."

Wallis, C. 1980. "Pastores de Llamas en Cailloma (Arequipa) y Modelos Estructuralistas para la Interpretación de su Sociedad." In R. Matos (ed.), *El Hombre y la Cultura Andina*, pp. 248–257. Lima: Actas y Trabajos del III Congreso Peruano, tomo III.

6

Gamonalismo After the Challenge of Agrarian Reform: The Case of Capacmarca, Chumbivilcas (Cusco)

Christiane Paponnet-Cantat

Traditionally, the province of Chumbivilcas has been a society prone to violence over both land and labor whenever new demands arose within the national economy. Indeed, in Chumbivilcas, violence has become part of the process of accumulation which accompanied economic expansion and political integration into the Peruvian nation-state. By the late nineteenth century, a combination of minimal state representation at the provincial level and a relatively weak articulation with the international wool trade had enabled the Chumbivilcano rural landholding elite to entrench its power locally. To control the rural labor force and to prevent disruption in the productive process, these landowners relied on paternalism, the manipulation of cultural codes and the use of brute force to exercise their authority (see Poole, this volume).

By the twentieth century Chumbivilcas constituted what Cardoso (1975) would call an "unnoticed" sector in agriculture, where smallholders produce in the shadow of the dominant *hacienda* economy. Typical of the underdevelopment of the region, districts like Capacmarca exhibited an illiteracy rate of 70 percent in 1972 and an average life expectancy of 40 years with more than one fourth of the deaths occurring before the age of two (Capacmarca's Municipal Death Registrar; DNEC 1972).

By the 1950s the power of the traditional landed class (or *gamonales*) had grown increasingly precarious as Peru's socio-economic structure underwent important changes (Havens et.al. 1983). This was partly due to capitalist penetration in the countryside through greater demands for wool on the world market and increased meat consumption in the urban centers. The political legitimacy of the *gamonal* class was also being severely undermined by peasant movements spreading throughout the region over land grievances and the new system of labor relations based on cash payment (Quijano 1967; Martínez-Alier 1977; Havens et.al. 1983). In an attempt to solve the many conflicts over land and labor relations and in order to dispose of the unproductive *hacienda* system, state authorities led by General Juan Velasco Alvarado implemented the 1969 land reform decree (Law 17,716). In the sierra, this law was intended to replace traditional latifundism with cooperative production to prevent recurring peasant insurrection. Since the state had an interest in supporting commercial agriculture, priority was given to export-driven regions such as Puno where former *haciendas* were converted into state-run associative enterprises (see Rénique, this volume; Caballero 1977; Skar 1981). In areas like Chumbivilcas, which were geared to supplying food to the growing industrial sector, the reform was designed to remove the *hacienda* landowners so as to promote the development of a more efficient agricultural sector (Quijano 1971; Yambert 1989).

This chapter will examine the impact of the 1969 agrarian reform law on power relations in the smallholder region of Capacmarca. Capacmarca is a remote, subsistence-oriented district in the northernmost part of Chumbivilcas. In the mid-1960s, Capacmarca became a major center of confrontation between *campesinos* (peasants) and *gamonales*. The reform sought to halt this climate of political instability by partially fulfilling the historical aspiration of *Capacmarcaños*: It gave these peasants the right to pursue subsistence agriculture through a legally more secure regime of private property. In the following pages, I will argue that, although the reform enabled a certain degree of tenurial up-grading, it failed to dislodge local *gamonales*. After reform, these rural lords lost access to some of their land and to the free work performed by peasants attached to their estates. However, they rapidly found alternative methods to re-assert their hegemony through authoritarian modes of imposition such as rustling and the educational system.[1]

Local Class Structure and Conflict

The district of Capacmarca is located between 2,860 and 4,522 meters above sea level and covers a total of 37,988 hectares. It is characterized by semi-tropical valleys, temperate uplands and the ever present *puna*—a broad expanse of flatland above 4,000 meters in elevation. Here, the Santo Tomás River and its tributary, the Collqa River, cut deeply into the *puna* terrain creating steep canyon walls some 1,000 meters deep. Below, protected ravines known as *quebradas* contain subtropical micro-climates particularly suited for maize (the most common agricultural crop of the district), citrus fruits, peaches, and apples which grow on the surrounding slopes.

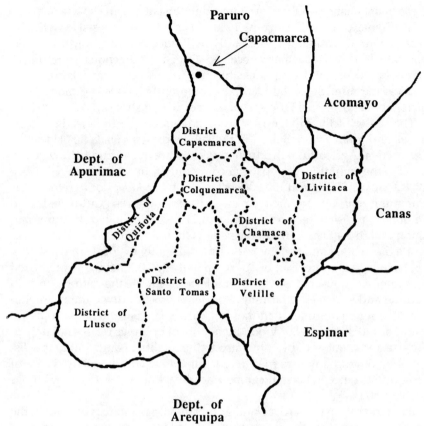

FIGURE 6.1   The province of Chumbivilcas.

As with so many other areas of the *provincias altas*, the overriding characteristic of Capacmarca is its geographic isolation (see Gade, this volume). A dirt track, usable only during the dry season, reached the area in 1986. The extreme ruggedness of the terrain, combined with sheer distance, make overland travel very difficult (usually on foot or horseback). Two routes lead to Cusco. One is a forty eight hour journey through the province of Acomayo. This requires one day on a bus and at least twelve hours of steady walking through the high plateaus. The second alternative, through Colquemarca, Velille, and Yanaoca, takes a minimum of four days of travel by truck or bus and on foot.

Some 4,370 inhabitants or approximately six percent of the overall population of the province live in the district of Capacmarca. The district consists of a central community of the same name and four others including Cancahuani, Huascabamba, Sayhua, and Tahuay. The community of

Capacmarca hangs on the mountain ridges just above the spectacular Río Santo Tomás canyon. During the 1930s, in an attempt to resist external encroachment, its residents successfully petitioned the state for official recognition. In 1938, Capacmarca received its legal "indigenous community" status based on land claims established in 1656 by Fray Domingo de Cabrera Lartaún.[2] Since the 1960s, the community has also become a "municipality" and, as such, the seat of district administration.

The center of the village is at 3,565 meters on the upper edge of the maize and grain zones. Below, in the sub-tropical *quebrada* lies Hacienda Percasenqa. Agricultural production takes place above and below the nucleus of the community—a pattern commonly found in the Andes (Isbell 1978; Orlove 1977; Urton 1984; Webster 1971). In 1968, prior to reform, the community of Capacmarca covered 10,850 hectares. Cultivated land amounted to 6,480 hectares of which 4,215 were irrigated. Pasture land amounted to 3,400 hectares in the *puna*.[3] However, much of this land was worked privately and some was occupied illegally by local landlords.

The village is comprised of approximately 1,970 inhabitants organized into some 430 households. These families concentrate their efforts on both herding and subsistence farming. Residents practice diversified exploitation at different altitudes. Landholdings are small. Several households are landless and many are landpoor. Inequality of holdings relates not only to the size and number of plots but also to the quality of land and to the distribution of crop holdings in different subzones. This inequality is not of recent occurrence; its origin can be traced back to at least colonial times (Poole 1987).

Based on the Spanish royal land grants that Capacmarca received in the seventeenth century, the community was able to recover part of its communal holdings after reform without incurring any agrarian debt. However, the precise amount of land affected by the law was still unknown in 1986; at the Ministry of Agriculture in Cusco, an official told me that cadastral surveys had yet to be completed.

Mestizo ranches and *haciendas* have long existed in this region. In 1689 the community of Capacmarca counted seven estates and two mills (Villanueva 1981:307). Later, in 1851, nineteen families owned a total of thirty six estates within the district.[4] Although no official record could be found on the exact number of *haciendas* in existence prior to the implementation of the reform, the 1972 census mentions the following: Mapay (with 35 tenant households), Percasenqa (19 tenant households), Patahuasi (13 tenant households) and, among others, Cachucalla, Chuchina, Canchura, Parcoray, Q'ehuayllo, Huascabamba, Pampa-Callanca, and Jukucha (which borders the province of Paruro).

In the fertile *quebradas*, medium-size *haciendas* predominate while peasant farms are scattered throughout the hills. The majority of these homesteads are tiny plots which are often too small to provide sufficient food-stuffs for their owners' families. Much of the available land is badly eroded and of poor quality. Generally speaking, water supply and irriga-tion systems are inadequate.

Cases of land conflict between communities and *haciendas* abound. For instance, in 1937 twenty parcels of mainly *puna* land were contested by the *comuneros* (members of a peasant community) who claimed that the peas-ant community of Capacmarca had lost them to nearby estates.[5] Sorting through the district archives, we find that peasants fought endless battles in the courts over disputed boundaries with local landlords who repeat-edly encroached on communal land. Usually, their lawsuits were to no avail. To express their frustrations, peasants had frequent recourse to acts of violence including banditry. In the latter case, it was chiefly cattle rus-tling that they practiced in order to resist exploitation by powerful land-owners. In the 1960s, local *campesinos* adopted a more political form of ac-tion which led to one of the major uprisings in southern Cusco.

The uprising originated with *comuneros* who lived independently in communities. Although these peasants provided labor services at estates held by the local elite, they were not resident workers on local *haciendas*. Land conflicts between *comuneros* and the owner of Hacienda Percasenqa had been seething below the surface for some time. The landlady, Doña Toribia Varzuelo de Ricalde, had the reputation of being a harsh person. Not only was she accused of encroaching on nearby community land, but also of demanding excessive working hours, beating and jailing peasants, and being ruthless in her market practices.[6] From the conversations that I had with local peasants in 1984, the uprising was triggered by Doña Toribia's decision to establish a wage-based system on her estate—a move which workers considered to be detrimental to their existing customary arrangements. Well aware of the unpopularity of her decision, the owner requested the help of the police to contain any possible "subversive" movement. Through her son, who was the Trial Division Judge, Doña Toribia obtained a detachment of thirteen civil guards, one sergeant and a lieutenant on her *hacienda* (*El Comercio* 1963). Their presence meant that the police were at the disposition of the landowning class; they would be ready to assist *hacendados* at any time and in any way necessary.

On October 11, 1963, an estimated five hundred *comuneros* from Capacmarca, Sayhua and Huascabamba marched to Percasenqa. Armed with only sticks and rocks, the rioters sought to take possession of the communal lands which they claimed belonged to Cancahuani. The two main leaders of the revolt were Victor Cruz from Huascabamba and Arcadio Hurtado Romero from the community of Capacmarca. Hurtado Romero, a twenty-four-year-old peasant, was the General Secretary of Peasants and became the political organizer of Capacmarca's peasantry.

He had received full support from major leftist organizations such as the Workers' Federation of Cusco (FTC), the University Federation of Cusco (FUC) and the Provincial Federation of Peasants from La Convención y Lares (FPCCL). The resulting clashes left three *comuneros* dead and some twenty five persons wounded including several policemen. After nightfall, the landlady, her sons and the police escaped by horse to Hacienda Huanso in Mara, a district of the department of Apurimac. The *feudatorios*, who were resident workers at Percasenqa, helped the owner fight off the invaders. However poor and destitute these tenants were, their dependence on the *hacienda* made it difficult for them to challenge directly the authority of the landlady. Within a few days, the insurgency was strongly suppressed when an additional 150 army troops, police reinforcements and even helicopters arrived in the district.

The uprising led to the arrest of Arcadio Hurtado Romero who was flown by helicopter to Cusco where he was sentenced to jail. After his arrest, he was interrogated by Coronel Carlos León who wanted him to provide compromising documents on other "ringleaders" such as Luis Bellota, Justo Huallpa and Belisario Santisteban. His assassination eight months after his arrest was the consequence of landowner retaliation. A financial deal had been worked out between local *gamonales* and a prison guard to plot Hurtado's killing. According to information gathered in 1984, the owner of Percasenqa gave twenty bulls. The two owners of Cachucalla (who were also Arcadio's uncles) paid S/15,000.00 (US $ 450.00). A third landlord, whose son later married the sister of Arcadio, added S/500.00 (US $ 15.00). The body of the peasant leader was never recovered by his family and, to date, nobody knows where he is buried.

This brief but bloody confrontation left local *hacendados* on their guard. Fearful of future violence, they banded together with landowners from the provinces of Canchis and Acomayo to form a regional league (Handelman 1981). Many renewed their membership in the Anti-Communist Front of Chumbivilcas which was created in 1953 and headed by the former provincial deputy to the national congress, Nicanor Berrío Márquez. They also acquired guns in case of other peasant uprisings.[7] Shortly after the rebellion, a police station was established in Capacmarca.

However, all Capacmarcaños were not united across the board. A petition dated December 5, 1963, presented by a group of *campesinos*, condemned the uprising. Their condemnation was justified by the persecutions that the signers and their families were facing. Indeed, reprisal was the *gamonales'* usual tactic of maintaining traditional power and playing peasants off against one another. Here is what the petition states:

> In order to clarify the invasion of Hacienda Percasenqa occurring on October 11 the present *comuneros* state that they had nothing to do with what hap-

pened. Notwithstanding, the police as well as the legal and political authorities commit acts of repression on ourselves and our families. … In regard to the event, it falls upon us to explain that the individual, Arcadio Hurtado, became a union member and he alone, acting under the instruction of some leaders of the FDCC [Departmental Federation of Cusco Peasants], took part in the invasion. Because he lived in our community, landowners and local authorities are using us for retaliation.[8]

The rebellion of Capacmarca was one of the most important peasant mobilizations in the province of Chumbivilcas. The seriousness of the events led the leftwing Peruvian newspaper *Voz Rebelde* (1963) to report that a civil war involving some 2,000 peasant rioters was underway in the district. This uprising focused on conflicting legal land claims and unwanted changes in payment practices. It was not meant to challenge the existing *hacienda* system. Nevertheless, it resulted in greater political organization at the regional level. For instance, in April 1964 peasant leaders managed to form a *sindicato* on Hacienda Cachucalla. This allowed tenants to buy the estate land they were occupying.[9] In Santo Tomás, the provincial peasant league was founded and named after Arcadio Hurtado Romero.

The Land Reform:
State Response to Peasant Violence

At the time when Capacmarcaños rose up *en masse* to confront *gamonalismo* similar violence was occurring throughout the highlands (Graig 1969; Mercado 1967; Blanco 1972). Peasants expressed their anger through strikes, invasions of *hacienda* lands, and insurgencies. The bloodshed that these violent confrontations generated provided an impetus for politicians to pay greater attention to the question of tenurial change at a time when 65 percent of Peru's agricultural land was owned by just 180 estates (Gitlitz 1977; Skar 1981). According to Montoya (1982), the national bourgeoisie was then forced to accept the idea of agrarian reform because of fears that resistance would lead to greater disruption of the rural class system. Clearly, this wave of peasant militancy was instrumental in the drafting and passing of a limited agrarian reform law in 1964. After General Velasco took power in 1968, it also helped put pressure on the officers in power to institute major changes if order was to prevail (Villanueva 1973; Havens et al. 1983; Rénique 1990; Montoya 1989).

In those regions where an export-driven economy previously existed, the military regime created state-run associative enterprises to promote animal husbandry through more economically rational farming practices. In Chumbivilcas, however, no associative entreprises were formed since the primary economic orientation of the province was meat for the domestic market rather than wool for agro-export (Villasante 1981).

At the provincial level, tenurial change was implemented first in the five districts nearest to the capital town of Santo Tomás and later in outlying areas such as Capacmarca which had been affected by the unrest of the 1960s (CICDA 1982). Reform initiatives did not reach the district of Capacmarca until 1976. By June 1981, the process of expropriation was stopped even though the mandate of the reform had not been completed.

Capacmarca's violent uprising in the 1960s played an important role in the implementation of a land distribution program. Within the district, several processes took place. Expropriated *haciendas* were (1) turned into communities (Tonabamba, Parcoray, Uyllullu, Q'ehuayllo), (2) occupied by peasants (Huascabamba), (3) assigned for collective use by peasant communities (Capacmarca) or (4) reduced in size and converted into "family units" under the provision of middle-sized properties (Percasenqa). Percasenqa, the *hacienda* which had experienced peasant unrest in the 1960s, was partially divided. Before reform, the *hacienda* had legally covered 1,046 hectares and had nineteen peasant families attached to the estate. In June 1981, tenants received 659.5 hectares, including 55 hectares of cropland and 570 hectares for pasture. The owners, however, were allowed to retain 387 hectares of the best land (Monje 1985:32). At the time of expropriation, the land was formally appraised at 42,577 *soles* to be paid by the beneficiaries. The owner received cash plus bonds. The total sum amounted to the equivalent of US $ 7,200.00. In 1984, one hundred and eighty hectares plus twenty seven cattle still belonging to the owner of Percasenqa were put on the market for 40 million *soles* (roughly, US $14,960.00).

Meanwhile, estates like Pataclay, Jukucha and Cachucalla were abandoned. Apparently their former owners had encroached on community lands claimed for decades by nearby villagers. The land of Jukucha was eventually sold to rich peasants, but the title to Pataclay was still being disputed in 1984 by the communities of Capacmarca and Tahuay. After reform, however, the landowner class retained control of a number of large properties including those of Mapay, Chuchina, Canchura, and Pampacallanca.

In the community of Capacmarca itself six communal *laymis*, where sectorial fallowing is practiced, were returned to Capacmarca which now has a total of twelve *laymis*. Furthermore, the community regained access to five collective parcels or 2.6 hectares of farmlands dedicated to maize and wheat cultivation. At the time of my fieldwork in 1984, these properties were being worked communally in *faenas* (collective work parties) and their surplus used to pay legal fees in ongoing suits against local landlords (Monje 1985:69).

The reform also affected four plots maintained by *cofradías* (Catholic lay associations). Prior to reform, the produce of *cofradías* went to the parish priests in the provincial capital of Santo Tomás. In 1984 the surplus generated by church lands was used to cover the cost of the annual religious *fiestas* for local patron saints. Lands belonging to the municipal council (1.80 hectares of irrigated land) have remained untouched and its surplus continues to finance administrative expenses.

Under the agrarian reform, the community received lands confiscated from the demesne of nearby *haciendas.* Soon after, these were broken up and distributed among members for private use. Usufructory land rights, found in communally supervised areas of cultivation, make such plots virtually the same as private property since they confer permanent use. In return, however, members have *corvée* labor to fulfill such as cleaning irrigation ditches, roofing the church, and building schools, roads or bridges.

Land tenure changes are difficult to evaluate. This is due in part to the peasants' failure to draw any sharp distinction between "ownership" and "land use" rights. According to my 1984 survey of 210 households (49 percent of the population), some 98 percent of the residents, or 206 households, have access to land while only four families are landless (see Table 6.1). The main result shows that tenure remains unevenly distributed and highly fragmented.

One way of determining the extent of recent land distribution is to reconstruct an approximation of the landholding pattern prior to reform. This is achieved by deducting the number of plots acquired through reform from the total number of plots to which each of the 210 families had access in 1984. Table 6.2 and Figure 6.2 show that, in recent years, a moderate decline in the concentration of holdings has occurred.

A comparison between Table 6.1 and 6.2 and Figure 6.2 show that, prior to reform, 6.5 percent (or fourteen households) were landless as opposed to the current 1.8 percent of the population. (It is possible that these landless peasants may not be members of the peasant community, and hence unable to benefit from post-reform communal land redistribution.) Table 6.2 and Figure 6.2 also show that before adjudication the majority of holders (63 percent of the surveyed population) would have had access to less than eight plots each. In 1984 we see that a certain degree of tenurial upgrading has taken place. My survey indicates that in fact 85 percent of the households sampled received an average of six parcels per family. However, the reform failed to ameliorate fragmentation since some 55 percent of these *minifundios* were divided into nine to sixteen parcels. In fact, the law proved to be a catalyst for the further subdivision of tiny holdings varying between one sixth to one third of a hectare each.[10] Thus, plot size has remained a major problem. In 1984, only 7 percent of the sampled population had parcels between 5 and 7.5 hectares. Some 87 percent of the

TABLE 6.1 Number of Plots by Household and by Percentage of Households, 1984

Number of Plots[a]	0	1–4	5–8	9–12	13–16	17–20	21–24	25–30	31+	Total
Number of households	4	12	45	54	60	20	6	6	3	210
Percentage	1.8	5.7	21.4	25.9	28.7	9.5	2.8	2.8	1.4	100

[a]The plots are "operated" rather than "owned" as individual access to land is determined as much through community usufructory rights as through ownership. As a result, peasants do not clearly differentiate between these two types of tenure.

SOURCE: Field survey based on a sample of 210 of the approximate 430 Capacmarca households.

TABLE 6.2   Estimated Pre-Reform Landholding Pattern

Number of Plots	0	1–4	5–8	9–12	13–16	17–20	21–24	25–30	31+	Total
Number of households	14	76	57	38	12	7	1	5	0	210
Percentage	6.6	36.2	27.3	18	5.8	3.3	0.5	2.4	0	100

SOURCE: Field notes, 1984.

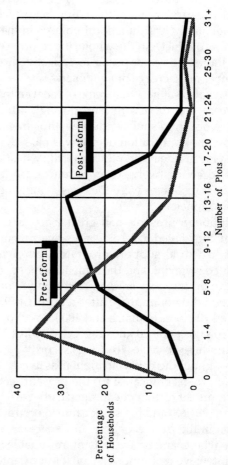

FIGURE 6.2   Comparison of pre- and post-reform landholding patterns.

respondents owned less than five hectares with the majority of them owning no more than 3.5 hectares of land. At the other end of the scale, 1.8 percent remained landless. If we compare these figures with the official pre-
reform census of 1972 when the typical Capacmarca *minifundio* amounted
to only 1.2 hectares, we see that a process of horizontal expansion has occurred: the number of landless households has decreased and average
family tenure has more than doubled in size. Although land continues to
be unequally distributed, differences in the number and size of holdings
are less distinct. On the whole, the reform consolidated the private micro-
holding sector as opposed to collective holdings by raising slightly the
number and acreage of *minifundios*.[11]

Data also suggest that some of the wealthier *Capacmarcaños* were able to
increase their access to land through a process of private parcelisation
which occurred shortly after the implementation of the law. For example,
before the confiscation decree was passed, the *gamonal* who owned Hacienda Percasenqa sold plots of fertile wheat and maize lands to local peasants receiving twelve oxen in return. Undoubtedly, cultivators with the
greatest resources were the ones gaining access to the most coveted ecological zones.

Although peasants had greater access to land ownership after the reform, they failed to receive any government technical assistance, credit or
infrastructural support programs. Consequently, crop productivity remained stagnant, and the hope to achieve food security seemed very distant to most *Capacmarcaños*. According to my data, potato and maize production did not improve after reform. In 1984 the average household produced 720 kilos of maize and 400 kilos of potatoes per hectare as opposed
to 750 kilos and 620 kilos respectively in 1972 (DNEC 1972).

Another obstacle to food security comes from livestock raising.
Throughout the Peruvian highlands livestock has traditionally been an as-
set of great significance for the peasant sector. Following the reform, the
government further encouraged cattle raising to cut down on beef imports
(Skar 1981:68) and livestock came to occupy an increasingly prevalent position in the rural economy. In Capacmarca, animals can be raised in the
puna where land is generally more suitable for long-term pasture use than
for intensive cropping. The most important herds are of sheep and cattle.
In 1984 some 63 percent of the sample households raised at least a few
head of cattle while 51 percent have sheep. Only two of the 210 families
surveyed had large herds of 50 to 150 head. Beef cattle are raised for their
market value on the coast in response to increased demands from the urban centers.[12] Sheep are bred because mutton is readily marketable within
the area. Animals are usually sold at the weekly fairs in Colquemarca
(Chumbivilas Province), Mara (Cotabambas Province), and Accha (Paruro
Province).

Since the reform, however, herd production has fallen drastically. Table 6.3, taken from the official pre- and post-reform censuses, gives an idea of the magnitude of the change—a fifty percent drop from 1972 to 1980. For the majority of the households, herding in its contemporary form is unable to contribute to any capital accumulation and is barely sufficient for the social reproduction of the household.

Numerous constraints have affected the development of adequate stock production: lack of peasant managerial capacity, shortage of capital and/ or bad weather conditions. The animals, which are poorly adapted to the environment, suffer from altitude stress, parasites, and nutritional deficiency (Browman 1987). Another likely cause is that before *haciendas* could be expropriated, local *hacendados* sold off their animals—a decapitalization that would have a long-term impact on local herds. Moreover, the granting of additional plots to *comuneros* has led to a more intense exploitation of the land and a subsequent reduction in livestock raising because family labor resources are withdrawn from herding.[13] Finally, animal stock theft continues to play a crucial role in preventing successful pastoralism. Rustling, which is linked to the *hacendados'* reaction to land reform, accounts for considerable animal losses.

Forms of Landlord Domination

Throughout the Peruvian highlands, landowners responded in various ways to the agrarian reform. Some subdivided their *haciendas* or abandoned their land, while others illegally dismantled their estates into small family holdings (Casos 1981; Yambert 1989). In Chumbivilcas, on the other hand, the counter-offensive was of a more violent nature. For instance, in 1980 the Cusco newsletter *Sur* printed the story of a Colquemarca *gamonal* who, upon learning that his estate (Hacienda Allpichiri) was to be adjacated to a nearby community, beat peasants, set their houses on fire, and used his personal influence to block expropriation. In Capacmarca, landowners resorted to outlawry, particularly livestock-rustling (*abigeato*), in response to state interference in their local affairs. In addition to their desire to hold onto landholdings and local power, this reaction also reflected the elite's regionalist identity and anti-state sentiments.

As Deborah Poole (1988) has pointed out, livestock-rustling has traditionally been endemic in Chumbivilcas and represents a major obstacle to the development of a profitable meat and wool producing economy. The high incidence of this type of brigandage has emanated from both peasants and local landlords. In a remote region like Capacmarca, rustlers can ruthlessly and successfully prey on herds and loot households by using their intimate knowledge of the rugged terrain.

TABLE 6.3   Pre- and Post- Reform Animal Production, District of Capacmarca

Type of Animals	1972	1980	Percentage Change
Sheep	56,279	23,000	−59%
Cattle	4,169	2,015	−51%
Horses	2,431	3,005	+24%

SOURCE: INS 1972 and 1980.

In the district of Capacmarca, rustling occurs mainly in the elevated, scarcely populated and notoriously unsafe high *punas* separating Capacmarca and Colquemarca. In these *punas*, shepherds and travellers are constantly at risk of being ambushed, beaten, and shot at. In an effort to protect themselves from this brutal form of violence, Colquemarca peasants have recently created a *ronda* or vigilante committee to patrol the region. In 1986, however, *Capacmarcaños* had yet to become organized. Rampant rustling presents such a major obstacle to the smallholding sector that peasants are gradually abandoning all livestock raising. Two major factors could be discerned for this resurgence in rustling: a worsening of the economic situation throughout the region and a black market in meat which developed in response to government restrictions on meat sales.[14]

Cattle-rustling, however, is also a practice of cultural significance. As Poole points out in Chapter 3 of this volume, cattle-rustling forms part of a regional identity associated with an ethos of anti-state rebellion and manly adventure. This ethos finds expression in the *qorilazo* as the personification of Chumbivilcas's unique male centered culture. This traditionalist, anti-state *rebeldia* and anti-progress ideology glorifies the past through the image of the *walaychu* or bohemian wanderer whose character is molded by the harsh *puna* environment in which he lives. The *walaychu* or *qorilazo* is also celebrated as a courageous and strongly individualistic cattle thief, who, whenever necessary, will not hesitate to take up arms to defend himself against state interference in his personal affairs.

Given this glorification of violence as part of a bohemian ideal, animal rustling earns respect as an activity that symbolizes the daring nature of herding. The atrocities it engenders are glossed over while the courage and fear it generates are greatly admired. Rustling thus represents an idealized portrayal of a local cultural identity which still holds considerable appeal to *gamonales* and peasants alike. The practice by local landowners, however, has reached such a critical level in recent years that peasant organizations are requesting government intervention to stop it. The report of a peasant forum held in 1985 states:

Ex-landlords socially and economically affected by the reform are the 'intellectual' authors of rustling. Their activity is directly supported and protected by official institutions. Rustling has considerably increased over recent years and is frequently carried out in the high zones where no state protection exists. Attackers use fire arms. *Puna* communities are most vulnerable to this type of crime which often leads to loss of human life. However, these settlements have no recourse as authorities refuse to put an end to this serious problem (FORUM 1985:26).

The local elite's involvement in rustling became evident to me during my fieldwork in Capacmarca. *Hacendados*, legal authorities, the police, and even teachers, all participated actively in livestock theft. On numerous occasions my assistant, himself a Chumbivilcano, was invited to drinking parties in Capacmarca where police, gunmen, and schoolteachers would boast endlessly about their criminal deeds. One individual at the center of these rustling activities was the community sergeant who also happened to belong to a leading *gamonal* family of Colquemarca. Although legislation prohibits Peruvian policemen from working in their community of origin, the law is ignored in both Colquemarca and Capacmarca.[15] This sergeant, who had been in charge of Capacmarca's police station since its creation in 1963, was one of the most powerful local bosses. He was notoriously mistrusted by the *comuneros* from whom he regularly stole. For instance, in 1983, he "bought" a cow from a widow for the equivalent of ten dollars that he still had not paid three years later. He was himself the *compadre* of a famous landlord/rustler and of several teachers as well as a close friend of the school director. With the help of his strongmen, he devoted the majority of his time to rustling and, for the last twenty years, had made it one of his most lucrative sources of livelihood. Once stolen, the animals were branded with the mark of the *guardia civil* (national police) and sold in Arequipa. Peasants in the village were well aware that the police, gunmen, and teachers operated together but felt that there was little they could do to change it.

Hacendados profoundly resented the land reform. They attributed the deterioration in their wealth to state interference and held the government responsible for the poverty afflicting the province (Poole 1987). Since state policies ran counter to their interests, they did not hesitate to justify their criminal activities as a way of making up for their loss of economic and political power. For landlords, rustling had become the reassertion of regional power based on *gamonalismo*.

Villagers told me on several occasions that rustling by landlords was by no means a new phenomenon. However, they were extremely concerned to see how much worse it had become in recent years. Rustling is costly for the peasantry. It prevents small landholders from becoming competitive as it discourages peasants from investing in herding. Those who are its prime targets are the somewhat richer peasants whose main source of accumulation lies in herding. As a result of rustling, a transfer of value takes place, with an appropriation of capital from higher income farmers to the coastal sector. Animal theft siphons off the surplus made by small producers to the urban meat markets of Arequipa and Lima. This illicit activity adds to the rapid erosion of the subsistence sector and has a levelling impact upon the peasantry, creating greater poverty. Rustling, therefore, has become a form of violence exercised against the expansion of the smallholder sector and its increasingly dependent ties to the labor market, both of which work to the detriment of the traditional forms of labor control characterizing the *hacienda* system.

Another important response of *gamonales* to the land reform has been their role in the educational system. The spread of formal schooling to rural areas was considered by President Velasco as part of the task of nation building. As such, it became one of the most important corollaries of the land reform. The new education law was promulgated in 1972. Its implementation resulted in the establishment of numerous rural schoolhouses; the district of Capacmarca now has six school centers.

During the 1970s, the powerful and very militant teachers' union SUTEP (Union of Education Workers of Peru), dominated by the Maoist Patria Roja party, was instrumental in expanding the political base of the left in the countryside by adopting an increasingly combative stance toward the rural social order. SUTEP activism became particularly important in Velille, Chumbivilcas, during the June 1979 national strike which lasted four months and ended with the arrest of several leaders. Many teachers who had played an important role in expressing peasant grievances were fired during the strike and never given back their jobs.

After reform, the expansion of state education and the leftwing teachers' union presented a double threat to a rural elite already losing access to crucial resources such as land and peasant labor. In an attempt to retain some control at the local level and to prevent the spread of outside political influence, members of the landed class increasingly occupied the available teaching positions which became important sources of power. As has also occurred in other regions of the *provincias altas* (see Gose, Chapter 5, this volume), in recent years schoolteachers of *gamonal* origin—sons and daughters of *hacendados*—have eagerly joined and now dominate the educational system in Capacmarca.

In 1984, two schools were operating in the center of the town—a primary school with five teachers and a secondary school with two teachers.[16] Five of the seven teachers came from the ranks of the local landholding elite. The most prominent propertied *mestizo* and well-known rustler of Capacmarca, Don Ricardo, had two of his children teaching in the community.[17] His son, Angel, was not only a teacher but also the mayor of Capacmarca and thus controlled municipal politics as well.[18] Teachers who were not themselves from *gamonal* backgrounds, were closely linked to traditional power either by marriage or fictive kinship. One schoolteacher couple (the wife from a prominent local landed family) chose as *compadres* the director of the *nucleo escolar* (school district) and the police captain of Capacmarca, who was himself of *gamonal* extraction. Nepotism and patronage dominate the educational system to the point of dictating community politics.

When I was in the community, supervision of the staff was neglected. Official visits supposedly taking place every three months had been scheduled three years apart in Capacmarca. One took place in 1985. During their two-day meeting in the community, officials worked no more than four hours checking out attendance and course matriculation. They were then wined and dined by the local elite from three in the afternoon to five the next morning.

Moreover, teachers themselves lacked expertise in their field; they had inadequate training, poor professional skills, and low formal schooling. Five out of the seven schoolteachers in the central school had only a grade five education. Clearly, they were not chosen for their academic qualifications. "To teach *indios*," as they said, "one only needs the right connection." They also displayed little commitment to their task. From my observation, none had regular work schedules. They seldom taught more than three hours a day and often never showed up. The findings of a two-month survey of the daily work load of elementary schoolteachers confirmed that all worked even less than half of the required four weeks per month and often spent most of their spare time drinking. Because peasant education is floundering at the hands of barely literate, corrupt, and frequently drunk or absent teachers, parents fail to see the point of sending their children to school. According to Monje (1985:37), in 1982 some 86 percent of the female population and 46 percent of the men remained illiterate. Of the 54 percent of the male students who usually attend school, no more than six percent reach the end of secondary school. This represents only three percent of the total male population.

Exploitation is endemic. The majority of the teachers are involved in graft, theft and corruption which continuously drain the *comuneros'* resources.[19] Various forms of extortion are employed as mechanisms of domination. Public funds are also misused. For example, in 1983 the Ministry of Education provided funds to complete the construction of a high school, but the director (who was also a rustler) preferred to use the money for installing community water taps near his home. This led to the closing of the secondary school in 1985. Also, goods intended for the children are confiscated by teachers for their own use.[20] Even worse, students frequently serve as domestics or carriers. This practice found the most tragic expression in a particular incident which took place in 1983. The following is a summary of the account as it was described to me by one of the witnesses.

Three teachers, together with one of the teacher's five-year-old daughter, were going to Cusco through Accha, a village located some ten walking hours from Capacmarca. The journey involves a long and arduous trek across the *puna*. A ten-year-old pupil—the child of a peasant family who was en route to sell his chickens at the weekly market in Accha—met them along the way. Shortly after leaving the community, the youngster was ordered to carry the teacher's daughter on his back. After complaining repeatedly of being extremely tired, he finally collapsed from exhaustion, lost his chickens, and was left behind. Another student from Capacmarca later found him and carried him on his horse to Accha. Upon arrival, the youngster was in a state of shock and sweating with high fever and exhaustion. While the teachers continued their journey to Cusco, the child was left at the police station. That night, the policeman on duty went drinking with village friends. When he came back to the station at 3 a.m., the child was dead. The powerful police corporal of Capacmarca, who was a *compadre* of the teachers, asked the police in Accha to state on the death certificate that the child had died of pneumonia. The following week a general assembly was held in Capacmarca during which *comuneros* publicly accused the teachers of continually exploiting their students and unfairly benefitting from their unpaid labor. The case was settled when Willy, the teacher, paid the youngster's father 150,000.00 *soles* (US $100.00).

Schoolteachers in Chumbivilcas do not always come from the *gamonal* class. Until the 1980s many belonged to SUTEP and were pro-peasant. In the remote villages of the *provincias altas*, however, rural schools have since become a bastion of the local landed gentry who keep SUTEP activists out of the region and prevent peasants from acquiring basic education and language skills in Spanish.

If the role of education in Capacmarca is to be interpreted in social terms, the teachers' abusive behavior is indicative of what is taking place outside the school, where a landed class and its allies still dominate. Education could potentially contribute to local patterns of peasant differentiation by encouraging motivated students to attain better paid jobs that would take them outside their social realm. However, schooling as practiced in Capacmarca, acts as a mechanism that prevents peasant children from becoming educated and potentially challenging *gamonal* power. The subversion of the school system by the interests of the landed elite is an institutional manipulation that parallels the manipulation of cultural practices such as rustling for economic gain and political control.

The agrarian reform has not only failed to dislodge the landed class, but has provided them with new and more modern avenues of power entrenched through the educational system. These and other such official positions within government institutions (for instance, the *sanitario* or medical assistant) validate both *gamonal* power in itself and exploitation by that power. Further, the transmission of culture is now under their control. In this way, they can distort the peasants' perception of reality. Here it is appropriate to refer to the concept of "cultural capital" developed by the New Sociology of Education.[21] Control over the cultural capital by a dominant group is crucial in the creation and perpetuation of inequalities:

> [T]he reproduction and legitimation of a social order go on in other than economic ways .... Rather, it assumes knowledge of the way in which both the form and content of the 'legitimate' culture, which is also partly reproduced in schools, act as instruments of power and as agents in the legitimation of power in society .... [O]ne must analyze the workings of cultural capital in much the same way as one would analyze the development of the ways schools can serve the interests of economic capital (Apple 1978:497).

In Capacmarca, schools have become environments where prejudiced attitudes reminiscent of a feudal mentality are perpetuated and legitimized. This way, the ruling ideas of the *gamonal* class are effectively reproduced to support the dominant group. Control over the educational system by the landed class has been an ideologically persuasive means of reproducing the symbolic order of pre-reform Capacmarca.

Whereas for a few years after reform the landowners were on the defensive, they have now regained their confidence and remain key figures in the economic and political operation of Capacmarca's rural life. To negate the effects of the reform, they are using counter-reform strategies that have enhanced their local power and prevented peasant socio-economic mobility. For instance, through rustling they effectively deprive the peasantry of the opportunity to acquire viable herds and to accumulate capital. Through education, they both prevent literacy from effectively reaching local communities and control the production of local culture. Their strength endures because the reform programs implemented by President Velasco have allowed this class to maintain and also develop new economic alternatives, thereby reinforcing their political power and, at the same time, retarding change in the *status quo*.

Conclusion

To conclude, I would like to make a few observations on the emerging agrarian structure of post-reform Capacmarca. Broadly speaking, the community now exhibits four types of social categories, namely (1) a small landless peasantry; (2) a large number of small *minifundistas*; (3) a limited number of wealthier *comuneros* and (4) an indigenous *gamonal* class.

The landless peasantry encompasses less than two percent of the sample and seems to be composed of migrants from neighboring communities who, as non-community members, cannot benefit from communal land redistribution. This group must subsist by hiring-out their labor within Capacmarca at times of peak agricultural activity and by providing seasonal labor outside the community. Further, they find themselves forced to take out loans with onerous terms and may often be indebted to local money lenders.

Small *minifundistas*, in some instances controlling up to sixteen plots per household, own a few head of cattle and sheep. They operate their farm on a family basis planting potatoes and maize for subsistence requirements. However, because they can barely produce enough to provide for their basic needs, these families are usually obliged to resort to wage labor outside the region on a seasonal basis. Richer peasants possessing up to thirty plots per family can grow maize and wheat in quantities over and above consumption requirements and raise sheep and cattle for a local and coastal market. Their holdings are often concentrated in ecozones of better soil quality and irrigation facilities. However, in no way can this group be considered a capitalist class of farmers "in formation." They are not entrepreneurial due to the impossibility of economies of scale, poor environmental conditions, lack of infrastructure and capital and, with regard to herding, rustling activities.

Finally, above the peasantry we find a *gamonal* class whose post-reform power has been enhanced. Today, it is of a more complex nature. Not only are they landlords, rustlers, teachers but, as always, they act as local shopkeepers, merchants, and moneylenders. As such, they continue to subject the *comuneros* to the same onerous and pervasive exploitation inherent in the pre-reform social system. Although the rent-in labor that they previously extorted from the peasants has been eliminated, they find other forms of surplus extraction.

Capacmarca's land redistribution to individual households came about as a political response to the violence of earlier peasant revolts. Such adjudication played a crucial role in consolidating rather than dissolving the smallholding system. Further, traditional power-holders have been able to retain control over *campesinos* through their own circuitous counter-offensive measures. This includes the use of physical violence. The fact that Capacmarca's *gamonales* continue to rule over local affairs contradicts the belief that *gamonalismo* is dead in Peru—a view that authors such as Montoya hold: "The former ideological and cultural dominance of the *gamonales* is being frontally challenged by every political sector in the country, and the land seizures have dealt the *coup de grace*" (1982:68). This study demonstrates that in regions where *gamonalismo* was previously entrenched and where state structures remain weak, *gamonal* bosses have managed to hold their ground and to preserve the *status quo* via old and new avenues within the context of a partially implemented package of reform.

Notes

1. This paper is based on fieldwork that I conducted in the region in 1983, 1984 and 1986. I am grateful to the International Development Research Center and the Social Science and Humanities Research Center for supporting this research which was part of my PhD thesis. Also, I would like to thank Marilyn Gates, Beverly Gartrell and Christopher Erickson for their comments on previous drafts.

2. Ministry of Agriculture, Sicuani, Expedientes de reconocimiento de la comunidad de Capacmarca, en el Distrito de Capacmarca, Provincia de Chumbivilcas; Expediente relativo al reconocimiento e inscripción oficial de la comunidad indígena de Capacmarca; Memorial que presentan los represantes de la comunidad de Capacmarca pidiendo la oficialización del Ayllo (1937).

3. Ministry of Agriculture, Sicuani, "Cuestionario al Jefe de la division de Promoción Comunal, Dirrección General de Comunidades, Lima."(1968).

4. Archivo General de la Nación (Lima): Sección: Tributos e Informes. Chumbivilcas, Cusco, Legajo 6; Cuaderno 186 (1851).

5. Ministry of Agriculture, Sicuani, Correspondencia: Ministerio de Salud Pública, Trabajo y Prevision Social; Sección Asuntos Indígenas: Expedientes relativo a la reclamación formulada por los indígenas de Capacmarca por usurpación de terrenosa (1936).

6. In the 1800s Hacienda Percasenqa belonged to the Mercederian Order in Cusco but was run by local landowning families. In 1918, the property was sold to a Catholic priest who paid 5,000.00 *soles* for 600 hectares of land. At his death in 1939, his common law wife and her two sons managed the *hacienda* which, in 1963, employed 28 tenant families.

7. *El Comercio*, October 14, 1963.

8. Ministry of Agriculture, Sicuani, "Expediente formulado por los comuneros del Distrito de Ccapacmarca, Provincia de Chumbivilcas al Señor Ministro del Estado en la Cartera de Trabajo y Asuntos Indígenas" (1963).

9. *El Comercio*, April 23, 1964.

10. One third of a hectare is equivalent to one *topo* and one six of a hectare equals one *tirapie*. *Yuntas, topos* and *tirapies* are local land measurements used in this southern part of Peru. One *yunta* corresponds to one *masa de toro* or the work that a

team of drafting oxen performs within a day. It corresponds to 1/2 topo or 1,650 square meters. One *masa de tirapie* is the work performed daily by a team of two men and one woman digging the field with the foot plow. It is equal to 1/2 *yunta* or 1/4 *topo*. It represents approximatly 800 square meters.

11. Uri Mendelberg (1985) observes a similar process taking place in Bolivia.

12. Camelids such as alpacas and llamas are best fitted to the environment. However, they are not bred in Capacmarca because their meat has little value in the national market.

13. To some degree, this situation has been exacerbated by the expansion of rural education which has indirectly affected pastoralism. In highland communities like Capacmarca, children are usually in charge of grazing herds in the *punas*. School attendance, however, is now compulsory which means that the size of the household labor force is further curtailed.

14. For example, David Browman (1987:134) mentions that in Cusco the black market handles more mutton than the official sector and the illegal sheep market in Arequipa is larger than the legal sector.

15. Within the police force, Capacmarca's police station is known as *"el castigo de la guardia"* (police punishment). I was told that policemen who are not from the region and who come to serve in Capacmarca have been sent there because their conduct had been reprehensible or even criminal.

16. In Capacmarca, I gained access to the school system by accepting a voluntary part-time position as an English teacher at the secondary school with the understanding that I would be conducting research in the village. This job allowed me to observe day-to-day teacher behavior through collective situations such as "social breaks" and their mid-day soccer games. Though the teachers knew that I was an anthropologist, they usually paid little attention to my work which greatly facilitated my observation.

17. All the names mentioned in this section are pseudonyms.

18. In 1985 Angel was buying animals for himself with municipal funds.

19. Teachers constantly ask contributions from the peasants mainly in the form of work and presents such as food, agricultural produce and animals.

20. I found a fifty kilo sugar bag sent by the United States for the students' breakfast being stored and consumed at a teacher's home.

21. Michael Apple (1978) defines cultural capital as the sum of meanings, language forms, and tastes that directly or indirectly are regarded by dominant classes as socially legitimate. This concept was coined by Pierre Bourdieu and Jean Claude Passeron (1970:21–2).

Bibliography

Apple, Michael. 1978. "The New Sociology of Education: Analysing Cultural and Economic Reproduction." *Harvard Educational Review*, 48:495–503.

Blanco, Hugo. 1972. *Land or Death, The Peasant Struggle in Peru*. New York: Pathfinder Press.

Bourdieu, Pierre, and Jean Claude Passeron. 1970. *Éléments pour une théorie du système d'enseignement*. Paris: Les Editions de Minuit.

Browman, David. 1987. "Pastoralism in Highland Peru and Bolivia." D. Browman (ed.), *Arid Land Use Strategies and Risk Management in the Andes: A Regional Anthropological Perspective*, pp. 121–51. Boulder: Westview Press.

Caballero, José María. 1977. "Sobre el carácter de la reforma agraria peruana." *Latin American Perspectives*, 4(3): 146–159.

Cardoso, Fernando H. 1975. *Autoritarismo e Democratizaíao.* Rio de Janeiro: Paz e terra.

Casos, Vickie. 1981. "SAIS Maranganí." Unpublished BA Thesis. Cusco: Universidad Nacional San Antonio Abad del Cusco.

CICDA (Centre International de Coopération pour le Développement Agricole). 1982. *Programme d'appui du développement agricole de la province de Chumbivilcas.* Cusco: CERA Bartolomé de Las Casas.

(El) Comercio. 1963. "*Comuneros se apoderan del pueblo de Capacmarca.*" October 14, 1963. Cusco.

_____. 1964. "*Policia reprime a comuneros en intento de desalojo.*" April 11, 1964. Cusco.

DNEC (Dirrección Nacional de Estadísticas). 1972. *Anuario Estadístico.* 2 Tomos. Lima.

FORUM. 1985. "*Chumbivilcas: Microregión y Desarrollo Alternativo.*" Santo Tomás, Chumbivilcas: Consejo Provincial Chumbivilcas, Liga Agraria. Taller CIE, Hatun Ccollana.

Gitlitz, John. 1977. "Impressions of the Peruvian Agrarian Reform." *Journal of Inter-American Studies*, 13 (3–4), 456–474.

Graig, Wesley. 1969. "The Peasant Movement of *La Convención.*" In H. Landsberger, (ed.) *Latin American Peasant Movements*, pp. 274–296. Ithaca: Cornell University Press.

Handelman, Howard. 1981. "Peasants, Landlords and Bureaucrats: The Politics of Agrarian Reform in Peru." In H. Handelman (ed.), *The Politics of Agrarian Change in Asia and Latin America*, pp. 103–125. Bloomington: Indiana University Press.

Havens, Eugene, Susana Lastarria-Cornhiel and Gerardo Otero. 1983. "Class Struggle and the Agrarian Reform Process." In D. Booth & B. Sorj (eds.), *Military Reformism and Social Classes: The Peruvian Experiences, 1968–80*, pp. 14–39. London: The Macmillan Press.

INE (Instituto Nacional de Estadística). 1972. *Boletín Estadístico Regional.* Cusco: Oficina de Estadística del ORDESCO.

_____. 1980. *Boletín Estadístico Regional.* Cusco: Oficina Regional de Estadística-Cusco.

Isbell, Billie Jean. 1978. *To Defend Ourselves: Ecology and Ritual in an Andean Village.* Austin: The University of Texas Press.

Martínez-Alier, Juan. 1977. *Haciendas, Plantations and Collective Farms: Agrarian Class Societies in Cuba and Peru.* London: Frank Cass.

Mendelberg, Uri. 1985. "The Impact of the Bolivian Agrarian Reform on Class Formation." *Latin American Perspectives*, 12:45–58.

Mercado, Rogger. 1967. *Los guerrillas del Perú.* Lima: Fundo de Cultura Popular.

Monje, Serafino. 1985. "Estructura económica de la comunidad campesina: El caso de Capacmarca, Chumbivilcas." Unpublished BA Thesis. Cusco: Universidad Nacional San Antonio Abad del Cusco.

Montoya, Rodrigo. 1982. "Class Relations in the Andean Countryside." *Latin American Perpsectives*, 9:63–78.

_____. 1989. *Lucha por la tierra, reformas agrarias y capitalismo en el Perú del siglo XX.* Lima: Mosca Azul.

Orlove, Bejamin. 1977. *Alpacas, Sheep and Men: The Wool Export Economy and Regional Society in Southern Peru.* New York: Academic Press.

Poole, Deborah. 1987. "Q'orilazos, abigeos y comunidades campesinas en la provincia de Chumbivilcas." In Alberto Flores-Galindo (Ed.), *Comunidades campesinas: cambios y permanencias,* pp. 257–295. Lima & Chiclayo: CONCYTEC Centro Solidaridad.

_____. 1988. "Landscapes of Power in a Cattle-Rustling Culture of Southern Andean Peru." *Dialectical Anthropology*, 12:367–398.

Quijano, Aníbal. 1967. "Contemporary Peasant Movements." In S. A. Lipset & A. Solari (Eds.), *Elites in Latin America,* pp. 301–340. New York: Oxford University Press.

_____. 1971. *Nationalism and Capitalism in Peru: A Study in Neo-Imperialism.* New York: Monthly Review.

Rénique, José Luis. 1990. *Los sueños de la sierra. Cusco en el siglo XX.* Lima: CEPES.

Skar, Harald. 1981. *The Warm Valley People: Duality and Land Reform Among the Quechua Indians of Highland Peru.* Oslo: Universitetsforlaget.

SUR. 1980. "Colquemarca: pobreza, gamonales y expression política." *SUR,* Año 3, 29:12–18.

Urton, Gary. 1984. "Chuta: El espacio de la práctica social en Pacariqtambo, Perú." *Revista Andina,* 3:7–56.

Villanueva, Horacio. 1981. *Cusco 1689. Economía y sociedad en el Sur Andino.* Cusco: Centro Bartolomé de Las Casas.

Villanueva, Víctor. 1973. *Ejército peruano.* Lima: Editorial Juan Mejía Baca.

Villasante, Marco. 1981. *Campesinado e industria doméstica.* Cusco: Universidad Nacional San Antonio Abad del Cusco.

Voz Rebelde. 1963. "Concentración de 2000 comuneros en actitud beligerante." *Voz Rebelde,* October 14, 1963.

Webster, Steven. 1971. "Native Pastoralism in the South Andes." *Ethnology,* 12:115–33.

Yambert, Karl. 1989. "The Peasant Community of Catacaos and The Peruvian Agrarian Reform." In B. S. Orlove, M. W. Foley, T. F. Love (eds.), *State, Capital, and Rural Society. Anthropological Perspectives on Political Economy in Mexico and the Andes,* pp. 181–209. Boulder: Westview Press.

7

Political Violence, the State, and the Peasant Struggle for Land (Puno)

José Luis Rénique

From a distance, Peruvian politics appear reduced to the violent confrontation between the state and the Communist Party of Peru "Shining Path" (PCP-SL, or Sendero Luminoso). This confrontation appears to be particularly severe in the rural highland areas where an old history of exploitation and injustice would seem to explain the PCP-SL's war against the state. According to this rationale, region after region has fallen in a spiral of violence generated, in the final analysis, by the uninterrupted hold of a social order in which peasant political participation has been suppressed and the PCP-SL's violent armed struggle would seem to form the only effective path towards change.

A more analytical vision has to go beyond such generalizations to identify with more precision the actors, contexts and nature of the conflicts. This chapter will use a local or regional approach focused on the Department of Puno to explore the roots of contemporary rural conflict in the southern Peruvian highlands. Specifically, I will look at the development of peasant organizations, their struggle for land over the last decade (1980-1990), and the ways in which this struggle has been compromised by the expanding violence of the PCP-SL.

Velasco's Legacy

In the context of contemporary Latin America, Peru's Andean area stands out as a stronghold of rural backwardness symbolized by the survival of feudal-like *haciendas* (estates) well into the second half of the twentieth century. Various reformist plans were attempted since the 1920s to remedy the situation. None, however, were of the scope and intensity of the agrarian reform applied by General Juan Velasco Alvarado's military junta between 1969 and 1975. In the view of the military reformers, agrar-

224

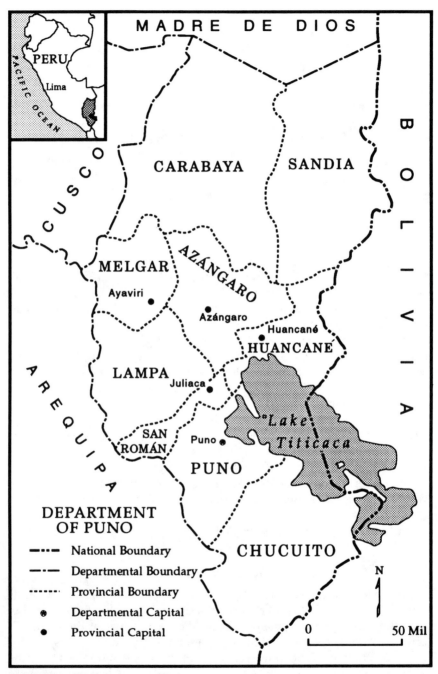

FIGURE 7.1   The Department of Puno.

ian change was an essential step towards replacing oligarchic domination with a "social democracy of full participation" which would be "neither capitalist nor communist" (Stepan 1978; Cotler 1980).

Velasco's agrarian reform swept the country creating enormous expectations. The National System of Support for Social Mobilization (SINAMOS) was established in 1973 to transform these expectations into government support by creating a network of state-regimented rural organizations. There were also, however, numerous conflicts, as many peasants became disenchanted by the government's decision to form "associative enterprises" (*empresas asociativas*) modelled after various types of cooperatives, rather than to restore the land in the form of individual or communal holdings. Rural discontent grew deeper when the overthrow of General Velasco in 1975 brought about a withdrawal of state support to the reformed agrarian sector. Begun under the so-called second phase of military government led by General Francisco Morales Bermúdez (1975–1980), this orientation was continued by the democratically elected administration of President Fernando Belaúnde Terry (1980–1985), an adamant opponent of Velasco's interventionist policies.

State withdrawal left behind a legacy of uncertainty. In the aftermath of Velasco's fall, leftwing parties occupied the space abandoned by SINAMOS while *hacendados* (land holders) tried to get back their expropriated property. Some of the highlands' largest associative enterprises virtually collapsed under pressure from peasant communities. Regional multiclass movements also emerged in cities throughout the highlands to demand public funds and decentralization.

The emergence of the Marxist Left as a national force was one of the most notable events in late 1970s Peruvian politics. Leftwing parties, however, were far from acting as a single block; factionalism and splintering was the norm among them. Only in 1980 did the pro-Soviet Peruvian Communist Party "Unity" (PCP-Unidad) join with other parties of the New Left such as Revolutionary Vanguard (VR), the Revolutionary Communist Party (PCR), and the Revolutionary Left Movement (MIR) to form the United Left (IU). This party coalition would become a national electoral force in the context of the transition to democracy made effective by two succesive national elections—one in 1978 for a constituent assembly and a second two years later for president and congress. The PCP-SL, however, remained critical of any sort of electoral participation. For them, the military's return to its barracks and the predictable weakness of the incoming government were instead seen as favorable conditions under which to launch their long awaited armed struggle (CSRP 1991:40).

By 1980, highland areas such as the department of Puno seemed to be ripe for expansion of the PCP-SL. There, the usually inefficient and corrupt associative enterprises offered a stark contrast with peasant communities starving for land in an area stricken by cyclical natural disasters. The PCP-SL, however, was not alone. Other leftwing parties had also been there, organizing rural discontent, since the late 1970s. By the time the transition to democracy was complete, Puno was a United Left stronghold and a leading advocate of regional governments ordered by the new 1980 Constitution.

Confrontations between Sendero and the United Left for control of Puno would be further complicated when, in 1985, a new president, Alan García, began a move to regain state initiative in rural areas where the PCP-SL's actions had been growing for the last five years. President García wanted to make Puno a showcase of how development policies focused directly on peasant communities could work to defuse the conditions that were feeding the PCP-SL's insurgency. For the United Left, on the other hand, Puno was to be the spearhead of a regional movement rooted in peasant mobilization from which a new brand of truly democratic and popular government could be born. Finally, for the PCP-SL, Puno—with its extensive high plateau stretching from the highlands of Cusco and Arequipa to the Bolivian border—was a militarily and politically strategic area for the protracted guerrilla war which they planned to fight at a national and, eventually, international level. By the mid-1980s, for all these political players, Puno had become a crucial testing ground.

Agrarian Politics and Peasant Movements

In Puno, hacienda expansion occurred during the late nineteenth and early twentieth century wool export boom and was based primarily on the forced seizure of community land (Giraldo & French 1978; Burga & Reátegui 1981; Flores Galindo 1977; Jacobsen 1982). The peasant communities opposed encroachments in a variety of forms and although they did not succeed, peasants held to the conviction that they were the legitimate owners of land taken by *hacendados*. In privileging the associative enterprises as a substitute for the traditional hacienda, Velasco's agrarian reform failed to resolve these historic demands for the return of lands stolen by *hacendados*. This was a demand of profound economic, as well as social and cultural significance.[1]

Three models of associative enterprises were designed to replace traditional haciendas: agrarian production cooperatives (CAP) were defined as indivisible units in which all assets were owned collectively; rural social property enterprises (ERPS) and agricultural social interest societies (SAIS) were especially designed for the highlands. In creating the ERPS, the land of a number of haciendas and adjacent communities were integrated into one single unit, while the old hacienda workers became workers on the new enterprise. In the SAIS model, the most productive lands of the ex-haciendas were put under the control of a hired manager and representatives of the state while, on the less-productive marginal lands, members of the community were allowed to engage in individual cultivation and/or to graze their own small herds (De Janvry 1981; Matos Mar and Mejia 1980). The SAIS were planned as cooperatives in formation; communities were to have a voice in their administration and access to the SAIS's services and facilities.

By taking the "associative" option, the government sought to preserve the administration and assets of the expropriated estates while at the same time defusing and controlling peasant demands for land. What actually happened, however, was that old tensions were transferred to the new units, where an administration concerned with maximizing profits clashed with peasant communities that wished to use the pastureland for their own production. As the state failed to provide effective arbitration, internal conflicts worsened and corruption flourished (Scurrah 1987; Caballero 1990). It was not uncommon for managers and government officers of the associative enterprises to establish alliances with the haciendas' old *majordomos* and administrators and run them to their joint profit (Caballero 1984; IIDSA 1983).

As SINAMOS withered away, organizations geared to peasant interests became stronger. With the assistance of leftwing parties such as the VR, PCR, and MIR, the national Peruvian Peasant Confederation (CCP) had provided, since the mid-1970s, coordination and representation for a variety of organizations struggling to recuperate land from associative enterprises in different regions of the country. In Cusco, the largest such enterprises had been virtually dismantled by 1978 after several waves of peasant land invasions (García Sayán 1982). Puno's enterprises, however, would survive for another decade. The gap between these contiguous departments went back to the 1960s. At that time, Cusco's leftwing peasant federation led dozens of land invasions. In Puno, on the other hand, peasant unions were controlled by the Cáceres brothers—a group of powerful merchants from the city of Juliaca. The Cáceres focused on salaries and working conditions and left the question of land untouched (Tamayo Herrera 1982). Later, as the Cáceres became General Velasco's supporters, unions under their leadership were swallowed by SINAMOS-sponsored organizations. By the late 1970s, as peasant impatience with the associative enterprises grew, the CCP was able to gain a foothold in Puno, especially in the provinces of Melgar and Azángaro which were home to more than half the associative enterprises in Puno.

Another departmental peasant federation—the Departmental Peasant Federation of Puno (FDCP)—was created in 1978 in affiliation with the CCP. Because the FDCP's foremost goal was to acquire land for peasant communities, its beginnings were closely associated with the problem posed by the approximately forty associative enterprises that owned most of Puno's productive land. Nevertheless, to avoid confrontations between *comuneros* (members of independent peasant communities) and *feudatarios* (workers from the haciendas and associative enterprises), the FDCP's leaders proclaimed their support for the latter's demands for better wages and union rights and emphasized that it was not their objective to dismantle the associative enterprises. At least in an initial stage of the struggle for land, they said, the peasant movement should target only those enterprises that were

> incapable of assuring stability to their workers, that owed them salaries, that paid badly, that were bankrupt, that did not give elemental services, [and] that, when faced with scarce capital, resorted to servile and semi-servile [i.e., unpaid] forms of labor. (FDCP 1978).

Inadvertently, Belaúnde's decision to end protectionist measures and subsidies for the agrarian sector would also contribute to the FDCP's and the CCP's expansion in Puno. Now, as never before, Puno's rural population was hit by inflation and rising interest rates on rural credit. The price of fertilizers, pesticides and other agricultural inputs rose sharply, while agrarian prices declined. Belaúnde's technocrats were eager to get rid of Velasco's "collectivist" heritage and open the agrarian sector to market forces. In their view, free competition would become the key factor in developing a modern agrarian order. For peasants, hacienda workers, and small agricultural producers, this policy meant an unacceptable abandonment of the highland countryside (Mejía 1980; Eguren 1980; Barrenechea 1982).

By 1983, when Puno was hit by another drought, rural discontent became even more acute. Pressures for invasion were running high. Although in 1979 there had been several land invasions, these had been mostly isolated cases. In 1983 numerous communities were pursuing costly and neverending trials for the adjudication of SAIS land. Legal disputes created an environment of conflict that lapsed many times into violence. In 1984, for example, the Sollocota SAIS in Azángaro province, organized

> nocturnal patrols [*rondas nocturnas*] with horsemen who circulated in the immediate surrounds of the community yelling insults and death threats to the 'lazy peasants and terrorists [i.e., Senderistas].' They constructed deep ditches along the community boundaries to stop invasions. They maintained a great number of peasants as temporary workers under the constant threat of losing even this assurance of work if they 'caused any troubles.' Finally they began to build a center on the west side of the community to house the herders who were members of the SAIS, for the sole purpose of using these herders as a means of social control [*instrumentos de contención social*] in case of an invasion by the community (IIDSA, 1982:108).

No less harmonious was the internal situation of the associative enterprises. In 1978 in the Buenavista SAIS, the general administrator made six times the wages of a herder. By 1986 this wage differential had more than doubled, and the SAIS had left its workers without pay on various occasions. In response, workers and *feudatarios* lost interest in the enterprise's future, concentrating their attention on their own household economies instead. In these circumstances, calls by the National Center of Peasant Enterprises (CENECAMP)—the national lobby of associative enterprise administrators—to close ranks against Belaunde's anti-peasant policies were not as appealing as the "second agrarian reform" proposed by the FDCP.

These conditions explain the formation of a network of organizations that were to play a major role in reshaping Puno's agrarian structure. In this endeavor, VR's militants received support from Catholic Church members who had sided with the peasant communities in what they perceived as a just and long overdue demand (Judd 1987). On several occasions during the stormy second phase of the military government, the bishops of Peru's southern highlands had publicly expressed their opposition to repression and anti-popular economic policies. This unusual step made by the provincial hierarchy of the Catholic Church was the beginning of a decade-long collaboration between priests and leftwing organizers united by the common goal of supporting peasant organizations.

Regarding the "peasant question," however, the CCP's pro-peasant stance was only one among many within the complex universe of the Peruvian Marxist Left. Since the early-1970s, for example, VR's approach to the land question had been strongly questioned by Maoist hard-liners such as those who would later form the PCP-SL. These differences would deepen during the following years. By agreeing to participate in the 1980 elections, VR became part of the legal left in the same year that PCP-SL was to launch its armed struggle. By that time, the PCP-SL had already labelled the VR as "revisionists" who stood in the way of Sendero's "popular revolution" (Arce Borja 1989:110). Later, the PCP-SL's leader, Abimael Guzmán, would declare that "revisionism" was a "cancer that has to be ruthlessly eliminated" (CSRP 1991:9). Given these ideological definitions, the clash between the legal left and Guzmán's followers seemed almost inevitable.

Regional Politics, APRA, and the Left

The emergence of peasant organizations, the arrival of party organizers and the growing commitment of the Church with peasant struggles were expressions of broader changes that, in turn, altered the links between Puno and the national political system. For the coastal oligarchy that had run the country since the turn of the century, Peru's highland area was the nation's backyard. Highland provinces were controlled politically by landowners who served as local representatives to the national congress. Most of the local authorities, including mayors and town council members were appointed by the Ministry of Interior. With few exceptions, government agencies did not have local branches in highland cities. In a context of this sort, politics in Puno were essentially a competition for the public funds that allowed the departmental elite of landowners and authorities to maintain enough order and stability to keep their haciendas alive (Bourricaud 1967; Tamayo Herrera 1982).

By the 1960s, these structures had deteriorated rapidly. Demographic growth and urbanization had created new interests and demands. In addition, crises such as the one generated by the droughts of 1956 and 1961, had opened the way for changes in the administration of the department and for international development projects (Dew 1969). Building upon these experiences, governments promoted significant growth of the state apparatus and public spending in Puno. The emerging public sector became the major source of employment for dozens of graduates from schools such as the Universidad Técnica del Altiplano (UNTA), which had opened in the city of Puno in the mid-1960s.

Under the second phase of military government, as state interventionism dwindled, non-governmental organizations (NGO's) slowly increased their presence in Puno (Palao Berastain 1988). They would rapidly become an important source of jobs for former government functionaries and new professionals. With links to both the Catholic Church and leftwing parties, the NGO's would play a substantial role in the regional movements of the 1980s (Carroll 1990). These movements were initially based on a coalition of urban interests represented by a variety of organizations, ranging from Puno's engineering school to mothers' organizations and public employees' unions. In large part because of their opposition to Belaúnde's handling of the 1983 drought, the United Left emerged as the political voice of these regional movements. This role was further reinforced by leftwing electoral triumphs in Puno's 1980 and 1983 municipal elections.

Municipalities would also play an important role in transforming the drought into a political issue as they organized forums and public debates to discuss possible solutions to its devastating effects. Debates on the drought focused on the department's socio-economic situation in connection with the issues of regionalization then under discussion in the national Congress. Proposals to create new regional governments were seen by these urban interests as an opportunity to gain the power and political autonomy necessary to redirect Puno's social and economic development. Participants in this debate stressed the necessity of promoting capital reinvestment in local industry, agriculture and mining. There was also wide agreement regarding the rural situation. What they called the "restructuration" of the associative enterprises was seen as a basic step to revitalize Puno's agriculture. Restructuration meant redistributing part of the associative enterprises' lands to the peasant communities and helping them to form communal enterprises (*empresas comunales*) by using labor intensive production, simple technology, and local resources (Robles 1987; Salas 1984).

Consensus existed that these should be the master lines of a program to be applied by the future regional government of Puno. By mid-1984, as congressional debate on regionalization was in a deadlock, the urban coalition took the initiative of establishing a regional popular assembly which their leaders expected to be an embryo of the future regional government. There was general agreement that peasant organizations and their struggle for land would play a central role within this regional movement.

By 1985, Puno's regional movement occupied a prominent place in the United Left's national strategy to become the leading opposition force by developing an alliance with the social movements emerging throughout the country. Placed in this context, the peasant struggle for land acquired a particularly strategic position. Backed by a wide array of political parties and civic organizations, the FDCP was assured of access to the congress, executive branch, and Lima's press as no other peasant organization had ever been. This fact helps to explain the FDCP's strength and dynamism at the moment when Alan García took office on July 28, 1985.

On more than a dozen trips to Puno as part of his electoral campaign, García had offered to reverse Belaúnde's policy towards Andean agriculture. He promised to deal with the associative enterprise problem, to supply interest-free credit for peasant communities, to implement a broad program of public works, and to make Puno the capital of the "Andean Trapezoid"—García's euphemism for the impoverished southern highland provinces of Puno, Apurímac, Cusco, and Ayacucho. Specifically, García proposed to develop a series of micro-regional projects as a means to promote the economic development that would presumably undermine Sendero's advance (Rojas 1988).

For Puno's Left, García's plan constituted a tough challenge. The regional popular assembly responded to García's initiative by proposing that the government adopt the FDCP's plan to restructure the associative enterprises. According to this plan, the government would declare Puno an agrarian reform zone managed by representatives from the FDCP, CENECAMP, and the central state. With the authority to intervene in Puno's forty-one associative enterprises, this committee would be responsible for certifying the beneficiaries and for redistributing land. The plan did not propose to eliminate the associative sector in its entirety but actually specified that:

> Once the enterprises are restructured and surveyed their productive units will proceed with entitlement, guaranteeing their functioning via the integral assistance of the state which guarantees the workers' rights to job stability and participation in the conduct and management of the restructured enterprises (Municipio de Puno 1985:4).

The plan also required the immediate creation of a regional government which would assume control over public investment in Puno to be handled through "an agreement between the organized social forces, state institutions, and public administration" (ibid.).

Other forces on the Left responded with yet more radical proposals to change the agrarian structure. These proposals were facilated by realignments within the Marxist Left. In mid-1984, VR, PCR, and MIR—the same parties which for years had vied for control of the CCP—came together to form the United Mariateguista Party or PUM. While other members of the United Left were taking a conciliatory position towards President García's government, PUM adopted a line of hard opposition based on rural and regional mobilization. PUM's peasant organizers inherited one decade of leftwing experience in different areas of Peru. As a result, PUM had an important presence in the CCP and its network of departmental and provincial federations. From a broader perspective, it might be said that the peasant activism of PUM's predecessors—particularly VR—served as a catalyst to the democratization of significant areas of Peruvian highland's rural society. By 1985, PUM was one of the largest political parties within the legal left. Besides its political work in urban and peasant organizations throughout the country, PUM was well connected to the national intelligentsia, the NGOs, and progressive sectors of the Catholic Church. Furthermore, electoral participation had rewarded PUM with a dynamic group of elected officers.

By the time Alan García was sworn in, these resources had been successfully mobilized by PUM in support of the movement for land in Puno. The case of the province of Melgar illustrates how this involvement took shape. Since its inception Melgar's peasant federation—FUCAM—counted with the combined support of PUM and the Wakrani Rural Education Institute (IER Wakrani), a research, teaching, and discussion center sponsored by the Catholic Church and located a few miles from Ayaviri, the capital of Melgar province. From Lima, PUM party leaders and the CCP's National Committee arranged for the participation of specialists on agrarian matters from NGOs and universities from Lima. In successive forums and seminars held at Wakrani peasant leaders, political advisers, and professionals developed a plan to transform associative enterprises into communal enterprises (FUCAM 1983). According to this plan, peasant communities were to serve as the base for a new kind of enterprise that, in turn, would be the cell of Puno's alternative model of regional development (Vega 1989). This model was adamantly opposed by the managers and administrators of the former associative enterprises. As the bishop of Ayaviri wrote to García a few weeks after his inauguration,

> for several years, [the peasants of Melgar] have promoted this request (*reclamo*) [for the formation of communal enterprises] through reports, studies, and documentation (*fundamentaciones*). The management and administrative sector of the [associative] enterprises, however, have blocked the process, when the only thing the community demands is more land to strengthen their communal enterprise [*empresa comunal*].[2]

In October, a commission was formed to resolve communities' demands against the Kunurana ERPS in Melgar. In its report, the commission recommended in rather vague terms that the enterprise be restructured.[3] That same month, another commission was formed in the national congress to investigate "irregularities committed by the associative enterprises."[4] This commission did not meet, however, for several more months.

Meanwhile, the peasant movement was moving ahead. In late October, 1985, FUCAM organized a march around the Kunurana ERPS. On November 4, the Popular Regional Assembly declared Puno a region, in a symbolic act meant to denounce the government's reluctance to speed up the process of establishing regional governments. In early December the Assembly called a regional strike on the same day that peasant communities from Macari and Santa Rosa (Melgar province) took over 10,500 hectares of land from the Kunurana ERPS. These moves foreshadowed the future confrontation between President García's governing party, APRA (American Popular Revolutionary Alliance), and PUM for control of Puno. They also signaled the beginning of a cycle of rural violence initiated by confrontations between former *feudatarios* and *comuneros* in Melgar, and followed by an intensification of PCP-SL's presence in the area.

The PCP-SL

Sendero's presence in Puno can be traced back to at least the late 1970s. As in other regions of the Peruvian highlands, the initial focus of Sendero's expansion in Puno was the normal schools, where rural schoolteachers were trained. After a period in which they consolidated forces in the cities,

Sendero began work in the countryside. They chose Azángaro province for this phase of organization because of its central location in the department and because of its history of peasant uprisings and land invasions. In the early twentieth century, *hacendados* from Azángaro often formed armed bands which terrorized peasant communities; more than one peasant uprising in the province had resulted in massacre. On the eve of the agrarian reform, Azángaro was the principal stronghold of *gamonalismo* in Puno. Thirteen associative enterprises replaced the old haciendas. By the early 1980s, the inefficiency and corruption of these enterprises contrasted sharply with the pressing needs of an impoverished peasantry who constituted approximately eighty percent of Azángaro's population. Beyond this, little headway had been made in breaking the hold of the wealthy *gamonal* families over the towns in Azángaro province. These families controlled commerce and monopolized public offices as a means to assure their privileged social position.

In 1979 a Limeño leader of the PCP-SL, who had been sent two years earlier to open a front in Puno, was working as a schoolteacher in the small town of San Antón (Azángaro province). Around 1981, "peoples' schools" were established in the San Juan de Salina district, especially in the community of Curayllo. Several dynamite bombings in Juliaca and Puno confirmed rumors that Sendero was operating in the area. Nevertheless, since national attention was focused on the department of Ayacucho—at that time, the epicenter for the PCP-SL's "peoples' war"—Sendero's armed actions appeared to be minor. It was in these circumstances that a PCP-SL column established itself in the high parts of Putina, Munani, and Pedro Vilcapaza districts in Azángaro Province. From there, Sendero began to launch attacks against police posts and associative enterprises, and to threaten local authorities by demanding their resignations and submission to party directives. Municipal offices, medical posts, bridges, and a number of official vechicles were also dynamited in mid-1981.

In the following years, Sendero's activities in Puno grew at a gradual and sustained pace. Police outposts scattered throughout the department were easy targets for a small but well disciplined detachment who had a good knowledge of the terrain and who could count on at least the passive support of some rural dwellers. By 1985, demoralization among the police rank and file was deep. With no strategy to contain Sendero's actions, authorities ordered police forces to withdraw into provincial capitals. Several rural outposts were closed down. Seen as symbols of the state, associative enterprises became targets of guerrilla actions supported by crowds of unarmed people. On some occasions, *feudatarios* organized themselves to fight off these attacks as happened in late August 1982,

when workers from the Sollocota SAIS captured several Sendero participants in an attack on the SAIS.

By 1983, Sendero had managed to mobilize what they called their "local
force" made up of peasants from the area. The local force participated in
specific armed actions in support of the "principal force" made up of non-
Puneño cadres who were primarily from Lima and Ayacucho. It was with
the land invasions, however, that Sendero's armed actions increased most
notably. During the first six months of 1986, while the peasant organizations fought to obtain a government decision regarding the restructuring
of the associative enterprises, Sendero's armed actions escalated. There
was an increase in assassinations of police and local authorities. At least
two mining centers were attacked. From these mines, Sendero obtained
the dynamite with which they then destroyed a number of old hacienda
houses that had been converted into administrative centers for SAIS and
ERPS. Soon the Lima press began to refer to Azángaro and Melgar as
Sendero's "liberated zone."

At times attracted by Sendero's line and at other times moved by the
threat of force, dozens of peasants participated in the massive attacks on
the associative enterprises and in the sacking of goods and livestock
which took place after the armed attacks. One of these cases occurred in
Macari in June 1986. Around 350 inhabitants of Macari were taken by a
PCP-SL column while on their way to the market in Ayaviri. For several
hours they were obliged to participate in the sacking of the Kunurana
ERPS, where seven workers were killed. This attack on Kunurana brought
police and military repression on a community which, until that time, had
been fighting for land through legal channels. It also brought with it an increased rift between community members and ERPS' *feudatarios*. Every-
where Sendero's message was the same: land could only be recuperated
through the use of arms. As in Ayacucho, Sendero was looking for a confrontation that would "heighten the contradictions" fuelling their "prolonged guerrilla war." They believed they could do this by obliging the
government to declare Puno under a state of emergency with military administration. Sendero's attacks against Aprista leaders in Puno and the
APRA's party headquarters in both Puno and Juliaca formed part of this
strategy.[5]

For a brief time, Sendero appeared to be achieving its objective. In
March and June of 1986, military troops carried out raids in Azángaro and
Melgar. More than a battle against Sendero, these operations were intended to intimidate those communities who, because they were involved
in land claims, were perceived by the military authorities as pro-Sendero
and therefore as potential "terrorists."

For Puno's Aprista leaders the spread of violence provided an ideal opportunity to strike a blow against their traditional political rivals on the

Left. Labelling PUM as the "legal arm of Sendero," Apristas threw the blame for Senderista violence on their closest political rival for control of Puno's peasant movement and regional government. Armed APRA defense groups were mobilized against both the Left and the FDCP, while a political campaign was launched by APRA's Congressman Rómulo León Alegría to denounce PUM's ties to the NGOs and international aid agencies who supposedly supported "subversive activities" in Puno. These confrontations between APRA and PUM contributed to the tense atmosphere that prevailed in the area by mid-1986. A journalist visiting Puno at that time compared the local situation to one of a country in a state of civil war (Gonzales 1986). Given the close bond between PUM and the FDCP, the Aprista accusations both clouded the legitimacy of the peasant struggle for land and gave renewed strength to the position of the associative enterprise managers, since they also alleged that the peasant federations maintained ties to the subversives.

Restructuring Committees and Land Invasions

By early 1986, doubts were beginning to be raised if there was in fact a serious proposal behind García's rhetoric (Montoya 1986). Given the ample support for reform of the associative enterprises, the case of Puno was considered a convenient opportunity for APRA's government to resolve the conflicts created by Velasco's reforms. By doing so García could send out the message that Belaunde's inertia was ending and that an activist government was now in power.

Already by late 1985 it was clear to many that the new government was incapable of making a real difference. An example of this was the meager results attained by the parliamentary commission—headed by the Aprista Congressman Cristóbal Campana—formed to investigate the associative enterprises' situation. The commission's field inspections were limited by the associative enterprises' reluctance to cooperate and by the conflictive atmosphere prevailing in Puno. The overall situation was further aggravated by a new cycle of natural disasters, including torrential rains and flooding. Despite repeated requests issued to the associative enterprises through the Puno branch of CENECAMP, the parliamentary commission was unable to make the enterprises hand over basic information about their administrative and financial status. Months later, only Rosaspata SAIS had cooperated with this request and the commission's final report included information only on this one enterprise. Nevertheless, the parliamentary commission concluded its report with a recommendation for restructuring the associative enterprises. In their final report, the commission would state that:

the direct testimony of many members [of the enterprises] ... gave evidence of a climate of intimidation and abuse against all those who wished to testify or give their opinion about anything against the enterprise; by contrast, there were prizes and rewards for those who testified on behalf of the managers and administrators.[6]

The deadlock was finally broken by a presidential decision in February 1986. García's Supreme Decrees 005 and 006 ordered that the associative enterprises in Puno be restructured and that up to one million hectares be distributed among the peasant communities.

In response, CENECAMP-Puno denounced the "uninformed bureaucrats and ill-intentioned political advisors" who had surprised the "highest levels of government" by making them commit an act contrary to the constitutional order (CENECAMP-Puno 1986). CENECAMP insisted that, instead of weakening the associative enterprises by ordering restructuration, the government's first duty was to re-establish order through the "presence of the Armed Forces in the provinces assailed by terrorism and a climate of violence" (ibid.). This first communiqué deploring the President's decision set the tone for further actions undertaken by managers and administrators of the associative enterprises. Playing upon the fears instilled by Sendero's growing presence in Puno, they claimed that peasant demands on associative enterprise land were expressions of "terrorism" and, as such, deserved a firm military response.

In the following weeks, however, CENECAMP would accept state intervention as an inevitable fact. In May, a restructuring commission formed in Lima began inspecting the associative enterprises. With President García's personal support, the commission's work proceeded rapidly without the obstacles faced by the parliamentary commission.

Once the decision to restructure the associative enterprises had been made, the implementation process became the principal point of disagreement between the managers, who sought to slow down and mediate the process, and the peasant organizations which sought both to speed up and to oversee the process. From the beginning, conflicts were common and the restructuring commission soon became an object of criticism. CENECAMP-Puno complained that the commission was headed by officials who lacked knowledge of Puno and who refused to negotiate criteria for restructuring the associative enterprises (CENECAMP-Puno 1986). For their part, the peasant organizations protested what they considered to be the marginalization of the FDCP, and the resultant inability of a commission subjected to pressure from managers and local political powers to guarantee an authentic restructuring.

Despite these objections, the restructuring commission sent from Lima managed to act with relative autonomy. Around July 1986, they concluded the task of determining which lands would be affected and issued resolutions ordering expropriation. In carrying out their work, the commission enjoyed direct relations with the communities involved and sought to avoid all intermediaries including the FDCP and the CENECAMP. In this way the government sought to put aside the leftwing's leadership of the peasant land movement, thereby allowing APRA, as the governing party, to become the only one able to capitalize on the political rewards of handing over the associative enterprises' land. For this, the government party also relied on a series of nationwide departmental-level meetings called Rimanakuys (from the Quechua verb "to converse") intended as forums for the discussion of peasant concerns. By personally attending these meetings, President García hoped to seal an alliance between his government and the peasant communities (Bravo 1987).

Sensing that a partisan political agenda was hidden behind both García's Rimanakuys and his restructuration proposals, the FDCP took a more radical approach in reference to the future of the associative enterprises. At Puno's Rimanakuy, they opposed what they termed APRA's "bureaucratic route" to reform the associative enterprises and stressed their own "democratic restructuring," the final goal of which would be the "total elimination of the SAIS, CAP, and ERPS models in the Department of Puno" and the creation of a departmental land fund to be turned over to the peasant communities in the form of communal enterprises (FDCP 1986b). They also demanded sanctions against the managers and officials who had committed "offences against their enterprises' economy" [Ibid.]. With respect to the work of the restructuring commission, they concluded that it had shown a "clear and open partiality in favor of the associative enterprises, and against the peasant communities." For this reason, they also requested sanctions against members of the commission, as well as the "immediate dismissal of the agrarian reform director of the XXI Agrarian Region-Puno" and the "total reorganization of said entity." They gave the authorities one month to carry out these demands.

Restructuration initially had a fast start and then proceeded slowly in the midst of political turmoil. It was not until late 1986 that the lands designated for redistribution began to be handed over to the state. Fifteen months after its announcement by the government, restructuration still showed poor results. In April 1987, many associative enterprises had not yet received official notification of the resolutions affecting their lands. By the same token, communities which had already received property titles had not been able to take possession of the land.

The case of the Chapioco peasant community exemplifies the problems faced by restructuration. During Puno's Rimanakuy, Chapioca had received property titles for lands it was to receive from the Parina CAP. Several months after, however, the community complained that:

> Today we have still not received the land. We only have the paper and no land, because the CAP's administrators refuse to hand the lands over to us and they say they don't want to hear anything about laws or restructuration …. Even the chief of restructuration for the Puno agrarian region tells us that Parina CAP cannot hand over the lands because they are not the owners, [and] this makes us think that Parina has a pact with the engineer [from the Ministry] and that there is a bribe by the enterprise.

According to the Chapioco peasants, in order to prevent the transference of land to their community, a group of Parina CAP's partners, headed by the cooperative's manager—a former majordomo of the old hacienda Parina—had applied for its recognition as a community. Workers of the Parina CAP had joined *chapioqueños* in denouncing this maneuver. Therefore, since the authorities had not attended to Chapioco's complaints, the community had decided to invade the land for which they held titles issued by representatives of the restructuring committee. Other testimonies refer to analogous situations in which old power groups managed to perpetuate their predominance, aided by the tacit or overt complicity of regional authorities.

In this context many communities turned to the peasant federations as the most effective means to break the deadlock. In February and March of 1987, land invasions occurred on the Kunurana ERPS, the Santa Lucia CAP, and the Mañazo SAIS, while the Peasant Federation of Aricoma (Carabaya Province) held a demonstration expressing their intention to take land from the Aricoma SAIS by force if no action was taken to satisfy their demands. In early April, the FDCP moved to hold massive land invasions on May 19, the day when the General Confederation of Workers of Peru (CGTP) had announced a national strike.

The weeks preceding the announced date were characterized by the feverish activism of peasant leaders coordinating dozens of communities and working out agreements between peasants and hacienda workers on the targeted lands. On the designated day, 156 communities representing 15,000 peasant families invaded 280,603 hectares belonging to 22 different *empresas* in an assertion of their rights to the land (FDCP 1987a). On the following days, the communities sent *memoriales* to President García, along with copies of the deeds to the lands which he himself had promised them.

As the peasant movement unleashed its force, Sendero's armed column attempted to use the opportunity to gain a foothold in Puno and lead the struggle for land as part of its national strategy. The PCP-SL had grown mostly among the younger population, including students and school-teachers, in provincial capitals such as Azángaro or Ayaviri, but also among young rural dwellers, part-time peasants with seasonal migration experiences, and the poorer members of communities who sympathized with the PCP-SL's promises to redistribute any livestock and goods taken from the associative enterprises. At the time that land invasions began Sendero had difficulty translating these levels of sympathy, tolerance, or passive support of armed actions into active support of their tactic to take the associative enterprises' land "con las armas en la mano." Conversely, PUM's successful mobilization for land and the FDCP's broad-based movement against the militarization of Puno were direct rebuffs of Sendero's line.

To drive home the differences between its own tactics and those of the "revisionists" in the FDCP and PUM, in April 1987 a PCP-SL column assassinated Zenobio Huarsaya, a founding member of the FDCP who, at the time of his death, was the United Left mayor of San Juan de Salinas. At that very moment, not far from San Juan de Salinas, the FDCP's board was deciding to begin the land takeovers. At Huarsaya's funeral, the FDCP's leaders reaffirmed the distance between their own strategy based on collective decisions and Sendero's based on the imposition of a militarized vanguard. Some weeks later, a PCP-SL column was decimated by the police in the town of Cututuni. During 1987, Sendero's armed action in Puno descended to its lowest point since 1985.

Under the stress of increasing violence and a hardening of new anti-terrorist laws, peasant organizations were obliged to clarify their positions with respect to Sendero. They did so by reaffirming their aims in community assemblies and by reiterating their commitment to the use of legal channels as a means to recuperate land which the PCP-SL asserted could only be obtained through the forceful and violent elimination of the associative enterprises. The peasant organizations also countered Sendero through their vocal opposition to military intervention. Because peasant federations would be subject to persecution if a state of emergency were to be declared, preventing the declaration of a state of emergency (and the consequent military presence) became a necessary condition for advancing the struggle for land. This concern was also voiced by the regional popular assembly and the Catholic Church, which joined forces with the popular and peasant movement to prevent the occurrence of another "dirty war" such as that which had unfolded in the Department of Ayacucho in the early 1980s. The resulting mobilization for peace brought Puno's situation to national attention as a case where the possibility existed for political forces and social organizations to present a united bloc against Sendero's insurgency. Although these expectations were not completely fulfilled, Puno's peace movement managed to contain partially PCP-SL violence and halt militarization until late 1990.

Conclusion

Although it brought about the disappearance of traditional haciendas in Puno, agrarian reform failed to address the peasant communities' histori- cal demands for land. In 1981, 42 associative enterprises had received 1,966,217.51 hectares of agricultural land and natural pastures while only 49,192.23 hectares were directly delivered to peasant communities (Caballero 1991:135). Thus, the formation of associative enterprises did not mean a significant alteration in Puno's historical landholding patterns as the enterprises kept control of 44 percent of the total amount of the department's land while the peasant communities possessed a meager 12 percent. While the former group comprised 18 percent of Puno's rural population, the latter made up approximately 70 percent of it (Caballero 1992: 110).

The amount of land distributed, however, was only part of the problem. The associative enterprises reproduced the oppressive traits of the traditional haciendas in a period when demographic growth and the effects of recurrent droughts and floods spurred the communities' demands for land. With no effective legal route for resolving their demands, peasants resorted to self-organization and struggle. In the process, the peasant community—despite factors of internal differentiation and relative decay—was reborn as an instrument of collective organization (Caballero 1992). Backed by a variety of supporters and allies and as part of a broader regional movement, the community-based struggle for land no longer suffered from the isolation that had traditionally affected Puno's rural movements. In a period when state authorities were withdrawing from the countryside as a result of both government policy and Sendero's insurgency, the FDCP became an effective authority in working out agreements among peasant communities and between *comuneros* and *feudatarios* to carry out a new distribution of land, this time to the benefit of the peasant communities.

The FDCP's power was severely tested, however, by both the managers and by García's Aprista administration. Under the cloak of an *agrarista* proposal, President García launched a plan to reassert governmental control in Puno's countryside. By defending a limited restructuration and by retaining control of positions of authority, local elites tried to reconstitute their power in the new context. The managers of the associative enterprises manipulated and controlled local level authorities and public opinion. They influenced provincial and departmental authorities, for example, by playing off the authorities' traditional and culturally engrained disdain for the peasants.

Another determining factor was the emerging disagreements between national and local instances of the APRA party. Although their organization—CENECAMP—had been effectively bypassed by the restructuring commission, in Puno the managers continued to hold influence over local Aprista leaders and authorities in the Ministry of Agriculture. While the central government could make concessions with relative autonomy, APRA's regional level representatives had a direct interest in keeping the enterprises and medium-sized properties intact.

The peasant movement, however, was strong enough to resist these attempts, both by forcing García to respond to their demands and by bypassing Puno's Aprista leaders (who were ultimately unable to displace their leftist rivals). As the Aprista administration lost popularity and entered into a rapid decline after July 1987, the ability of state officers to regulate the distribution of land was also diminishing while the peasants began to conduct the process on their own.

As the 1990 national elections approached, however, divisions within the United Left and debates within PUM resulted in a division that affected the cohesiveness of the FDCP. In PUM's Second Party Congress in mid-1988 it was decided that peasant communities and organizations should use arms to defend themselves against Sendero. This development affected Puno's regional bloc as some members became reluctant to be linked to PUM's self-defense initiative at a time when calls were growing to harden counterinsurgency measures (Rénique 1991).

In November 1990, a state of emergency was declared in several provinces of Puno and, although Puno did not become another Ayacucho, a gradual process of militarization began at that point. By discouraging peasant organizations, military presence could well aid Sendero's growth in Puno.

Notes

1. In June 1986, Puno's associative enterprises controlled 1,765,116.14 hectares with 19,000 families. (Other sources suggest they may have controlled up to 30,000 families.) The peasant community sector, on the other hand, which represented over 100,00 families, controlled only 565,785 hectares and the *parcialidades* (peasant communities which have not been officially recognized by the state) controlled only 774,415 hectares.

2. Letter from Monsignor Francisco d'Alteroche to President Alan García, Ayaviri, Sept. 7, 1985.

3. *SUR*, #92 (February 1986), p. 11.

4. Ibid.

5. Information on Sendero's actions is from interviews done in Puno and Azángaro in 1987. In particular, I would like to thank Ricardo Vega, Fernando Gonzales, Ronald Llerena (parish priest from Azángaro) and Martha Giraldo of the Puno Human Rights Committee for sharing their information and insights with me.

6. Peru, Chamber of Deputies, draft of the "Informe final de la Comisión investigadora de irregularidades cometidas en las Empresas Asociativas del departamento de Puno," Lima, May 1987.

Bibliography

Arce Borja, Luis. 1989. *Guerra Popular en el Perú, El Pensamiento Gonzalo.* Brussels: Edición Luis Arce Borja.

Barrenechea, Carlos. 1982. "Las nuevas condiciones del subdesarrollo agrario en el Perú," *Cuadernos de Debate.* Lima: Centro Nacional de Estudios y Asesoría Popular.

Bourricaud, Francois. 1967. *Cambios en Puno.* México: Instituto Indigenista Interamericano.

Bravo, Gonzalo. 1987ms. "La reestructuración de las empresas asociativas de Puno." Lima: Cepes, 1987.

Burga, Manuel and Wilson Reátegui. 1981. *Lanas y Capitalismo Mercantil en el Perú.* Lima: Instituto de Estudios Peruanos.

Caballero M., Víctor. 1984. *Las Crisis de las Empresas Asociativas en el Agro Puneño.* Puno: Servicios Populares/Escuelas Campesinas.

_____. 1991. "La realidad de la reestructuración de las Empresas Asociativas en Puno." In V. Caballero & D. Zurita (Eds.), *Puno: Tierra y Alternativa Comunal,* pp. 133–157. Lima: Instituto de Apoyo Agrario.

_____. 1992. "Urbanización de la sociedad rural puneña, crecimiento y cambios en las comunidades campesinas," *Debate Agrario,* 14:107–120.

Calla, Hermogenes, *et.alia.* 1986. *Problemas socio-económicos de una Empresa Asociativa en el proceso de Reforma Agraria. Estudios de Caso: SAIS Buenavista Ltd. No. 23.* Puno: Escuela de Post-grado, Maestria de Desarrollo Rural de la Universidad Nacional de Altiplano.

Carroll. Thomas, Denis Humphreys and Martin Scurrah. 1990. "Oranizaciones de apoyo a grupos de base en el Perú: Una radiografia," *Socialismo y Participación,* 50:23–39.

CCP-FDCP. 1986a. Reestructuración democrática del agro puneño. Via campesina comunero. Puno: CCP-FDCP.

CENECAMP-Puno. 1986. *CENECAMP-Puno a la Conciencia Nacional.* Puno: CENECAMP.

Committee to Support the Revolution in Peru (CSRP). 1991. *Interview with Chairman Gonzalo.* Berkeley, California:CSRP.

Consejo Unificado Nacional Agrario (CUNA). 1983. *Documentos.* Lima: CUNA.

Cotler, Julio. 1980. *Clases, estado y nación en el Perú.* Lima: Instituto de Estudios Peruanos.

de Janvry, Alain. 1981. *The Agrarian Question and Reformism in Latin America*. Baltimore: The Johns Hopkins University Press.

Eguren, Fernando. 1980. "Ley de promoción agraria: Grandes problemas siguen en pie," *Quehacer*, 9:23–28.

Federación Departamental de Campesinos de Puno (FDCP). 1978. Moción sobre tomas de tierras presentada al II Congreso de la FDCP, San Juan de Salinas, Azángaro.

――――. 1986b. *Acuerdos* del III Congreso de la FDCP presentados al Rimanacuy. Puno: FECP.

――――. 1986c. *Carta abierta al Sr. Presidente de la República Dr. Alan García Pérez.* Ayaviri, 4 April 1986.

――――. 1987a. *Informe presentado al Ministerio de Agricultura.* Puno:FDCP.

――――. 1987b. *Nuevo plan aprista: Cerrar la reestructuración y reprimir al campesinado.* Puno: FDCP.

Flores Galindo, Alberto. 1977. *Arequipa y el Sur Andino, siglos XVIII-XX*. Lima: Editorial Horizonte.

FUCAM. 1983. *Comunidad campesina Acari. Diagnóstico para la reestructuración democrótica del Fundo U. Milloni de la ERPS Kunurana.* Puno: Comité Técnico FUCAM.

García Sayán, Diego. 1982. *Tomas de Tierras en el Perú*, Lima: Desco.

Giraldo, Martha & Ana Liria Franch. 1978. Hacienda y Gamonalismo, Azángaro, 1850–1920. Tésis de Magister, Universidad Católica del Perú.

Gonzáles, Raúl. 1986. "¿Qué pasa en Puno?" *Quehacer* 43:31–52.

Instituto de Investigaciones para el Desarrollo del Altiplano (IIDSA). 1983. *Desarrollo Rural Andino y la Problematica Sur Andina.* Puno: Universidad del Altiplano & IIDSA.

――――. 1982. *Informe final del proyecto Economía Campesina y Movimientos Sociales.* Puno: IIDSA.

Judd, Stephen. 1987. The Emergent Andean Church: Inculturation and Liberation in Southern Peru, 1968–1986. Unpublished Ph.D. dissertation, Graduate Theological Union, Berkeley, California.

Matos Mar. José & José Manuel Mejia. 1980. *La Reforma Agraria en el Perú.* Lima: IEP.

Mejia, José Manuel (ed.). 1980. *Promoción Agraria Para Quien? Análisis de la Ley de Promoción y Desarrollo Agrario.* Lima: Tiempo Presente.

Montoya, Rodrigo. 1986. "La misma política de siempre," *La República* (Lima), 14 Jan. 1986.

Municipio de Puno. 1985. *Hagamos realidad nuestra propia alternativa de desarrollo.* Documento de trabajo elaborado electivamente por el equipo de programa especial de promoción de la regionalización y asesoría los gobiernos regionales. Octubre 1985.

Palao Berastaín, Juan. 1988. *Programas, Proyectos, Micro-regiones y Desarrollo Rural: El Caso de Puno, 1947–1987.* Lima: Fundación Friederich Ebert.

Peru. Ministry of Agriculture. Agrarian Region XXI (Puno). 1987. *Comunicado Oficial.* Puno, May 29, 1987.

Rénique, José Luis, "La batalla por Puno: violencia y democracia en la sierra sur" in Debate Agrario 10, March 1991, pp. 83–108.

_____. 1982. "Violencia y Democracia en la sierra sur del Perú: Puno en la era post-velasquista." In C.I. Degregori (ed.), *Perú: el problema agrario en debate/ SEPIA IV*, pp. 441–458. Lima: Seminario Permanente de Investigación Agraria.

Robles, Fernando. 1987. *Reestructuración y Desarrollo Regional de Puno*. Puno: Universidad Nacional de Altiplano.

Rojas, Telmo. 1988. "Límites y posibilidades del desarrollo microrregional," *Perú: el problema agrario en debate*, pp. 386–391. Lima: Seminario Permanente de Investigación Agraria.

Salas, Enrique. 1984. "Desarrollo y penetración neocolonial en las comunidades campesinas," *Problematica Sur Andina*, 6:19–59.

Scurrah, Martin (ed.). 1987. *Empresas Asociativas y Comunidades Campesinas, Puno después de la Reforma agraria*. Lima: Gredes.

Stepan, Alfred. 1978. *State and Society: Peru in a Comparative Perspective*. Princeton: Princeton University Press.

Tamayo Herrera, José. 1982. *Historia Social e Indigenismo en el Altiplano*. Lima: Ediciones Treintaitres.

Vega, Ricardo. 1989. "Empresa comunal y vía campesina comunera (Apuntes desde la experiencia de Puno)." *Allpanchis*, 33:84–107.

8

Peasant Culture and Political Violence in the Peruvian Andes: Sendero Luminoso and the State

Deborah Poole

On March 15, 1986, a twelve year old boy died of natural causes in a small house outside the community of Llusco in the province of Chumbivilcas. The boy's grandparents, with whom he had lived, covered the body—which lay inside their dark, one-room adobe house—with an assortment of rags and old clothes, and set off for the four hour walk to Santo Tomás. Before moving or washing the body, they were required by law to fulfill a legal act called the *levantamiento de cadaver* (removal of the corpse). Before burying it, they were then further required by the state to perform a medically supervised autopsy. Both needed to be witnessed by Señor Alvis, the current Justice of the Peace and former ruling *hacendado* of Llusco. Señor Alvis, who was in Santo Tomás for business and personal pleasure, arrived to the house some four days later to find the body exactly where the boy's grandparents had left it. Without examining the body, he ordered and signed the *levantamiento* and authorized an autopsy to be supervised by the nurse stationed at Llusco's medical post. On the day of the funeral, however, the nurse declared that, in order to perform the autopsy, she would require the assistance of the district's *rezador* (prayer). The *rezador*, an old, landless and kinless peasant, performed the legally required autopsies for peasant burials in return for a small fee paid by the family. For an additional sum, he also agreed to pray over the body and perform the funeral rites, since there was no priest in either Llusco or Santo Tomás. For his instruments he used an ax and a tin cooking knife. As he performed the autopsy in the cemetary, a large circle of curious neighbors and onlookers from the community gathered around the body to comment on the various internal organs which the autopsy gradually revealed. The

247

various organ parts were then gathered up in small plastic bags to be shipped by truck to a laboratory in far-off Lima.

*   *   *

On the evening of July 25, 1987, a large crowd of people gathered in the dusty open space which passed for the central "plaza" of Antuyu, a small peasant community in the high plateau above Llusco in the province of Chumbivilcas. They were there to celebrate the feast of Saint James (Santiago), a mounted saint known in Spain as the Moor Slayer, in other parts of Peru as the patron of lightening and thunder, and, in Antuyu, as the patron saint of livestock rustlers. As in other patronal festivals in the Andes, the principal activity was drinking alcohol and beer and dancing to music paid for by the *carguyuq*, or fiesta sponsor, an office filled each year by a member of one of the district's more notorious livestock rustling families. Unlike other Andean patronal feasts, however, in Antuyu the *carguyuq* and his family were conspicous in their absence. The town celebrated the saint under their auspices, and in the shadow of their well known violent power, but, perhaps as a means to heighten that power, without their personal presence. Also absent was the saint himself, because his image had burned along with the church some years before. Loyal to their saint—and cautious of his links to the rustlers who continually stole their animals— the peasants of Antuyu nevertheless paraded the ashes and few remaining pieces of wood left from his once revered and holy statue. A gesture meant to appease the rustlers who presumably watched from their *estancia* (ranch) outside the town, this procession also served to pass the saint's image over offerings which some victims of livestock-rustlers had clandestinely buried in the four corners of the square as a precautionary measure. Perhaps these offerings served as well to dilute the iconic power of the all too human *carguyuq* who, that evening following the procession, galloped on horseback into the plaza with his face and chest smeared with fresh blood.

*   *   *

On April 24, 1990, twenty-six armed and mounted Peruvian military personnel, led by an army lieutenant nicknamed "Negro," entered the peasant community of Qasahui, near Antuyu in the Chumbivilcano district of Quiñota.[1] As one of the *patrullas volantes* (roving patrols) sent out from the regional military headquarters in Antabamba (Apurímac), the soldiers' ostensible mission was to round up "subversives," locate arms stashs and gather intelligence on activities of the Peruvian Communist Party "Sendero Luminoso."[2] In Qasahui, the patrol arrested eight peasants, claiming that, because they were outside the boundaries of their community, they were terrorists. Following their detention, they were stripped naked and tortured by dunking in a nearby lake for four hours. The following day (April 25) a group of six soldiers rode patrol in the various sectors of Qasahui, taking three additional prisoners, all of whom were later beaten.

At 9:00 A.M. April 26, sixteen prisoners (ten from Qasahui and six who had been brought with the soldiers from the neighboring department of Apurimac) were made to form a column. Four individuals were selected from the column and locked in a house. The remaining twelve were made to drink alcohol which had been laced with an unidentifed substance put in it by one of the soldiers. The following day, one of the twelve died. The eleven remaining prisoners were taken to Ccapallullu hill and forced to stand in a row. The soldiers then dynamited and shot machine gun rounds at the peasants, killing all eleven. The bodies were hidden in caves on Ccapallulu and covered with dry grass.

The soldiers then left Qasahui, taking with them the remaining four prisoners, whom they had tied to their pack horses. One year after their departure from Qasahui, no arrests have been made despite positive identification of the military personnel involved and concerted attempts by a parliamentary investigatory committee, a national human rights organization (APRODEH), and Amnesty International. Instead, in March 1991 the entire province of Chumbivilcas, along with those of Canchis, Canas and Espinar were declared under a military state of emergency that would last for nearly a year.

*   *   *

Blood smeared on an *abigeo*'s face; a decomposing child's body; a mass grave; military rule and suspension of constitutional rights: As I look at my fieldnotes and archives from Chumbivilcas, these images of horror move alongside and intertwine with all my more cherished pastoral memories of potato harvest rituals, music-filled fiestas, and family dinners around the hearth. These images invade my thoughts when I come to write about Chumbivilcas. They are the images which I feel need to be explained not merely because they have now come to be the focus of anthropological memory in Peru, but, more importantly, because they are, increasingly, the stuff of daily life in Chumbivilcas and many other areas of the southern Peruvian highlands. Perhaps stronger still than the experientially constant and psychologically diffuse sentiments of community and family, these emotionally charged moments of brutality and blood constitute the elusive utterances and evocative symbols by which physical violence comes to authorize the many forms of state, ethnic, and class power that infiltrate peasant daily life.

Seen against this background, the incident in Qasahui, shocking as it is, does not, unfortunately, form a substantive break with the burials and rustlers' fiestas which preceded it or, for that matter, with either Chumbivilcas's or Peru's historic past. Rather, from the point of view of the peasants themselves, it might better be thought of as a continuation— or perhaps culmination—of a historical experience in which power has traditionally been negotiated through the use of physical violence. Accostumed—though by no means resigned—to the violent extremes of *gamonal* behavior they have witnessed in their lives, peasants throughout Chumbivilcas and other parts of Peru's southern highlands have come to understand that power is something which is negotiated and inscribed on the body. This process of negotiation and inscription, moreover, is not just episodic. It is not restricted to such moments of extreme brutality as that in which eight Qasahui peasants tragically died. It is continually under construction in events such as those at Antuyu and Llusco where peasant bodies are symbolically encoded as the passive victims of forces beyond their control.

Both the immediate horror of events such those at Qasahui, Antuyu, and Llusco and their historically imaginable connections with the ongoing traditions of violence characterizing Peru's southern highlands, bring into vivid focus the difficulty and necessity of rethinking the notion of a "culture of violence." Do the peasants' shared and oft repeated experiences with the brutality of a state required and primitively performed "autopsy," for example, in some way prefigure their understandings of the physical mutilations and massacres enacted by other agents of the state? Is there a shared understanding of the nature of physical violence and blood underlying the symbolic gestures of an *abigeo* in Antuyu and an army lieutenant? Does an understanding of the symbolic and expressive elements of Chumbivilcano peasant experience assist us at all in understanding the meaning of the massacre in Qasahui?

The answers we formulate to such questions depend very much upon the ways in which we understand and confront a series of presuppositions regarding the nature of cultural perception, historical determination, and violent action. These in turn depend upon how we reconcile the semantically polarized fields assigned in our social science literature and political traditions to the competing constructs of culture and violence. In these traditions, culture is characterized as symbolic, diffuse, ethereal, and unconscious or unmotivated. It is seen to be a natural phenomenon tied to concepts of appropriateness and order. This is true as well of those theories of culture which understand it to be constructed as a historial consequence of individual actions and beliefs. In these theories, individual actions and creations are understood to be "cultural" precisely *because* they draw on and contribute to some shared understanding of symbolic or imaginative expression. Violence, by comparison, is frequently understood to be instrumentally motivated, physically concrete, and focussed

or targetted. It is seen to be an inherently *un*natural phenomenon related
conceptually to disorder and chaos. It is usually also considered, by virtue
of its physical concreteness, to be an individual (and hence asocial) act: Violence is both enacted by individuals and does harm to discrete individual bodies. This individual ascription placed on violence is brought out by
the complementary notion of "collective violence" in which a group or
crowd is considered to have acted "of one mind" to effect an act of violence.

Consideration of the quite different fields of meaning assigned to the
two terms "violence" and "culture" renders even more problematic their
unification in the notion of a "culture of violence." Does this phrase mean
that the collective or symbolic sphere of culture somehow relates to, or
motivates, the instrumental and individual act of violence? Or that the instrumental physicality of concrete violent acts has somehow prefigured
the collective symbolic domain of culture? Even a preliminary reflection
on these two different possible readings of a single phrase makes clear the
extent to which the commonly heard, and even popular, notion of "a culture of violence" is in need of serious consideration if it is to be of any use
in historical or anthropological inquiries into the forms and meanings of
contemporary political and social violence.

In this concluding essay, I want to reflect upon some of the ways in
which the historical experience of the *provincias altas* can assist us to rethink critically the relationship between violence and culture in 1980s and
1990s Peru. First I examine the historical vision and philosophy of violence of the Communist Party of Peru ("Sendero Luminoso" [Shining Path
or PCP-SL]) and its roots in European rationalism. Whereas many popular
and academic representations of Sendero's violence have attempted to explain it as an irrational or emotional expression of the frustration of ethnically or racially marginalized youth, within the party's elaborated historical teleology, violence figures not as a byproduct of ethnic or national
identity, but rather as the principal force giving shape, order, and meaning to the history of both Peru and the working classes. As an ordering
force in history, violence becomes, in this partisan historical vision, not
only the principal "cultural" determinant of Peruvian political and historical identity, but a powerful ideological form shaping PCP-SL militants'
commitment to both the party and its armed struggle.

Next I examine the role of racial ideologies in shaping the Peruvian
state's military response to the PCP-SL. In the popular image of a "cycle of
violence," state violence is seen to occur in response to that of the PCP-SL
or some other insurgent force. The racial forms assumed by state repression are then seen to be expressions of an underlying colonial heritage of
racial discrimination which surfaces in moments of social crisis. Closer
consideration of the history of state formation in republican Peru, how-

ever, reveals the importance of racial ideologies and practices to the consolidation and structuring of the modern Peruvian state.

Finally, I examine how both the PCP-SL's authoritarian violence and the racist violence of the state relate historically to popular, or "cultural," understandings of power and conflict in Andean Peru. I suggest that Andean peasants do not simply accept the authoritarian equations of violence and power offered to them by both the PCP-SL and the state's counterinsurgency forces. Rather, the historical experience of *gamonalismo* and associated forms of racial and class violence has provided peasants with a cultural understanding of violence in which the relationship between violence and power is seen to be a highly fragile and contested one.

The PCP-Sendero Luminoso

On May 17, 1980, during the first presidential elections in Peruvian history in which illiterate peasants had been allowed to vote, several masked and armed individuals appeared in the Ayacuchano provincial capital of Chuschi and burnt the ballots. Hours later a local schoolteacher and several students were arrested and charged with the incident. They were members of the Communist Party of Peru "Sendero Luminoso" (PCP-SL). This Maoist political party had been formed ten years earlier following a dispute between a small group within the Partido Comunista del Perú "Bandera Roja"(Peruvian Communist Party-Red Flag, or PCP-BR) led by Abimael Guzmán and the majority group within the same party led by Saturnino Paredes. As a result of this dispute and the defeat of Guzmán's faction of the party in the congress of one of Ayacucho's regional peasant federations, Guzmán and his followers consolidated in 1970 to form the PCP "Sendero Luminoso," a party which from its early years would privilege clandestine organisation and armed struggle over work with the "masses."[3]

Over the next ten years Guzmán and his fellow party members worked out of the University of Huamanga in Ayacucho, where they controlled at different moments sections of the student federation and the education program. In the 1978 Ninth Central Committee Plenary of the PCP-SL, Guzmán and other party leaders declared that their party had completed its process of consolidation and was ready to assume its role as the revolutionary vanguard for the Peruvian working class. Clandestine military training schools were formed and, on April 19, 1980—one month before the action in Chuschi—Abimael Guzmán announced to his party the initiation of the armed struggle (Guzmán 1989c). Shortly after the events in Chuschi, the party carried out armed actions and bombings in Lima and other coastal and highland cities (DESCO 1989; PCP-SL 1982).

At the time, journalists and politicians in the coastal capital of Lima dismissed the event in Chuschi as a relatively meaningless gesture of provincial factionalism and political infantilism. It was, they argued, an act of symbolic and hence harmless violence performed by an irrelevant splinter party, in an impoverished part of the country where peasants, in any case, represented a relatively insignificant political force. In short, like the peasants for whom the PCP-SL claimed to speak, the charred remains of Chuschi's ballots were viewed as a curious, even exotic, sign of the wildness and incivility which marks the Andean highlands in Peruvian national discourse.

This initial reading of Sendero's violence reflects the strength of prevailing beliefs about both violence and the sierra. As a form of political or social action, violence is often equated with an explosive spontaneity or unthought out mode of action more appropriate to the non-political realm of the emotional or infantile, than to the mature domain of politics. Thus, for example, it is not unusual to hear violent acts characterized as expressions of "frustration" or as irrational "outbursts." Through such expressions, violence is marked as an act appropriate to the emotional (and hence irrational) domain of the adolescent, immature, or feminine. Such characterizations are particularly common in cases of violence carried out by Third World or colonial populations who have already been marked in the discourse of European paternal or colonial rule as "childish" or "immature." It is precisely this association which has been used by the press and terrorism "experts" to distinguish Third World "terrorist" violence from the supposedly more reasoned acts of war carried out by "Western" nations (Chomsky 1988b; Herman & O'Sullivan 1989; Said 1988). Unlike the violence of the irrational "terrorist," military acts of violence carried out by Western nations are routinely described as acts of retaliation, prevention, self-defense or—even more revealingly—as "punitive strikes."

In the case of Sendero, the association between violence and immaturity has been strengthened by dominant images of the Andean highlands and the Andean highland peasantry, and by the assumption that the PCP-SL—because it originated and carried out many of its most visible early actions in the highlands—was in fact a highland political or peasant movement. Since at least the late eighteenth century when the *mestizo* muleteer and Inca descendant, José Gabriel Tupac Amaru, threatened the Peruvian colonial state with his armies of Indian rebels, Lima has lived with the fear of Indian masses sweeping down from the mountains to invade the coastal *creole* capital. Such fears strengthened the Lima elite's royalist resistance to independence in 1821, and they continue to fuel modern day fears of the migrant poor who have invaded the streets and households of Lima in the guise of *ambulantes* (street-vendors), taxi-drivers, and maids. As part and parcel of this coastal dread of the Andes and its peoples, the highlands have been portrayed in both popular literature and scientific discourse in Peru as a harsh and inhospitable environment, whose geological, ecological, and climatic conditions predispose its inhabitants to violence, delinquency, and crime (Poole 1988 & 1990).

Today such images continue to inform popular racist images of Andean Indians and *cholos* as violent or agressive, as well as the more occasional "scientific" attempts to explain Senderista violence. As recently as October 1992, an influential Peruvian magazine wrote that Senderista violence could be explained physiologically by the young age of many of the party's members, their excess hormones, high stress levels, and blood pressure, and psychologically by their resulting ability to "focus the conscience on a single objective (the party dogma), by blocking out their surroundings." In the highlands these effects were heightened, the magazine continued, because "people who live in the altitude—above 3,500 meters—are more prone to violence" due to the fact that a "lack of oxigen predisposes them to aggressivity."[4]

Such associations between the highlands, violence, and Sendero helped to shape Peruvians' early expectations that the PCP-SL was a childish, and hence passing, phenomenon. Nine years after the initiation of the PCP-SL's armed campaign, the Peruvian Senate Special Commission on Violence wrote a report in which violence carried out by groups in arms was classified as a form of "symbolic violence." Sendero's armed struggle, the Commission members argued in their report, was *aberrant* precisely because it had gone beyond this domain of the "symbolic" to encompass a truly "political" form of violence (Peru, Senado 1989:40). Similarly dichotomized models of Peruvian political behavior emerge from the paradigms of modernization theory that continue to dominate much political science writing on Sendero and Peru. Within these paradigms, a rational, modern, or "civilized" center (Lima) is opposed to a less developed periphery (the Andes) whose peoples are described as "traditional." Using this model, political scientists have attempted to explain Sendero's existence and actions as an expression of the resentment or frustration felt by a "peripheral population" towards a modernizing center which has been unable to meet their increased expectations for development and improved life conditions. Not only do such theories dovetail easily with popular Peruvian images of a childlike and irrational traditional peasant population, but, in the case of Sendero, they have been further strengthened by the widespread notion that Sendero's Maoist military strategy consists of a unidirectional "encirclement" of the cities from the countryside.[5]

Sendero's actions, however, have belied both Peruvian racist stereotypes of highland or Andean society, and the political scientists' equally simplistic models of "traditional" versus "modern" forms of political behavior. The party's leaders—including Guzmán—have come predominantly either from provincial urban elites or from Lima, and not from peasant backgrounds. Its political-military strategy is derived from philosophical and military sources having nothing whatsoever to do with either Andean indigenous culture or sociological theories of peasant rebellion. Nor was the party at any point in its history an exclusively—or even predominantly—rural movement. From the beginning of their armed struggle, Sendero's actions have been divided almost equally between urban and rural theaters of military operations. In later years, the party has increasingly privileged urban actions as the groundwork for a planned final insurrection that party members believe will lead to a seizure of power and the collapse of the Peruvian state. Moreover, far from depending on the support of the rural "peasant base" hypothesized by some analysts of Sendero's guerrilla war (e.g., McClintock 1984 & 1989; Woy-Hazelton & Hazelton 1989), many of the rural areas the PCP-SL "controls" have been so severely depopulated as to render such a "base" physically impossible.[6] In other, less isolated regions, such as Puno described by Rénique in Chapter 7, Sendero has taken advantage of local political conflicts or contradictions to infiltrate and temporarily work through existing movements for social justice. Work on party recruitment, by comparison, has focussed on urban labor unions and on students in both coastal and highland cities, and only secondarily on peasant and rural populations.[7]

Clearly the ethnic and class dynamics underlying Sendero's war are more complex than any dualistic models of a Peruvian society divided between Spanish and Indian, center and periphery, coast and highlands, or modernity and tradition would lead us to believe. How then to explain the extreme forms of violence and brutality that have characterized Sendero's actions if not through such models of ethnic divisiveness and its attendant feelings of hatred and revenge? From the beginning of its war, the use of violence and terror has formed an integral part of the PCP-SL's overall political and military strategy.[8] This strategy is designed to eliminate competing organizations and forces in the national arena of popular and left-wing political struggle and to polarize the political situation such that the only two political agents are the PCP-SL and a militarized Peruvian state. For this reason, the PCP-SL's principal targets have moved from state elected local office holders under the governments of Fernando Belaúnde (1980–1985) and Alan García (1985–1990), to leftwing activists and grassroots union and peasant leaders in the later years of García's administration and under current president Alberto Fujimori. Through the physical elimination or intimidation of elected authorities, Sendero hopes to cut the state's ties to local populations and provincial level organizations; by targeting popular leaders, the party hopes to eliminate or weaken those organizations who provide the peasant and working classes with an alternative to the PCP-SL's authoritarian leadership. To under-

stand Sendero's relationship with the Peruvian peasantry, it is important
to note that it is this goal of political polarization through both the elimination of state authorities and the purging or "cleansing" of the Peruvian
"revisionist" Left that constitutes the PCP-SL's military *raison d'être* and
not the revindication of Andean cultural or ethnic nationality.[9] As a strategic military tool, the role of violence in the PCP-SL's war is instrumentally
related to this purging drive; it is assassination and terror (through, for example, car bombs and exemplary executions) which serve as the most effective means to either eliminate or debilitate competing political forces.

But how to explain Senderistas' willingness to carry out such acts of violence? One mode of explaining this phenomenon has been to invoke the
youthfulness of the party's recruits, their relatively high levels of education and hence expectations, and the frustration they have experienced as
provincial, often darker-skinned youth seeking employment in Peru
(DeGregori 1989; Degregori & López Ricci 1990). Such explanations have
parallels with the arguments for cathartic racial violence proposed by
Frantz Fanon (1961) in his analysis of violence in French colonial Algeria.
Indeed, the models of racial or ethnic relations informing these psychological and sociological explanations of violence frequently posit racial
and ethnic discrimination in Peru as a *colonial* tradition, or archaic trace,
rather than as a component of *modern* Peruvian society. Both racism and
the violence it provokes are seen to be irrational or attitudinal vestiges of
a social order which has not yet become fully modern.

Another, more convincing, way of explaining the PCP-SL's commitment to violence as both an instrument for enacting political change *and* a
doctrine or motivating ideology, is to reevaluate the party's ideas regarding violence not as part of a *colonial* racial or ethnic rage, but rather as an
outgrowth of the party's hyper-rationalist—or what Guzmán himself calls
"scientific"—commitment to carrying out a preordained program of revolutionary change. Here the most important vehicles for conveying party
ideology—and the party's commitment to violence—are Abimael Guzmán's compelling vision of history and his concept of contradiction. For
Guzmán, history is a material force devoid of human agency. As such, the
course of history can be neither stopped nor questioned by individuals.
"The done is done, it cannot be reopened," Guzmán has written. "How
can grains detain the millstone? They will be reduced to dust." (Guzmán
1989b:142–3) This vision of history represents one of Guzmán's most significant departures from the Marxist tradition. For Marx, and for the vast
majority of the Marxist theorists and intellectuals who have built on his
work, it is human agency (e.g., the actions of the working classes) and the
contradictions between oppposing sectors of human society (e.g., the
struggle between capital and labor) which constitute the unpredictable

motor force of history. Socialism and communism are conceived as the products of an ongoing human struggle to alter the course of history, rather than as the necessary or predetermined outcome of History itself. For Guzmán, by comparison, history moves along a predestined path which individuals are incapable of either altering or resisting. The PCP-SL and its armed struggle are both the inevitable expressions of this historical force, and the means by which individuals will be selected to take part in the inexorable progress of History as it moves towards its final goal of a communist society.

> Many are called and few chosen. We stand alone. We are all subject to the storm; the wind carries away the chaff, but the grain remains. In 1927 [there was] a great storm and the Chinese Communist Party was sifted out. The Party [the PCP-SL] has entered a great storm, everything is going to burn; for some time we have been ready to become the polar center; the convergence has already begun. Our road is set; all the problems will be resolved.(Guzmán 1989b:141; translation mine)

As the inheritor of the revolutionary mission of the "true" Chinese Communist Party, the PCP-SL and its armed struggle have come to constitute (what Senderistas' understand to be) the inevitable epicenter of world revolution not as a result of concrete human actions, but as an <u>act of historical destiny</u>.[10]

Guzmán also departs from the Marxist-Leninist tradition in assuming that *all* contradiction is antagonistic. According to Marx, contradiction is manifested in society through the struggle between opposing classes. The fundamental characteristic of these contradictions is that they are dialectical because both terms of each contradiction existentially presuppose the other. As such, social contradictions imply a form of inclusive opposition which must be worked out—like history itself—through the concrete actions and struggles of human beings. For Guzmán, by comparison, *all* contradiction is conceived as a mutually exclusive antagonism. Because the two poles of a contradiction are in essence different from and external to the other, the necessary and only resolution to the antagonism or contradiction between the poles is through the total irradication of one of the two poles. Contradiction is not resolved, as in the Marxist dialectic, through the synthesis between two opposing poles, but rather through the physical annihilation of one of the two poles (Arce Borja 1988; Guzmán 1989b).

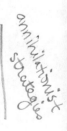

annihilationist strategy

It is this concept of absolute contradiction, together with Guzmán's theory of history, that has provided the philosophical or conceptual apparatus around which the party has been able to articulate its commitment to violence as a form of enacting—or hastening—political and social change.

When conceived of as the opposite pole of an antagonistic contradiction, other social classes and political forces are construed as a sort of absolute "other" which can be dealt with only through their complete elimination. Thus, for Sendero, dialogue is impossible either with what Sendero refers to as the "revisionist left" or with the "old state"; purging becomes the only mechanism through which History and the armed struggle can advance towards the inevitable victory of the PCP-SL and the establishment of its "New Democracy."[11]

Similarly, when conceived as the necessary and irresistible motor force of history, the party's armed struggle and its use of violence cease to be moral dilemmas and assume the form of necessary historical actions. Violence is consistently described by Guzmán as a material force external to the individual. Far from an act of individual moral or political will, violence becomes a force which must be *assumed* by the individual as an act of historical destiny. It is an external—or in Guzmán's language, a *material*—fact in which the party member must immerse him or herself as an act of revolutionary faith. "We reaffirm ourselves in revolutionary violence as the universal law to take Power," Guzmán has written. "We communists must empower ourselves ideologically, politically and organically *to assume* [violence] properly." (PCP-SL 1989:310; emphasis mine) From the point of view of party members, Guzmán's historical teleology and its invocation of violence as a supra-human historical fact have had a powerful ideological effect. The personal decision to take part in the party's armed struggle surpasses the realm of the political, to encompass a broader philosophical commitment to allow oneself to be swept up—and possibly destroyed—by both History and the violence that propels historical change. As described in a Senderista document captured in 1984, "Blood fortifies us and if in the 'bath' which the Armed Forces have given us blood is running, it is not harming us but rather making us stronger (Gorriti 1990:168)."[12]

Contrary to popular invocations of either the Andean roots of Sendero or the non-Western "terrorist" fanaticism of Guzmán, this vision of history is neither that of Peru's many indigenous rebellions—all of which were directed towards the reform, as opposed to total destruction of the state—or that of the frustrated and irrational terrorist. Rather, the single most important elements of the hybrid political culture upon which Guzmán draws for his vision of history and the armed struggle are an anti-state insurrectionary tradition inherited from the French revolution (Billington 1980; Hobsbawm 1990a & 1990b) and the rationalist philosophies of progress inherited from the European Enlightenment (Adorno & Horkheimer 1972). Building upon Rousseauian conceptions of utopian community and the unnaturalness of social division, the eighteenth century French bourgeois revolutionaries invented the language of totalitar-

ian politics and terrorist purges (Hoffman 1987). Guzmán's program for violent revolution in Peru picks up on each of the fundamental elements of this eighteenth century discourse of revolution—its myths of unanimity (or harmony), utopian teleology of progress, politics of paranoia, and conception of war as a mechanism for the purification and unification of society—to sculpt a Jacobin-like program for the total destruction of the Peruvian state and all its "reactionary" accomplices.[13] To attribute the totalitarian aspects of Guzmán's philosophy either to the "Marxist tradition" or to the supposedly dichotomized arena of Peruvian ethnic politics is fundamentally to misrepresent the nature, and importance, of Sendero's violent program for the destruction of Peruvian society.[14]

While the similarities between Guzmán's totalitarian worldview and that of, for example, Robespierre or Condorcet, are striking, an anthropological explanation of Sendero's use and understanding of violence must go beyond simply tracing its broad discursive genealogies, to question how these (European) traditions were shaped by the specific history of Peru and, in particular, by the forms of social and political violence which have characterized that history. Here we need, in turn, to examine not just the history of violence in Peru, but the manner in which Sendero's ideologues have interpreted and represented that history to their followers. In a 1978 text, Guzmán lays out the basic elements of this partisan historical vision of Peru:

> Violence is inscribed in the essence of our history. The *conquistadores* used violence to subjugate these lands and to submit them to colonial domination; Tupac Amaru unchained violence in defense of the rights and demands that mobilized hundreds of thousands of indigenous peasants; today and yesterday violence is the peasantry's usual means in their unfinished fight for 'the land for those who work it'. Violence is in our society's centuries of history, principally in that of the peasantry who continue to confront the landlord-bureacratic State [and] especially against the *gamonalismo* which is its base and sustenance. (Guzmán 1989a:97; translation mine)

In this and other Senderista texts, violence surfaces as something more than a conjunctural or episodic feature of Peruvian history: In conformance with Guzmán's vision of History, it is seen to be the determining and historically constant force which has propelled a popular struggle of which Sendero forms but the latest, and final, stage. In this vision of history, the natural, or "organic," link between the party and the masses is neither nationalism nor cultural and ethnic revindications, but rather violence itself.

It is on the basis of this historical understanding of violence that Guzmán has reworked the Maoist concept of the "mass-line." As outlined by

Mao, the first element of this concept asserts that the party should have a deep reverence for the "political and inspirational powers of the masses"; the second element "sets out a technique for coordinating the efforts of the party and the masses in the formulation and execution of policy. This technique requires party cadres to study and synthesize the unsystematic views of the masses on questions of policy ... and to exhort the masses to ... translate [their views] into action" (Tiruchelvam 1978). In Mao's China, the mass-line concept was used to develop forms of popular justice based on traditional community modes of democratic decision making. Through study of the traditional forms of social sanction used by the masses, the Chinese Communist cadres developed institutional forms of "popular justice" under the guidance of the party.

For Guzmán and his followers, however, it is violence, and not the peasants' traditional forms of democratic community, which is the "universal law" of Peruvian history (Guzmán 1989a:97). Indeed, Guzmán has exorcized all traces of such democratic or community based forms of social struggle from a historical vision which instead isolates, privileges, and *naturalizes* violence as the principal motor force in Peruvian social and political history. He sees this historically proven yet unsystematic use of violence by the masses as a force which can be channeled into "revolutionary violence" under the authoritarian guidance of the PCP-SL (Arce Borja 1988; Guzmán 1989a & 1989b).

It is in defence of this perception of violence as the organic link uniting the masses and the party, that Sendero has also modified classic Maoist military and political strategy. Unlike Mao, who gave priority to his war against the state by forming strategic alliances with other opposition forces, Guzmán's version of prolonged guerrilla war adopts an exclusionary or Jacobin politics of paranoia to define all those who do not participate in or condone his party's use of violence as "enemies of the revolution"who must, therefore, be eliminated (*Amauta* 1989). These "enemies" include the leftwing parties, development organizations, labor unions, peasant federations, *rondas* (peasant patrols against rustlers), *frentes de defensa* (unarmed community defense groups), neighborhood and mothers' clubs, church groups, research centers, and electoral campaigns whose historical legitimacy Sendero denies. Rather than develop forms of popular justice based on the democratic practices of these organizations, the PCP-SL has exclusively privileged violence in the form of corporal punishment, massacres, and the exemplary executions euphemistically referred to as "popular trials."

Guzmán's philosophical (or historical) emphasis on violence and his party's targeting of popular political organizations and leaders thus go hand-in-hand: They are the direct and logical outcome of Guzmán's teleological vision of History and historical progress, his heuristic isolation of violence as the "universal law" of Peruvian history, his refusal to build upon existing forms of popular democratic organization, and his under-standing that it is violence which forms the historical or cultural link be-tween party cadres and the popular masses. From the beginning of their actions in the Ayacuchano countryside, Sendero has been unwilling to work with or through any existing forms of community organization. Rather, upon entering communities, the party sets to work to reorganize completely the peasant community (Isbell 1992; del Pino 1991). This un-willingness stems, in part, from Guzmán's refusal to acknowledge the role of democratic and non-violent forms of popular political struggle in the course of Peruvian political history and his consequent inability to accept community traditions of democratic decision-making as the basis for the forms of popular justice which he envisions as part of Sendero's "New Democracy." Rather than acknowledge and work through these popular democratic organizations, Guzmán's reading of Peruvian history empha-sizes the violence which has been a feature not so much of peasant histori-cal agency as of the Andean *gamonales* and provincial elites from whose ranks Sendero draws its leaders and many of its cadres.

The State

Seeking to match force with force, the Peruvian military has battled the PCP-SL's nearly invisible insurgent army by targetting a peasant civilian population from whom they—like some political scientists and Sendero "experts"—mistakenly believe the party draws both its strength and membership. Surveillance, disappearance, torture, massacre and arrest without charge, are by now the standard weapons in this counterinsur-gency campaign.[15] With the increasing prominence accorded to Sendero's activities in national political discourse, other groups have mounted com-peting insurgencies directed against both Sendero and the state.[16] The more recent appearance of rightwing death squads—who work in alliance with the military to eliminate these competing guerrilla forces and other non-armed union and leftist leaders—places Peru firmly within the esca-lating cycle of violence said to characterize such other Latin American societies as Colombia, Guatemala and El Salvador.[17]

But what does it mean to speak of a "cycle of violence?" Popular and journalistic accounts of political violence in the Third World describe a systemic process in which violent acts by insurgent forces feed those per-formed by state or military agents, and vice versa. In this vision of the world, the motor force propelling violent practices through time is pre-sumed to be a reactive process occurring between equal or matched oppo-nents. As these practices continue over time, a narrative of escalation is generated in which we are led to expect (as in all Western European derived forms of narrative) a resolution or outcome, and in which relative power advantages appear to result from the playing out of military moves and countermoves. The opposing sides thus come to be identified with their positioning in a give and take of violent activities, while violence itself acquires a narrative ontology divorced from the specific social and historical contexts in which it unfolds.[18] As a structurally mimetic, and hence universally similar, ontological force, the logic, organization and meaning of violence is then assumed to be the same in Peru, Lebanon, Liberia, Mozambique, El Salvador, or Guatemala. At the basis of many of these academic and popular representations of Third World violence lurk classic anthropological theories relating political and social violence to the internal working of "tribal" (or non-modern) social organization.[19] Yet other theories further naturalize the violence of others by positing that all human psychology (and therefore social organization) is inherently mimetic and therefore aggressive by nature.[20]

Such universalizing theories go far in explaining the mimetic rationalities of retaliation and revenge informing the proliferation of violence in such countries as Peru. In their reliance on a representational structure by which violence is assigned its own narrative ontology or internal logic, however, they do little to explain the specific forms which violence assumes. Similarly, by defining opponents as equally matched and power differences as a result of the temporal play of violence itself, they do little to explain the nature of the historical events, class structures, racial ideologies, and political cultures through which civilian populations are drawn—both physically and ideologically—into the particular "cycle of violence" that afflicts them.

To answer these more challenging questions, it is necessary to distinguish the distinct forms of violence practiced by different agents in each society. In the case of Peru in the 1980s and 1990s, for example, this would require recognition of the fact that the targeted political assassinations performed by the PCP-SL form a qualitatively different mode of violence from the collective punishments and massacres performed against peoples of highland or "Indian" origins (lumped in Peru and other Andean countries under the racialized ethnic label of *cholo*) by the predominantly white/*mestizo*/Spanish-speaking members of the state-backed counterinsurgency forces.[21]

These actions respond to a historically specific form of racism which permeates all levels of Peruvian society and history. Since the conquest and colonial period, when Peru, like Spain's other New World colonies, was divided into two ethnically constituted and juridically separate "republics," the opposition of Indian and Spanish (or "*blanco*") has been the dominant calculus of social classification and cultural practice. Following independence, the juridical distinction between the two "republics" was abolished and Indians were declared equal citizens of the state. In practice, of course, such equality failed to emerge as Indians throughout Peru were forced off their newly alienable lands and denied the support of their traditional community institutions which, under liberal ideology, were denied juridical status.

With the emergence of the modern state, these systemic contradictions between the liberal discourse of equality and a liberal economy based on unequal access to both wealth and power, were transformed into the basis of a constitutively new form of racist ideology and practice. Whereas earlier colonial understandings of race had been based on notions of caste (*casta*) transmitted through blood, nineteenth century racial discourse located racial difference in biology and the human body (Banton 1987). As the object of scientific scrutiny, the new biological definitions of race became a subject for the new technologies of social engineering and regulation by which modern states sought to improve their populations, construct uniform (and singular) national identities, and achieve economic and political "progress." In the case of Peru, Indians were viewed, for the first time, not simply as a culturally distinct and inferior "Republic," but as racially distinct beings whose biologically inferior bodies literally stood in the way of Progress and the Nation. In Peru, as in the US, Europe, and other parts of Latin America, the explosion of ideas and discussions of race went hand in hand with the need to define new national identities and the goals of national growth and progress (Demelas 1981; Graham 1990; Saxton 1990; Takaki 1979). Thus, while certain shared understandings of race remained a constant throughout the nineteenth century period of nation formation in Peru, it was during precisely those moments of national crisis and reconsolidation—the early nineteenth century post-Independence period, the late nineteenth century period immediately following the war with Chile, and the early twentieth century modernizing state of Augusto Leguía—that the most active debates concerning the meaning of race and the status of Peru's Indian citizens surfaced (Poole 1990 & 1992). In each case, discussions of race centered around the need to resolve the discrepancy between the presence of a culturally *and biologically* distinct population, and the dominant understandings that the Nation must have a *singular* national culture.

This modern Peruvian racial discourse and its attendant forms of racism were both similar to those forms of racial ideology (and racism) inscribed in other modernizing liberal states, and tailored to Peru's specific history of conquest and state formation. As Michel Foucault (1991) has argued for Europe, modern forms of European racism differ substantively from earlier ancestral forms of racism, which had been based on "the simple hate or disdain of races for each other." This new form of modern racism, Foucault argues, emerged from the contradiction between the normalizing technologies through which liberal states promised to guarantee the conditions of life for *all* its citizens, and the fact that these same states depended on military apparatuses in which their citizens must be asked, not to guarantee life, but to kill for the state. By dehumanizing the enemy, racism provided the means whereby individuals could be made to kill for a state whose legitimacy was supposedly based not on violence, but on its visible role as guarantor of continuing social and biological life. Racism does this, moreover, without at the same time undermining the discursive legitimacy of state power, since modern or "scientific" racial thought is based on the same forms of biological classification and control as are the regulatory technologies of censuses, statistics, welfare, demography and hygiene through which the state retains its claims over the minds and bodies of a specific population.

As an example of the centrality of this racial and racist logic to the functioning of liberal state power, Foucault cites the case of German Fascism. As an extreme case of the normalizing state, the Fascist state sought to penetrate all aspects of its citizens lives through highly developed institutions and technologies of normalization (see also Passerini 1987). The success with which the Nazi state carried out these programs, Foucault argues, was due to their equally successful campaigns of racist mobilization, wherein citizens were incited to fight *for* the state and against a set of non-German others (Jews, Poles, Communists). The arbitrariness of the racial and ethnic categories upon which such campaigns of victimization were constructed, contradicted the calculus of individual culpability encouraged by the liberal discourse of democracy and law. (As such, racism mimicked the same contradiction between political equality and economic inequality found in even the mildest forms of liberal political rule.) In the case of the Nazis, the arbitrariness of state supported racial victimization spawned a form of psychological control through terror. This terror was the product of the German people's—both victims and victimizers—inability to reconcile their understandings of liberal individuality and culpability with the highly visible and pervasive forms of arbitrary violent punishment carried out by the Nazi state in the name of German law and the nation state (Lowenthal 1946).

This digression in European political history is useful for understanding the relationship between Peruvian state supported violence in the 1980s and 1990s and racism, as an ideological and cultural expression of Peruvian national and social identity. Both Peruvian nationalism and the Peruvian state have been consciously modelled after the nationalist and liberal projects of nineteenth century Europe. These projects, however, were shaped in fundamentally different ways in Peru. Pre-existing forms of authoritarian power such as *gamonalismo* offered a persistent and overtly oppositional force with respect to the Peruvian state's early attempts to regulate the national population through taxation, censuses, education, and so forth. As pointed out in the chapters by Gose, Rénique, Paponnet-Cantat, and Poole, these forms of violent authoritarian power have impeded effective central control on the part of the state. They came to constitute the nexus between state power and the peasantry in those regions, such as the southern *provincias altas*, where *gamonales* often constituted Indians' sole contact with the state. It was on this level of local state structuring, rather than in the military nationalism and war machines in which Foucault locates the racism of the European state, that racial ideologies and practices became inscribed in the Peruvian state.

However, with the military dismanteling of the oligarchic state in 1968, the rise of General Velasco's corporative and normalizing state, the decline of the landholding elites, the electoral democracies of Belaúnde and García, the advent of Sendero, and, finally, the authoritarian "democracy"of Alberto Fujimori, the locus of Peruvian state racism has come to conform more clearly to the European pattern sketched by Foucault: The state has consolidated its disintegrating hold over civil society through a politically *and* racially defined internal enemy in the form of the PCP-SL and the Andean peasantry who supposedly supports it. The racist nature of the early counterinsurgency campaigns has been well documented: Military personnel were instructed to regard all Andean peasants or *cholos* as potential "terrorists" or as supporters of the PCP-SL. Under the current regime of President Alberto Fujimori, the politics of fear associated with the counter-insurgency state have become even clearer. Since his *autogolpe* or "self-inflicted coup" of April 5, 1992, Fujimori has repeatedly invoked the terrorist threat of Sendero to justify a series of repressive measures designed to consolidate his own hold on power. These measures have included closing congress, dismanteling the judiciary, and instituting a special system of trial by anonymous judges for suspected "terrorists." Facilitated by Fujimori's sweeping new anti-terrorist laws, detentions of human rights workers, and popular leaders have also become more frequent. Conversely, victories over the PCP-SL—including most prominently the capture in September 1992 of PCP-SL leader Abimael Guzmán together with much of the political bureau of his party's central committee—have been used by the president and members of his administration to confirm the legitimacy of Fujimori's near dictatorial powers.[22]

As the Peruvian state continues to crumble with the onslaught of Sendero, the domestic economic crisis, and the crushing burden of international debt payments, the centrality and national character of its fight against Sendero conforms increasingly to the forms of arbitrary (because racially defined) victimization underwriting European Fascist attempts to unify their national populations through terror. In the case of the inci-

dents in Qasahui described earlier in this chapter, the military forces responsible for the massacre in Qasahui preceded the final murders with a
series of arbitrary punishments and arrests intended to induce terror in
the local population. These measures included the specific techniques of
random imprisonment, arbitrary victimization, entrapment, physical deg-
radation through nudity, rape, inebriation and bondage, confiscation of
property, and the use of masked peasant prisoners to inform publically
(and under coercion) on their neighbors and families. These techniques of
terror—all of which were also practiced in Nazi Germany—were not directed towards suspected armed "terrorists." (Indeed, those peasants
who did hand over arms—probably hunting rifles—to the soldiers were
immediately released.) Nor were they intended to enlist popular peasant
support for a "democratic" state. Rather, as in fascist states, their intended
effect is to use abritrary victimization to demobilize the Peruvian people
as a whole: As visible acts of collective punishment carried on outside the
boundaries of legally recognized zones of military jurisdiction (where
such activities, though still illegal, are nonetheless common practice), the
incidents in Chumbivilcas provided a clear message that the military's
ability to define and punish victims conforms to no recognized legal or juridical rationale.

   Although comparisons with European forms of state racism and violence—especially of the essentialized sort which Foucault proposes—
must be approached with caution, they are valuable in pointing out the
ways in which racism and racist violence are not epiphenomenal or aberrant attributes of a liberal state apparatus which has somehow "gone
wrong" in Peru.[23] Rather, such comparisons reveal that racism is a constitutive aspect of both the normalizing technologies and absolutist and/or
militarized forms of power posited in those liberal projects of national
state formation upon which Peru's state has been historically modeled.
Racism has been engrained in the Peruvian state and civil society from the
early years of the Republic by virtue of both the systematic exclusion of
the Andean highlands from dominant Peruvian national projects *and* the
state's reliance on such forms of coercive and racially defined local power
as *gamonalismo*. The forms of violence generated by both *gamonal* and state
(or military) racism are like that of Sendero because they are founded on
polarizing or exclusionary modes of thought and because they generate
absolutist equations between power and the excercise of physical violence. They are fundamentally unlike that of Sendero, however, in the extent to which they deny, rather than glorify, violence. Thus, while Guzmán singles out violence as the "universal law" of Peruvian history, the
state, as maintainer of order in society, legitimizes its power by asserting
the illegitimacy and abnormalcy of violence, including its own.

The Peasants

In preceding chapters, we have traced some of the historical relationships between the authoritarian and racist political cultures that have given birth to both the PCP-SL and the Peruvian state's counterinsurgency campaigns, and the daily lives of people in southern Peruvian highland society. Through these case studies we can begin to decipher the historically specific understandings of conflict, power, and authority that influence the ways in which people in the Andean highlands interact with each other and with the Peruvian state. These "understandings" about the ways in which power and authority are expressed and legitimated derive, on the one hand, from a shared discourse of racial, sexual, ethnic, and social difference, and, on the other, from peoples' concrete historical experiences with, and memories of, locally specific forms of conflict and dispute. The discursive categories or representations of the oppositions Indian-Spanish, highland-coast, *cholo-mestizo*, worker-patron, female-male provide Andean peoples with a basic calculus for negotiating and recognizing (or naturalizing) the distribution of real power in Peruvian society. Nonetheless, it is only by looking at the second factor—the concrete and locally specific forms of conflict resolution—that we can see how these discursive, or "cultural," idioms of difference are negotiated as the distinctive political cultures wherein discourse is transformed into modes of real political action, including violence.

In the Peruvian Andes, there exist various, overlapping strategies for the expression and resolution of conflict. They are based on concrete forms of historical experience and on popular, or collective, memory of locally specific incidents of class conflict, inter-community confrontations, and intra-group disputes. These experiences or memories informing political culture include such democratic or communalist processes of conflict resolution as the community assemblies, peasant unions, and elected municipal governments described by Rénique in Chapter 7. They also include, however, such inherently violent and conceptually diverse events as the land invasions, retaliatory raids and murders, *chaqwas* and *tinkuys*, and livestock and property theft, described in the other chapters of this book.[24]

To understand the relations of dominance and dependence existing between these seemingly opposite, yet coexisting, modes of conflict resolution, it is necessary to understand how individuals in Peruvian society negotiate the topography and contemporaneity of their different yet overlapping strategies and perspectives. As we have seen in the ethnographic portraits of rural life presented in the chapters by Orlove, Gose, Paponnet-Cantat and myself, individuals' identities, political strategies and understandings of power are not divided into neatly segregated

zones of *misti* versus *campesino*, or Spanish versus Andean. The constant—
one might almost say, obsessive—use of these labels in daily life, however, means that, while individuals can rarely be made to fit absolutely
into any one empirically-bounded ethnic category, the oppositional constructs and exclusionary calculus of racial or ethnic categories is very real
at the level of discourse and therefore of "culture." In other words, even
as individuals constantly construct new identities to fit differing political
and social contexts, all identity is phrased (or referred) for validation or
authorization, to a discourse of opposing ethnic, cultural or racial categories.[25]

The polarizing logic of these ethnic, racial, and cultural oppositions
functions in Peruvian society as what Raymond Williams (1977) has
termed "the ruling definition of the social." This "ruling definition of the
social" exercises its dominance on the level of discourse. Yet what renders
it dominant (i.e., what authorizes its universality) is the fact that in everyday life and in popular memory, such oppositions as "*misti*" and "Indian"
are inscribed in both individual memories and the social imaginary as labels inscribed on the body through concrete acts of physical violence.
Thus, even the most mundane understandings of ethnic or racial identity
in Peru contain within them an imminently conflictual dynamic. In regions such as the southern *provincias altas* with particularly marked histories of *gamonal* violence, this inherently confrontational logic constantly
threatens to subsume the moral and consensual strategies of community
(which are based on these same understandings of ethnicity) to the dominant culture of violence and authoritarian power. In this sense, such historically Andean cultural forms as the *ayllu*, the community, or the reciprocity ideal must be seen not as essentialized survivals from a
communitarian past, but rather as contested arenas within a national political struggle centered on the need to control the meaning of local level
"democratic" or community practices and beliefs.

The many different levels at which this contest over the meaning of Andean cultural practices occurs, are attested to in the case studies presented
in previous chapters. In Huaquirca (Chapter 5) and Capacmarca (Chapter
6) these struggles over meaning were fought out in the realm of daily life
and in the semiotics of property-holding and class distinction. Orlove's
analysis of the events at Mollocahua in Chapter 2, and my own analysis of
Chumbivilcano folklore in Chapter 3, in turn pointed towards the ways in
which violence itself has been subjected to recurrent forms of politically
motivated interpretation. Even the ritual battles described by Orlove in
Chapter 4 emerge as a site for conflicting interpretations of the meaning
and importance of such Andean cultural values as reciprocity and resistance. Perhaps the most striking case of this battle over the meaning of
peasant cultural forms, however, is provided in Rénique's account of

events in Puno, where an armed guerrilla organization, various legal leftwing parties, and an array of national and provincial level government agents have turned to violence as a means to influence the shape of peasant political culture and agrarian organization.

The importance of shifting the concept of Andean culture back into the realm of the political, the national, and the conflictual, and away from the isolated archaism or essentialism of much cultural anthropological analysis, is evident if we turn, once again, to the problem of recent political violence in Peru and its representation—or "explanation"—in the social sciences. As I have suggested in the introduction to this volume, historical and ethnographic studies of the Andes have traditionally approached culture as a system of order rather than of disorder or conflict. Within this approach to culture, violence is seen to occur when culturally patterned understandings of natural or social order are disrupted. Violence is something which exists outside of, rather than within, the cultural order.

Efforts to define the nature of peasant support for Sendero's activities have followed this lead. They attempt to trace the ways in which Sendero's discourse of order—its political and moral ideology—speaks to what are taken to be "Andean" ideas of social and cultural order. The outcome has been some very peculiar arguments in which academic observers—forgetting the inherently *political* nature of the PCP-SL as a splinter party motivated by it historical enemity with other Peruvian leftwing parties—attempt to find parallels between Sendero's internationalist political discourse and glorification of violence, and such supposedly eternal "Andean" cultural values as communal agriculture, verticality, reciprocity, and the peasant "moral economy" (e.g., Berg 1987; McClintock 1984 & 1989).

Closer consideration of the PCP-SL's Maoist strategy and geographic spread, however, suggests a much more likely scenario in which its limited means of communication with peasants resides in a shared discourse of authoritarian power—though not necessarily in the violence which Guzmán proposes as the basis for his party's mass-line linkage (Degregori 1989; Manrique 1989). As the chapters in the volume have made clear, Andean peasants are all too familiar with authoritarian forms of power. Their history has been one of alternating confrontation, cooperation and coexistence with such social phenomena as *gamonales, pandillas,* debt peonage, corrupt state officials, summary justice, and political assassination. Sendero's strategy utilizes a similar vocabulary of authoritarian control. It calls for organizing "pandillas" in the form of peasant armed militias, economic coercion in the form of prohibiting peasant market participation, summary justice in the form of "peoples' trials," taxation in the form of "revolutionary contributions," and assassination of "unreformable elements" including elected office-holders, appointed authorities, abusive merchants, landlords, police, and other representatives of the state. In short, it is a construction of power which is all too easily recognized by the peasant both for its possibilities for abuse—in, for example, economic coercion and retributive killings–*and* equally important, for its *efficacy.*

Such an analysis is upheld by the record of peasant support for PCP-SL's actions. This analysis suggests that it was indeed a shared vocabulary of violent power, and not shared models of either order or cultural community, which gave the party entry into those communities with whom they worked for brief periods in the initial years of armed struggle in Ayacucho and Apurímac (Degregori 1989; Manrique 1989). Since that time, Sendero has moved largely in areas of the highlands like Ayacucho, Huánuco, Apurimac, Puno and the *provincias altas* of Cusco and Arequipa, which have been historically dominated by the politics and culture of *gamonalismo*. In these areas, peasant support for the party's presence in their communities is articulated as a highly conjunctural or non-binding agreement regarding both the necessity, or efficacy, of employing physical violence to resolve certain types of local grievances, and the desirability of having outside agents (i.e., the party) who are willing and able to perform these illegal acts (Berg 1987; Degregori & López Ricci 1991; del Pino 1991; González 1982 & 1983; Isbell 1992; Poole & Rénique 1992:60–64). These include such tactics as the elimination of particularly abusive local authorities; the banishment of unscrupulous merchants; the recuperation of cooperative lands from the State as in the case of Puno described in Chapter 7; the trial and punishment of rustlers, thieves and irresponsible schoolteachers as has occurred in the Cusco high provinces of Chumbivilcas and Canas; or the forced regulation of market prices for coca leaf and other commercial crops as has occurred in the coca producing Huallaga Valley of northern Peru (Poole & Rénique 1992:185–187).

In these same areas, more long-term political support has been effectively limited, however, by the extent to which the PCP-SL—on the basis of Guzmán's idiosyncratic reading of Peruvian history—has attempted to expand the boundaries of this shared vocabulary of limited authoritarian intervention as a charter for either expanding its use of physical violence or dismantling traditional forms of political and community organization. Peasants throughout the highlands have condemned and rejected Sendero's assassinations of peasant political leaders, their use of retributive and destructive violence, their attempts to prevent the sale of cash crops, their prohibitions on peasant participation in markets and national politics, and their destruction of development projects and collectively owned breeding stock, tractors, and buildings (e.g., CCP 1988 & 1989; CEPES 1989; Ticama 1989a & 1989b; Sánchez 1989). In these activities, Sendero reveals its political nature as a vanguard or cadre party dedicated to disrupting all competitive forms of political organization—including such popular democratic institutions as community assemblies and peasant federations—which do not answer to its authoritarian party structure.

In this respect, the PCP-SL both draws on and participates in a dominant political culture of exclusionary or oppositional logic which is fundamentally alien to such forms of popular democracy as the peasant community. This culture and its exclusionary logic is manifested as racism in the case of the Peruvian military. In the PCP-SL, it is all too clearly manifested in Guzmán's Stalinist vision of the vanguard political party and in Sendero's simplistic understanding of a Peruvian class structure which they envision as being neatly divided between an urban working class and a backward rural peasantry (Arce Borja 1988; PCP-SL 1989). As Isbell (1992) has suggested for the case of Ayacucho, the clear lack of fit between this essentialized or dualistic cosmology of class and the complex ethnic and class realities of Andean peasant life explains in some part Sendero's failure to mobilize a more permanent base of rural, peasant support.

Rethinking Andean Culture in the 1990s

As the chapters of this book make clear, both cultural identity and political violence in the Peruvian highlands are legacies of a historical experience in which violence has been equated with the domains of political action and discourse, and in which violence has gone largely unpunished. Like today's army patrols and Senderista columns, the *gamonales* and *abigeos* who have victimized peasants for decades have simply ridden away when their acts were done. Peasants by the thousands have turned to the state and its laws to redress such crimes. Yet, immune to the sanctions imposed on peasants for similar acts of violence, the violence practiced by such actors as the *gamonal*, the *abigeo* or the army has instead gone to consolidate concrete forms of economic and political power.

To speak of a "culture of violence" in Peru is to speak of this dispersed and continually re-enacted process of perception and authorization. It is not to speak of "a culture" constituted by some inherited set of interpretive codes or by the symbolic meanings attached, for example, to notions of blood, the body or power. Nor is it to speak of the hypothetical process by which such essentialized symbolic meanings have led people somehow to accept violence, to rationalize it in the form of symbolic codes, to practice it without scruples or reflections, to think—as journalists like to imagine Third World peoples do—that "life is cheap." Rather it is to recognize that, like us, peasants themselves perceive two historical facts about violence in Peru: First, it leads to real political power; and second, when it is accompanied by real power, it will remain immune to punishment by the state. As the chapters in the volume make abundantly clear, both these perceptions have formed a very real part of the historical experience of the people who live in Peru's southern *provincias altas*.

Such is not to say, however, that Peru's Andean peasants are resigned to the historical inevitability of either power or violence. It is precisely *because* peasants themselves see that violence is mediated by this inherently negotiable and historically contingent domain of political power, that they do *not* come to attach fixed symbolic meanings to violence or much less to accept violence as a "value" or "norm" of their cultural tradition. By recognizing that violence is politically contingent and dependent on the moment in which it occurs, they come instead to perceive that power is itself inherently contestable and unstable.

This perception stems, on the one hand, from the recurring nature and theatricality of physical violence in the Andes and, on the other, from the peasants' perception that the immunity of powerful people to punishment for these displays, contradicts both the values of legal justice and peaceful dispute settlement advocated by the state *and* the state's claims to monopolize power in Andean rural society. Because of the first factor—the seemingly necessary resort to displays of physical violence that we have seen at work in *gamonal* culture—the peasant does not see power as something essential to any single ethnic group or class fraction. Rather power is seen as something which can or must be repeatedly won or "slugged out." *Mistis* or *gamonales* are not considered to "own" (or have) power as the result of an inherited or historically stable cultural or social tradition. Similarly, the *gamonales'* use of violence in the past is not seen to legitimize or connect necessarily with their descendants' use of violence today. Rather, the fact that *gamonales* must constantly restage acts or displays of physical violence, makes it apparent that the symbolic statements which these acts of violence generate about the *gamonales'* relationship to power are, in fact, highly contingent utterances about the inherent *fragility* of their power. As pointed out in my own chapter on Chumbivilcas, the *gamonales'* efforts to construct a folklore or popular fiesta culture which might produce a "traditional" set of non-contingent or eternal symbolic truths about manhood, violence, and the *gamonales'* eternal right to power, are relatively recent. They correspond to a historical moment when the *gamonales'* ability to restage displays of real physical violence has been threatened by increasing state intervention in their traditional territories. Similarly, Guzmán's attempts to validate his own political agenda by eternalizing the naturalness and distinctiveness of violence *per se* in Peruvian history, conforms to a moment when the naturalness of absolute authoritarian power had been called into question by the expanding network of popular social movements that has characterized Peruvian politics for the past two decades.

Such attempts at constructing tradition or at eternalizing racial categories are efforts to naturalize categories of social experience by decontextualizing the specific contexts or set of social relations within which violence occurs or utterances about racial or class categories are made. Our analyses of culture in the Andes must not, however, use this same technique. That is, we must not naturalize either violence or racial language by explaining their meaning solely in terms of the historical embeddedness of these categories of perception and behavior. As the diverse case studies presented in this volume make clear, each act of violence is experienced—and therefore interpreted—in terms of the immediate set of political and social references it elicits. It is not interpreted by the peasant as a statement whose meaning is about the origins or naturalness of violent power. Rather what unites these various perceptions, understandings, and interpretations into what we might call "a culture of violence" is the way in which each interpretation and (violent or non-violent) negotiation of power is referred back for authorization to the set of utterances or discourses about ethnicity, race, and power which have been generated, in the past, by other specific acts of violence. In order to understand the nature and intransigeance of this "culture of violence," anthropologists and historians will have to examine carefully both the specific acts of violence which have gone into the making of Peruvian history and the narratives of ethnic and cultural encounter which have been used to legitimate and explain violence in the Andean world.

Notes

1. The following highly condensed description of the events in Qasahui is taken from the more detailed reports contained in: Liga Agraria Arcadio Romero de Chumbivilcas & APRODEH, *La Matanza de Chumbivilcas* (Cusco, 1990); Policia Técnica del Perú. Departamento Contra el Terrorism (DIRCOTE), Sede Cusco. "Atestado DIRCOTE sobre Matanza Chumbivilcas Abril 1990." (Cusco, 1990); Fiscal Superior Cusco, "Informe a la Comisión Investigador de los sucesos de Chumbivilcas," Cusco, 28 January 1991.

2. Sendero has been active since the early 1980s in the Apurímac provinces of Andahuaylas, Aymaraes and Antabamba. As a result, the entire Department of Apurímac has been declared in a state of emergency since November 1982. This more or less permanent state of emergency has brought with it a suspension of basic civil rights for Apurímac's 361,000 inhabitants, the establishment of military bases in several of the provincial capitals, and a high rate of out migration.

The neighboring Cusco province of Chumbivilcas, however, was not at that time an emergency zone. Sendero columns, probably originating from Apurímac or Ayacucho, had on separate occasions tried and executed a livestock rustler in Livitaca (1986), redistributed livestock in Colquemarca (1987), distributed propaganda and death lists in Santo Tomás (1986) and assassinated three policemen in Velille. The party, however, enjoys very little popular support among the peasantry of Chumbivilcas, in part due to the strength of the Provincial Agrarian

League 'Arcadio Romero,' an affiliate of the Departamental Peasant Federation of Cusco (FDCC), which is, in turn, an affiliate of the Peasant Federation of Peru (CCP). Sendero's presence in the zone may have increased following the events in Qasahui as evidenced by two armed actions in Ingata (Chamaca) and Livitaca, where Sendero organized a mock trial and public execution in May 1990.

3. For histories of the PCP-SL, see Degregori 1990, Gorriti 1990, Harding 1987, Poole & Rénique 1992 and Taylor 1981.

4. "Instinto Asesino," *Caretas*, October 8, 1992, p. 19.

5. For an extended critical analysis of the center-periphery paradigm in U.S. political scientists' analyses of the PCP-SL, see Poole & Rénique 1991. For an analysis of how Sendero's military strategy and concept of "complementary theatres of operation" differ from both Mao's theories of guerrilla warfare and the image of an encirclement, see Poole & Rénique 1992:55–56.

6. Peasants have fled from both Sendero and the Peruvian armed forces who have conducted a counterinsurgency war against Sendero. For information on the resulting refugee population, see Kirk 1991. The issue of territorial "control" must also be looked at differently for Sendero than for most other guerrilla armies, since the PCP-SL does not seek to construct "liberated zones." Instead, the party has sought to construct strategic corridors in sparsely populated areas through which its military columns can move more or less freely.

7. For analyses of the class and educational background of PCP-SL members, see Chávez de Paz 1989 and Degregori 1989, 1990 & 1991.

8. For Sendero's military program, see PCP-SL 1982 & 1989 and Arce Borja 1988. For critical analyses of their program see, Gorriti 1990, Degregori 1990, González 1982 & 1984, and Poole & Rénique 1992.

9. In this, the PCP-SL follows the Maoist line set in 1967 in the Fifth Conference of the PCP-BR, of which Guzmán was at that time a member. At this conference it was resolved that class was the determining contradiction within Peruvian society and that national, ethnic, and racial factors were of only secondary importance in the determination of Peru's historical development and revolutionary struggle (PCP-BR 1967 and 1969). Since that time, none of Guzmán's or the PCP-SL's public discourse or published statements privilege ethnic, racial or cultural factors as elements shaping the historical vision, political philosophy and military strategy of their party (Degregori 1990:205; Manrique 1989; Montoya 1992:78–79). In fact, in those documents where PCP-SL spokespersons and leaders do mention "Andean culture" they disparage such "folklore" as "nacionalismo mágico-quejumbroso" [magical-whining nationalism] and as archaic survivals which must be *eliminated* in the construction of the PCP-SL's "New Democracy" (*El Diario* 1988 & 1989; Fokkema 1990). Other party documents reveal Abimael Guzmán's orders that Quechua *not* be the language of instruction in the "popular schools" set up by the party in Peru's Andean highlands (J-L. Rénique, personal communication); and, on at least one occasion, a PCP-SL leader has announced that Sendero will seek to "eliminate the Quechua language" (Montoya 1992:80). The PCP-BR's and PCP-SL's dismissal of ethnic and racial factors distinguishes them from the political tradition of José Carlos Mariategui, who posited race or "the Indian question" as a fundamental determining contradiction in Peruvian society (Flores-Galindo 1989;

Mariátegui 1980 (1928)). Despite this and other discrepancies with Mariátegui's thought, the PCP-SL—along with all other political parties descended from Mariátegui's shortlived Socialist Party and the original Communist Party of Peru—claim Mariátegui as their intellectual and political founder.

10. The PCP-SL considers itself to be the true embodiment of Maoism, and as such a continuation of the revolutionary struggle begun by Mao in the Chinese Commmunist Party. They consider the present Chinese Communist Party to be "revisionists" who have betrayed the correct Maoist line. To make clear its differences with the present-day Chinese government, Sendero has frequently targetted the Chinese embassy in Lima.

11. In conformance with Guzman's understanding of contradiction, in this "new democracy" all forms of political, social and cultural difference will have been eliminated. It will be, Guzmán writes, "the society of great harmony, the radical and definitively new society towards which fifteen billion years of matter in movement ... is directed necessarily and irrepressibly" (PCP-SL 1982:14).

12. For other accounts by Senderistas of the so-called "quota of blood" required by the party from its members and of the ideology of self-sacrifice and martyrdom with which the party has prepared its members for war, see Gorriti 1990:167-9 and Degregori & López Ricci 1990.

13. Elsewhere I have argued for the similarities between Guzmán's understanding of history and contradiction and the notions of historical causation and exclusive contradiction posited by Immanuel Kant (Poole & Rénique 1992:50–51). While reducing Guzmán's political and philosophical influences to any one source—and particularly to any one thinker so complex and varied as Kant—would be an oversimplification, consideration of the parallels between Kantian philosophy and Guzmán's totalizing metaphors of historical causation and absolutist political will does much to dispel the popular notion that Guzmán's philosophical training as a Kantian scholar is somehow at odds with his political philosophy and rhetoric. Far from an aberrant or "non-Western" mode of thought and action, the same ideas of historical telos, progress and authoritarian rule posited by Guzmán can readily be located in the Enlightenment thinkers such as Kant whom Guzmán read and studied (Habermas 1991:101–116; Hoffman 1989; Michalson 1990).

14. These two interpretations are common currency in the Sendero literature. In an otherwise thorough history of Sendero, Peruvian journalist Gustavo Gorriti, for example, incorrectly attributes the invention of totalitarian politics and terror to Marx and the Marxist tradition (Gorriti, *Sendero*, pp. 158–69). Such an ideologically informed reading of Sendero's political formation, however, misrepresents both the complexity and diversity of Marxist thought and its place as *one of many* descendents of a European political tradition founded upon the totalizing discursive formations and experiences of the French Revolution. The ethnic argument, on the other hand, is much more common in U.S. political scientists' attempts to fit Peruvian ethnic politics into the polarized fields of "center and periphery." See, for example, Palmer 1985a & 1985b.

15. Over 27,000 deaths and disappearances have been reported during the twelve years of war between the PCP-SL and the Peruvian armed forces. The material cost of the violence is estimated at over ten billion dollars, or four times the

country's export earnings. See, Amnesty International 1988 & 1989:144–7, Peru. Senado 1989, and DESCO 1989.

16. Sendero's principal armed opponent on the left was Movimiento Revolucionario Tupac Amaru (MRTA), which began its armed initiative in 1984. Following internal factional strive and the arrest of several of its leaders, the MRTA has ceased most armed actions.

17. For a chronology of actions by the right-wing paramilitary groups, see DESCO 1989:252–8, and Peru. Senado 1990.

18. This in turn gives way to the depoliticization and irrationalization of third world violence in such empty signifiers as "terrorist," "subversive," and "fanatic" (Chomsky 1988a & 1988b and Said 1988). Regarding the discursive power of such representations of violence, see Taussig 1987 & 1992.

19. Anthropological models of "segmentary systems" and blood feuds explain the logic which both initiates and propels a cycle of violence, or "feud," in terms of the social structure, which is supposedly prone to fissioning or "segmentation." See among others, Black-Michaud 1976; Chagnon 1968; Gellner 1969; Sahlins 1961. Since at least the 1930s when Evans Pritchard formalized Durkheim's concept of the segmentary society as a model for African kinship based societies, such models have informed both anthropological and popular representations of third world violence as "tribal," and as therefore caused by the social organization and culture of the people involved. Tribal explanations are, for example, widely used in the U.S. press to explain violence in Africa and the Middle East.

20. Universalizing psychological models of violence include those of René Girard (1977) who traces the origins of culture to the mimetic rationalities inform-ing sacrifice and mythic violence (see also Hamerton-Kelly 1987). Frantz Fanon's (1961) theory of cathartic revolutionary violence is based on a similar notion of mi-mesis, yet situates the mimetic rationality of violence within the historically spe-cific context of racially divided colonial societies.

21. The racist component of Peru's recent counter-insurgency campaigns has been largely ignored in the literature. For important exceptions see Degregori & Lopez Ricci 1990, Manrique 1987 & 1989, Manrique & Flores-Galindo 1986, and Montoya 1992.

22. The arrests of Guzmán and the other central committee members were made by the Peruvian intelligence agency, DINCOTE, following years of surveillance and intelligence gathering. Fujimori's attempts to claim credit for the arrests are rendered even more problematic given the existing animosity between DINCOTE and the military hardliners who support Fujimori. Because the counterinsurgency tactics and harsh repressive measures proposed by Fujimori and his military advi-sors target suspected "supporters" rather than the military and political leaders of Sendero, they are sharply opposed by DINCOTE, which favors a strategy based on intelligence gathering and aimed towards decapitating the party apparatus through the surveillance and arrest of high-ranking party members. Of the two strategies, that of DINCOTE has proven the most effective in delivering blows to Sendero's formidable military and political apparatus.

23. This type of analysis is common in Peruvian sociological and juridical analy-ses of state sanctioned violence and racism. See, for example, Peru. Senado 1989:34.

24. Such violent public acts and gestures overlap in critical ways with the forms of agression and gender identities characterizing the "private sphere" in the form of domestic violence, violence against women, intra-familial disputes, and petty forms of intra-community strife (Harvey 1993). To date insufficient attention has been paid to problems of domestic and sexual violence in Andean culture, including in this volume.

25. Individuals in Andean society shift ethnic allegiances and linguistic and cultural markers according to contexts dictated by the constant struggle for power in social life. See, among others, de la Cadena 1991, Harvey 1987, Smith 1989, and Stein 1985.

Bibliography

Adorno, Theodor W. & Max Horkheimer. 1972. *Dialectic of Enlightenment*. Trans. John Cumming. New York: Continuum.

Amauta (Lima). 1989. "Las reglas militares que violó Sendero," 16 Nov. 1989; reprinted in R. Wiener (ed.), *Guerra e Ideología. El Debate entre Amauta y El Diario*, pp. 58–67. Lima: Ediciones Amauta.

Amnesty International. 1988. *Peru: Violations of Human Rights in the Emergency Zones*.

_____. 1989. *Report l989*. New York: Amnesty International.

Arce Borja, Luís. 1988. "Entrevista del Siglo," [interview with Abimael Guzmán], *El Diario* (Lima), 24 July 1988.

Banton, Michael. 1987. *Racial Theories*. New York: Cambridge University Press.

Berg, Ronald H. 1987. "Sendero Luminoso and the Peasantry of Andahuaylas," *Journal of Interamerican Studies and World Affairs*, XXVII(4):165–96.

Billington, James H. 1980. *Fire in the Minds of Men. Origins of the Revolutionary Faith*. New York: Basic Books.

Black-Michaud, J. 1976. *Cohesive Force: Feud in the Mediterranean and the Middle East*. Oxford: Blackwell.

CEPES. 1989. "Organización campesina contra la violencia," *Alerta Agrario*, 33 (Dec. 1989):1–2.

Chagnon, Napoleon. 1968. *Yanamamo:The Fierce People*. New York: Holt Rinehart and Winston.

Chávez de Paz, Dennis. 1989. *Juventud y Terrorismo. Características de los condenados por terrorismo y otros delitos*. Lima: Instituto de Estudios Peruanos, 1989.

Chomsky, Noam 1988a. "Middle East Terrorism and the American Ideological System." In E.W. Said & C. Hitchens (eds.), *Blaming the Victims. Spurious Scholarship and the Palestinian Question*, pp. 97–147. London: Verso.

_____. 1988b. *The Culture of Terrorism*. Boston: South End Press.

Confederación Campesina del Perú (CCP). 1988. *Acuerdos del VII Congreso Nacional Agosto 1987*. Lima: CCP & Instituto de Apoyo Agrario.

_____. 1989. *Movilización Campesina: Respuesta Democrática*. Lima: CCP.

Degregori, Carlos Iván. 1989. *Qué difícil es ser Dios. Ideología y violencia política en Sendero Luminoso*. Lima: El Zorro de Abajo Ediciones.

———. 1990. *Ayacucho 1969–1979. El Nacimiento de Sendero Luminoso.* Lima: Instituto de Estudios Peruanos.

———. 1991. "Jóvenes y campesinos ante la violencia política: Ayacucho 1980–1983." In H. Urbano (ed.), *Poder y violencia en los Andes*, pp. 395–417. Cusco: Bartolomé de las Casas.

Degregori, Carlos Ivan & José López Ricci. 1990. "Los Hijos de la guerra: Jóvenes andinos y criollos frente a la violencia política." In DESCO (ed.), *Tiempos de Ira y Amor*, pp. 183–219. Lima: DESCO.

de la Cadena, Marisol. 1991. "'Las Mujeres son mas indias': Etnicidad y género en una comunidad del Cusco," *Revista Andina*, 17:7–29.

Demelas, Marie-Danièle. 1981. "Darwinismo a la criolla: El Darwinismo social en Bolivia, 1880–1910," *Historia Boliviana*, 1/2:55–82.

DESCO. 1989. *Violencia Política en el Perú, 1980–88.* 2 vols. Lima: DESCO.

[El] *Diario.* 1988. "IU con la perestroika y la utopia andina: Residuos de la moribunda ideología burguesa," *Cresta Roja. Suplemento dominical de El Diario* (Lima), *Año* II, No. 62, July 1988, p. iii.

———. 1989. "Editorial." 9 June 1988, p. 12.

Fanon, Frantz. 1961. *Les Damnés de la terre.* Paris: Maspero.

Favre, Henri. 1984. "Sentier Lumineux et Horizons Obscurs," *Problèmes d'Amérique Latine*, 72:3–27.

Flores Galindo, Alberto. 1989. *La Agonia de Mariategui.* 3ra. edicion. Lima: Instituto de Apoyo Agrario.

Fokkema, Anita. 1990. "Interview with Luís Arce Borja," *NACLA Report on the Americas*, Vol.XXIV, no.4 (Dec/Jan, 1990–1).

Foucault, Michel. 1991. "Faire vivre et laisser mourir: La Naissance du racisme," *Les Temps Modernes*, 535:37–61.

Gellner, Ernest. 1969. *Saints of the Atlas.* Chicago: University of Chicago Press.

Girard, René. 1977. *Violence and the Sacred* (1972). Baltimore: Johns Hopkins University Press.

González, Raúl. 1982. "Ayacucho: Por los caminos de Sendero," *Quehacer*, 19 (Oct.):36–77.

———. 1983. "Crónica Inconclusa. Las Batallas de Ayacucho," *Quehacer* 21:14–27.

———. 1984. "Especial sobre Sendero. El Terror en Ayacucho. El Terror Senderista. Sendero: El Maoismo y una revolución para exportar," *Quehacer* 30 (August):6–29.

Gorriti, Gustavo. 1990. *Sendero: Historia de la Guerra Milenaria en el Perú.* Vol. I. Lima: Editorial Apoyo.

Graham, Richard (ed.). 1990. *The Idea of Race in Latin America, 1870–1940.* Austin: University of Texas Press.

Guzmán, Abimael. 1985. "Inicio de la lucha armada (1980)," in R. Mercado (ed.), *Los Partidos Políticos en el Perú*, pp. 89–91. Lima: Fondo de Cultura.

———. 1989a. "Contra las ilusiones constitucionales y por el estado de Nueva Democracia" (1978). In Luís Arce Borja (ed.), *Guerra Popular en el Perú: El Pensamiento Gonzálo*, pp. 95–111. Brussels: Edic. Luís Arce Borja.

———. 1989b. "Por la nueva bandera" (1979). In Luís Arce Borja (ed.), *Guerra Popular en el Perú: El Pensamiento Gonzálo*, pp. 141–145. Brussels: Edic. Luís Arce Borja.

_____. 1989c. "Somos los Iniciadores" (1980). In Luís Arce Borja (ed.), *Guerra Popular en el Perú: El Pensamiento Gonzálo*, pp. 163–175. Brussels: Edic. Luís Arce Borja.

Habermas, Jürgen. 1991. *The Structural Transformation of the Public Sphere. An Inquiry into a Category of Bourgeois Society* (1962). transl. T. Burger. Cambridge, Mass.: MIT Press.

Hamerton-Kelly, R. 1987. *Violent Origins*. Stanford: Stanford University Press.

Harding, Colin. 1987. "The Rise of Sendero Luminoso." In R. Miller (ed.), *Region and Class in Modern Peru*, 179–207. Liverpool: University of Liverpool, Institute of Latin American Studies, Monograph Series No. 14.

Harvey, Penelope. 1987. *Language and the Power of History: The Discourse of Bilinguals in Ocongate (Southern Peru)*. Ph.D. Thesis, London School of Economics.

_____. 1993. "Domestic Violence in the Peruvian Andes." In. P. Harvey & P. Gow (eds.), *Sex and Violence: Issues of Representation and Experience*. London: Routledge (in press).

Herman, Edward & Gerry O'Sullivan. 1989. *The 'Terrorism' Industry. The Experts and Institutions that Shape our View of Terror*. New York: Pantheon.

Hobsbawm, Eric J. 1990a. *Echoes of the Marseillaise*. New Brunswick, NJ: Rutgers University Press.

_____. 1990b. *Nations and Nationalism since 1780. Programme, Myth and Reality*. Cambridge: Cambridge University Press.

Hoffman, Piotr. 1989. *Violence in Modern Philosophy*. Chicago: The University of Chicago Press.

Hoffmann, Stanley. 1987. "A Note on the French Revolution and the Language of Violence," *Daedalus*, 116:149–56.

Isbell, Billie-Jean. 1992. "Shining Path and Peasant Responses in Rural Ayacucho." In D.S. Palmer (ed.), *The Shining Path of Peru*, pp. 59–81. New York: St. Martin's Press.

Kirk, Robin. 1991. *The Decade of Chaqwa. Peru's Internal Refugees*. Washington: U.S. Committee for Refugees.

Lowenthal, Leo. 1946. "Terror's Atomization of Man," *Commentary*, I(3):1–8.

Manrique, Nelson. 1987. "Política y violencia en el Perú," *Márgenes*, 2: 125–58.

_____. 1989. "La Década de la Violencia," *Márgenes*, III(5/6):137–82.

_____. 1990. "Violencia e imaginario social en el Perú contemporáneo." In DESCO (ed.), *Tiempos de Ira y Amor*, pp. 47–75. Lima: DESCO.

Manrique, Nelson & Alberto Flores-Galindo. 1986. *Violencia y Campesinado*. Lima: Instituto de Apoyo Agrario.

Mariátegui, José Carlos. 1980. *Siete Ensayos de Interpretación de la Realidad Peruana* (1928). Lima: Biblioteca Amauta.

McClintock, Cynthia. 1984. "Why Peasants Rebel: The Case of Peru's Sendero Luminoso," *World Politics*, 37(1984):48–84.

_____. 1989. "Peru's Sendero Luminoso Rebellion: Origins and Trajectory," in S. Eckstein (ed.) *Power and Popular Protest. Latin American Social Movements*, pp. 61–101. Berkeley: University of California Press.

Michalson, Gordon E. 1990. *Fallen Freedom. Kant on Radical Evil and Moral Regeneration*. New York: Cambridge University Press.

Montoya, Rodrigo. 1992. *Al Borde del Naufragio. Democracia, violencia y problema étnico en el Perú*. Lima: Cuadernos del SUR.

Palmer, David Scott. 1985a. "The Sendero Luminoso Rebellion in Peru." In G. Fauriol (ed.), *Latin American Insurgencies*, pp. 67–85. Washington: Georgetown University CSIS & The National Defense University.

———. 1985b. "Rebellion in Rural Peru. The Origins and Evolution of Sendero Luminoso." *Comparative Politics*, 18(1):127–46.

Partido Comunista Peruano-Bandera Roja (PCP-BR), Comité Central. 1967. *Quinta Conferencia Nacional*. Lima: Bandera Roja.

———. 1969. "Polémica entre Saturnino Paredes y 'Alvaro' [Abimael Guzmán]." Lima:Bandera Roja.

Partido Comunista del Peru (PCP-SL), Comité Central. 1982. *Desarrollemos la Guerra de Guerrillas*. Lima: Bandera Roja, 1982.

———. 1989. *Bases de discusión* (1988). In Luís Arce Borja (ed.), *Guerra popular en el Perú. El Pensamiento Gonzalo*, pp. 307–392. Brussels: Edicion Luís Arce Borja.

Passerini, Luisa. 1987. *Fascism in Popular Memory*. Cambridge & New York: Cambridge University Press.

Peru. Senado. 1989. *Violencia y Pacificación*. Comisión Especial sobre las causas de la violencia y alternativas de pacificación en el Perú. Lima: DESCO & Comisión Andina de Juristas.

———. 1990. *Informe*. Comisión Investigadora de Grupos Paramilitares. Lima: Sendado del Perú.

del Pino, Ponciano. 1991. "Los Campesinos en la guerra." Unpublished ms., Seminario Permanente de Investigación Agraria (SEPIA), agosto 1991, Iquitos (Peru).

Poole, Deborah. 1988. "Landscapes of Power in a Cattle-Rustling Culture of Southern Andean Peru," *Dialectical Anthropology*, 12:367–398.

———. 1990. "Ciencia, peligrosidad y represión en la criminología indigenista peruana." In C. Walker & C. Aguirre (eds.), *Bandolerismo, Criminalidad y Sociedad en Peru y Bolivia, siglos XVIII–XX*, pp. 335–367. Lima: Instituto de Apoyo Agrario.

Poole, Deborah & Gerardo Rénique. 1991. "The New Chroniclers of Peru: US Scholars and their 'Shining Path' of Peasant Rebellion," *Bulletin of Latin American Research*, X(1):133–191.

———. 1992. *Peru: Time of Fear*. London: Latin America Bureau.

Sahlins, Marshall. 1961. "The Segmentary Lineage: An Organization of Predatory Expansion," *American Anthropologist*, 63:322–45).

Said, Edward W. 1988. "The Essential Terrorist." In E. W. Said & C. Hitchens (eds.), *Blaming the Victims. Spurious Scholarship and the Palestinian Question*, pp. 149–58. London: Verso.

Sánchez, Rodrigo. 1989. "Sendero declara guerra a comunidades campesinas," *Sur*, 124 (August 1989):13.

Saxton, Alexander. 1990. *The Rise and Fall of the White Republic. Class Politics and Mass Culture in Nineteenth-Century America*. London: Verso.

Smith, Gavin. 1989. *Livelihood and Resistance. Peasants and the Politics of Land in Peru*. Berkeley: University of California Press.

Stein, William. 1985. "Countrymen and Townsmen in the Callejón de Huaylas, Peru: Two Views of Andean Social Structure." In W. Stein (ed.), *Peruvian Contexts of Change*, pp. 211–331. New Brunswick, NJ: Transaction.

Takaki, Ronald T. 1979. *Iron Cages. Race and Culture in Nineteenth-Century America.* New York: Knopf.

Taussig, Michael. 1987. *Shamanism, Colonialism and the Wildman. A Study in Terror and Healing.* Chicago: Univ. of Chicago Press.

_____. 1992. "Terror as Usual: Walter Benjamin's Theory of History as a State of Siege." In *The Nervous System*, pp. 11–35. New York & London: Routledge.

Taylor, Lewis. 1981. *Maoism in the Andes Sendero Luminoso and the Contemporary Guerrilla Movement in Peru.* Liverpool: Centre for Latin American Studies.

Ticama, Juan. 1989a. "Violencia y terror contra los pobres del campo," *Sur*, 122 (June 1989):4

_____. 1989b. "Violencia, militarización y desinformación," *Sur*, 123 (July 1989):7–19.

Tiruchelvam, Neelan. 1978. "The Ideology of Popular Justice." In C.E. Reasons & R.M. Rich (eds.), *The Sociology of Law: A Conflict Perspective*, pp. 276–277. Toronto: Butterworths.

Williams, Raymond. 1977. *Marxism and Literature.* New York: Oxford University Press.

Woy-Hazelton, Sandra & William A. Hazelton. 1989. "Sendero Luminoso and the Future of Peruvian Democracy," *Third World Quarterly*, 12:21–35.

About the Contributors

Daniel W. Gade is professor of Geography at the University of Vermont. He has researched and published extensively on the cultural and historical grography of the Central Andes, Southern Europe, Madagascar, and North America. His principal work on the Andes is *Plants, Man and Land in the Vilcanota Valley of Peru* (1975).

Peter Gose is associate professor of Anthropology at the University of Lethbridge (Alberta). He did fieldwork in the high provinces of Peru in the early 1980s and has since published on various aspects of Andean culture and economy in *American Ethnologist* and *Man*. He is currently preparing for publication a manuscript on ritual and class formation in the rural Andes.

Benjamin Orlove is professor of Environmental Studies at the University of California (Davis). He has conducted field and archival research on the political economy and culture of the high provinces of Cusco and Puno since the early 1970s. His principal works include *Alpacas, Sheep and Men* (1977) and articles in *American Ethnologist, Current Anthropology, American Anthropologist,* and other journals. He is currently researching the history of Peruvian geography and preparing a book manuscript on the fishermen of Lake Titicaca.

Christiane Paponnet-Cantat is assistant professor of Anthropology at the University of New Brunswick (Canada). She did research on the Peruvian agrarian reform in the high provinces in the mid 1980s and has published on violence and peasant conflict in *The Canadian Revuew of Sociology and Anthropology* and in *From the Margin to the Center.* She is currently working on a monograph on land and the hunger crisis in peasant communities of southern Peru.

Deborah Poole is assistant professor of Anthropology at the Graduate Faculty of the New School for Social Research (New York). She has done field and archival research in the Cusco region since the mid 1970s. She has published articles on violence, *gamonalismo,* and Sendero Luminoso in *Dialectical Anthropology* and the *Bulletin of Latin American Research,* and is the co-author with Gerardo Rénique of *Peru: Time of Fear* (1992). She is currently completing a monograph on European and *indigenista* photography in the Andes.

José Luis Rénique is associate professor of History at Lehman College of the City University of New York and a research associate at the Centro Peruano de Estudios Sociales (CEPES) in Lima. He is the author of *Los Sueños de la Sierra: Cusco en el siglo XX* (1991) and co-author with José Deustua of *Intelectuales, indigenismo y descentralismo en el Perú, 1897–1931.* He is currently completing a book on regional politics and the peasant movement in Puno.

About the Book and Editor

Violence forms a part of the daily rhythms of life in the Peruvian Andes—from the "play" of everyday life to the political actions of the Shining Path. This volume explores how violence has affected the daily lives, cultural identities, and political futures of the inhabitants of Peru's southern high provinces. In their case studies, the contributors consider how violence has inflected the historical geography of the region; popular discourses of race, ethnicity, and gender; and the forms of local power that perpetuate landlord rule. *Unruly Order* makes a powerful argument for extending our understanding of this particular regional culture of violence to the social and cultural processes at work in many other parts of Latin America.

Deborah Poole is assistant professor of anthropology at the Graduate Faculty of the New School for Social Research.